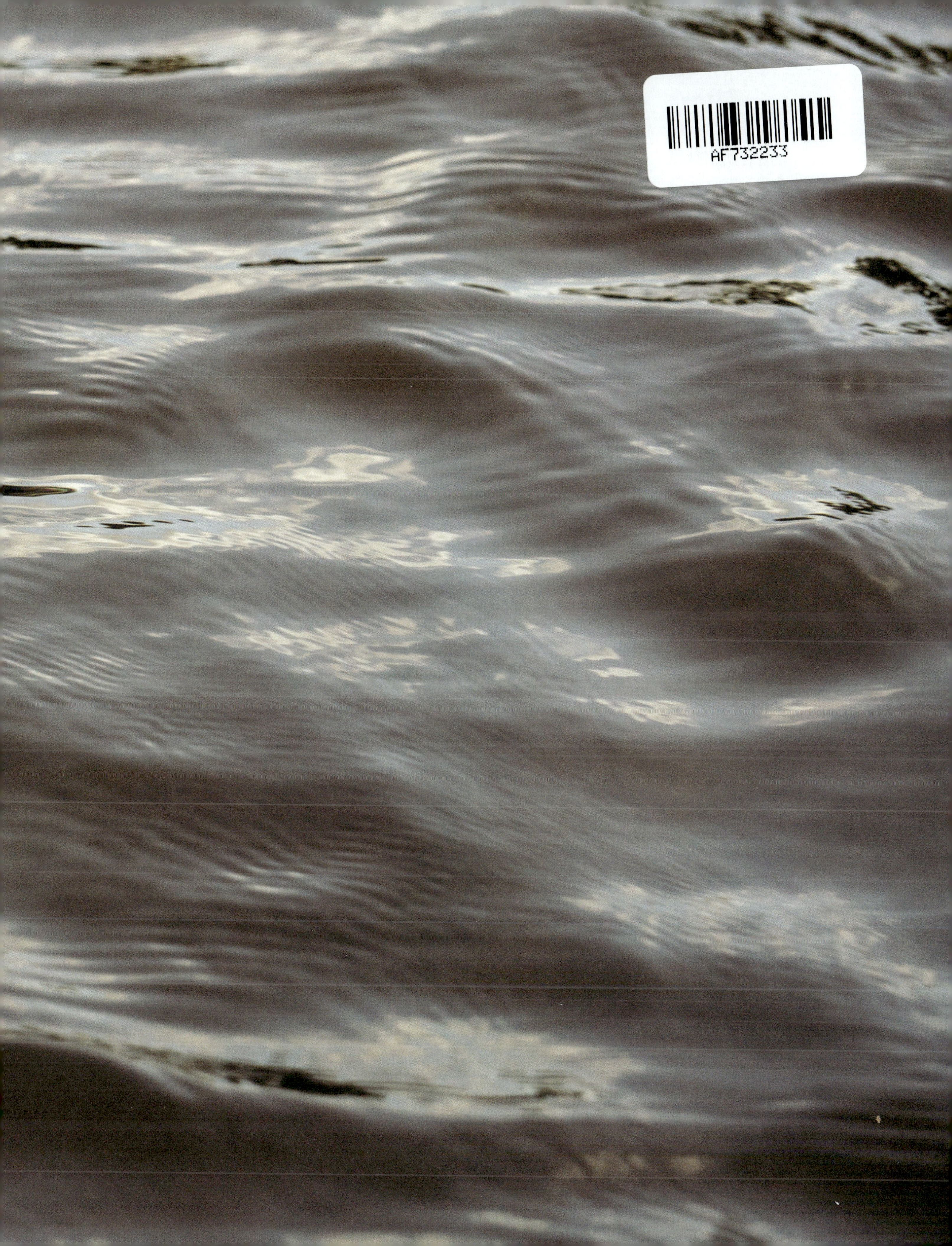

# INVENTING ACADIA

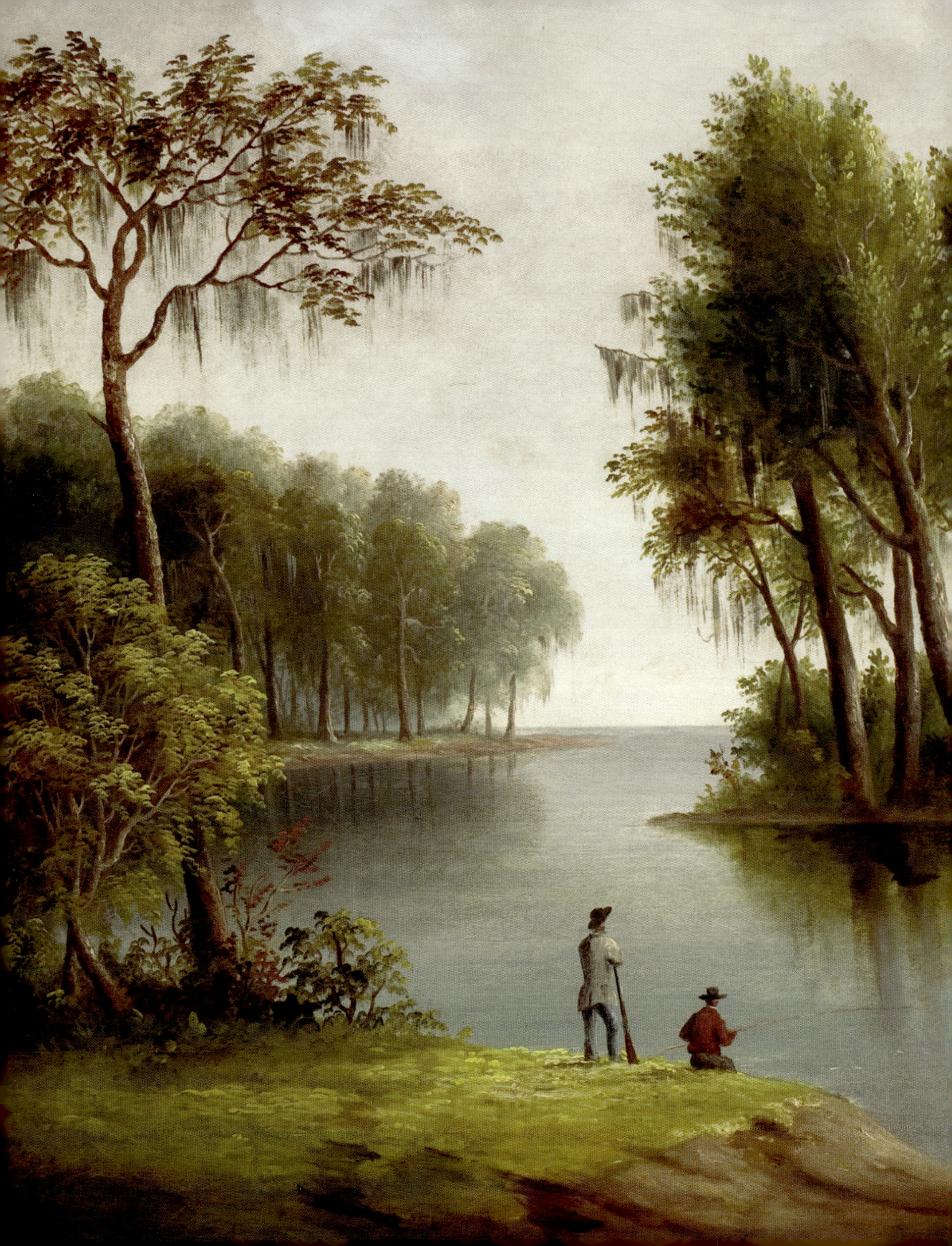

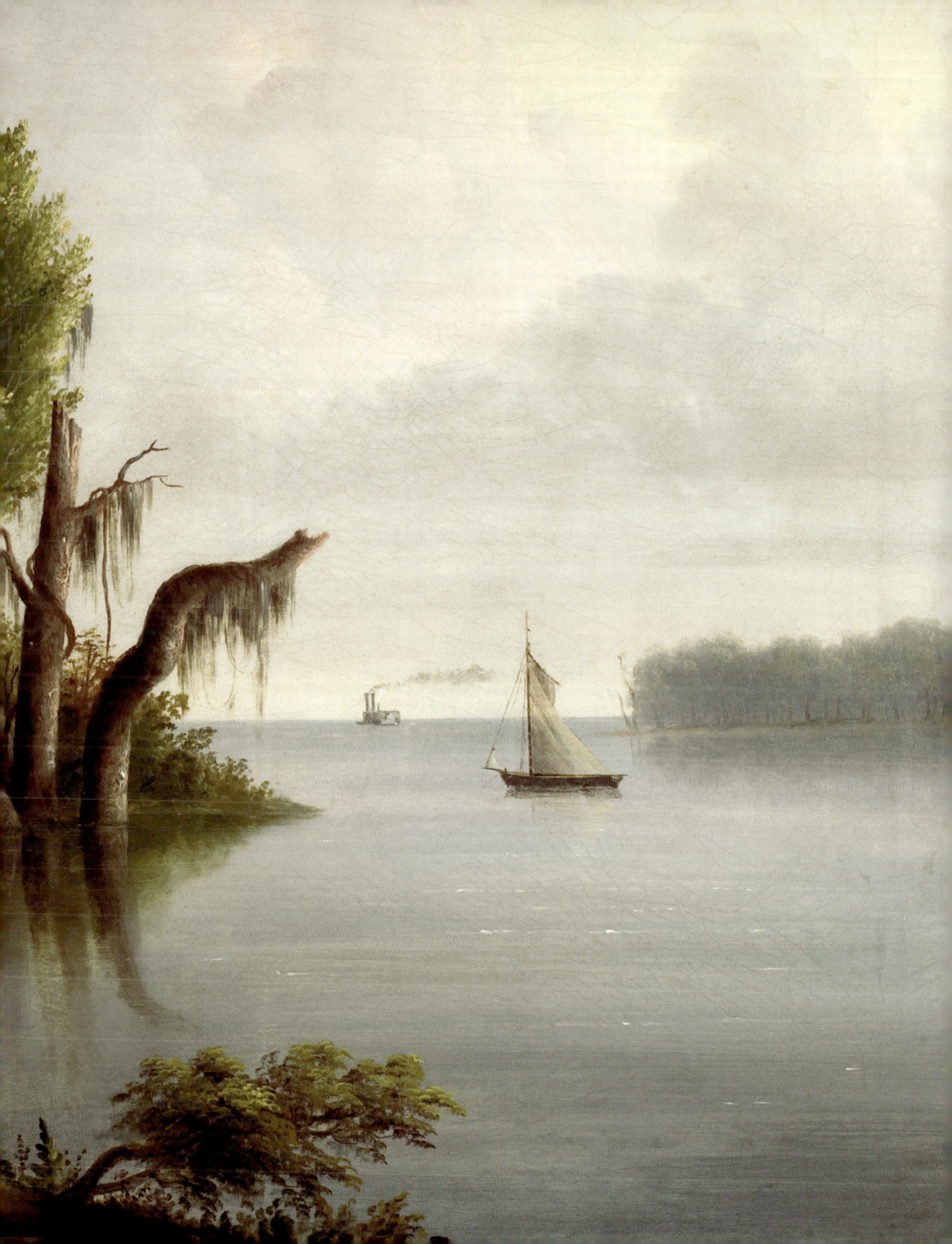

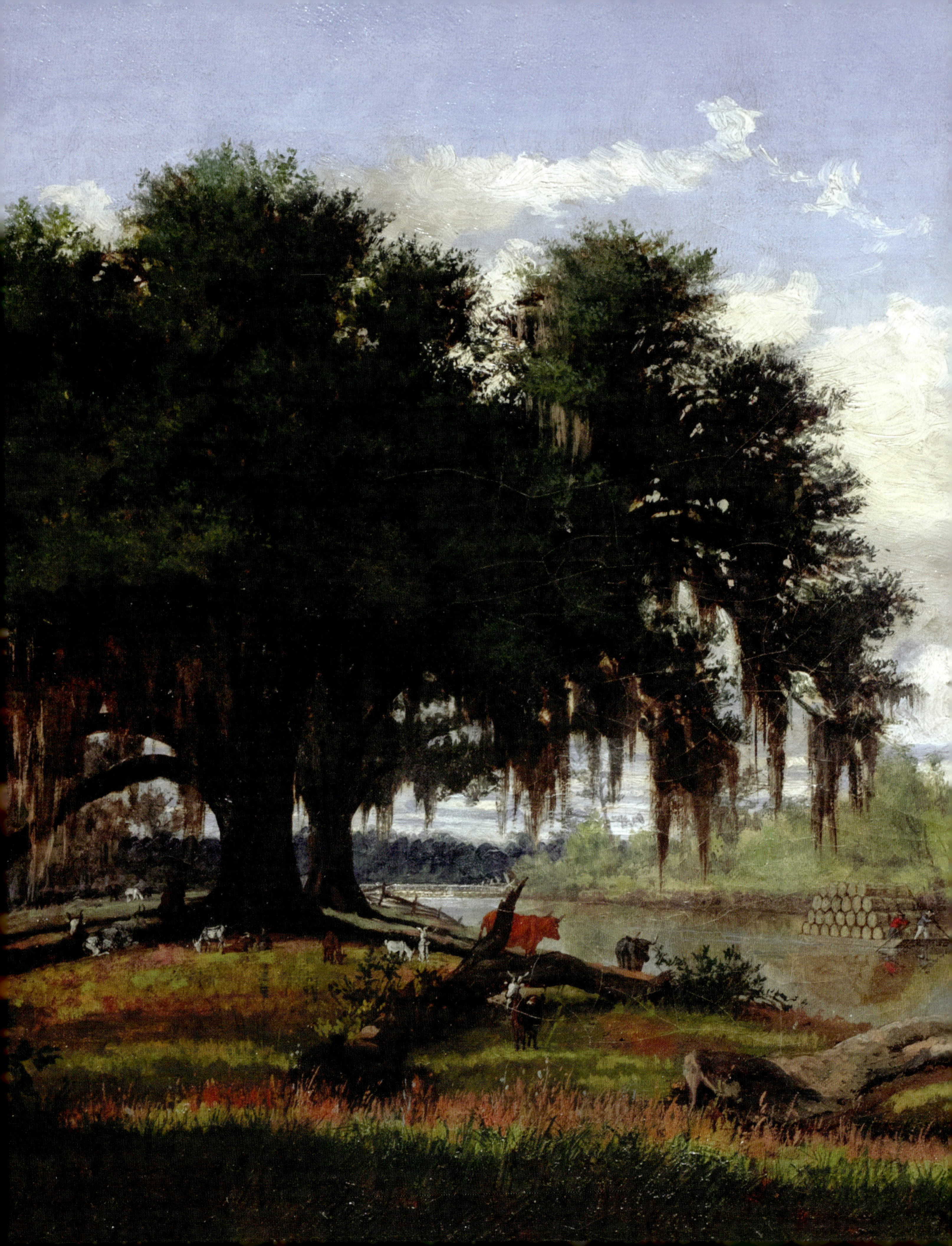

# INVENTING ACADIA

*Painting and Place in Louisiana*

Edited by Katie A. Pfohl

New Orleans Museum of Art

Distributed by Yale University Press,
New Haven and London

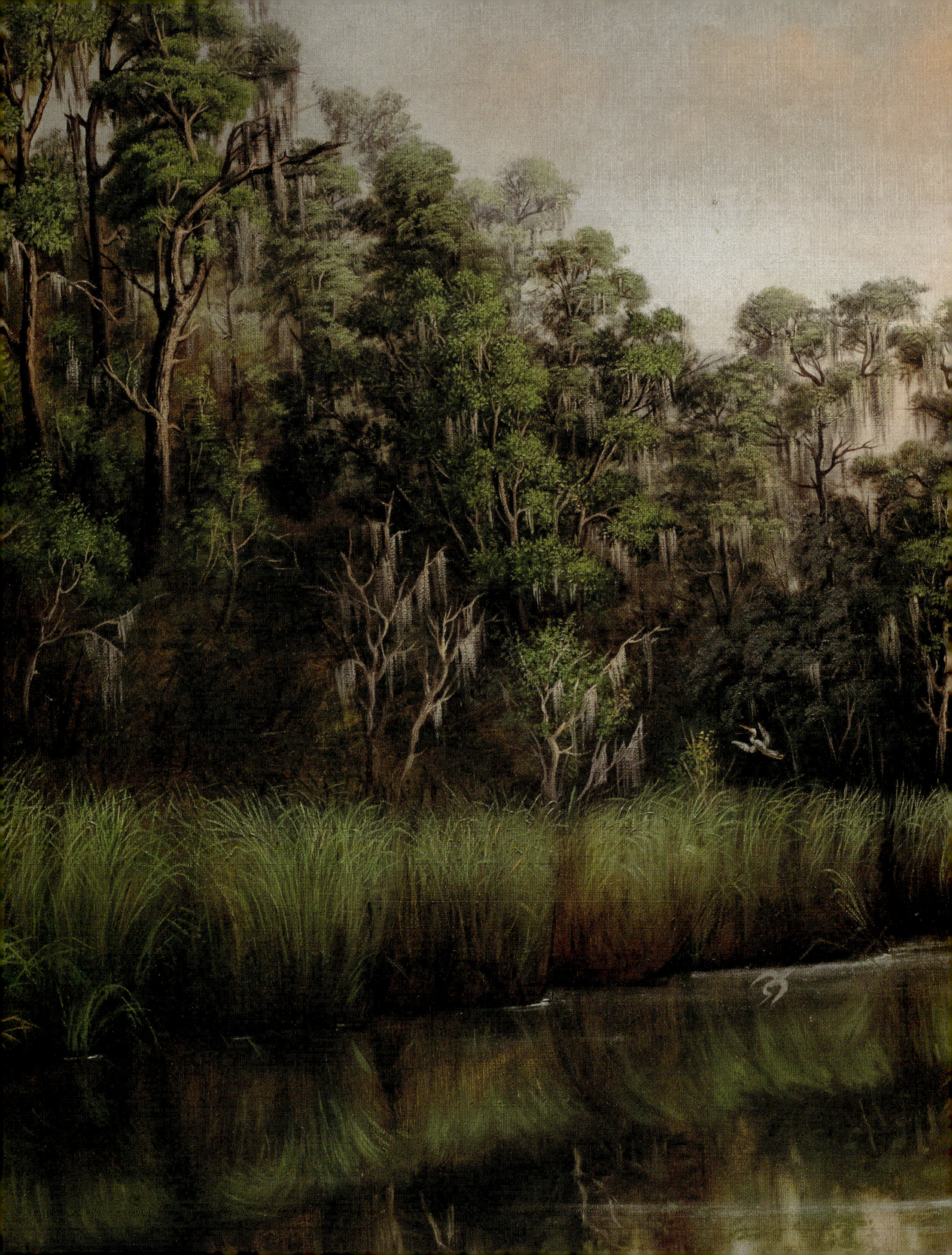

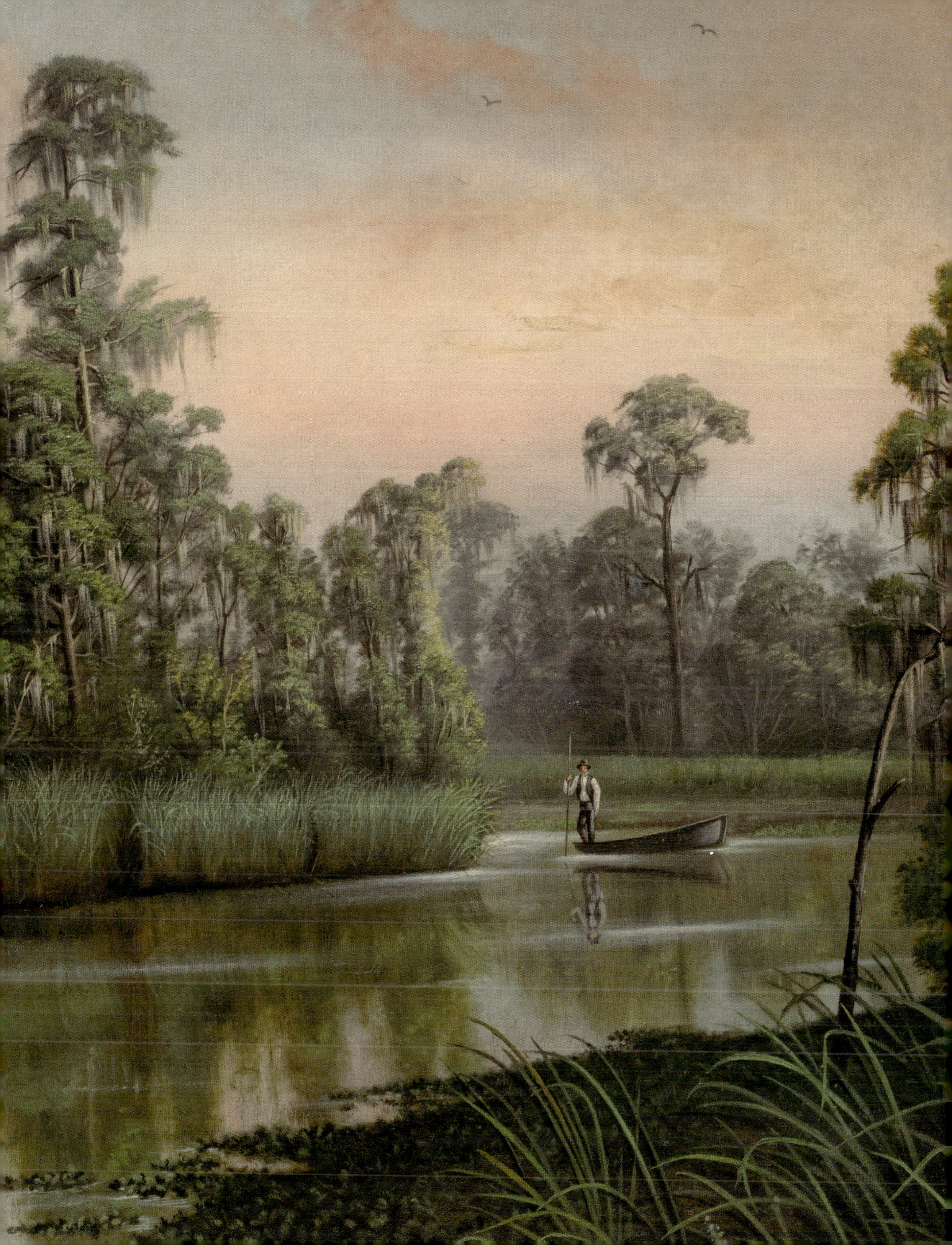

Published on the occasion of the exhibition *Inventing Acadia: Painting and Place in Louisiana,* organized by the New Orleans Museum of Art and presented from November 16, 2019 to January 26, 2020



Published by
New Orleans Museum of Art
1 Collins Diboll Circle, City Park
New Orleans, LA 70124
noma.org

Distributed by
Yale University Press
302 Temple Street
P.O. Box 209040
New Haven, CT 06520-9040
yalebooks.com/art

Library of Congress Control Number: 2019948589
ISBN 978-0-300-24731-2

Designed by Katrina Andry
Printed in the United States of America by
Four Colour Print Group

COVER:
Joseph Rusling Meeker, *After a Storm–Lake Maurepas,* 1888, Oil on canvas, 32 ¾ x 45 ¼ x 1 ¼ inches (framed), Louisiana State University Museum of Art, Gift of the Phi Gamma Chapter of Chi Omega Sorority, 98.14, Photography by David Humphreys.

PP. 2-3 Robert Brammer, *Mississippi Panorama,* 1842-1853, Oil on canvas, 29 x 36 inches, Collection of Stacy and Jay Underwood. Image courtesy of the Mississippi Museum of Art.

P. 4 Everett B.D. Fabrino Julio, *Life Along a Louisiana Bayou,* n.d., Oil on canvas, 15 ¼ x 30 ¼ inches, Roger Houston Ogden Collection, Courtesy of Ogden Museum of Southern Art. Photography by Patrick Barnes.

PP. 6-7 George David Coulon, *Bayou Beauregard, St. Bernard Parish,* 1887, Oil on canvas, 24 x 33 inches, Roger Houston Ogden Collection, Courtesy of Ogden Museum of Southern Art. Photography by Patrick Barnes.

P. 10 William Henry Buck, *Swamp Scene,* 1887, Oil on canvas, 16 x 28 inches, New Orleans Museum of Art, Gift of Miss Mary Bell Swanson Mayer, 80.41

P. 17 George Henry Clements, *Louisiana Swamp,* 1879, Oil on canvas, 26 ½ x 22 ½ inches (framed), Collection of Donna and Bubba Hines, Photography by Roman Alokhin.

P. 232 F. Arthur Callender, *New Orleans from Algiers Point,* 1893, Oil on canvas, 15 x 24 inches, Roger Houston Ogden Collection, Courtesy of Ogden Museum of Southern Art. Photography by Patrick Barnes.

ENDPAPER:
Regina Agu, *Documentation of Site Visit to Lake Maurepas (Water),* 2019, Digital image, Collection of the Artist © Regina Agu 2019

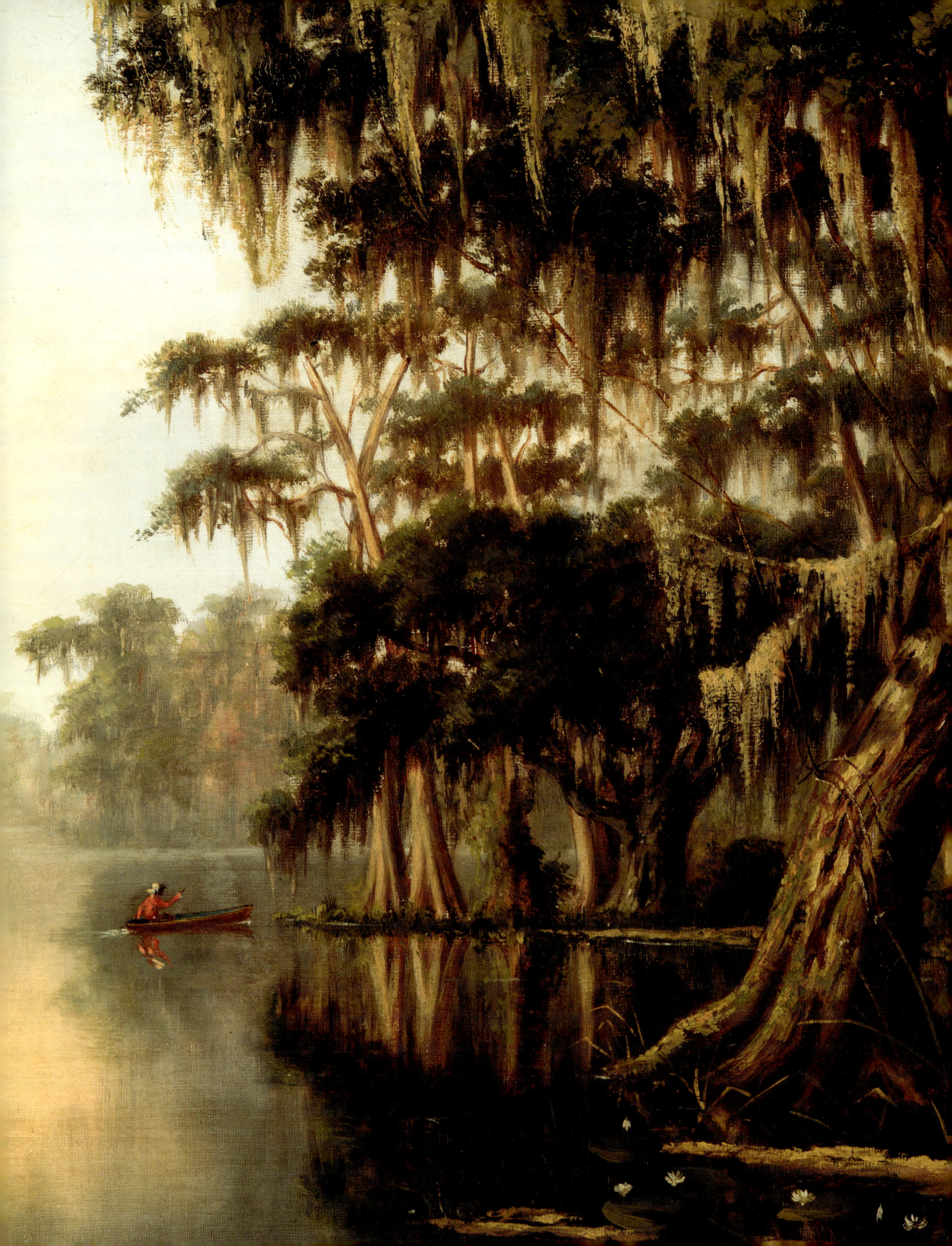

# FOREWORD

*Inventing Acadia: Painting and Place in Louisiana* explores the rise of landscape painting in Louisiana during the nineteenth century, when landscape painters from across the globe came together to form a new school of landscape painting that rivaled any other in the country. The exhibition marks the first time in more than forty years that Louisiana will be the focal point of a landscape exhibition, and the first time that Louisiana landscape painting has been placed in a wider national and international context. More than sixty nineteenth-century landscape paintings from American museums and private lenders, as well as NOMA's permanent collection, are included in *Inventing Acadia*. Offering a newly expansive view of the American landscape and its people, *Inventing Acadia* reveals Louisiana's role in creating a new vision for American landscape art vastly different than that to be found in the rest of the United States or Europe.

From the early nineteenth century onwards, Louisiana's dense forests and tangled, impenetrable swamplands—branded as *Acadie*, or Acadia—represented the apotheosis of the American fascination with untamed wilderness, resulting in landscape paintings that brought American art into conversation with a new type of landscape as well as Louisiana's complicated political terrain. Painters, poets, and writers of the period envisioned Louisiana's swamps, marshes, deltas, and riverbanks at once as a paradise, and as places profoundly marked by the fraught political, racial and environmental realities of Louisiana before and after the Civil War. Painters from all across the world—Toussaint François Bigot, Alfred Boisseau, Richard Clague, William Henry Buck, and others—came together to capture Louisiana's landscapes on canvas, creating paintings of great importance within global landscape traditions.

*Inventing Acadia* would not be possible without the generosity of the many individuals who supported the exhibition and this catalogue. NOMA extends its utmost gratitude to the corporations, foundations and individuals that have supported the exhibition, including Hyatt Regency New Orleans, the Eugenie and Joseph Jones Family Foundation, The Robert Lehman Foundation, Bill and Martha Gunther, Robert J.A. and Norris S.L. Williams, Delta Airlines, Neal Auction Company, Sally E. Richards and Amanda Winstead Fine Art. This project is supported in part by a grant from the National Endowment for the Arts. Research for this exhibition was supported by the Terra Foundation for American Art. NOMA thanks the National Endowment for the Arts for their support of exhibition research in both Paris and Mexico City, and the Terra Foundation for American Art for funding a first—and crucial—research trip to France.

We also wish to thank the many institutions and private collectors that have lent key artworks to the exhibition, thereby allowing us to share wonderful examples of landscape art with the public. We thank The Art Institute of Chicago, The Brooklyn Museum, Detroit Institute of Arts, The Historic New Orleans Collection, Louisiana State Museum, Louisiana State University Museum of Art, Minneapolis Institute of Art, Montgomery Museum of Fine Arts, Morris Museum of Art, Saint Louis Art Museum, and The Walters Art Museum for lending works from their collections, and also acknowledge Walter O. Evans, Don Fuson, Martha and Bill Gunther, Jennifer and Fred Heebe, Donna and Bubba Hines, Roger Ogden and Ken Barnes, Tommy Spinosa, Stacy and Jay Underwood, Virginia and Michael White, and Mr. and Mrs. Dwight Winstead for lending works from their private collections.

This catalogue features five texts from scholars of French, American, Mexican, and Caribbean landscape painting who represent important and timely new approaches to the field. Their essays uncover little-known regional histories, while at the same time demonstrating the importance of this art for landscape scholarship in Europe and the United States more broadly. We thank Katie A. Pfohl, NOMA's Curator of Modern and Contemporary Art, and curator of this exhibition, for her work on both this exhibition and catalogue. NOMA has had this project in mind for several years, but it was only when Katie joined the NOMA curatorial staff that we could take on such an important project. Her talent and insightful scholarship has resulted in a superb exhibition. We wish to especially acknowledge Roger Ogden and Ken Barnes for their sponsorship of this exhibition catalogue, and for being such tireless advocates and collectors of Louisiana landscape painting for the last fifty years, inspiring a generation of collectors, curators, and scholars to study and celebrate Southern art. Their lead gift ensured this project's success.

Capturing the unique landscape and ecology of the region, *Inventing Acadia* grapples with questions that continue to inform our contemporary connections to the environment, culture, and history of Louisiana, the place so many of us call home. Shedding new light on Louisiana's landscape history, this exhibition and catalogue also looks forward, to consider how this history shapes art and life in Louisiana today.

Susan M. Taylor
The Montine McDaniel Freeman Director
New Orleans Museum of Art

# ACKNOWLEDGEMENTS

This exhibition is both an act of recovery, and a recognition of loss. Because these paintings have, up until recently, been less widely known, they have not been as carefully researched, documented, and preserved as landscape painting from other places. Much art from this genre—especially work by Indigenous communities, women, and people of color—have been lost to floods, fire, and the ravages of time. Due to the dedication of public museums and private collectors from this region and beyond, some paintings have survived to be shared with the public for this exhibition, which offers new interpretations that illuminate the complex histories of which these landscapes are a part. We first wish to thank the many museums, collectors, curators, and scholars who have helped steward and protect the works in this exhibition over the course of the last two centuries, and also acknowledge the many voices and perspectives that have been lost. The works in this exhibition picture precarious landscapes, and also reflect the precarity of history itself in a place of constant flooding, where land itself is constantly being built, and lost.

Our gratitude also goes to the distinguished group of scholars and curators whose voices are assembled in this catalogue, and whose interpretations have been so crucial for shaping this exhibition. Thank you to Anna Arabindan-Kesson and Mia L. Bagneris for helping us understand how the legacy of slavery informs our view of these landscapes; Kelly Presutti for showing the startling connections between the French Barbizon School and Louisiana-based landscape artists; Aurora Yarazeth Avilés García for shedding light on the artistic ties between Louisiana and Mexico; and Ryan N. Dennis for her interview with contemporary artist Regina Agu. We also thank Zarina Martínez Lacy for her sensitive translation of Aurora Yarazeth Avilés García's essay into English. We wish also to acknowledge the work of the many fellows and research assistants who have been part of this show, including María Beatriz Haro Carríon, Caroline Cox, Nicole J. Lampl, Lucia O. Momoh, Mónica Ramírez, Marjorie A. Rawle, Anne C. B. Roberts, Paris Willoughby, and Allison K. Young. Special thanks goes to Anne C. B. Roberts for helping to get this catalogue over the finish line.

We thank New Orleans-based artist and graphic designer Katrina Andry for her vision for the catalogue design. Phillip Collier and Chris Williams were instrumental in helping to bring this catalogue to completion in the final stages of the project.

Contemporary artist Regina Agu's installation in NOMA's Great Hall brings new depth and perspective to the historical paintings in the exhibition. We thank Regina for bringing such great creativity and passion to this project, and for braving humidity, snakes, and alligators to create stunning new landscape imagery for this exhibition. Regina's project at NOMA is produced in partnership with A Studio in the Woods, an artist residency program focused around art and environment, and we also wish to thank A Studio in the Woods for their collaboration and friendship. Ama Rogan, Managing Director; Cammie Hill-Prewitt, Residency Coordinator; Grace Rennie, Residency Technician; and David Baker, Environmental Curator, have been wonderful partners for this project, providing us with invaluable connections to artists, scientists, and communities across the region, and teaching us about the political and environmental issues affecting Louisiana's landscapes today. We also wish to thank David Baker at A Studio in the Woods; Richie Blink, the Plaquemines Community Outreach Coordinator for the National Wildlife Federation; and Dr. Robert Moreau at the Turtle Cove Environmental Research Station for leading us on deeply fun and informative trips across the region's waterways.

This exhibition would not have been possible without the expertise, talent, and dedication of NOMA's staff. This exhibition and catalogue have benefited greatly from the vision and direction of Susan M. Taylor, The Montine McDaniel Freeman Director, and Lisa Rotondo-McCord, Deputy Director for Curatorial Affairs, who has overseen every aspect of this project with the grace, insight, and good humor she brings to all that she does. We also thank Anne Baños, NOMA's Deputy Director, and NOMA's development team, especially Jenni Daniel, Director of Development; Margaux Krane, Director of Branding and Communications; and Elisabeth Rietvelt, Monique A. Tourres, and Bridget Raburn. Jennifer Ickes, Head Registrar, expertly led the exhibition's installation and NOMA's installation team, including Tony Garma, Matthew Hance, Tao-nha Hoang, Geoff Vick, and Tim Morales. We especially want to acknowledge Elizabeth Bahls, Laura Povinelli, and Marie-Page Phelps. Our gratitude goes also to Mary Degnan and David Johnson for their editing and graphic design work on the exhibition; and NOMA's supurb visitor experience team, gallery attendants, and maintenance staff.

NOMA's Learning and Engagement team has played a pivotal role in bringing new interpretations, voices, and perspectives to the show. Gabrielle Wyrick, NOMA's Deputy Director of Learning and Engagement, has been a thoughtful partner in considering how to present these landscapes—and the issues and questions they raise—to today's audiences. Jennifer M. Williams, Public Program Manager, has worked tirelessly to develop and realize these programs, and we thank her for her vision and dedication. Nic Brierre Aziz, Community Engagement Curator, has helped bring this art and its history beyond the museum's walls through community outreach programs in schools across the city. We also thank Tracy E. Kennan, Chantell Nabonne, Danielle Rives, and Connor Kilian.

NOMA has developed a range of public programs around this exhibition, and we wish to extend our greatest thanks to our partners in this work, as well as to The Robert Lehman Foundation for sponsoring these programs. Southerly Gold, an artist ensemble of three female photographers—Aubrey Edwards, Ariya Martin and Elena Ricci—will create a visual field guide and interpretation space for the exhibition. We are also pleased to partner with Deltaworkers, a New Orleans-based artistic production and residence program, on a four-part film series entitled *Fragmented Landscapes/Beyond Acadia* that brings together artists from across the world to consider our changing landscape and environment, and thank Maaike Gouwenberg for her work on this series. We also thank Hannah Chalew, artist, and Jane Bleeker, perfumer of XODO Botanicals, for working with us to develop a scent for the exhibition, and for related programming that explores the relationship between scent, landscape, and memory. Tom Beller, Professor of English at Tulane University, has brought together Monique Harden, Assistant Director of Law and Policy and the Community Engagement Program Manager at the Deep South Center for Environmental Justice, and Shannon Rainey, President of the Residents of Gordon Plaza, Inc., for a panel on environmental justice in New Orleans. We also extend our gratitude to Les Cenelles, a New Orleans-based musical collective, for performing a special closing-night concert for the exhibition that will fuse historical Creole music with original contemporary compositions.

*Inventing Acadia* has already inspired productive conversations about Louisiana's landscape history—and future. We thank everyone who has been part of this dialogue so far, and invite all of the readers of this catalogue and viewers of this exhibition to be part of this evolving conversation.

Katie A. Pfohl
Curator of Modern and Contemporary Art
New Orleans Museum of Art

# LENDERS TO THE EXHIBITION

The Art Institute of Chicago

The Brooklyn Museum

Detroit Institute of Arts

Walter O. Evans

Don Fuson

Martha and Bill Gunther

Jennifer and Fred Heebe

Donna and Bubba Hines

The Historic New Orleans Collection

Louisiana State Museum

Louisiana State University Museum of Art

Minneapolis Institute of Art

Montgomery Museum of Fine Arts

Morris Museum of Art

Roger Ogden and Ken Barnes

Saint Louis Art Museum

Tommy Spinosa

Stacy and Jay Underwood

The Walters Art Museum

Virginia and Michael White

Mr. and Mrs. Dwight Winstead

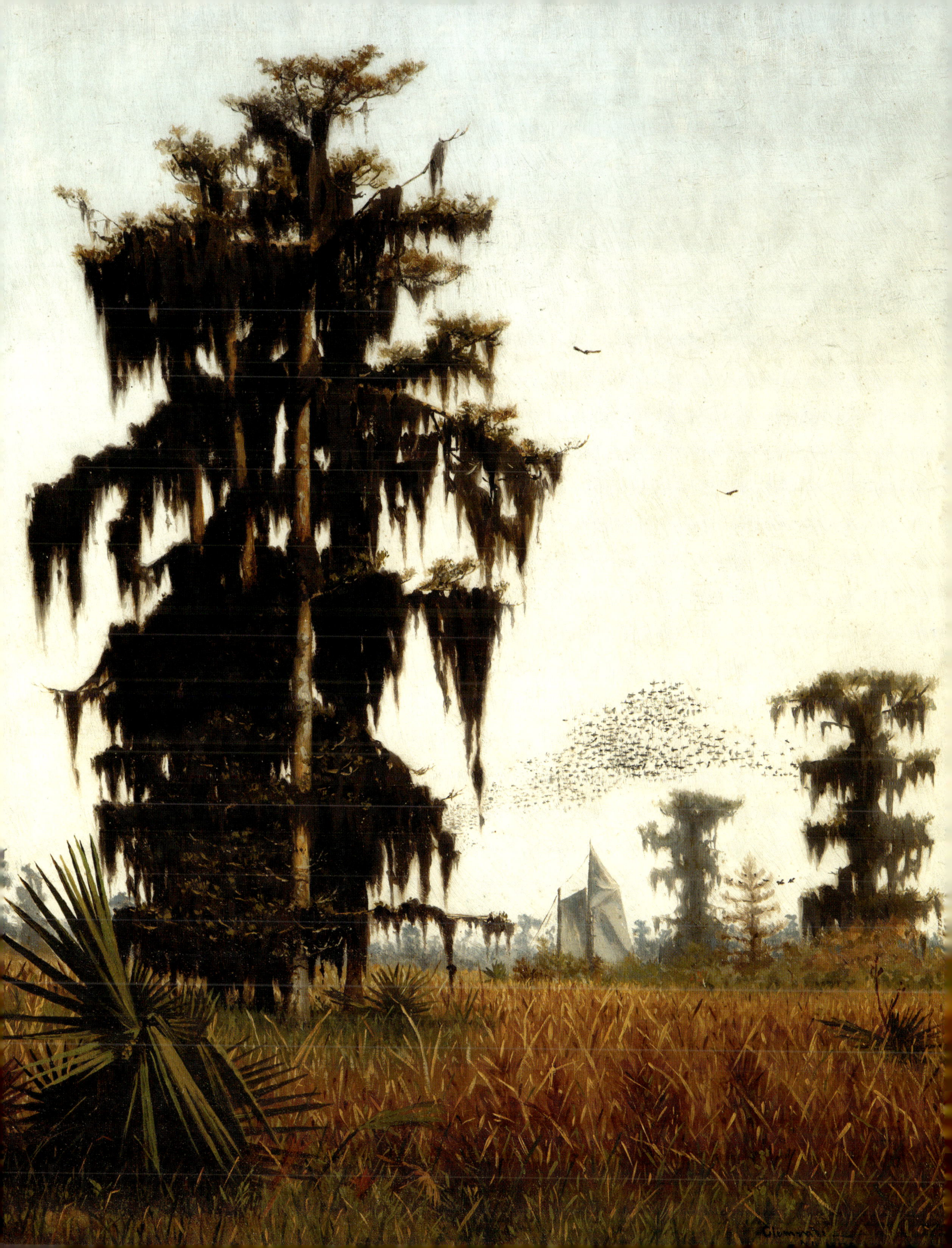

# TEXTS

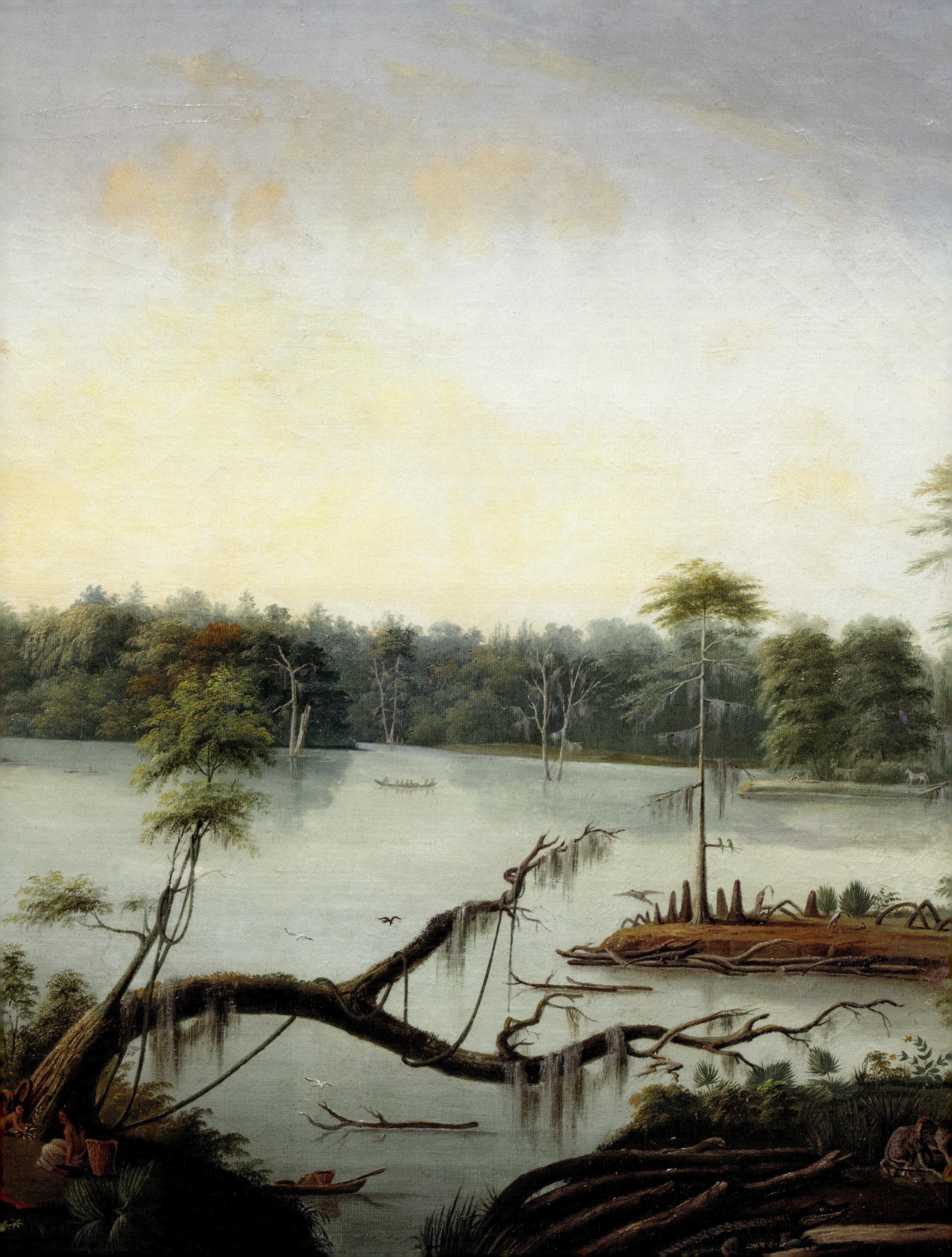

# In Land, Sea: Louisiana's Shifting Landscape

Katie A. Pfohl

In south Louisiana, no one can ever precisely define the difference between land and sea. They never could. Early visitors often described the region—its vast network of swamps and bayous that give way to coastal marshes, and rivers that flow into oceans—as a place somewhere between land and water: "a vast alluvia in a semi-liquid state," that, as French geographer Élisée Reclus wrote during his 1853 visit to the region, "was not even part of the continent yet."[1] As many recognized in the eighteenth and nineteenth centuries, to be in Louisiana was to be in a state of constant flux, a landscape in which it was impossible to fix the boundaries between delta and marsh, swamp and bayou, or river and sea. Louisiana was a place where, in the words of another nineteenth century writer, "the normal relations everywhere of land and water are reversed, or at least interchangeable."[2] To some, this reversal caused Louisiana's river deltas and swamplands "to bear the most striking resemblance to the ocean; when you are in them you readily fancy yourself at sea."[3] As a result, Louisiana seemed to many to be less of a landscape, and more—in the words of Louisiana State Representative Lionel A. Sheldon, in his 1892 argument for the establishment of a levee system—of an "inland sea."[4]

The painters who came to this region—from Europe, the Caribbean, and the broader Americas—encountered a landscape utterly unlike the mountains and valleys around which the very idea of landscape painting had been formed. In Louisiana, these artists travelled through boundless wetlands that barely looked like land at all, places that appeared, in the words of nineteenth-century historian Charles Gayarré, "as if they wish to sink back into the sea, from shame of having come into the world prematurely, before having been shaped and licked by nature into proper objects of existence."[5] This radical indeterminacy made many wonder whether Louisiana could even be referred to as land, much less painted as a landscape. For to treat "a country [that] is but so much flotsam and jetsam" as a landscape, many worried at the time, would be to disturb the very definition of land itself.[6] To take it one step further, and imagine such a place as a subject fit for a landscape painting, as one writer proclaimed in 1848, was "daring the wrath of Academicians Durand and Doughty"; famed American painters who—it is implied—would be none too happy to see this "waste of waters" rendered in paint.[7]

To paint this place, then, was an act of invention—a transformation of water into land, and a revisioning of the medium of landscape painting itself. Focusing on some of the

Fig. 1
Toussaint François Bigot, *Alchapalia, Louisiana*, 1848, Oil on canvas, 29 ½ x 36 inches, Roger Houston Ogden Collection, Courtesy of Ogden Museum of Southern Art. Photography by Patrick Barnes.

earliest representations of Louisiana's territories by European and American artists, this essay explores the way these artists navigated the act of painting Louisiana, a landscape that seemed, to many, to be "spilled out and spread out in almost limitless extent."[8] As these artists grappled with how to bring to canvas a landscape that knew no such bounds, they drew upon many different systems of knowledge culled from sources ranging from European cartography and mapmaking, to Indigenous art and elements from both European and American painting. In the works of artists such as Alexandre de Batz, Toussaint François Bigot, Alfred L. Boisseau, Robert Brammer, Blanche Virginia Blanchard, and Harriet Goodhue Hosmer, many different systems of knowledge collide, showing how art that is not typically considered alongside painting—such as Indigenous basketry—often, in fact, lead the way. Precisely because Louisiana's landscape proved so resistant to traditional practices of landscape painting, these works possess a level of aesthetic innovation and openness rare in European or American art of this time. Bringing together artistic influences from many diverse sources, these artworks push beyond the frame of landscape painting to become more akin to the fluid form of the wetlands themselves. With water streaming across, around and through them, these paintings make evident their connection to the vast aqueous landscape of the Mississippi River Delta, the Gulf of Mexico, and the ocean beyond.

Unlike even other representations of coastal wetlands, for instance Martin Johnson Heade's paintings of the marshes of New England in works such as *Newburyport Marshes: Approaching Storm* (circa 1871; Fig. 2), these paintings lay bare many clashing ideas about land and water management in the nineteenth century.[9] Painted concurrently with new efforts to control and commandeer Louisiana's landscape—through levees and logging, the digging of canals, and the displacement and enslavement of people—these artworks picture a landscape actively refusing to be reshaped, either by painterly perspective or through land reclamation. In 1816, the year a major flood hit New Orleans, a correspondent for the *Niles' Weekly Register* wrote with "water rising at [their] door" that "the most considerable work of art, yet constructed for the purpose of rendering this country habitable, is the embankment of the river, usually called the levee."[10] Calling the levee a work of art, this early writer showed his awareness of the connection between the two, hinting at the ways that, in Louisiana, art was working alongside real land development to reshape the landscape—to bring it into form. In not allowing their work to become a simple or easy tool of this reshaping, the artists explored in this essay show the stakes of trying to transform Louisiana's amorphous land into a painted landscape, and reveal the many voices and perspectives that, as a result of this transformation, have been lost.

## The Arrival Of Painting

One of the first known landscape paintings of the region now known as Louisiana is Alexandre de Batz's *Desseins de Sauvages de Plusieurs Nations, New Orleans* (1735; Fig. 3), a watercolor that is now in the Peabody Museum of Archaeology and Ethnology at Harvard University. A French architect, draftsman and artist in the employ of the French colonial government, de Batz was one of the first European artists to represent the landscapes

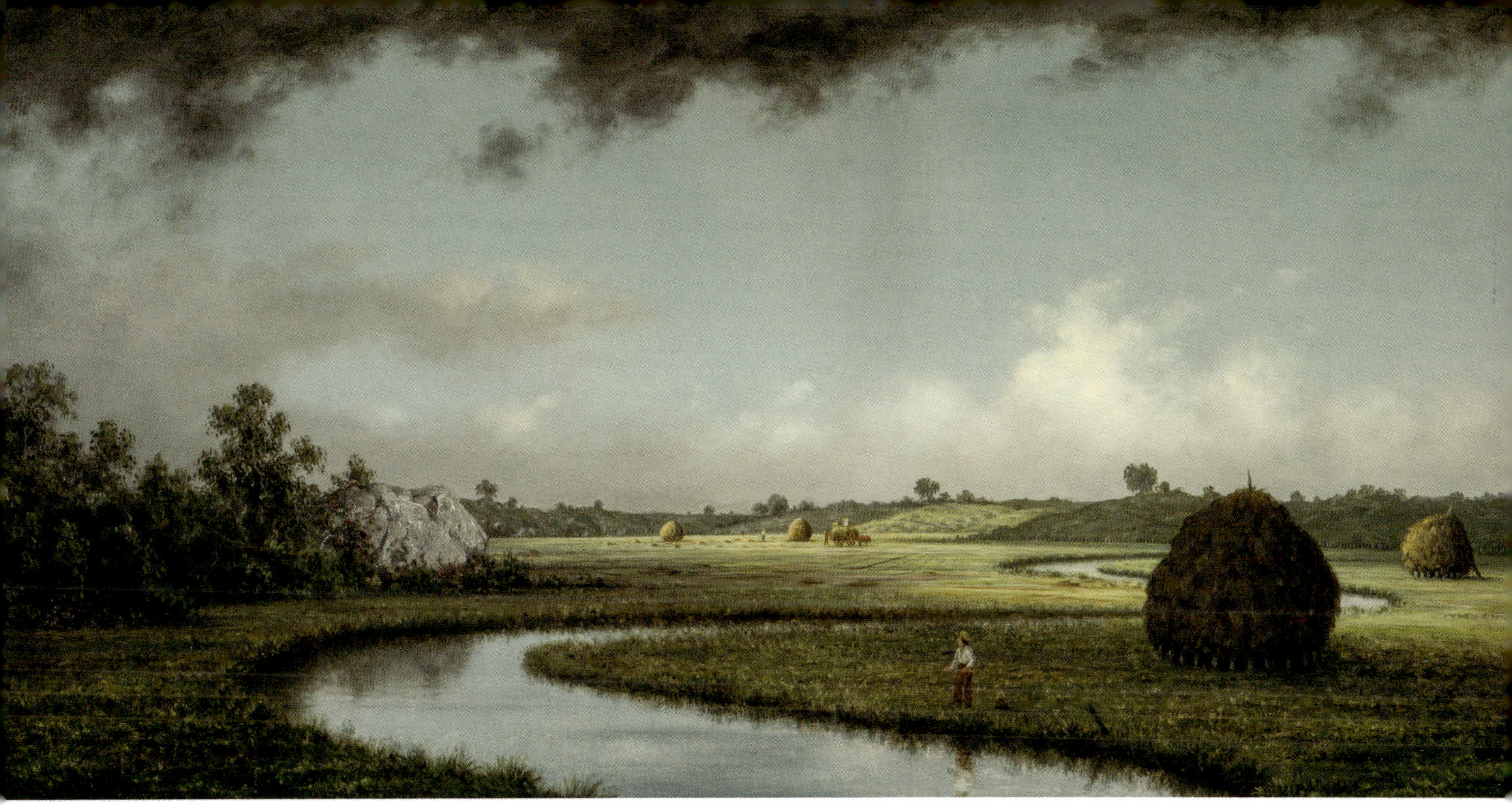

Fig. 2
Martin Johnson Heade, *Newburyport Marshes: Approaching Storm*, circa 1871, Oil on canvas, 15 1/4 x 30 1/8 inches, Terra Foundation for American Art, Daniel J. Terra Collection, 1999. 68, Photography © Terra Foundation for American Art

and people of what eventually became Louisiana. Arriving to the Louisiana Territories in 1730 to serve as the "Engineer to the King," de Batz designed one of New Orleans's first scientific observatories, and is today best known as one of the chief architects of the Ursuline Convent—the last remaining structure built during the French occupation that still survives today.[11] During his time in New Orleans, de Batz also created a group of watercolors and pen and ink drawings of Louisiana's Indigenous populations that are at once ethnographic studies and landscape representations in their own right. In these early paintings and drawings, de Batz grapples with a problem that informs the work of nearly all of the painters that followed: how to capture Louisiana's landscape through forms of composition and perspective developed for firmer ground.

In de Batz's *Desseins de Sauvages de Plusieurs Nations, New Orleans* a group of Indigenous people occupy a sliver of land set directly between two dark, shaded lines. One line represents the flow of the Mississippi River, and the other a tree line that follows the meandering pathway of the river back into the painting's background. Likely showing the high ground around the Mississippi River upon which Indigenous communities built some of the region's first settlements—the crescent from which New Orleans takes its name—the painting includes a diverse group of Indigenous people from across the country, including at least one member from the regional Atakapa-Ishak Nation. At once an ethnographic document and a landscape study, the painting places these figures within complex topography of the Mississippi River Delta, documenting how French colonists were attempting control both the landscape and its Indigenous inhabitants under colonial rule.

The logic of the composition owes much more to the maps of the Mississippi River Delta that de Batz was creating concurrently, such as his widely published *Carte general de toute la côte de la Louisianne* (1747; Fig. 4), than to any precedent from European landscape painting he might have brought over from France. During this time, French landscape paintings typically presented idealized scenes in which the landscape was clearly

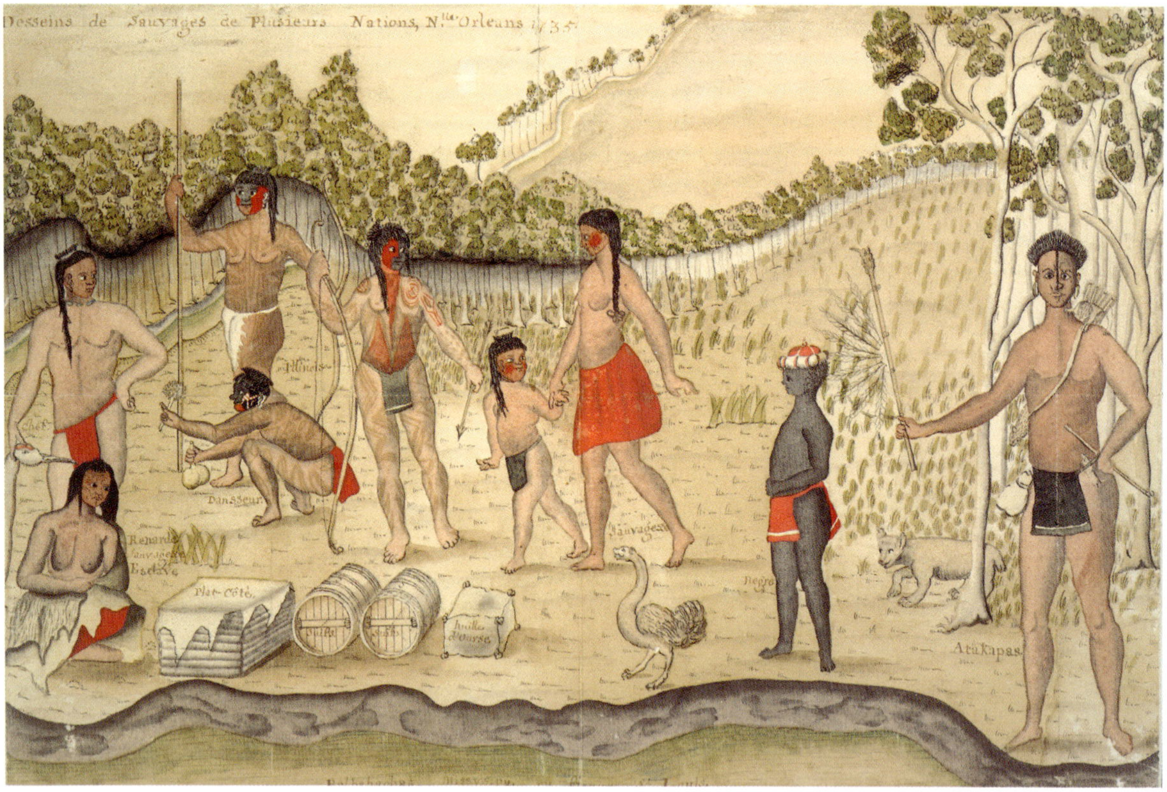
Desseins de Sauvages de Plusieurs Nations, Nlle Orleans 1735
Atakapas

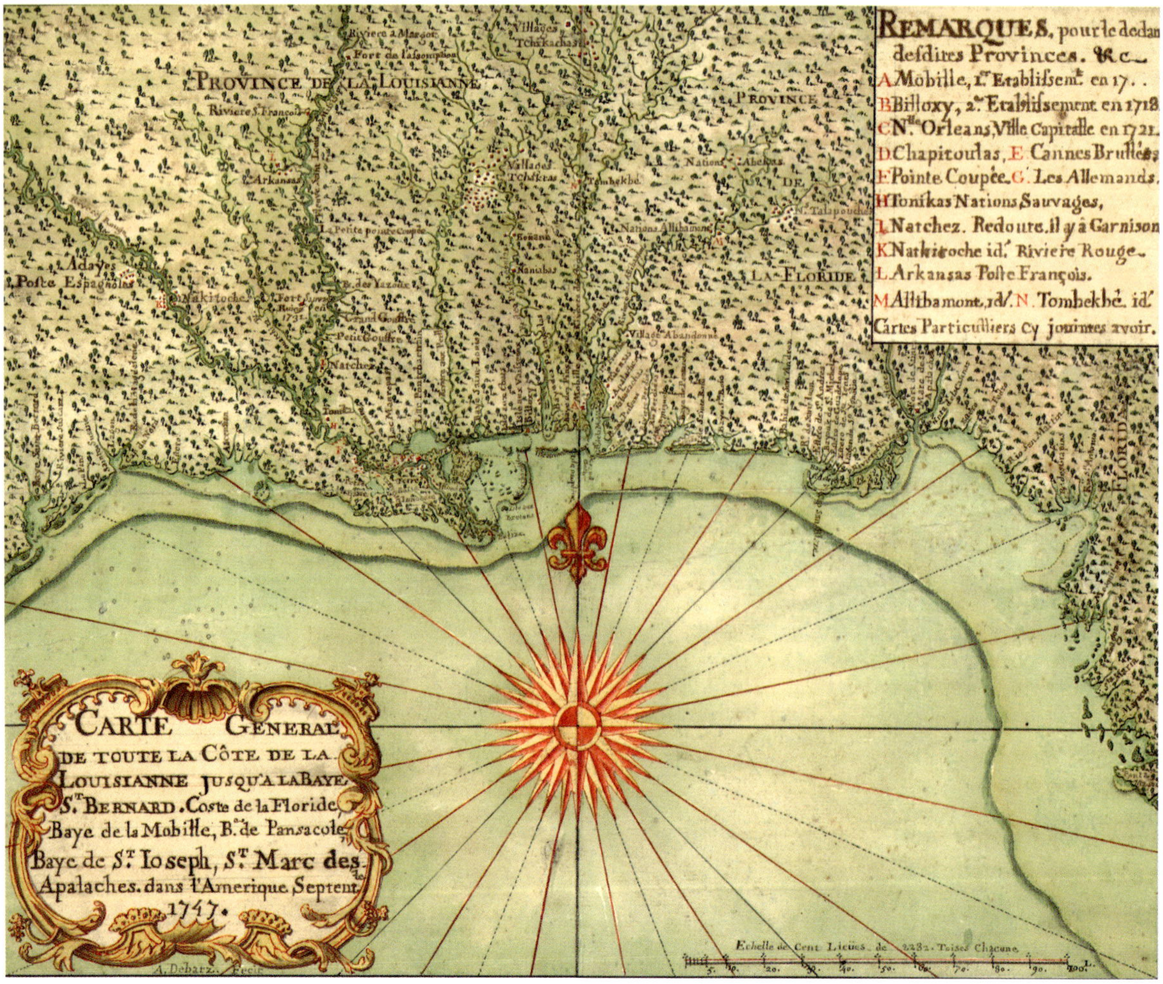
REMARQUES, pour le dedan desdites Provinces. &c.
A Mobille, 1er Etablissemt. en 17. .
B Billoxy, 2e Etablissement en 1718
C Nlle Orleans, Ville Capitalle en 1721.
D Chapitoulas, E. Cannes Brullés,
F Pointe Coupée. G. Les Allemands.
H Tonikas Nations Sauvages,
I Natchez. Redoute. il y a Garnison
K Natchitoche id. Riviere Rouge.
L Arkansas Poste François.
M Alibamont. id. N. Tombekbé. id.
Cartes Particulliers cy jointes avoir.
PROVINCE DE LA LOUISIANNE
PROVINCE
LA FLORIDE
CARTE GENERALE DE TOUTE LA CÔTE DE LA LOUISIANNE JUSQU'A LA BAYE ST. BERNARD. Coste de la Floride, Baye de la Mobille, Bie. de Pansacole, Baye de St. Ioseph, St. Marc des Apalaches. dans l'Amerique Septent.
1747.

Fig. 3 (opposite)
Alexander de Batz, *Desseins de Sauvages de Plusieurs Nations, New Orleans*, 1735, Watercolor, gouache, Iron gail ink, Carbon-based ink, and Graphite on medium weight blue laid paper, 11 3/4 x 17 13/16 inches, Gift of the Estate of Belle J. Bushnell, 1941, Peabody Museum of Archaeology and Ethnology, Harvard University, 41-72-10/20

Fig. 4 (opposite)
Alexandre de Batz, *Carte general de toute la côte de la Louisianne jusqu'a la Baye St. Bernard, coste de la Floride, Baye de la Mobile, Be. De Pansacole, Baye de St. Joseph, St. Marc des Apalaches. Dans l'Amerique septentle.*, 1747, 84 x 104 inches, Library of Congress, Geography and Map Divison.

organized both by perspective—a clear progression from foreground to background—as well as calming signs of human control over nature, such as the bridge that directs the flow of water in French painter Claude Lorrain's *Ideal View of Tivoli* (1644; Fig. 5). Copies of Lorrain's paintings were on view in New Orleans as early as 1845, and reviewers marveled at their "aerial perspective," which offered elevated vistas impossible to achieve within the flat landscape of a river delta.[12] de Batz, in contrast, organizes *Desseins de Sauvages de Plusieurs Nations, New Orleans* just like his map: the flow of the river in the foreground of his painting follows the shape of Louisiana's coastline, with the receding line of trees in the painting's background even mirroring the pathway of the Mississippi River as it flows inland. Organizing his painting like his map—or, perhaps, his map like his painting—de Batz captured the conflict between European systems of order—like painting and cartography—and the landscape's own patterns. Showing how the region's wild flow of water ultimately escaped all these forms of way-finding, de Batz draws a clear visual connection between the lines of the fanned-out feathers on the calumet (pipe) being held by the Atakapa-Ishak person on the painting's far right, and the points of the compass on his map. So doing, his painting points away from mapmaking and European perspective, and toward the knowledge systems de Batz found within the region's Indigenous communities.[13]

Making him more attuned to the lived complexities of the river delta, de Batz's maps helped him gain perspective on how to represent a place so antithetical to Lorrain's idealized views. It wasn't, of course, that these maps made sense of the delta—in many ways they also visually presented the problem—but they allowed de Batz to see how this landscape

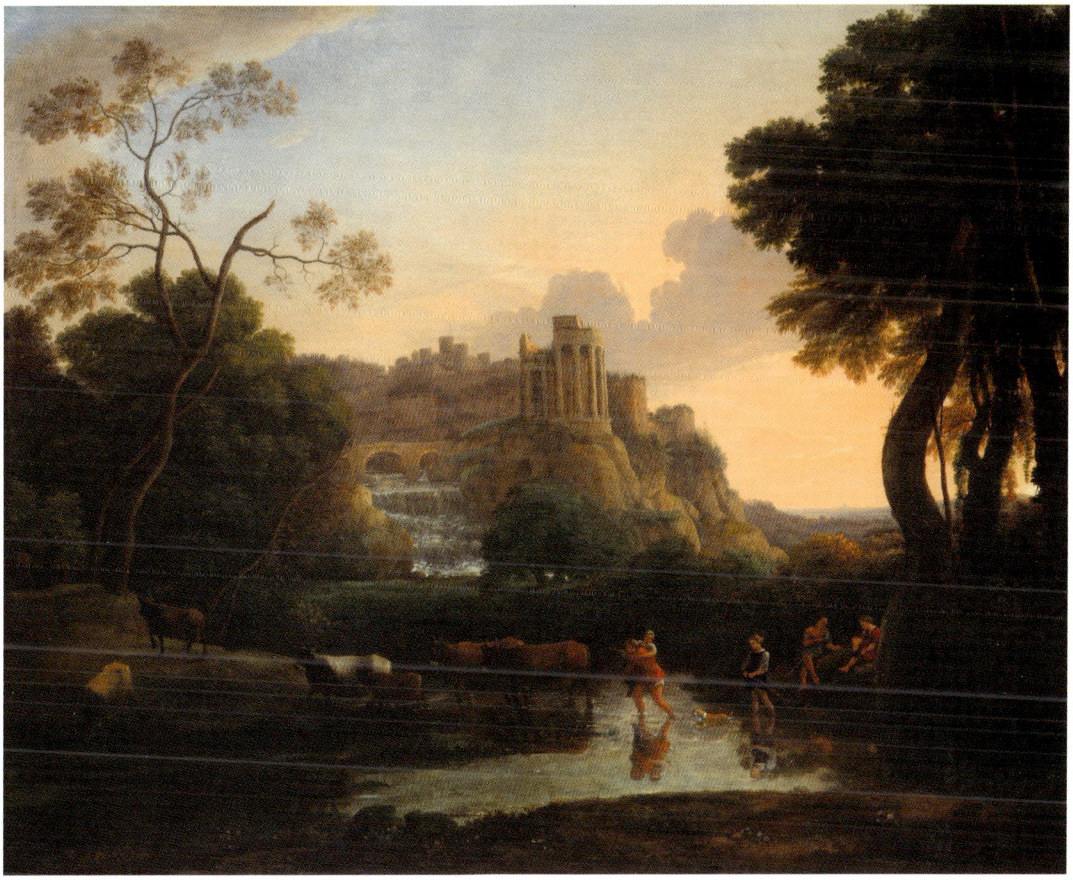

Fig. 5
Claude Lorrain, *Ideal View of Tivoli*, 1644, Oil on canvas, 55 1/8 x 67 1/2 inches, New Orleans Museum of Art, Museum Purchase, Art Acquisition Fund Drive, 78.1, Photography by Roman Alohkin.

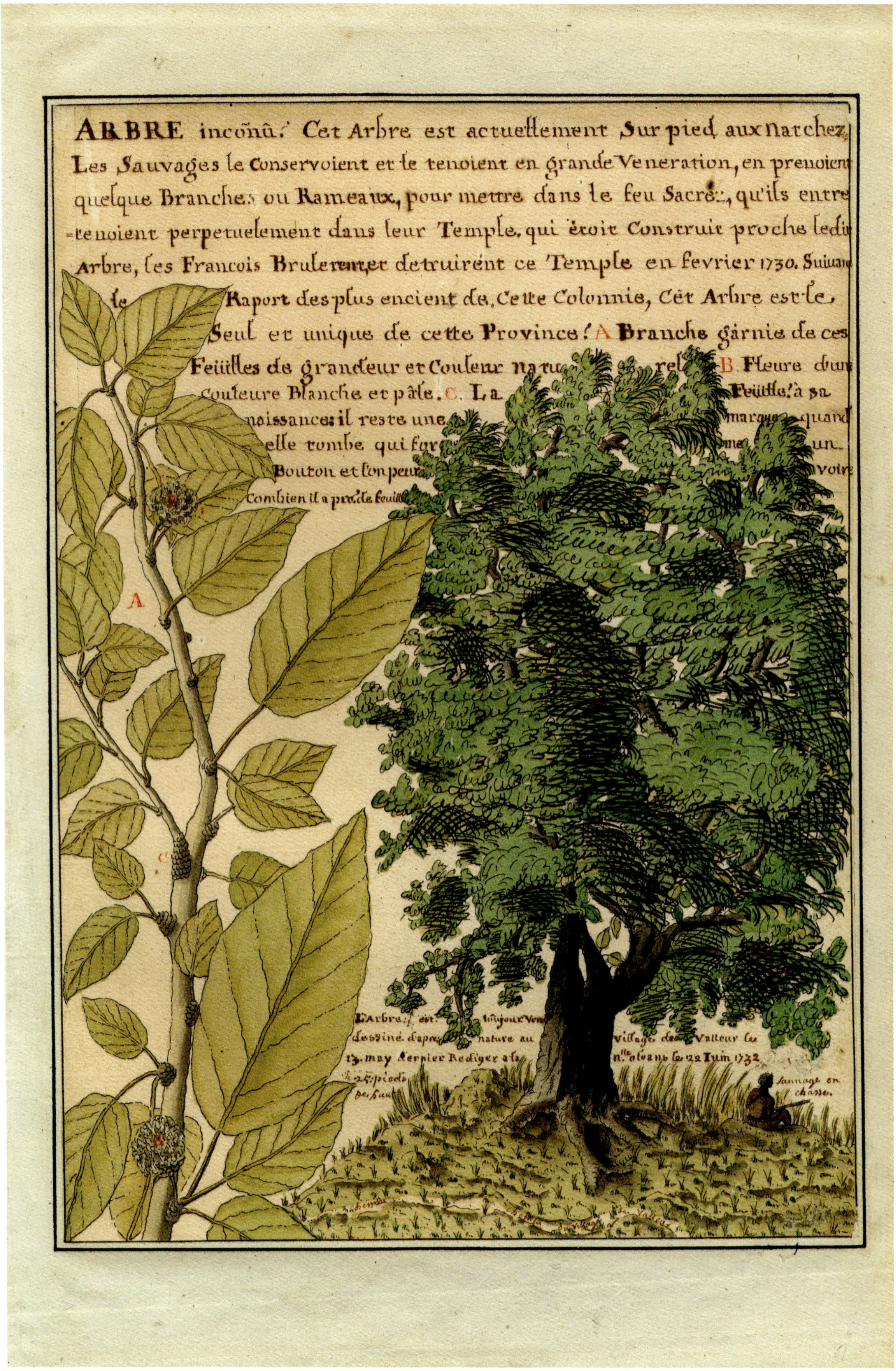
ARBRE incoñû. Cet Arbre est actuellement Sur pied aux Natchez
Les Sauvages le Conservoient et le tenoient en grande Veneration, en prenoient
quelque Branches ou Rameaux, pour mettre dans le feu Sacré, qu'ils entre
=tenoient perpetuelement dans leur Temple, qui etoit Construit proche ledit
Arbre, les Francois Brulerent et detruirent ce Temple en fevrier 1730. Suivant
le Raport des plus encient de Cette Colonnie, Cet Arbre est le
Seul et unique de cette Province. A Branche garnie de ces
Feüilles de grandeur et Couleur natu rel B. Fleure d'un
Couleure Blanche et pâle. C. La Feüille à sa
naissance: il reste une marque quand
elle tombe qui for me un
Bouton et l'on peut voir
Combien il a pro. de feuill
A
C
L'Arbre est toujour Vert
dessiné d'apres nature au village des Valleur le
13. may dernier Rediger a la Nlle orleans le 22 Juin 1732
25 pieds
de haut
sauvage en
chasse.

**Fig. 6 (opposite)**
Alexander de Batz, *Arbre Inconnu, Nouvelle Orleans, Le 22 Juin, 1732*, 1732, Colored pen and ink sketch, 12 11/16 x 9 5/16 inches, Gift of the Estate of Belle J. Bushnell, 1941, Peabody Museum of Archaeology and Ethnology, Harvard University, 41-72-10/17

ran counter to European systems of order, and document that difference in his work.[14] In composing *Desseins de Sauvages de Plusieurs Nations, New Orleans,* de Batz may have been thinking not just about European mapmaking as a model, but also about the close studies of natural history specimens he was making alongside his maps and paintings. In one extant pen and ink sketch from his time in Louisiana, entitled *Arbre Inconnu (Unknown Tree)* (1732; Fig. 6), de Batz places a drawing of a tree specimen, embedded within the landscape, alongside a detailed study of that tree's leaves and stomata, their branching veins—so much like his map of the river delta—ostensibly serving as a kind of finding aide for the tree.[15] Placed side by side, tree and stomata are an analogue for the connection between de Batz's painting and his map, and demonstrate de Batz's awareness of this landscape as a site of conflict. As de Batz writes in the text that accompanies this drawing:

> *The savages preserve this tree and hold it in great veneration, and took its branches and twigs to put in the fire that they perpetually kept burning in their temple. François Brulerent destroyed this temple, which was built near the city, in February 1730. According to reports, this tree is the most ancient of this colony, is the only one [left] in this province.*

Nineteenth-century French painter Alfred L. Boisseau could have known de Batz's early maps and drawings, some of which were still being published as lithographs in France through at least the 1850s.[16] Perhaps Boisseau even studied them in preparation for his own voyage to Louisiana in the 1840s. While Boisseau only lived and worked in Louisiana for two short years, between 1845 and 1846, he returned to Louisiana subject matter throughout his career, driven, in part, by the international recognition he received for his painting *Marche d'Indiens de la Louisiane (Louisiana Indians Walking Along a Bayou)* (1847; Fig. 7), which won a gold medal at the 1848 Paris Salon and was also shown at the National Academy of Design in New York in 1849.[17] While in Louisiana, Boisseau, like de Batz, focused much of his attention on the region's Indigenous populations, perhaps inspired by the success of American artist George Catlin's *Indian Gallery*, which had premiered in Paris to great acclaim shortly before Boisseau left the city in 1845.[18] However, Catlin's *Indian Gallery,* a collection of over 500 ethnographic portraits, genre paintings and landscape studies of Indigenous communities across the Americas, diverged from Boisseau's painting *Marche d'Indiens de la Louisiane* in nearly all respects. Catlin's portraits largely consisted of closely cropped portraits with distant, blurry landscape backgrounds, as in his 1832 portrait of a Plains Cree mother and child (1832; Fig. 8). Boisseau, in contrast, imbeds his figures within Louisiana's densely forested wetland terrain, painting them amidst thick impasto that replicated the look and the feel of the swampy landscape.

**Fig. 7 (pp. 28-29)**
Alfred L. Boisseau, *Marche d'Indiens de la Louisiane (Louisiana Indians Walking Along a Bayou)*, 1847, Oil on canvas, 28 1/4 x 44 3/8 x 2 inches (framed), New Orleans Museum of Art, Gift of William E. Groves, 56.34

Like de Batz's earlier painting, *Marche d'Indiens de la Louisiane* follows the flow of water. A river ripples across the composition from right to left, following five people—a man, two women, a young child, and a baby—as they walk along the river's path, heading west. Water moves throughout the entire scene: even in places where the river is mostly obscured by the dense foliage of the surrounding swamp, water still peeks through tropical plants as glistening blue and white paint that pools upon the canvas's surface so that the river seems,

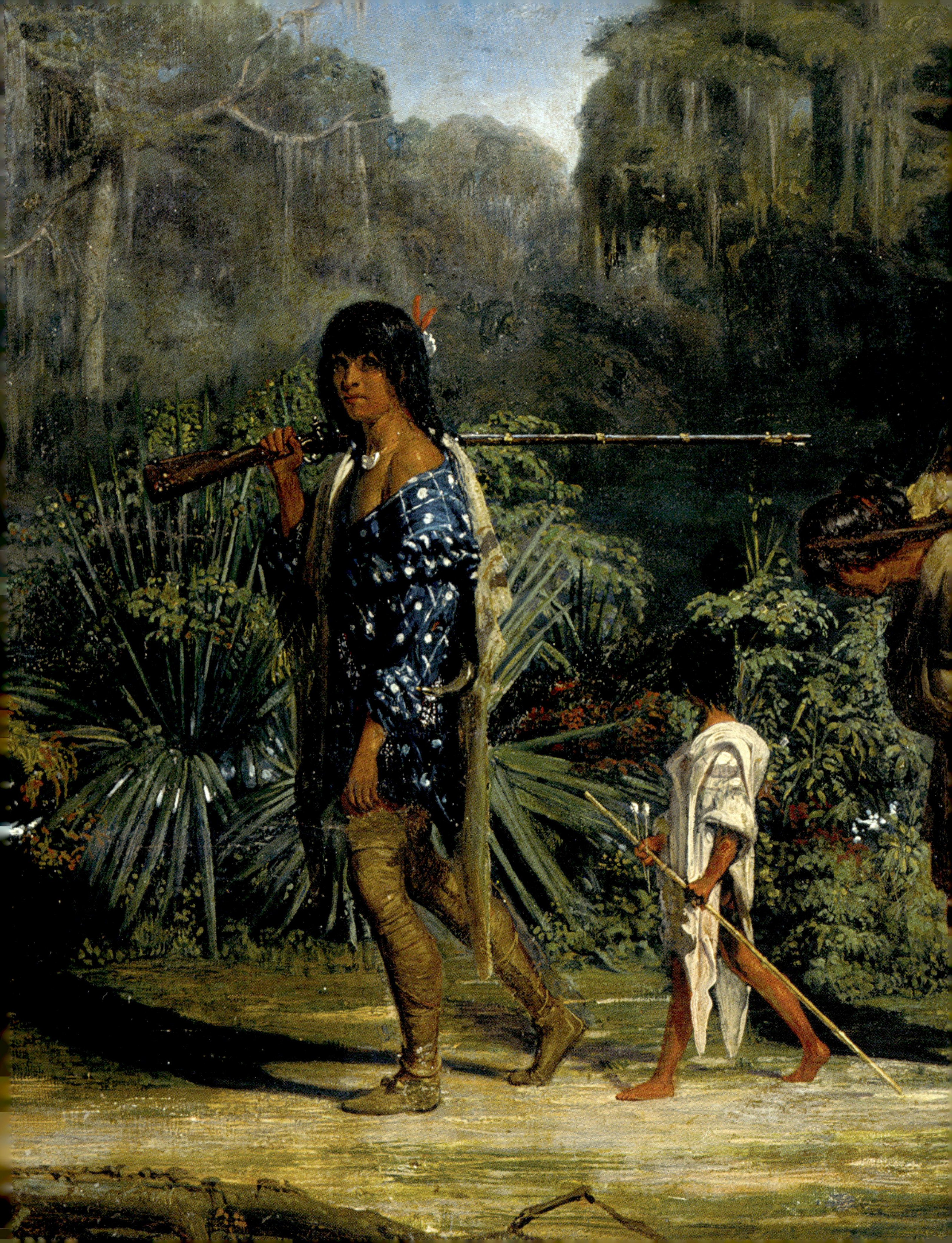

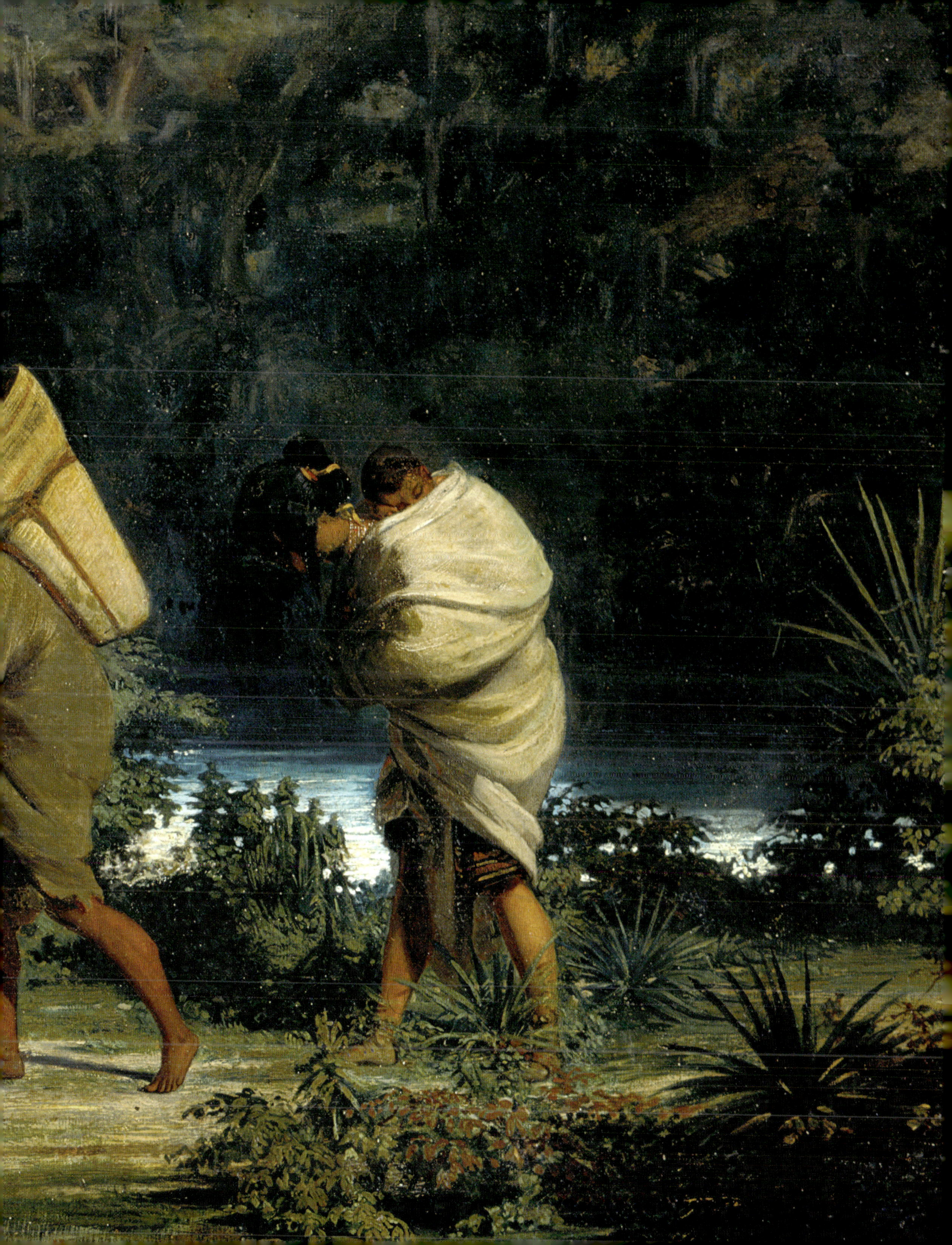

in places, almost to flow outwards from the canvas. Boisseau's swampy painting style—the thick layers of paint so different from the smooth, slick surfaces of the paintings of his teacher Paul Delaroche, or his fellow student in France, Jean-Léon Gérôme—registers the *feeling* of Louisiana's wet, humid landscape.[19] This reflects Boisseau's absorption of techniques he likely gleaned from the Barbizon School, a movement he probably first encountered in France, and then likely saw again in New Orleans in the work of fellow French émigré Richard Clague.[20] Bringing Barbizon's emphasis on close observation of nature to bear on Louisiana's swamplands, Boisseau viscerally conveyed the bayou's dense humidity, draping moss and muddy ground in a manner similar to French Barbizon artist Jules Dupré's painting *Sun Setting Over a Swamp* (1852; Fig. 9). So doing, Boisseau brought the techniques of the French Barbizon to bear on the landscapes of Louisiana, capturing the complexities and contradictions of a landscape that—at the time Boisseau painted it—was already a battleground.

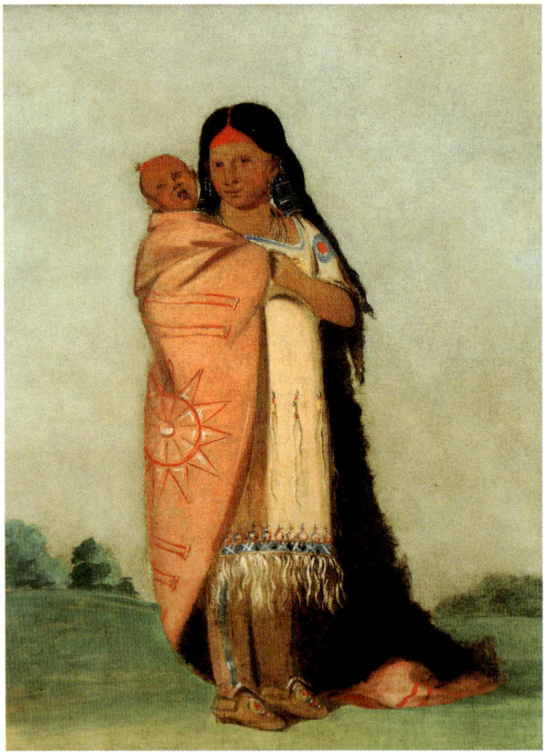

**Fig. 8**
George Catlin, *Tsee-moúnt, Great Wonder, Carrying Her Baby in Her Robe*, 1832, Oil on canvas, 29 x 24 inches, Smithsonian American Art Museum, Gift of Mrs. Joseph Harrison, Jr., 1985.66.177

In *Marche d'Indiens de la Louisiane*, the "walking" of the painting's translated English title belies the forced "march" that is more implied in its French translation. This (mis) translation into English has obscured the painting's likely reference to the Indian Removal Act of 1839, and especially to the Trail of Tears, which was already violently displacing Indigenous communities east of the Mississippi by the time of Boisseau's arrival in Louisiana. While we do not have any words from the artist himself to confirm his intentions, the specific landscape that Boisseau chose to paint certainly indicates his awareness of these issues. Period accounts name that place as the Tchefuncte River, a word derived from the Choctaw word *Hachofakti*, which refers to a medicinal plant often found along the banks of that waterway.[21] By the time Boisseau painted it, the Tchefuncte River—and many of the region's other surrounding bayous—were already heavily trafficked commercial waterways. The Tchefuncte, in particular, had a lighthouse—still extant—installed with much fanfare in 1837, to guide the vessels bringing lumber cut from ancient cypress forests in the bayous across Lake Ponchartrain to New Orleans, and points beyond.[22]

When Boisseau painted the Tchefuncte, then, it was already an active logging site: a landscape being reordered by the displacement of Indigenous people, the re-routing of water, and the extraction of natural resources. Perhaps in recognition of this unfolding transformation, Boisseau juxtaposes the pooling daubs of blue and white paint representing water in *Marche d'Indiens de la Louisiane* with the gridded blue and white dot pattern on the European checkered shirt worn by the Indigenous man holding the musket. Placing

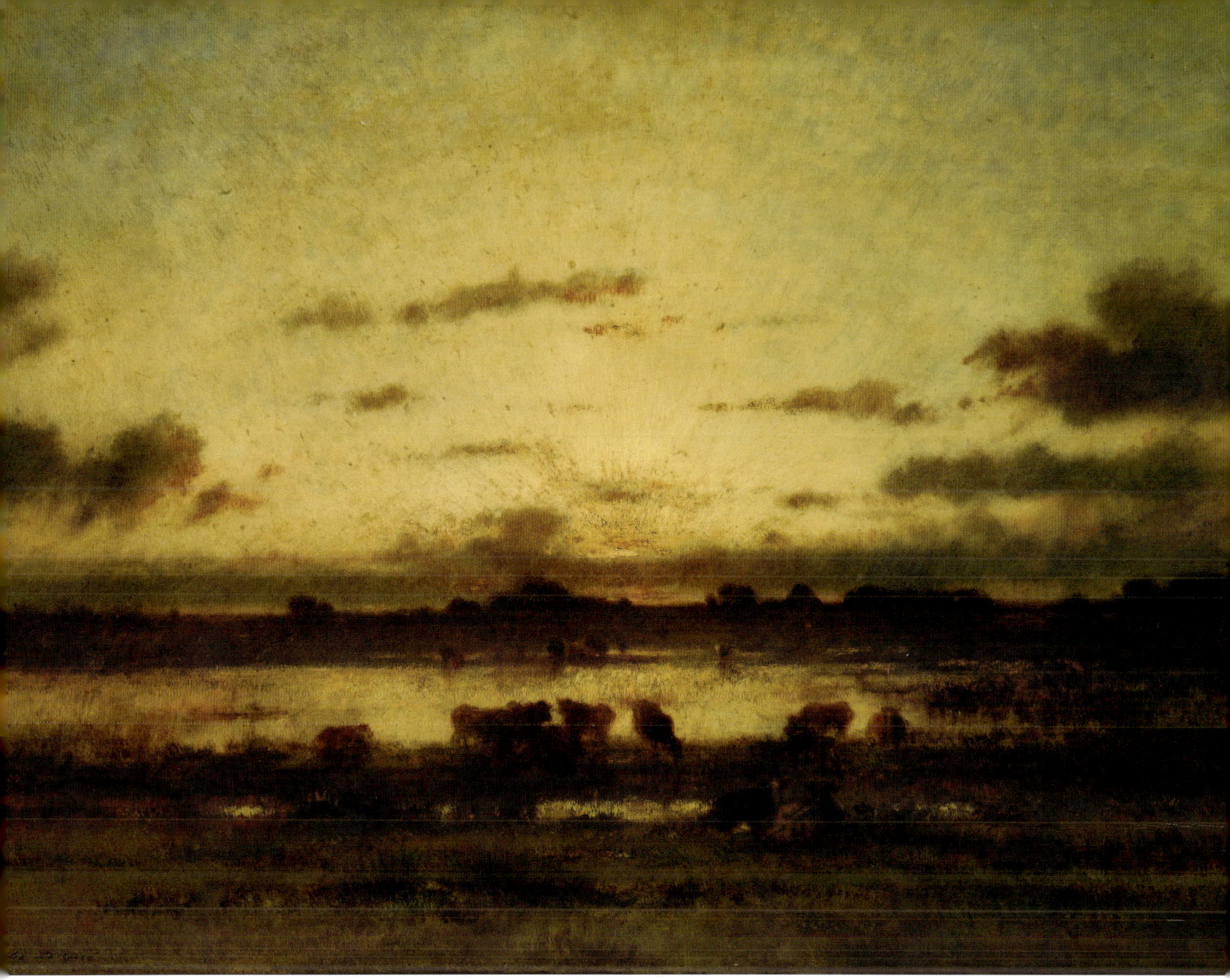

**Fig. 9**
Jules Dupre, *Sun Setting Over a Marsh*, 1852, Oil on wood, 20 ½ x 30 inches, Musee D'Orsay, Photo. Gerald Blot ©RMN – Grand Palais / Art Resource, NY

dense dollops of paint alongside the ordered grid pattern of European fabric, Boisseau shows the way this grid exists in opposition to—rather than alignment with—the surrounding landscape, the dots of the shirt almost an echo of the neatly stacked piles of lumber in other period paintings like Robert Brammer's *Wooding Up, Rodney, Mississippi* (circa 1842-53; Fig. 10). Unlike de Batz's earlier work, however, this grid in the painting's center—in some ways so like a map—is utterly at odds with the surrounding landscape, showing the stark contrast between European systems of order and the surrounding swamp.

Existing in contradistinction to the ordered grid of fabric in the composition's center, the thick impasto in *Marche d'Indiens de la Louisiane*—in which paint itself blurs the lines between water and land—captures the contingency of a landscape in a constant state of both disappearance and becoming. Although very few of Boisseau's other paintings survive—and none in which landscape elements are so dominant—the title of another one of Boisseau's paintings, cited in historical accounts as *Flood on the Mississippi* (ironically now lost, possibly to one of New Orleans's many floods), indicates the artist's attentiveness to water's power to disrupt and disorder the landscape, and to make and unmake land.[23] For in choosing to paint a bayou at all, Boisseau was representing a place that people in the

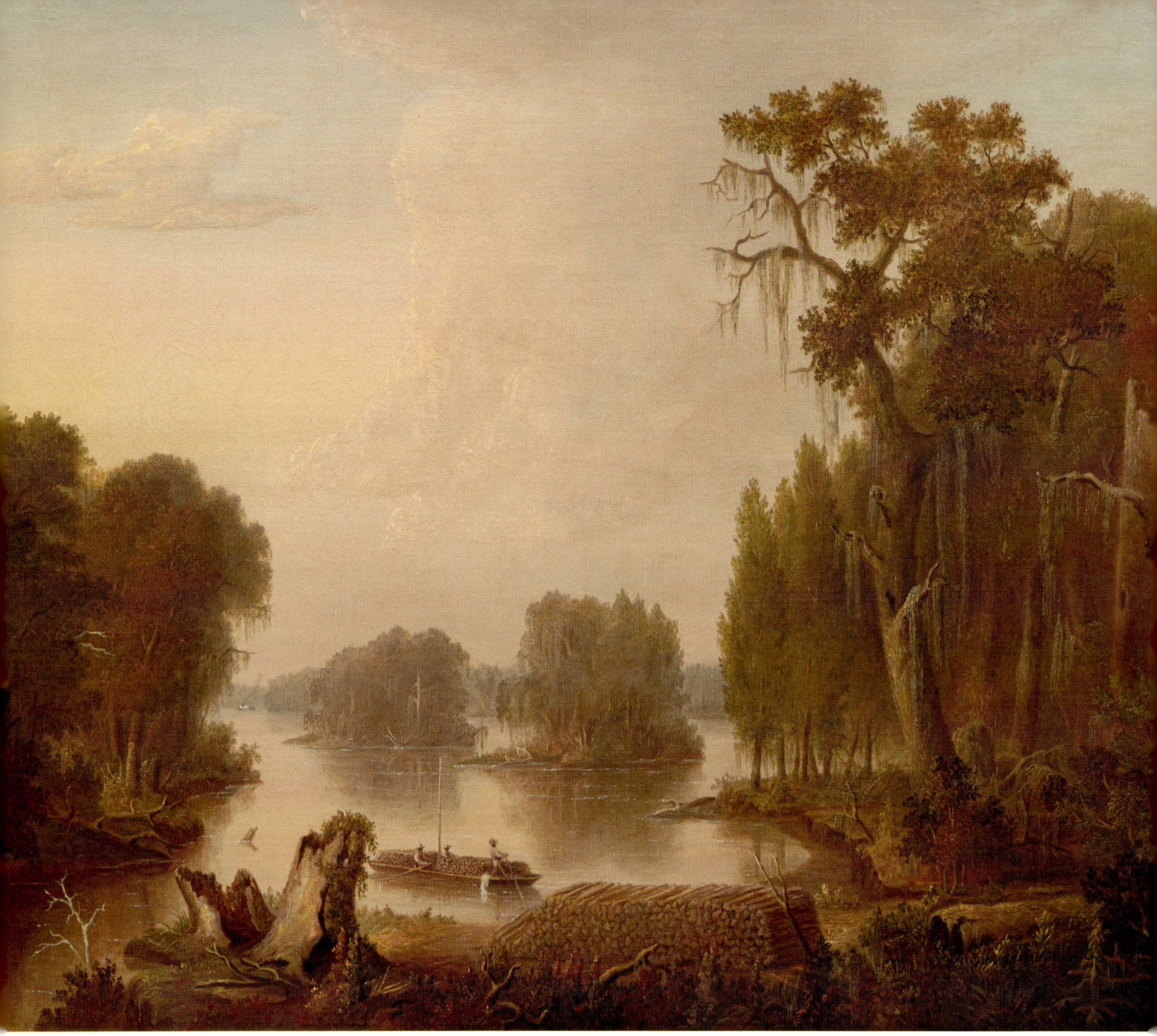

Fig. 10
Robert Brammer, *Wooding Up, Rodney, Mississippi*, circa 1842-53, Oil on canvas, 41 x 48 inches (framed), Collection of Bill Gunther, Photography by Roman Alokhin.

nineteenth century already understood could not be "rendered secure," to borrow a phrase from a nineteenth century account:

> *I have known several acres of land to disappear in a single night. I have seen primeval forests of sycamores and cotton-woods, which but yesterday towered a hundred feet in the air, now toppled in the boiling flood, as weeds by the road-side are washed down by a summer shower. There they would remain, swayed to and fro by the eddies, till the roots detached from the soil in which they had been rooted for centuries, and the gigantic trunks were swept away by the current.*[24]

Such descriptions of Louisiana's waterways often dramatically describe acres of land disappearing in a single evening as the result of flooding from heavy rain and hurricanes. During this time, erosion was only being sped up by the digging of logging canals and the removal of trees, whose root systems were so crucial for holding land in place—keeping the soil from sliding into the water—during heavy storms and flooding.

The cleared patch of earth upon which the Indigenous people tread in *Marche d'Indiens de la Louisiane* is a path that has seemingly been pounded down and worn thin by the movement of many other feet. Is there, perhaps, within this painting, a recognition of the stakes of clearing this land, of Europeans trying to turn this place from swamp to solid ground? Could this painting have been an emotional call to recognize this twinned disappearance of land and people in Louisiana, already so far underway by the time Boisseau arrived in the region? Did Boisseau somehow look past the prejudice of his time to see, on his trips to the bayou, a connection between the plight of the people he met and painted there, and the French people living in Barbizon's forests, who were also, at the same time, rapidly loosing the woodlands on which their lives and livelihoods depended to deforestation?

There were some Europeans who visited Louisiana during Boisseau's own time that seemed to comprehend the nature of this struggle. Perhaps Boisseau encountered—either on the bayou, or back home in France—the missionary Adrien Emmanuel Rouquette, whose 1879 novel *La nouvelle Atala, ou, La fille de l'esprit legende indienne*, written in French and distributed in both New Orleans and Paris, helped energize emerging environmental movements in both places.[25] The novel, based on Rouquette's experiences in Louisiana living among the Choctaws as a Catholic missionary for almost thirty years, makes a powerful emotional plea for the connections between people and land through the experience of the novel's central character, an Indigenous woman named Atala:

> *The trees spoke to her, sang for her, and animated and identified with her, as though they were sympathetic creatures. They covered her in thick foliage and flooded her…the sound of the axe that cut them down, the roar of the flame that consumed them [and] the hurricane that uprooted them felt to her like she was being ripped apart. She herself felt the effects of all of the attacks that wounded them…her trees! Oh! Her trees!*

Mobilizing the feel and feeling of paint to capture a similar spirit of interconnection between people and landscape, Boisseau's painting diverges from more conventional ethnographic representations like Catlin's in conveying both the complexities of this landscape and the realities of its political and environmental conquest. In Boisseau's *Marche d'Indiens de la Louisiane*, the material qualities of paint become, in some sense, a form of resistance—a way of keeping both landscape and people present, a refusal to allow them to be worn thin. Although maps and missionaries are—like the forced removal of people and trees, like painting itself—tools of political and environmental conquest, within these early renderings of Louisiana's landscape there is a certain unwillingness—or, at the very least, inability—to allow the landscape to be completely subsumed within these systems of control.

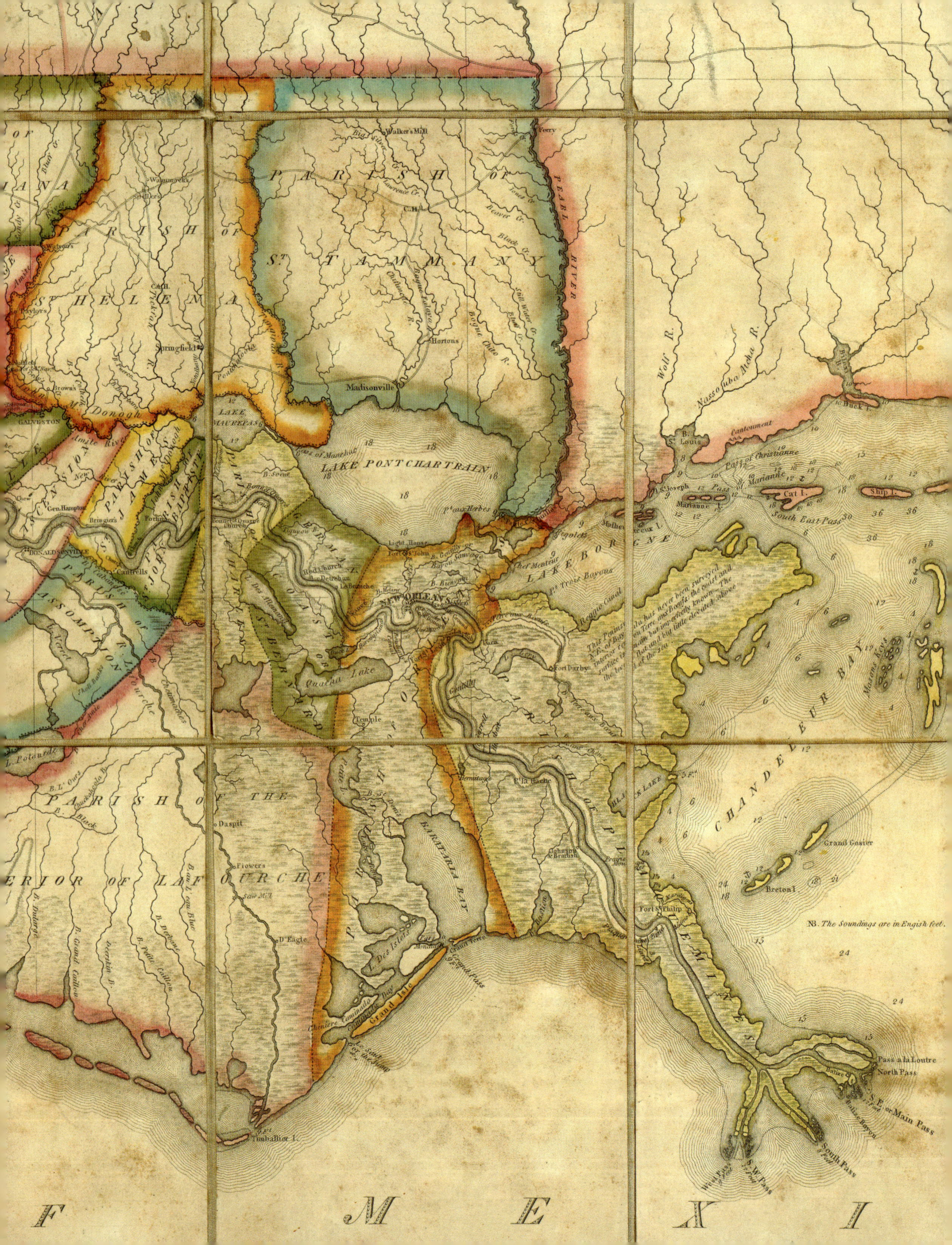

PARISH OF ST. TAMMANY
PEARL RIVER
PARISH OF ST. HELENA
Madisonville
Springfield
LAKE PONTCHARTRAIN
LAKE MAUREPAS
NEW ORLEANS
LAKE BORGNE
Quacha Lake
Fort Darby
CHANDELEUR BAY
Cat I.
Ship I.
Pass Christianne
Pass Marianne
South East Pass
Cantonment
St. Louis
Wolf R.
Nassouba Acha R.
PARISH OF THE INTERIOR OF LAFOURCHE
BARATARIA BAY
Grand Isle
Grand Terre
Grand Pass
Timballier I.
Fort St. Philip
Grand Gosier
Breton I.
Pass a la Loutre
North Pass
S.E. or Main Pass
South Pass
S.W. Pass
N.B. The Soundings are in English feet.
Madisonville
DONALDSONVILLE
GALVESTON
ASSOMPTION
PARISH OF ST. JAMES
Hortons
Walker's Mill
This Peninsula has never been surveyed
Daspit
Temple
Hermitage
F M E X I

**Fig. 11 (opposite)**
William Darby, *A Map of the State of Louisiana with Part of the Mississippi Territory, from Actual Survey by Wm. Darby, Philadelphia, Published May the 1st 1816, by John Melish* (detail), David Rumsey Map Collection © 2000 by Cartography Associates

## The Mouths Of The River

In 1816, almost seventy years after de Batz published his map of the Louisiana territories, cartographer William Darby published the first widely distributed map of Louisiana to appear after it officially became an American state in 1812 (1816; Fig. 11).[26] Based on much more extensive surveys of the region than de Batz would have had access to, Darby's map—and his accompanying travelogue—presented a considerably more complex view of the region's topography. Conveying Louisiana's landscape as a "vast labyrinth of water," Darby described Louisiana as a land composed of "river uniting to river in a thousand mazes." Emphasizing the landscape's almost "inexplicable intricacy," Darby's map pictured the region's myriad intersecting waterways, showing the ways in which water seemed to run in a continuous "stream over an immense canvass [*sic*]" of land.[27] Capturing the landscape's complexity, Darby also insisted on its navigability. For in incorporating Louisiana, Darby wrote, "the citizens of the United States [had] opened themselves to an almost unlimited field": a vast network of water that would link the United States to Latin America, Europe, Africa, and points beyond. In gaining the territory of Louisiana, America also got unfettered access to the Mississippi River—one of the largest and most powerful waterways in the world—and a new point of connection to the Gulf of Mexico: a conduit for shuttling people, goods, and natural resources back and forth from the country's interior out into the open sea.[28]

Darby's maps, however, told a more complicated story. Until Darby's map, most available representations of Louisiana depicted its main waterway—the Mississippi River—as a single stream with one primary commercial port, much like the cartouche on John L. Boqueta de Woisseri's map *A Plan of New Orleans & Its Environs* (1803; Fig. 12), which shows the river as a single, steady stream despite the clear evidence to the contrary in the much more unwieldy map of the Mississippi River Delta in the upper left. Darby's more detailed map of the Mississippi—its many mouths and branches, and endless twists, turns, and tributaries—went against the stated goal of nearly all of the region's early explorers—Iberville, DeSoto, LaSalle—of identifying *the* mouth of *the* river, as well as America's goal of controlling this waterway as a commercial port. Darby's map, in contrast, presented the river with no less than *six* mouths, surrounded by an "infinite variety" of other waterways that branch off from the river's main path. So pervasive were these early imaginings of the Mississippi River as a single stream with *one* mouth that many people outside of the region who saw Darby's map resisted the visual evidence it presented to the contrary. In 1816, the year the map was published, one reviewer based in Baltimore wrote of being profoundly "confused [by] the infinite interlocking of lagoons and bayous that chequer [*sic*] the mouth of the river…[and by all of] the rivers running in and running out of [the river], uniting with each other, separating, and winding into a thousand mazes."[29]

Presenting this more complex view of the Mississippi River, Darby's map also pictured a kind of landscape that had no real precedent in American landscape representation. During this period, American landscape paintings were typically more like rivers with one mouth:

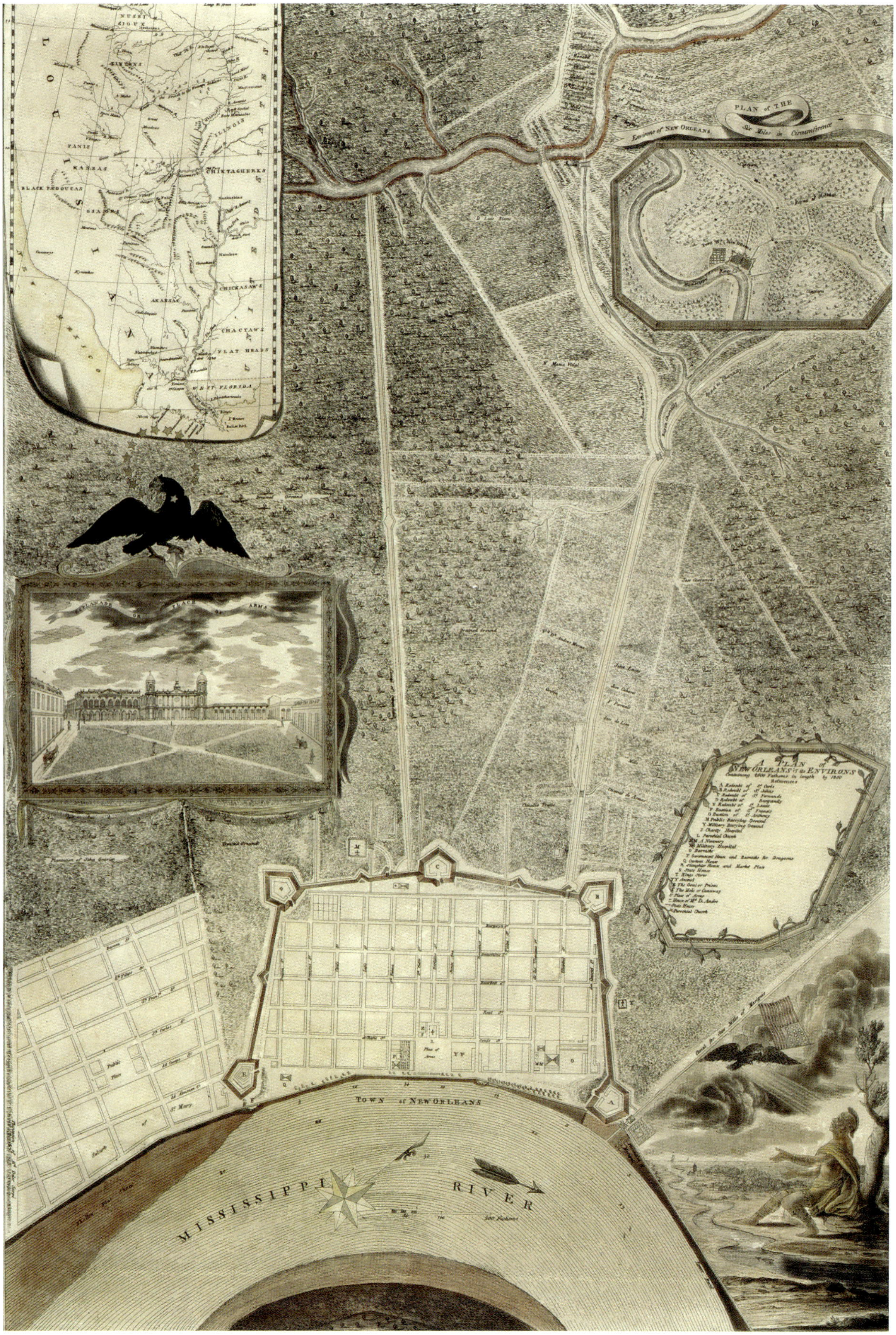
PLAN of THE
Environs of NEW ORLEANS
Six Miles in Circumference
TOWN of NEW ORLEANS
MISSISSIPPI RIVER
LOUISIANA
KANSAS
PANIS
BLACK PADOUCAS
CHICKASAWS
CHACTAWS
FLAT HEADS
WEST FLORIDA
ILLINOIS
A PLAN of NEW ORLEANS & its ENVIRONS

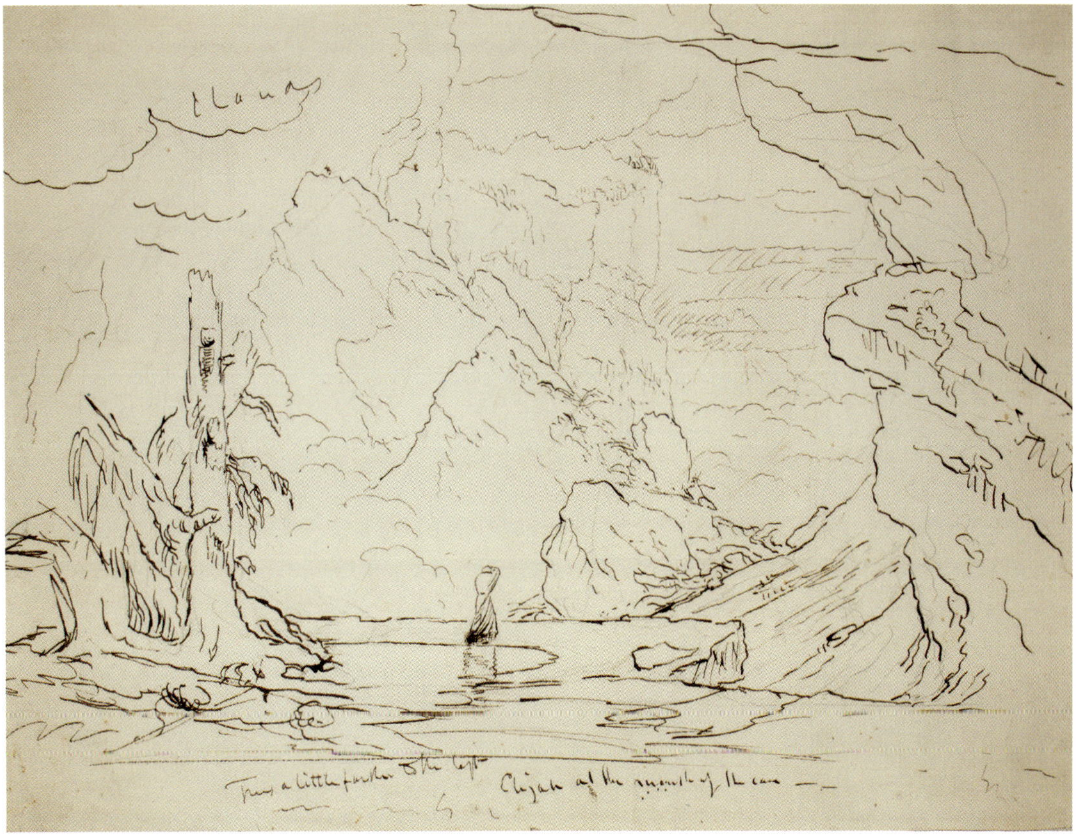

**Fig. 13**
Thomas Cole, *Elijah at the Mouth of the Cave*, 1828 or 29, Pen and brown ink over graphite pencil on off-white wove paper, 10 ⁵/₈ x 14 ³/₄ inches, Detroit Institute of Arts, Founders Society Purchase, William H. Murphy Fund, 39.342.A

emphasizing a singular perspective and point of view, their carefully composed foregrounds, middle grounds, and backgrounds set viewers out on a steady course out to the horizon, not unlike European works by artists such as Lorrain discussed earlier. The scant landscape paintings from elsewhere that people in New Orleans might have seen during the nineteenth century, such as Thomas Cole's *Elijah at the Mouth of the Cave*, reinforced exactly this view.[30] While Cole's painting itself is now lost, preparatory sketches indicate the likely arrangement of the scene. In one sketch (1828/9; Fig. 13), land wraps around the entire perimeter of the composition, tunneling both water and vision straight from foreground to background through the mouth of the cave, which neatly frames the mountainous landscape scene beyond. In 1845, one New Orleans based reviewer noted Cole's placid, peaceful, and clear representation of water, writing, "Mr. Cole is justly famous for his water scenes, and never has he painted it more limpid," describing a quality—limpid—which water in New Orleans has arguably never possessed.[31] Indeed, in *Elijah at the Mouth of the Cave* the painting's titular figure is, according to the Bible, supposed to be lost, but the painting's composition tells him—and us—exactly where to go, with Cole's note on the sketch—"Try a little farther to the left"—indicating how carefully he engineered the perspective to make it clear that Elijah, as he waded through the pooling water at the mouth of the cave, was not lost at all.

Toussaint François Bigot, another one of Louisiana's first landscape painters, could have seen Cole's paintings in New Orleans as early as 1845, when they first started being exhibited at George Cook's National Gallery of Paintings, just around the corner from where Bigot taught art classes at the time.[32] Arriving to New Orleans in 1826, Bigot was, alongside his fellow painter and wife Stephanie Wilkinson Bigot (whose paintings have apparently not survived),

**Fig. 12 (opposite)**
John L. Boqueta de Woiseri, *A Plan of New Orleans and its Environs*, Engraving with hand-colored ink and watercolor, 27 ³/₁₆ x 18 ⁷/₈ inches, The Historic New Orleans Collection, The L. Kemper and Leila Moore Williams Founders Collection, 1858.41

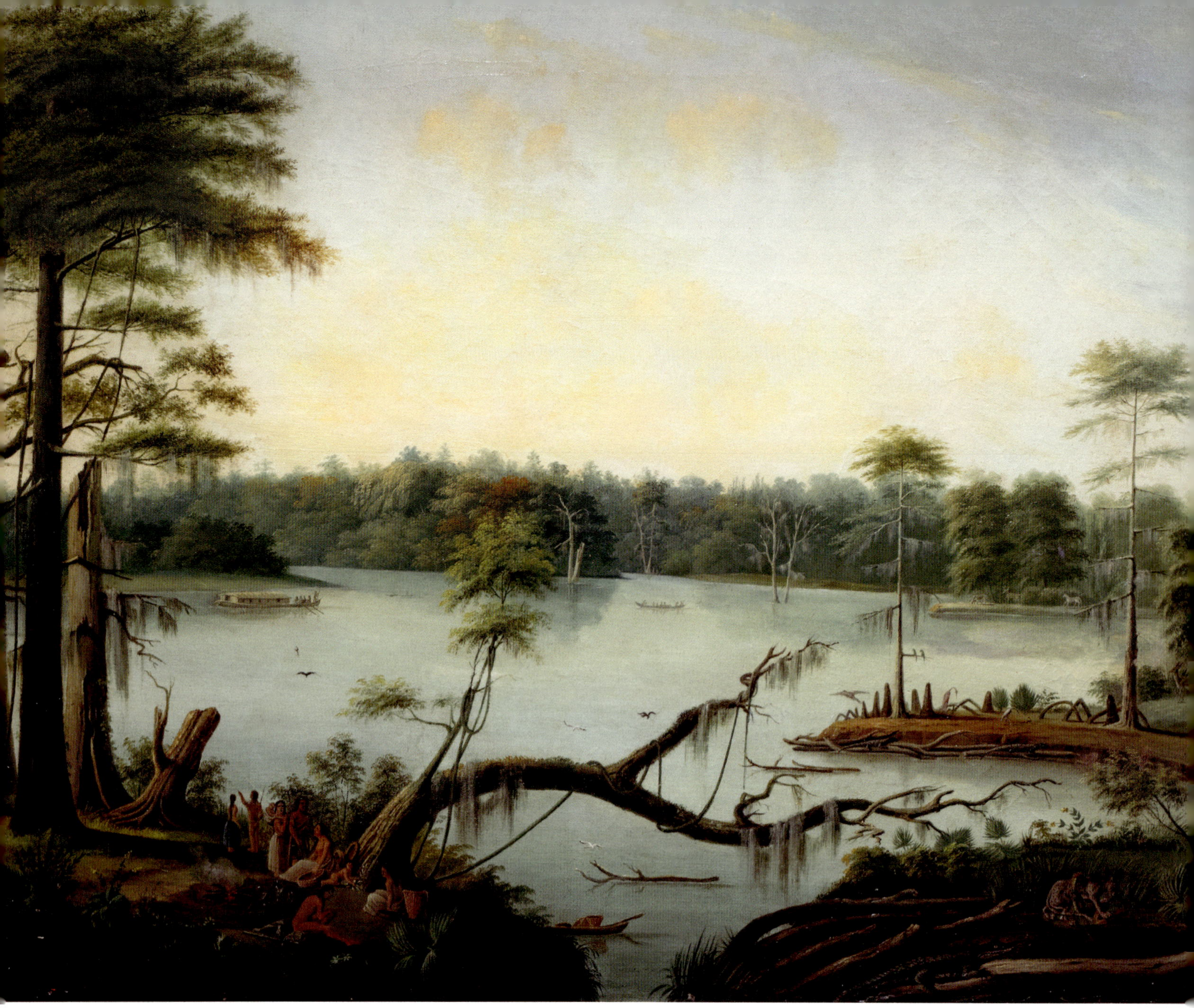

one of the city's earliest practitioners and teachers of traditional painting and drawing.[33] Painted just a few years after Boisseau's *Marche d'Indiens de la Louisiane*, Bigot's *Alchapalia, Louisiana* (1848; Figs. 1 and 14) is one of the artist's few surviving paintings.[34] Like Boisseau's earlier work, Bigot's painting reflects the challenges he faced in trying to paint a landscape organized much more like Darby's map than Cole's painting.

*Alchapalia, Louisiana* pictures the landscape of the Atchafalaya Basin, which is still today the largest wetland swamp in the United States. Formed by the meeting of the Atchafalaya River with the Gulf of Mexico, it stretches out over a million acres of wetland swamps and river deltas. Like so many of Louisiana's landscapes, it contains a mixture of both fresh and salt water in which the line between land and sea is murky at best. Correspondingly, Bigot's painting includes what seems like an improbable array of wildlife, at least to anyone who has never been to Louisiana. Deer, horses and wildcats—creatures we might associate more with inland landscapes—exist alongside swamp dwellers like alligators, serpents, and birds. All of these move amidst a landscape that includes both fresh and saltwater tree and plant species, some

**Fig. 14**
Toussaint François Bigot, *Alchapalia, Louisiana*, 1848, Oil on canvas, 29 ½ x 36 inches, Roger Houston Ogden Collection, Courtesy of Ogden Museum of Southern Art. Photography by Patrick Barnes.

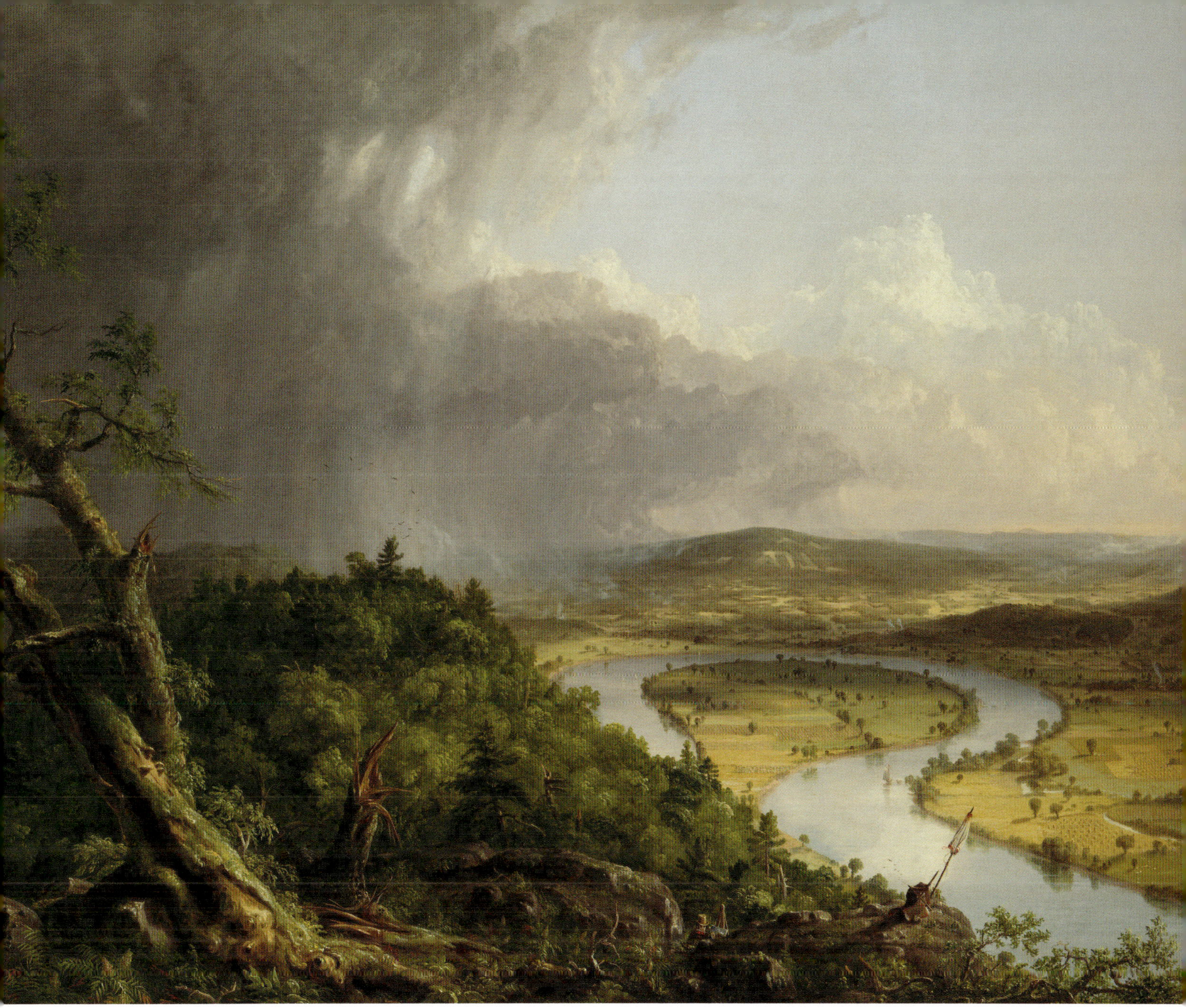

**Fig. 15**
Thomas Cole, *View from Mount Holyoke, Northampton, Massachusetts, after a Thunder Storm—The Oxbow*, 1836, Oil on canvas, 51 ½ x 76 inches, The Metropolitan Museum of Art, Gift of Mrs. Russell Sage, 08.228 © The Metropolitan Museum of Art

of which are newly growing, others recently toppled by a storm, and still others in an advanced state of decay.[35] Following a curve of tangled trees in the foreground, the painting meanders from right to left and back again, so that its perspective aligns more with the curve of the serpent in the painting's foreground than the directed view that would come from looking out at a landscape from the mouth of a cave. On the lower left, a group of Indigenous people—pictured with a plethora of baskets, woven from river cane or oak—sit at the base of a large fallen tree whose branches reach out over the water.

Extending out over the water, the branches of this fallen tree look just like the many mouths of the Mississippi River in Darby's map, as if Bigot had overlaid a map of the region's waterways onto his landscape of the swamp. Like a map, each of the main branches of this fallen tree point outwards to the painting's no less than *six* vanishing points, as the painting's waterway branches off into five different channels in the background, and one stream of water flows outward towards the viewer. Unlike even other American paintings of waterways made during the same period, such as Cole's *View from Mount Holyoke, Northampton,*

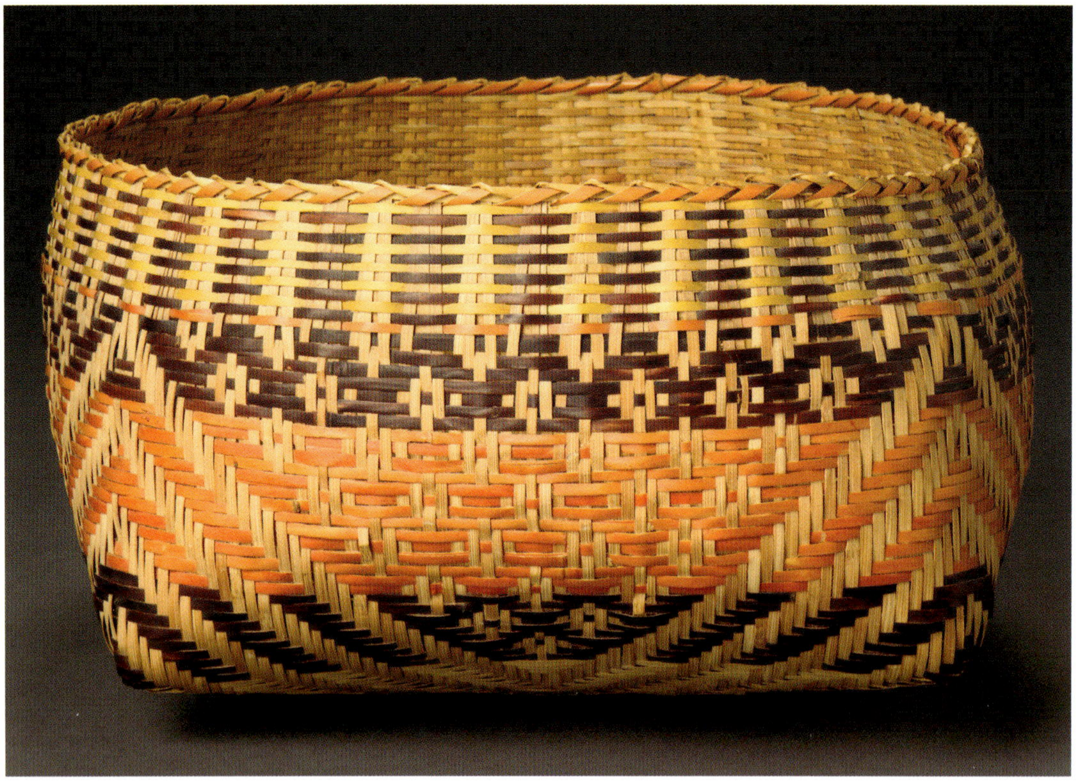

**Fig. 16**
Chitimacha Peoples, *Basket*, circa 1850-1900, Natural fibers, 8 x 14 x 14 inches, Collection of Don Fuson. Photographed by: David Humphrey.

**Fig. 17 (opposite)**
Unidentified Artist, *Oak Basket*, circa 1900, Natural fibers, 42 x 20 x 20 inches, Collection of Don Fuson. Photographed by: David Humphrey.

*Massachusetts, after a Thunderstorm—The Oxbow* (1836; Fig.15), water determines the flow of the composition. Cole's painting, by contrast, is organized—against the flow of water—from foreground to background, giving the painting a clear perspective from high ground that the waterway that weaves through the composition would otherwise lack. Cole even pictures himself within the painting, looking out over the landscape, showing himself—the American painter—in the act of structuring the view.

Bigot, in contrast, puts us in the water with the alligators and snakes, forming his painting around the flow of the many different intersecting waterways that weave through the composition. In Bigot's painting, there is no American artist, perched high above the landscape, but instead a group of no less than seven Indigenous baskets positioned throughout the painting's foreground, likely made by the group of people who sit around a small fire at the foot of the painting's fallen tree. Based on the painting's location in the Atchafalaya Basin, these are likely Chitimacha, Atakapa-Ishak or Choctaw baskets. Their lands once encompassed the entire Atchafalaya Basin, which is so named for the Choctaw word *hacha falaia*, or "long river." Woven from local river cane, the single and double weave baskets of the Chitimacha (circa 1850-1900; Fig. 16) are formed through a complex process splitting, scouring, soaking, dying, and weaving of cane.[36] In Bigot's painting most of the smaller baskets appear to be river cane, but a few of the larger baskets look like they might be made from oak, similar to the basket illustrated here (circa 1900; Fig. 17).[37] One particularly large basket—possibly oak—sits on a canoe in the painting's foreground, nearly at the composition's center, so that the weave of the basket is reflected in the water, and carried through the rest of the composition by the rippling waves that follow from the design of the basket's weave.

**Fig. 18 (pp. 42-43)**
Chitimacha Peoples, *Lidded Double Weave Trunk*, circa 1920, Split cane (arundinaria), natural dyes, 6 ½ x 10 ¾ inches, New Orleans Museum of Art, Gift of Mercedes Whitecloud in memory of Dr. Thomas St. Germain Whitecloud, III, 97.94.a,.b. Photography by Tom Simpson.

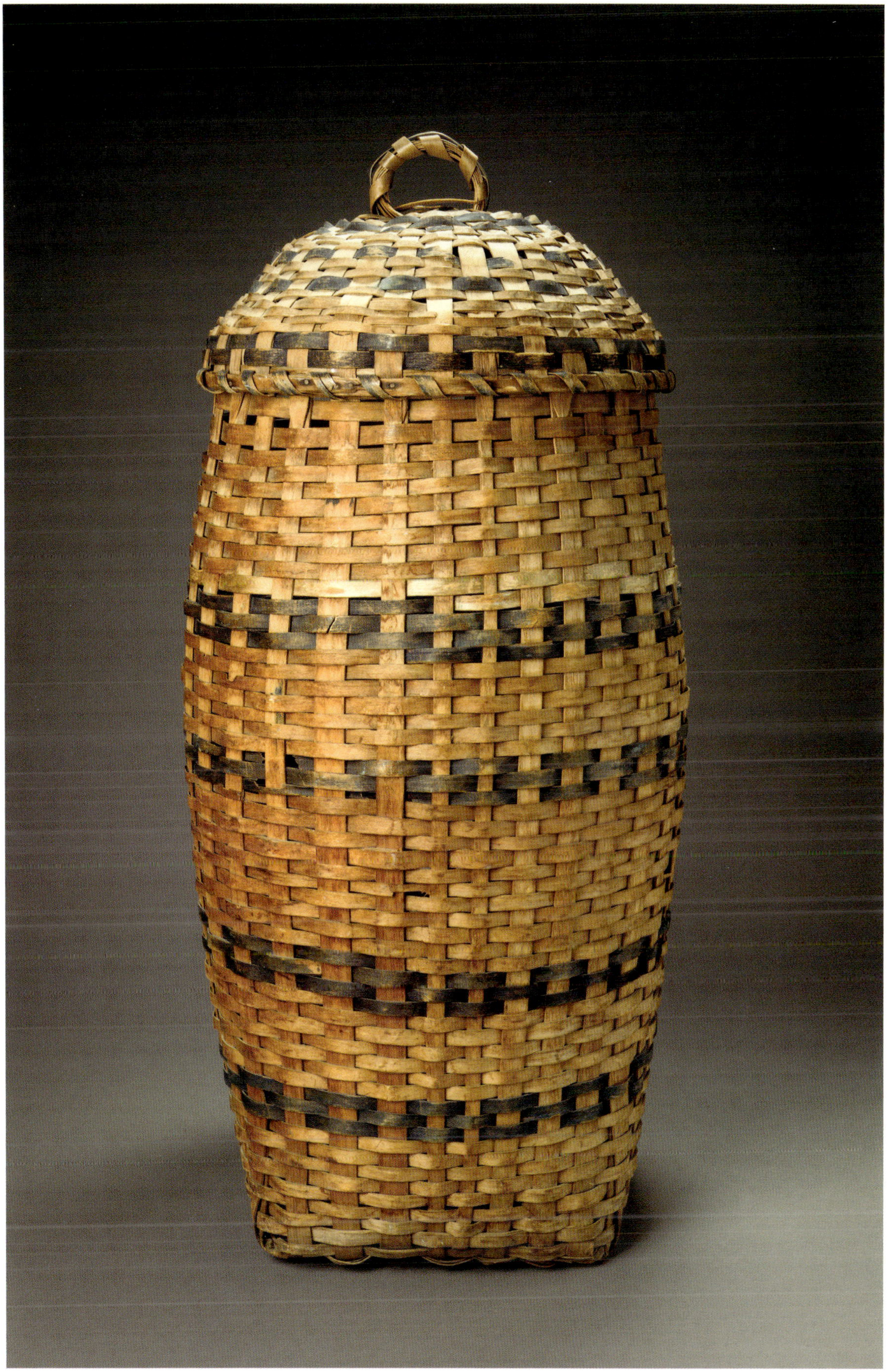

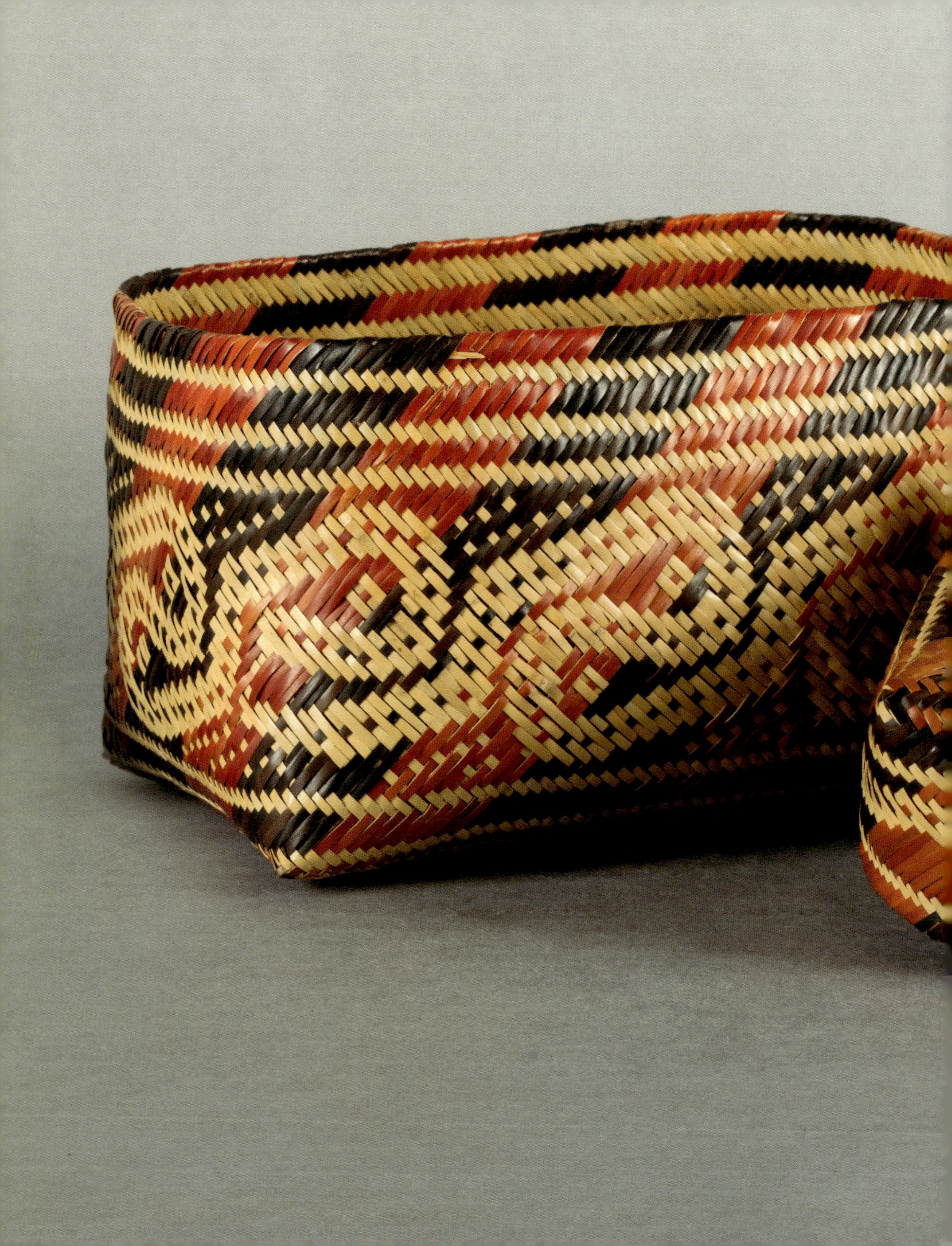

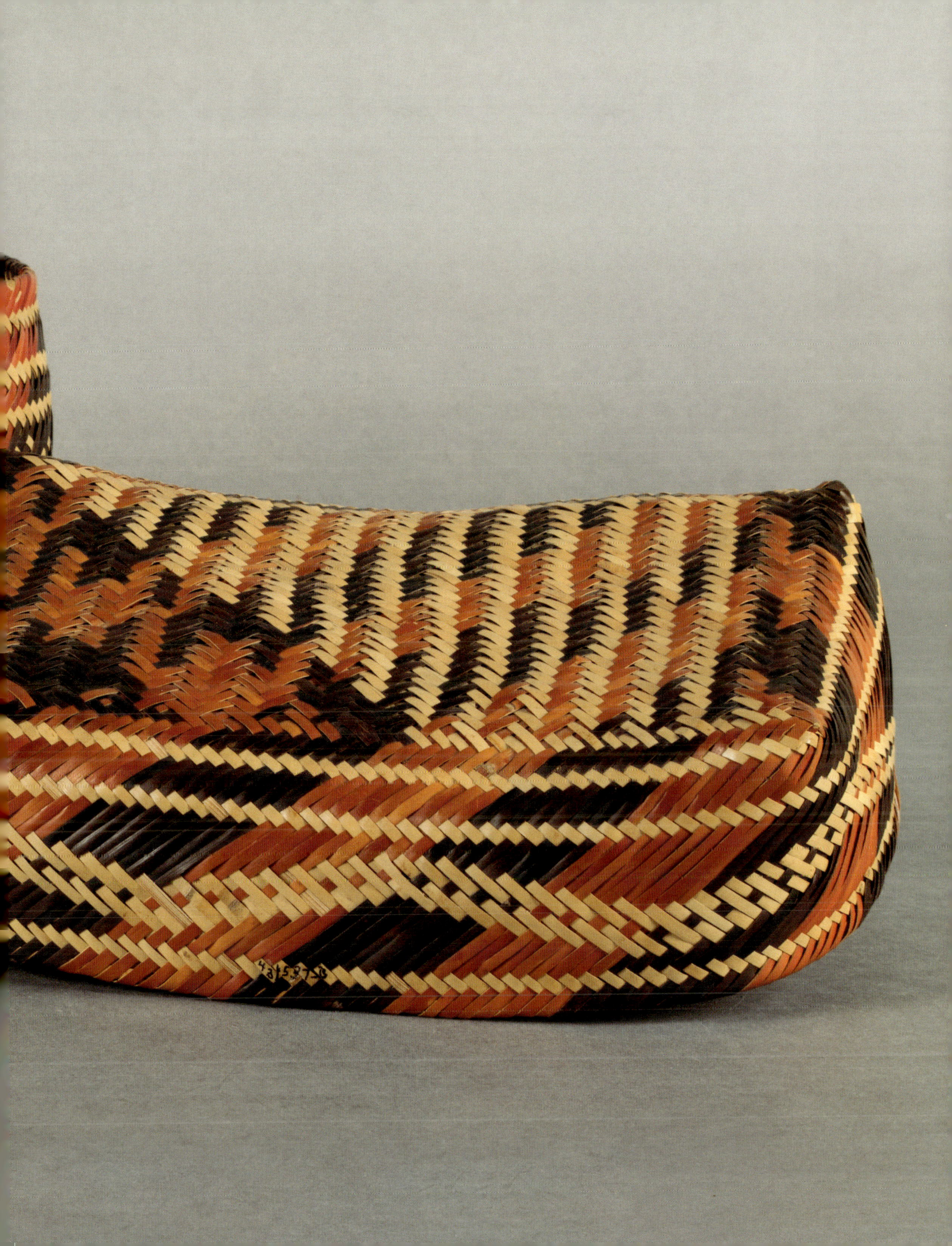

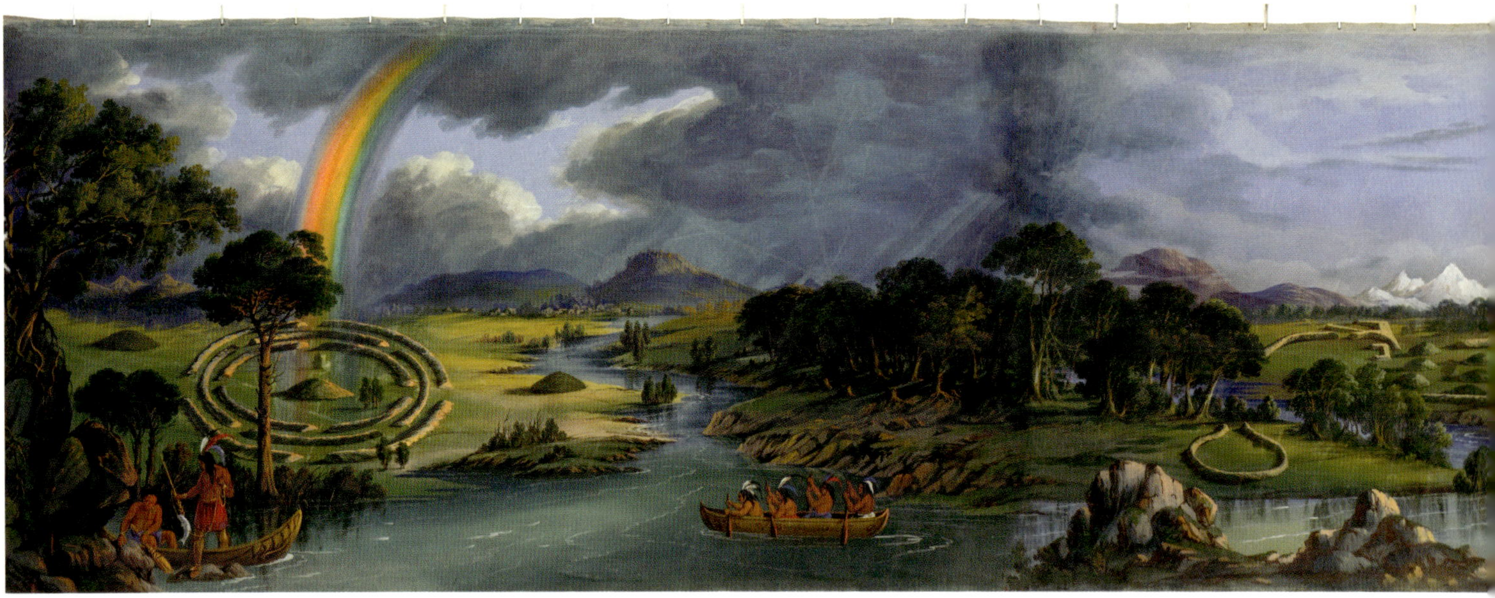

Fig. 19
John J. Egan, *Panorama of the Monumental Grandeur of the Mississippi Valley* (detail), circa 1850, Distemper on cotton muslin, 90 inches x 348 feet, Saint Louis Art Museum, Eliza McMillan Trust, 34:1953, Image courtesy Saint Louis Art Museum.

Placing Indigenous basketry at the entryway to his composition, Bigot—like de Batz and Boisseau—sets up a contrast between vastly different systems of ordering and apprehending the landscape: the map referenced by the branching tree, the weave of the basketry found throughout the composition, and the practice of landscape painting itself. In representing a place woven together by the convergence of so many different water sources, it is tempting to speculate that the form—and action—of weaving might have been for Bigot a more powerful point of reference than painting. Could Bigot have seen the baskets he placed so prominently at his painting's center as a source of inspiration for his art, perhaps even more so than European painting and maps? We have no words from Bigot to better understand his motives, but certainly the methods of making these baskets, and the forms and patterns found upon them, are in many ways more compositionally akin to Bigot's painting than the compositions of an artist like Cole.

At least forty-nine named basket patterns have been passed down by Chitimacha basket weavers and recorded by anthropologists. Many of the forms, like *nish-tu wa-ki* (alligator entrails), *cous-pi si-ou* (muscadine rind), and *tcish mish* (worm track), take their inspiration from the winding forms of alligator intestines, serpents, and the movements of worms. In Chitimacha baskets like Figure 18, which features the alligator entrails design, one sees not only references to natural form, but also a complex representation of the interwoven pathways of the region's waterways (circa 1920; Fig. 18).[38] Often treated by Indigenous communities themselves as tools of diplomacy—a way of drawing attention to legal efforts to protect their land—the baskets seem to serve a similar function in Bigot's painting.[39] In one of the few recorded interviews with Mathilde Johnson, one of the last basket weavers in Bayou Lacombe, she recalls crossing Lake Ponchartrain on the steamer *Camilia* almost every day with basketry to sell at the French Market, the baskets a tool for bringing visibility, awareness and resources to her community.[40] Positioned at the entrance to Bigot's painting, the basket in the foreground, reflected in the water—along with the fallen tree—exists as both a guide for the landscape beyond, and also a kind of gatekeeper. Telling

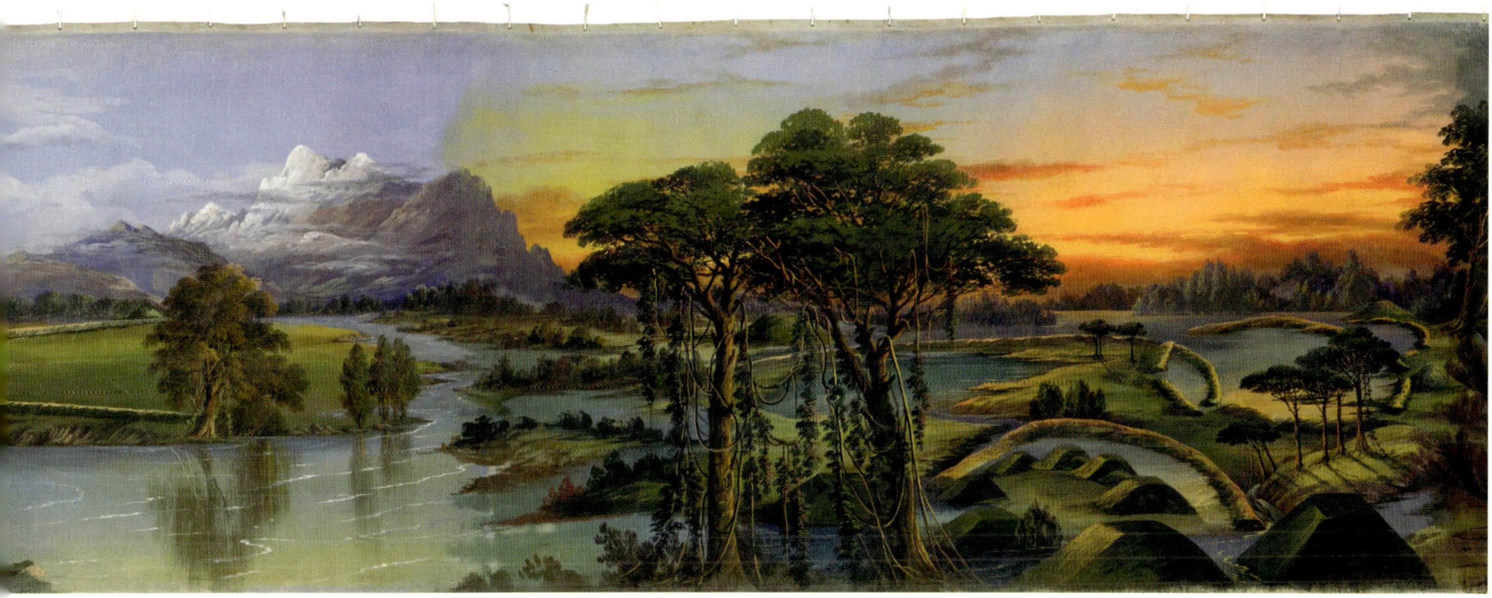

of the landscape's complexity, the basket also, perhaps, strikes a cautionary note about this land's ability to be brought into line with European systems of order.

## Moving Panoramas

Many of the first landscape painters in New Orleans—including Toussaint François Bigot—were what were called "scene painters": artists who painted moving panoramas and large-scale landscape backdrops for theater and opera. Many of the earliest landscape painters in the city painted these large-scale moving panoramas alongside their more traditional works in oil on canvas. During the nineteenth century, these moving panoramas were a popular form of entertainment in which artists would paint a series of landscape views on a long roll of canvas, and then present them to paying audiences in sequence by slowly unrolling the canvas on a crank. These moving panoramas sought to replicate the act of traveling through a landscape, as if one was watching the landscape unfold from a the car of a train or the deck of a ship.[41] New Orleans was a major center for both the production and presentation of these moving panoramas, and had a Cosmorama—a special theater designed specifically to show them—in continual operation on the corner of Orleans and Bourbon Street in the French Quarter as early as the 1820s.[42] During this time, Louisiana-based artists could have encountered any number of nationally and internationally practicing panorama artists in the city, such as John Vanderlyn, whose panorama of Versailles—now on permanent display at the Metropolitan Museum of Art—was shown in a building on Rampart Street in 1829, and John Banvard, who made many trips to New Orleans both before and after the production of his monumental *Panorama of the Mississippi River,* which traveled the world as one of the most celebrated panoramas of its day.[43]

One of the most popular pathways for these panoramic journeys to follow was that of water, and particularly rivers. The Mississippi River, alongside journeys up the Nile and the approach to Niagara Falls, were among the most popular and successful panorama subjects, with the Mississippi becoming particularly wed to the panoramic medium after the premiere of Banvard's *Panorama of the Mississippi River.* Painted on what Banvard advertised to be "three miles of canvas," although its real length was much more modest, the panorama covered over 1200 miles of landscape. New Orleans was Banvard's last stop after completing his 400 day journey down the river in a small skiff boat making preparatory sketches for his panorama—an adventure which was full of storms, unexpected stops and starts, and many near drownings.[44] In the book Banvard published to document his journey, he described the river thusly:

> *Thence it glides, alternately through beautiful meadows and deep forests, swelling in its advancing march with the tributes of a hundred streams. In its progress, it receives a tributary, which of itself has a course of more than a thousand leagues. Thence it rolls its accumulated, turbid and sweeping mass of waters through continued forests in lonely grandeur to the sea. No thinking mind can contemplate this mighty and restless wave.*[45]

Moving panoramas—at first glance—seem uniquely suited to capture the sensation of sailing down a river and witnessing a seamlessly unfolding succession of different views. However, as Banvard indicates in the above statement, the real experience of rivers, as well as the panoramas that claimed to navigate them, was something quite different. Because of the frequent use of such waterways as the organizational principle for these panoramic journeys, it is easy to imagine the experience of watching the panorama unfold as akin to how we envision the flow of a river—a steady stream of images similar to the contemporary experience of watching a movie. Although very few of these moving panoramas still exist, one of the few that does can help us better understand the real experience. John J. Egan's *Panorama of the Monumental Grandeur of the Mississippi Valley* (circa 1850; Fig. 19), now in the collection of the Saint Louis Art Museum, presents not a smooth, continuous view, but rather a collection of discrete scenes that offer a bewildering array of different perspectives, seasons, times of day, and even centuries.[46] Despite the physical and temporal distance between many of the individual vignettes, almost all of them are linked by water, which flows across and between the painted divides that seperate individual scenes. The resulting panorama creates an experience—likely true to many of the moving panoramas of the day—that feels like the apotheosis of the many descriptions quoted earlier in this essay regarding the labyrinthine, maze-like quality of the Mississippi River Delta, showing different waterways meeting, merging and tangling together across almost 350 feet of canvas.

It is perhaps no coincidence that Toussaint François Bigot also painted panoramas, for the many different vanishing points in Bigot's painting recall the sensation of looking at a continuous span of two or three of Egan's paintings side-by-side. The same is true of Bigot's fellow panorama painter Robert Brammer, who frequently titled even his more traditional oil paintings as panoramas, as in his *Mississippi Panorama* (1842-53; Fig. 20). Brammer's obituary notes that the "beautiful scenery of the mighty rivers of America, were his favorite studies," and, perhaps in reference to his panoramic work, describes his paintings as "embodiment[s] of pure poetry, glowing with all of fervid genius, of brilliant fancy and rich and racy language,

**Fig. 20 (opposite)**
Robert Brammer, *Mississippi Panorama*, 1842-53, Oil on canvas, 29 x 36 inches, Collection of Stacy and Jay Underwood. Image courtesy of the Mississippi Museum of Art.

**Fig. 21 (p. 48)**
Asher Brown Durand, *Forenoon*, 1847, Oil on canvas, 73 1/4 x 61 1/4 x 5 3/4 inches (framed), New Orleans Museum of Art, Gift of the Fine Arts Club of New Orleans, 16.4

**Fig. 22 (p. 49)**
Asher Brown Durand, *Landscape, Composition, Afternoon*, 1847, Oil on canvas, 60 1/2 x 47 3/4 inches, Mead Art Museum, College Purchase, AC 1947.40, Image courtesy Mead Art Museum at Amherst College

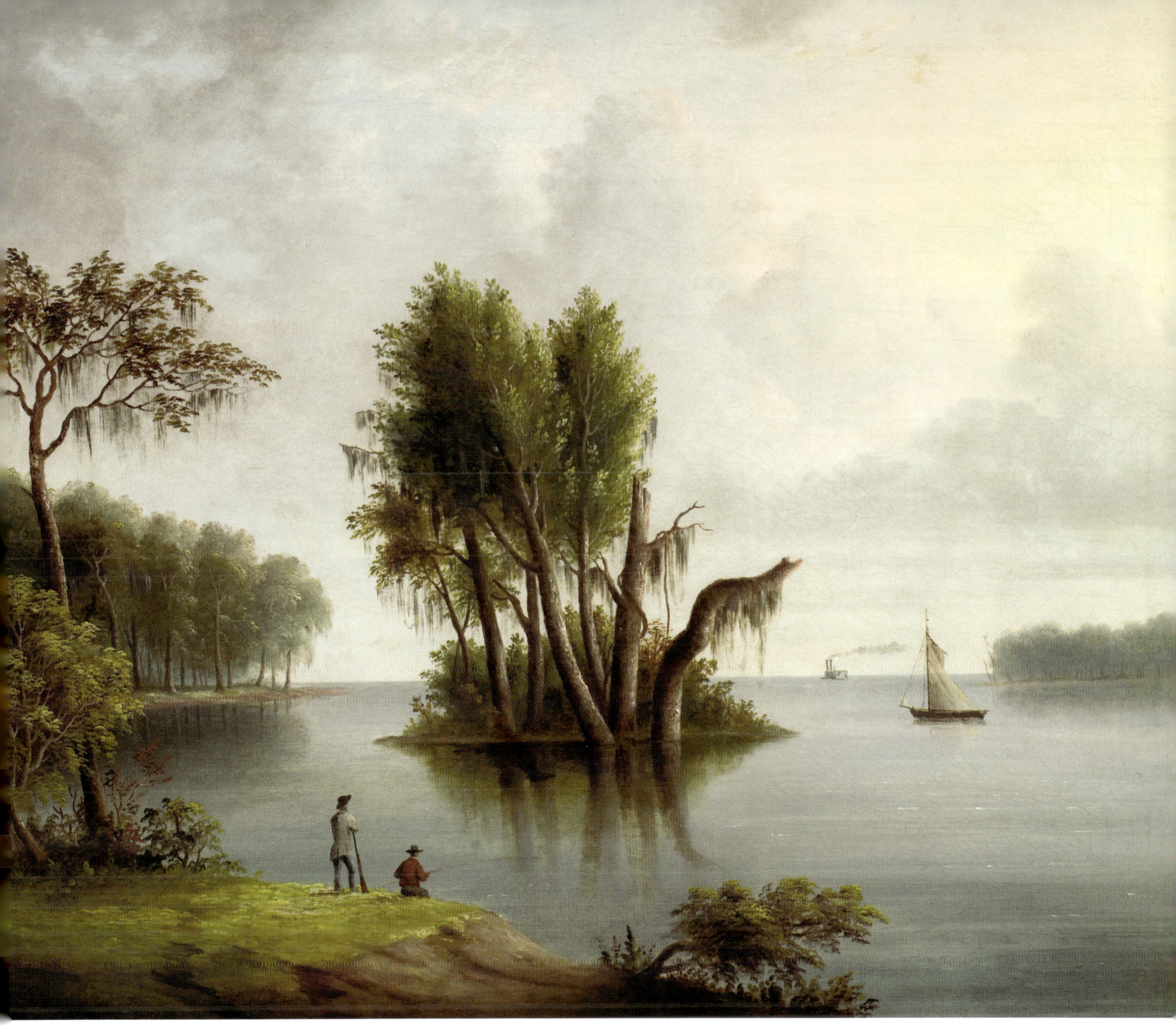

on the speaking canvas."[47] While none of Brammer's full-length panoramas survive, many of his paintings of river landscapes still do. At least two of these surviving works are titled as panoramas, reflecting their connection to the larger moving panoramas he was also making during this time. In *Mississippi Panorama,* Brammer paints the river with a small island of trees in the center. This island of trees, locatedright in the middle of the river, obscures the painting's horizon and blocks access to its vanishing point, making it appear, like Bigot's work, as if there are multiple bodies of water intersecting on the canvas, rather than just one river. Compounding this sense of multiple streams colliding are the two different kinds of vessels that Brammer juxtaposes in both paintings: a steamship and sailboat, which indicate that this painting was made not just at any point along the river, but rather, very deliberately, close to where the Mississippi River meets the Gulf of Mexico.

The island of trees in the center of Brammer's painting recalls a pendant pair of paintings by the Hudson River School painter Asher Brown Durand, *Forenoon* (1847; Fig. 21) and

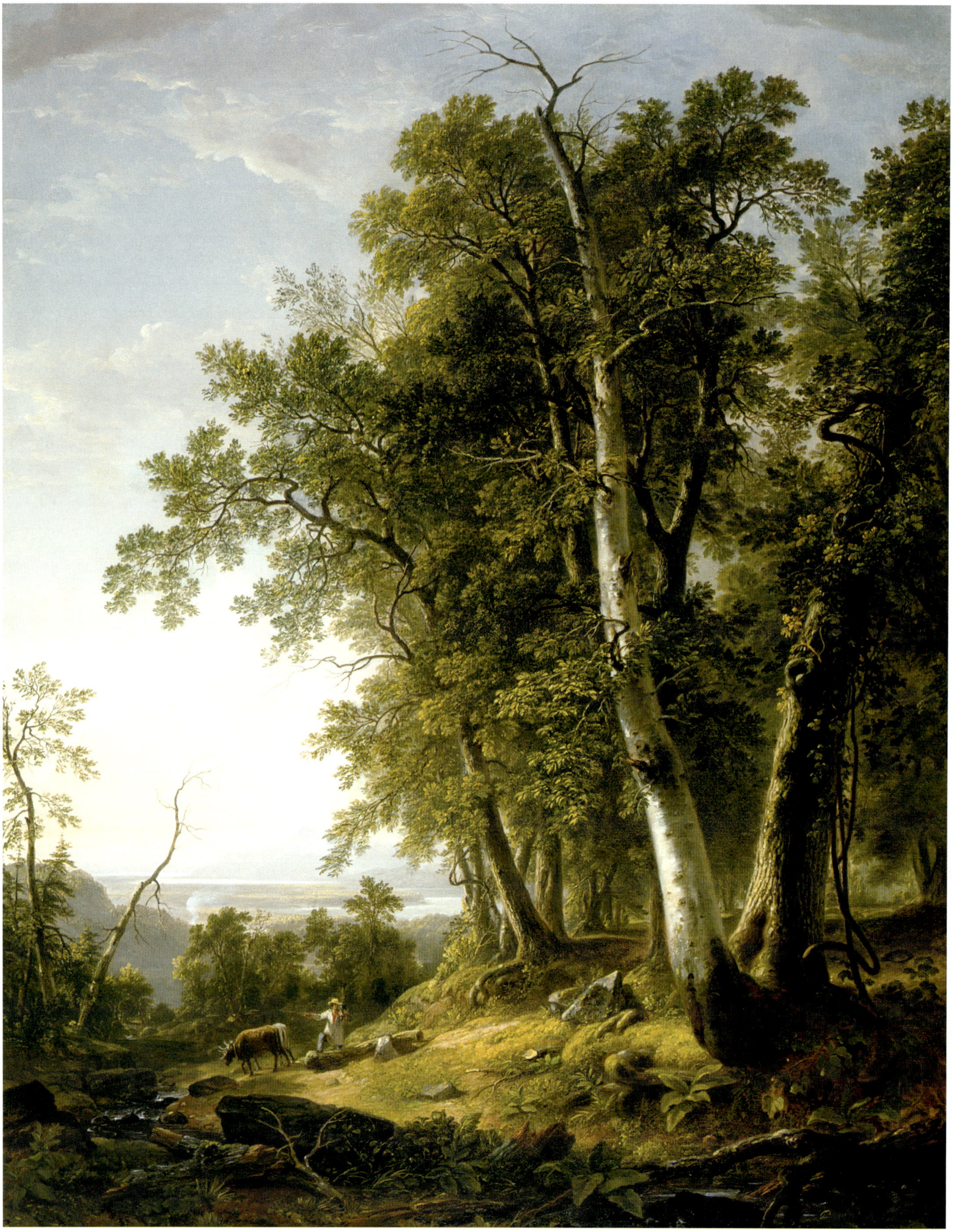

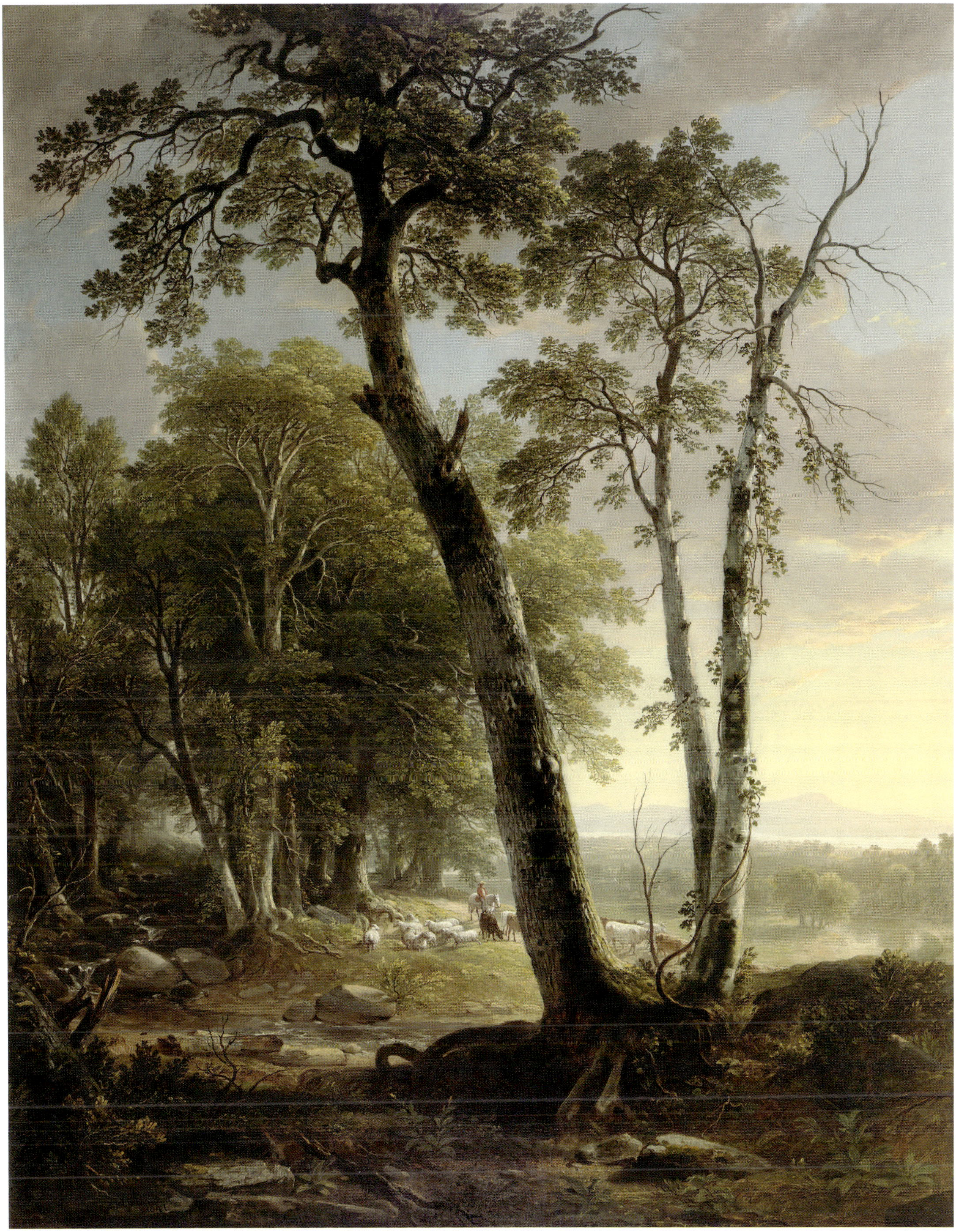

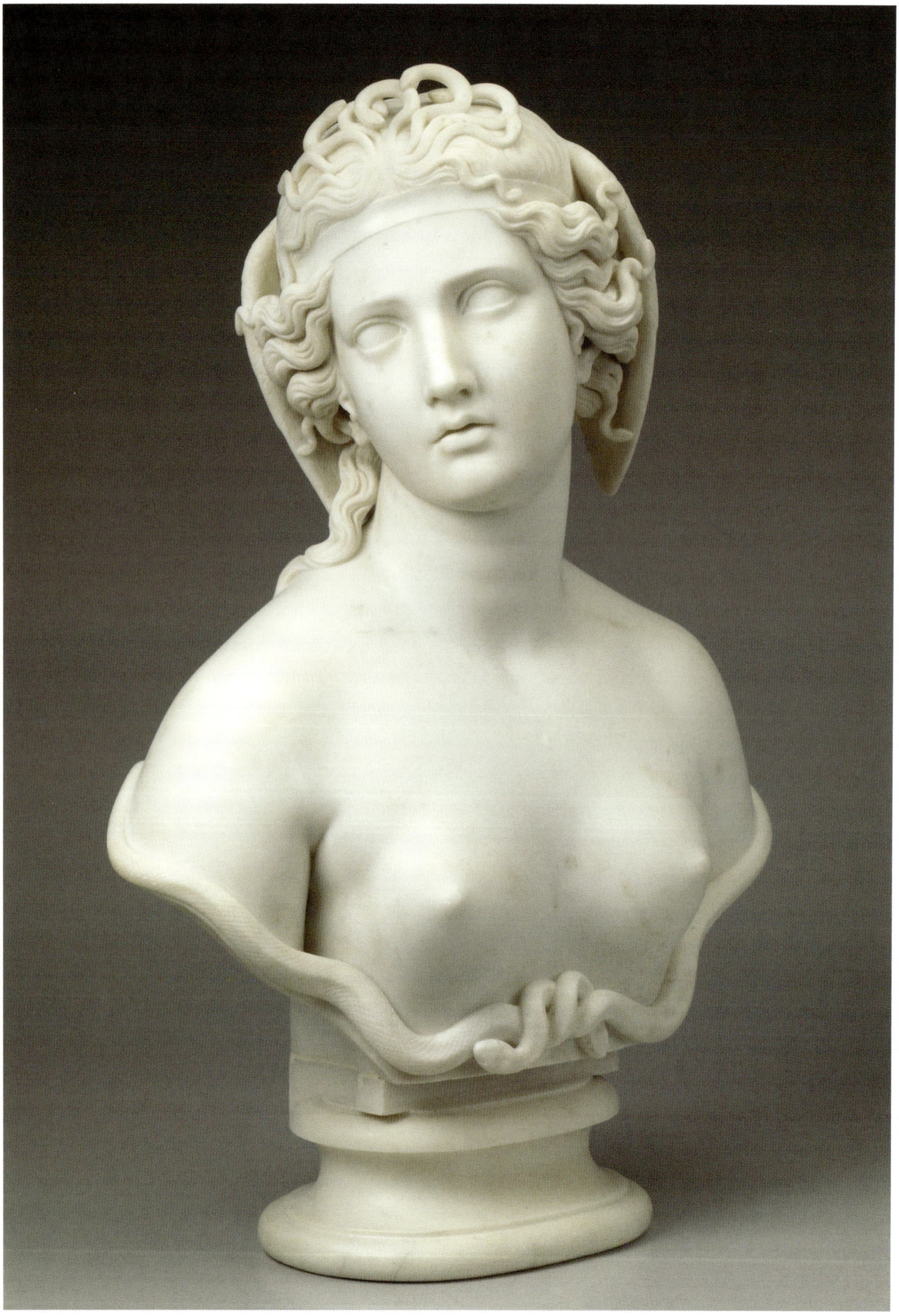

**Fig. 23**
Harriet Goodhue Hosmer (1830-1908), *Medusa*, circa 1854, Marble, 27 ¼ x 21 x 9 ½ inches, Minneapolis Institute of Art, MN, USA, The Walter C. and Mary C. Briggs Purchase Fund/ Bridgeman Images, 2003.125

*Landscape, Composition, Afternoon* (1847; Fig. 22) that Brammer could have seen in New Orleans at the Magazine Street mansion of business magnate and art collector James Robb as early as 1847.[48] These paintings both focus on a central group of trees, first painted by the light of morning and then by the shade of afternoon. The perspective of the paintings shift with the sun, so that one sees both sides of the scene as one moves from one canvas to another. Durand's trees are noticeably similar to the island of trees that Brammer painted into the center *Mississippi Panorama*, except that Durand's trees are set on land, while Brammer's are in water. In Brammer's painting, the clear reflections of the trees in the water below make it hard to tell where the water ends, and the land begins. Similar to the tree branches draped over Bigot's painting, the myriad reflections from these trees recall the larger structure of the river delta, as if Brammer meant to represent not just the particular scene being shown, but also the many pathways of water that branch off from this point in the river.

Insisting on the connectivity of these landscapes—showing the ways in which each of these singular landscapes is part of a larger water system—Brammer's painting is itself like a panorama. Extending beyond the borders of the frame to indicate the vast circulatory system of water of the river delta, Brammer's painting recalls the way water moves across and between the otherwise discrete scenes in Egan's moving panorama. Like so many other paintings during this period, Brammer's painting seems to insist that there is no way to paint, or see, just one part of this landscape. All of the landscapes of this region, Brammer seems to tell us, are moving panoramas, with water constantly streaming through them, around them, and far beyond them. Describing the way Louisiana was interlinked by water, one author in 1819 described the region thusly:

> *…the whole country is an alluvation of the gulph [sic] of Mexico, and of the rivers that have shifted their channels in successive ages. The Mississippi rolls majestically along through the state from North to South. With this stream are connected most of the navigable water courses of the country; others flow into the sea at different points. They are all so intimately interlocked as to form a general groupe, combining more singular varieties [of waterways] than is exhibited on the same extent of surface, in any other country of the globe.*

Many of these early painters of this region—Boisseau, Bigot, Brammer—demonstrate an openness to this more expansive vision of land through this connection *to* water, and this connection *through* water to perspectives beyond the typical purview of a single landscape scene.

Alongside Banvard and Egan, one of the other artists to produce a work of art connected to the experience of journeying up and down the entire length of the Mississippi River was sculptor Harriet Goodhue Hosmer. Her sculpture bust of *Medusa* (circa 1854; Fig. 23) was made in Rome in the years immediately following her 1851 voyage from St. Louis to New Orleans along the Mississippi River.[49] Hosmer embarked upon this journey with another female friend right after graduating from school. Her friend turned back after travel proved too difficult, but Hosmer continued on all the way to New Orleans. As described by her friend and biographer Cornelia Carr, her travels were defined by water's deceptiveness and even treachery:

> *The mighty Mississippi was not to be counted upon. Owing to its swift current and its soft bed of sand and clay, it changed course at will, moving suddenly from side to side, sometimes overlapping its legitimate borders and leaving sand bars and banks today where yesterday deep water had been.*[50]

Snakes were one of the main symbols for Louisiana's waterways—and especially the Mississippi River—during the nineteenth century. Artists such as Bigot, as discussed earlier, often rhymed their representations of Louisiana's waterways with the shapes of snakes and alligators, and period accounts often describe the landscape as akin to snakes, serpents, or alligators, as in Darby's description of the Mississippi's "serpentine meander."[51] Hosmer's sculpture, similarly, shows snakes streaming through the hair of a beautiful woman as she is being transformed into a gorgon, a monster with snakes for hair so fearsome that looking upon her turns people to stone. The resulting sculpture asks us to re-envision our relationship to female strength and power, and also recalibrate our relationship to the natural environment.[52] Hosmer cast Medusa's hair from live snakes that she captured outside of Rome, which she anesthetized and kept in plaster for three and a half hours, but then released back out into the wild. The sculpture, then, reverses the typical dynamics of both natural history and landscape painting, in which to represent is also, often, to destroy—or unmake—wilderness.

Hosmer's sculpture reflects a sense of environmental awareness that may have come, at least in part, from her voyage up and down the Mississippi River, and her experience of the landscape of the river delta.[53] The tangle of snakes that wind throughout Medusa's hair—twisting, turning and intertwining—echo the wild and unwieldy landscapes Hosmer encountered along the river shortly before making this work. Very few representations of women's experiences along the river remain—much less those cast, like Hosmer's sculpture, in stone—and this work provides some reflection of Hosmer's experience. It also connects to the work of nineteenth-century painter, Blanche Virginia Blanchard. Like Bigot and Brammer, Blanchard also painted large-scale decorative landscape works, in her case for homes and churches.[54] In one of her few surviving works, *Untitled (Louisiana Landscape)* (n.d.; Fig. 24), alligators and fallen trees snake through the foreground of a composition that branches off into several different pathways that weave backwards in echo of these serpentine forms.[55] While certainly *Medusa*—a sculpture made in Rome, with references to Greek mythology and classical Italian sculpture—looks far past the landscape being depicted in Blanchard's painting for its frame of reference, both Hosmer's sculpture and Blanchard's painting possess a shared sensibility that seems to reflect something of the landscape of the river delta, and what it meant to be a woman navigating it in the nineteenth century. The twisting branches and writhing alligators in Blanchard's painting, so like the serpents flowing through *Medusa*'s hair, confront perceptions of female power, but also question our power over land.

Blanchard's painting appears to be composed in large measure of *flotant*, or floating marsh—a term for the entangled roots and leaves of floating plants that often give the illusion of land within deltas, marshes and swamps. Great was the danger, in navigating many of Louisiana's

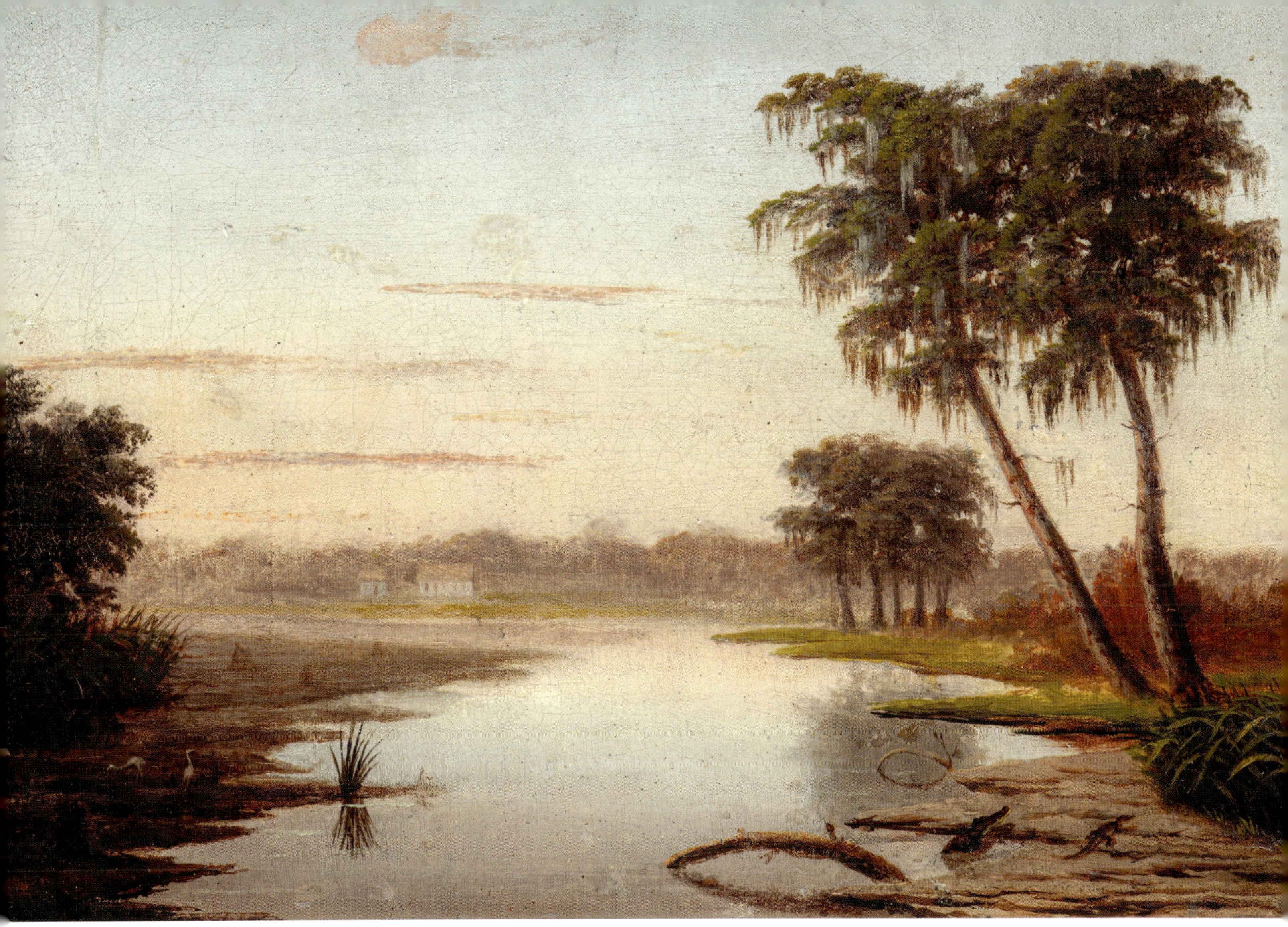

**Fig. 24**
Blanche Virginia Blanchard, *Untitled (Louisiana Landscape)*, circa 1880, Oil on canvas, 13 x 17 inches (framed), Collection of Tommy Spinosa, Photography by Roman Alokhin.

landscapes, of encountering *flotant*—a term unique to Louisiana that describes land that is not land at all: land in which to step is to sink, sometimes head deep. The entire left side of the bank of Blanchard's painting appears to be *flotant*, one of the most treacherous and unstable forms of land in the world. Painting a landscape in which it is impossible to discern where water ends and land begins, Blanchard shows this land's inability to become permanently solid, demonstrating the ways it could never—to reference back to Hosmer—be turned to stone. In painting the landscape's precarity, perhaps Blanchard was also thinking about her own perspective on this land as a female artist, and wondering about her own painting's chances of preservation.

## Vanishing Perspectives

As the century wore on, these early scenes of Louisiana's wetlands, swamps, and river deltas gave way to more conventional landscape imagery: representations of developed land in paintings that correspondingly ascribe to much more traditional landscape formats. In plantation pictures by artists such as Marie Adrien Persac, we witness the Louisiana landscape transforming into a place of precise order and systemic exploitation of both land and people, as discussed in later essays in this book. Even paintings of swamps and bayous—the very places artists like Boisseau, Bigot, and Brammer painted—show a landscape increasingly being brought under control, reordered by agriculture and industry as well as painterly perspective. In later paintings by Joseph Rusling Meeker such as *The Land of Evangeline* (1874; Plate 45), for instance, the landscape is nearly always hemmed in by trees that hug nearly all sides of the composition, its vistas foreshortened by thick fog. In many of these later paintings, the six vanishing points we saw Bigot's painting give way to just one.

In the hard-and-fast banks of the bayous that cut across paintings by George David Coulon, or the developed plantation landscapes of William Henry Buck, we witness a closing down of the more open, exploratory perspectives of these earlier artists. Crucially, these more expansive compositions made room for some trace—although often faint and hard to find—of the women, Indigenous communities, and enslaved people so often absent from these later works. This catalogue and essay has sought to recover some of these stories—both by finding within the paintings that have been preserved echoes of the voices that have been lost, and also by searching for artworks that have not previously been part of the story of Louisiana landscape painting. The process of searching for these missing voices has, more than anything, made clear all that has been lost: to the floods, fires, and hurricanes that have long made Louisiana such a precarious place for preservation, and to the privileging of some voices over those of others. This catalogue and essay are at best an incomplete attempt to find within this art some vestige of the many different people that once formed the landscape and history of this place.

The path to uncover more perspectives on this land has led to many dead ends: accounts of Blanche Virginia Blanchard's work that stake her claim to fame mostly on her role as assistant to male painters such as Charles Giroux; the apparent loss of almost all of the landscape work made by Haitian and African American artists for the 1884 World Cotton Centennial Exposition, described in accounts from the fair to have "ranged in the thousands"; the scant information that exists, either from the nineteenth century, or within contemporary scholarship, about the region's Indigenous art history; and the endless lists of women who were students of artists like George David Coulon and Andres Molinary—Marie Seebold, Edith Sansum, M.B. Smythe, A. McConnell, L, Bellot, among others—who, because very few traces of their work exists, never became recognized in the same way as artists.[56]

One painting in particular, itself now missing, shows how these histories and perspectives have been quite literally effaced from Louisiana's landscape (n.d.; Figs. 25 and 26). Variously attributed to painters Franz Fleischbein, Trevor Thomas Fowler or Theodore Sydney Moïse, this painting—titled *Four Children in a Louisiana Landscape*—for many years appeared to have only three.[57] When it was deaccessioned by the New Orleans Museum of Art in 2005, there existed in the painting the shadow of a fourth child, which subsequent conservation uncovered to be a young African American boy, leaning against a tree. This boy, at some point in the painting's history, was painted over, hidden beneath the landscape of the surrounding scene.[58] Despite extensive searching, the current owners of this painting—which subsequently passed through several different auction houses and dealers—could not be found. As a result, the nature and extent of the conservation work could not be confirmed or verified, and this work could not be included in this exhibition.[59] Today, it exists as a reminder of the many voices that were covered over by landscape painting during the nineteenth century, emphasizing the importance of finding within the incomplete records and scant objects that do exist some trace of the many perspectives that have been lost, or deliberately disappeared.

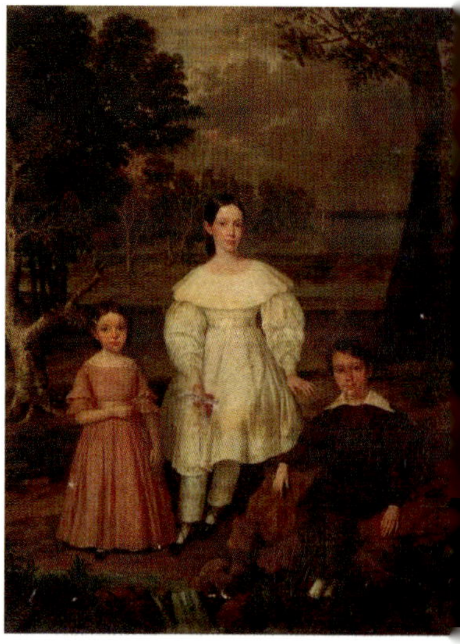

**Fig. 25**
Attributed to Franz Fleischbein, Trevor Thomas Fowler, or Theodore Sydney Moïse, *Four Children in a Louisiana Landscape*, Oil on canvas, 47 1/8 x 36 inches, Location unknown, Image courtesy New Orleans Museum of Art

**Fig. 26 (opposite)**
Attributed to Franz Fleischbein, Trevor Thomas Fowler, or Theodore Sydney Moïse, *Four Children in a Louisiana Landscape*, Oil on canvas, 47 1/8 x 36 inches, Location unknown, Image courtesy Brunk Auctions, Asheville, North Carolina

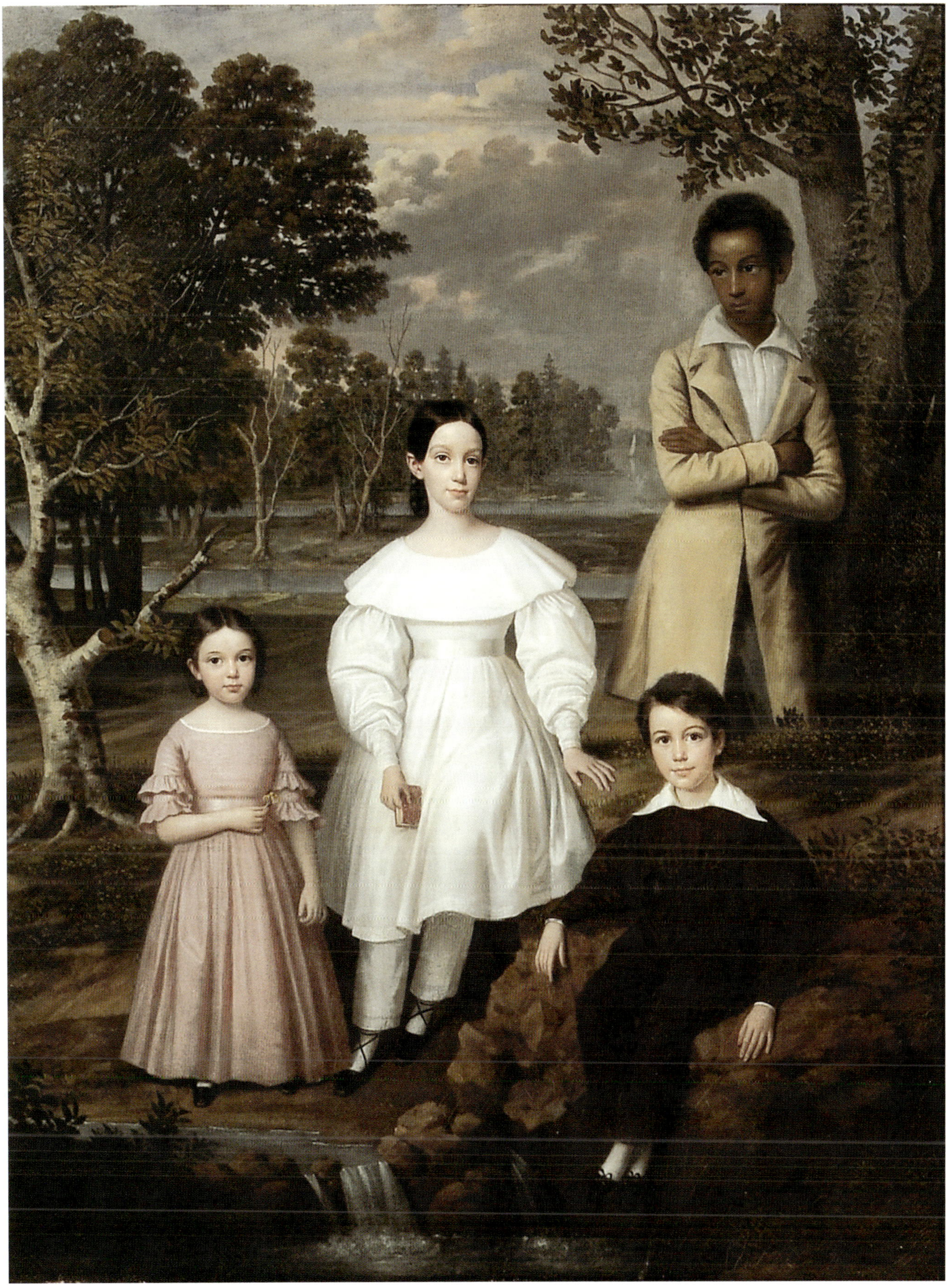

1 Élisée Reclus, *Fragment of a Voyage to Louisiana,* 1855, trans. John Clark, *Mesechabe # 11* (Winter 1993): 16.

2 "A Little World," *Scribner's Monthly*, August 1881, vol. 22, issue 4.

3 "Scenes in Louisiana," *Christian Watchman*, April 18, 1828, 1.

4 Lionel A. Sheldon, "Louisiana and the Levees," *The Arena*, January 1892, no. 26, 187.

5 Charles Gayarré, *Romance of the History of Louisiana: A Series of Lectures* (New York, NY: D. Appleton & Company, 1867), 232.

6 "A Little World," *Scribner's Monthly*, August 1881, vol. 22, issue 4.

7 "A Manhattaner in New Orleans," *The Literary World,* October 28, 1848.

8 "New Orleans: Memories of a Lost Cause," *New York Evangelist,* April 1884, 1.

9 See Kimia Shahi, "Entanglements of Land and Water: Picturing Contingency in Martin Johnson Heade's *Newburyport Marshes: Approaching Storm*" in *Nature's Nation:American Art and Environment*, eds. Karl Kusserow and Alan C. Braddock, exh. cat. (New Haven, CT: Yale University Press, 2018), 304-312.

10 "New Orleans," *Niles' Weekly Register,* June 8, 1816.

11 Samuel Wilson, Jr., "Louisiana Drawings by Alexandre De Batz," *Journal of the Society of Architectural Historians,* vol. 22, issue 2 (May 1963), 75.

12 "National Gallery of Paintings, Review of Paintings in the Gallery," *Daily Tropic,* February 14, 1845, 2.

13 Thank you to Jeffrey U. Darensbourg, Ph.D., Tribal Councilperson from the Atakapa-Ishak Nation, for drawing my attention to the calumet in this painting. See Jeffrey U. Darensbourg, "Travelling Light," Situate Magazine, June 1, 2016 http://www.situatemagazine.com/issue/new-orleans/409/traveling-light

14 "The High River," *The Louisiana Planter and Sugar Manufacturer,* May 21, 1892.

15 The painting depicts an Osage orange tree, which was venerated by the Natchez people. This tree was close to the Natchez's great temple, near what became the village of Valleur, which was destroyed in February 1730 during a conflict between the French and the Natchez. See *American Art at Harvard,* eds. Theodore E. Stebbins Jr and Melissa Renn (New Haven, CT: Yale University Press, 2014), 167.

16 Wilson, 88.

17 E. Benezit, *Dictionnaire critique et documentaire des peintres, scultpteurs, dessinateurs et graveurs de tous les temps et de tous les pays par un groupe d'ecrivains specialists francais et etrangers*, vol. 1, ed. Ernest Grund (Paris: Ernest Grund, 1924), 348.

18 See Emily C. Burns, *Transnational Frontiers: The American West in France* (Norman, OK: University of Oklahoma Press, 2018).

19 Benezit, 348.

20 See Kelly Presutti's essay in this volume for a more detailed discussion about the French Barbizon and its influence in Louisiana through the work of Richard Clague, and particularly its connection to emerging environmental movements.

21 Clare D'Artois Leeper, *Louisiana Place Names: Popular, Unusual and Forgotten Stories of Towns, Cities, Plantations, Bayous and even some Cemeteries* (Baton Rouge, LA: Louisiana State University Press, 2012), 244.

22 Jay C. Martin, "Sentinel of Centuries: The Tchefuncte River Light Station," *Lighthouse Digest*, October 2008.

23 Martin and Margaret Wiesdendanger, *Nineteenth Century Louisiana Painters and Paintings from the Collection of W.E. Groves* (Gretna, LA: Pelican Printing Company, 1971), 16.

24 Erastus Everett, "The Mississippi River, Its Delta, Its Bayous, Its Levees, Its Floods," *Appleton's Journal of Literature, Science and Art,* July 11, 1874, 45.

25 Adrien Emmanuel Roquette was born in New Orleans in 1813, and was sent to France in 1829 to study in Paris. Between 1829 and 1846, Rouquette traveled frequently back and forth between New Orleans and Paris, where he became well known for the poems and essays about Louisiana he wrote while living among the Choctaws. See Chris Michaelides, "The Tree of the Choctaws: Live Oaks in the Sacred Poetry of Father Adrien Emmanuel Rouquette," in *Mapping the Catholic Cultural Landscape*, eds. Sister Paula Jean Miller and Richard Fossey (Lanham, MD: Rowman & Littlefield Publishers, 2004).

26 Darby's was the first detailed American-printed map of the state after French cartographer Barthelemy Lafon's maps of 1805 and 1806.

27 William Darby, *A Geographical Description of the State of Louisiana, The Southern Part of the State of Missippippi, and Territory of Alabama; Together with a Map from Actual Survey and Observervation, Projected on a Scale of Ten Miles to an Inch, of The State of Louisana and Adjacent Countries* (New York, NY: James Olmstead, 1817, sold also by B. Levy &Co Booksellers, New Orleans), 43.

28 Darby, 22.

29 "Darby's Louisiana," *Niles' Weekly Register,* July 27, 1816.

30 Judith H. Bonner, "Artists' Associations in Nineteenth Century New Orleans: 1842-1860," *Southern Quarterly*, (Fall-Winter 1985): 128 and 133.

31 "Notices," *New Orleans Daily Tropic*, September 22, 1845. Another 1845 review mentions the work on display by Cole that year as *Schroon Lake*, which the artist painted in 1840 and is now in a private collection. See "National Gallery of Paintings: Review of Paintings in the Gallery, *Daily Tropic*, February 14, 1845, 2.

32 One of the first and best-documented art galleries in New Orleans was the National Gallery of Paintings, founded by George Cooke in 1844, and later renamed the Union Gallery. Although the painting is now lost, Thomas Cole's

*Elijah at the Mouth of the Cave* was exhibited at the Union Gallery in New Orleans in 1857. See Bonner, 128 and 133.

33 Toussaint François Bigot and his wife Stephanie were among the first artists to offer painting and drawing classes in New Orleans. Toussaint ran a painting and drawing academy from 1826-27, and taught at the central public school in the Ursuline Convent in the French Quarter from 1827-41. Advertisements for his painting and drawing instruction (at various locations throughout the French Quarter) appear in New Orleans papers through 1853.

34 Four other paintings by Bigot are documented and illustrated in the exhibition catalogue for the 1950 exhibition *Mississippi Panorama* at the City Art Museum in St. Louis. See Perry T. Rathbone, *Mississippi Panorama*, exh. cat. (St. Louis, MO: City Art Museum, 1950), 54-57.

35 Thank you to botanist David Baker, the environmental curator at A Studio in the Woods, for this assessment of the tree and plant species in this painting.

36 Stephen W. Cook, *By Native Hands: Woven Treasures from the Lauren Rogers Museum* (Laurel MS: Lauren Rogers Museum of Art, 2005).

37 Research has not conclusively demonstrated the origin of this oak basket, which is believed to have been made before the end of the nineteenth century in the Atchafalaya Basin. There are scant records or written histories about Southeastern basket traditions, which make many of the baskets that remain hard to conclusively identify or attribute to a specific region or culture. Thank you to Carl Bennett, Don Fuson, Danny Lee Petrella and basket weaver Tom Colvin for helping to research the origin and story of this basket, whose history and identity remains inconclusive.

38 See Dana Bowker Lee, "The Ties that Bind: Cane Basketry Traditions Among the Chitimacha and the Jena Band of Choctaw," in *The Work of Tribal Hands: Southeastern Indian Split Cane Basketry* (Natchitoches, LA: Northwestern State University Press, 2006), 48.

39 Citing extant letters between Chitimacha chiefs, and in particular the letters of Second Chief George A. Gemarest, Bowker Lee discusses how these baskets were mobilized by the Chitimacha both as tools of cultural diplomacy, and tools of cultural preservation.

40 See Daniel H. Usner, *Indian Work: Language and Livelihood in Native American History* (Cambridge, MA: Harvard University Press, 2009), 112.

41 See Lee Parry, "Landscape Theater in America," 1971.

42 See Rathbone, 20.

43 Estill Curtis Pennington, "Light on Louisiana Landscape," in *Downriver: Currents of Style in Louisiana Painting, 1800-1950* (Gretna, LA: Pelican Printing Company, 1991), 73.

44 Banvard had a strong presence in New Orleans, describing painting "views" there as early as the late 1830s. See John Banvard, "Adventures of an Artist," *Banvard's Geographical Panorama of the Mississippi River, with the Adventures of the Artist* (Boston, MA: John Putnam, Printer, 1847), 7.

45 John Banvard, "Mississippi River," *Banvard's Geographical Panorama of the Mississippi River, with the Adventures of the Artist* (Boston, MA: John Putnam, Printer, 1847), 15.

46 See Lisa Lyons, "Panorama of the Monumental Grandeur of the Mississippi Valley," *Design Quarterly,* No. 101/102, The River: Images of the Mississippi (1976), 32.

47 "Robert Brammer," *The Daily Orleanean,* August 6, 1853, 2.

48 Jason T. Busch, Christopher Monkhouse, and Janet L. Whitmore, *Currents of Change: Art and Life Along the Mississippi River, 1850-1861*, exh. cat. (Minneapolis, MN: The Minneapolis Institute of the Arts, 2004), 117.

49 William Gerdts, "The *Medusa* of Harriet Hosmer," *Bulletin of the Detroit Institute of Arts,* vol. 56, no. 2 (1978): 96-107

50 *Harriet Hosmer: Letters and Memories,* ed. Cornelia Carr (New York, NY: Moffat, Yard and Company, 1912), 9.

51 Darby, 86.

52 Many have written about the ways in which Hosmer conveyed "themes of female power" through this work. See Kate Culkin, *Harriet Hosmer: A Cultural Biography* (Amherst, MA: University of Massachusetts Press, 2010), 36

53 *Medusa* was a commissioned work, which Hosmer replicated three times. It is unclear how much of a role Hosmer played in the selection of the subject, but one imagines it was considerable, or at the very least that this particular subject was especially resonant for her.

54 See "Miss Blanche Blanchard," *The Times Democrat*, May 11, 1890, 9 and "A Precious Painting: It has been Skillfully Copied and placed in a New Orleans Church," *Times Picayune*, April 23, 1894, 3.

55 Blanchard was often singled out for the continual presence of serpents and alligators in her art, much of the rest of which has been lost. Martin and Margaret Wiesendanger write that "an alligator lying on a bayou bank is a recognizable mannerism of her art." See Wiesendanger, 14.

56 Pennington, 98; Herbert S. Fairall, "The Colored People: Their Exhibit," *The World's Industrial and Cotton Centennial Exposition, New Orleans, 1884-85* (Iowa City IA, 1885), 379; "The Art School," *Times-Picayune*, May 7, 1887.

57 Thank you to collector Jeremy K. Simien for bringing this painting and its history to my attention.

58 The painting was deaccessioned by the New Orleans Museum of Art and sold via Christies New York, March 1, 2005, lot 54. It was then resold at Brunk Auctions in Asheville, North Carolina in September 2010, lot 254.

59 According to conservation reports completed by Brunk Auctions, the African American figure is over fifty percent retouched, due to the difficulties of removing the landscape overpaint.

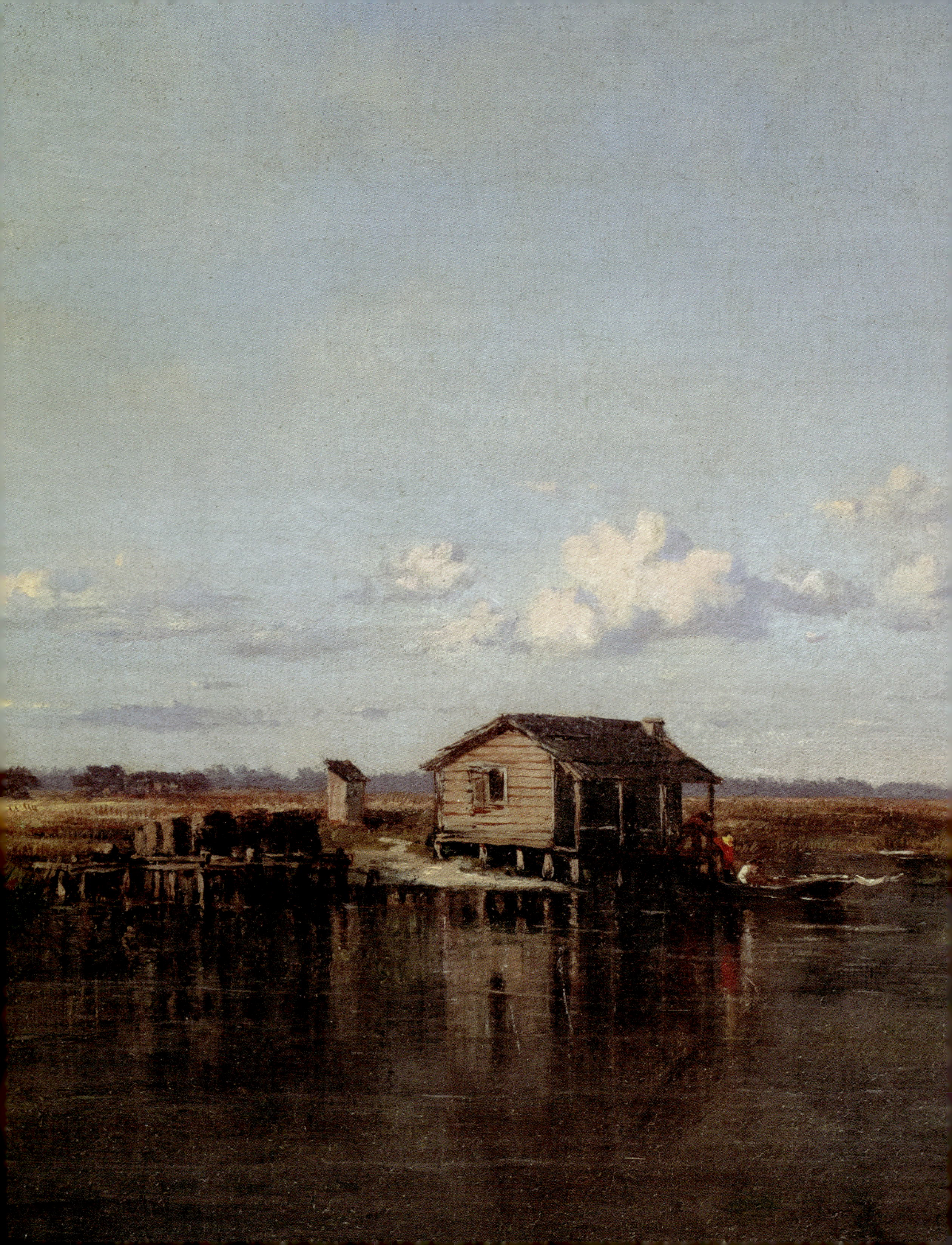

# Barbizon in New Orleans: Richard Clague's Site-Specific Practice

Kelly Presutti

Richard Clague's *Trapper's Cabin, Manchac* (1870; Fig. 1) is set, like so many of the artist's paintings, in an uncertain zone between water and land. At the painting's center, a cabin rests on the very edge of a body of water, elevated by stilts. Hovering over marshy ground, three figures board a boat stationed directly outside the door, moving from their provisional dwelling out into the vast network of waterways that bisect the Mississippi River Delta. The scene reads today as a tranquil painterly study in light, reflection, and sky, but in the context of mid-nineteenth-century Louisiana, it documents a contested environmental reality: the need to manage water, and the people who live on—and make their living from—it. Capturing both the beauty and the precarity of Louisiana's wetlands, Clague overlaps with a tradition of painting in France likewise concerned with close observation of nature, known as the Barbizon School.

The term "Barbizon" is first and foremost a place name—a town on the edge of the Fontainebleau forest in France where a group of loosely-gathered French landscape painters began congregating in the 1830s. These artists, who later came to be known as the Barbizon School, were some of the first French painters to make landscape the primary subject of their art. Living and working within the landscapes they painted, they countered the prevalent idea that painting was something to be done in a studio. Rendering the Fontainebleau forest with a startling sense of immediacy and specificity, they helped a generation of artists understand landscape painting's potential to capture the unique culture, topography, and politics of a place.

Among this group of artists was French-born, Louisiana-raised painter Richard Clague, one of the first Barbizon painters to practice in America. As early as the 1840s—long before Barbizon was well-known in major American art centers like New York and Boston—Clague was among a group of French émigré painters who moved to Louisiana to begin painting Louisiana landscapes in a French Barbizon style. As Clague worked to adapt the Barbizon aesthetic to Louisiana's swampy wetland landscape, he contended with how to practice a style of painting developed for the particularities of the Fontainebleau forest within Louisiana's vastly different terrain. In painting Louisiana, Clague certainly drew upon the forest-bound landscapes of Barbizon painters such as Charles-François Daubigny and Camille Corot, but he likely found more potent models in the work being made by their contemporaries Théodore Rousseau and Jules Dupré in the swampy Landes region of

**Fig. 1**
Richard Clague, *Trapper's Cabin, Manchac*, 1870, Oil on canvas, 14 x 20 inches, Roger Houston Ogden Collection, Courtesy of Ogden Museum of Southern Art. Photography by Patrick Barnes.

southwestern France. For—at the same time Clague began painting Louisiana's wetlands—France was involved in a political, aesthetic and ecological battle to manage its own wetland terrain in the Landes. As Barbizon painters like Rousseau and Dupré began painting in the Landes, they began developing aesthetic strategies more suited to swampy ground. Comparing Clague's Louisiana paintings to works made in the Landes during roughly the same period shows how painters were part of a broader political and representational struggle—in Louisiana as well as France—to contain and control wetlands. Together, their work shows how the Barbizon attention to the specificity of a region's landscape and topography could also help amplify the associated ecological and political concerns. As these artists adapted to a new kind of landscape that was as much water as land, what they took from the Barbizon was not so much a style of representation, but rather a new understanding of the political potential of site-specific landscape representation.[1]

Born in Paris in 1821, Clague lived briefly in New Orleans as a child. He was sent at a young age to study art in Switzerland before returning to New Orleans, where he worked under the panorama painter Leon Pomarede.[2] By 1844 he was back in Paris at the École des Beaux-Arts, and it was here that he was exposed to the work of Barbizon artists like Rousseau and Dupré. After decades of rejection from the French Academy, Rousseau was gaining newfound acceptance in the early 1850s, just as Clague began to exhibit his work in Paris. Clague exhibited at the Paris Salon in 1848, 1849, and 1853—the same year Rousseau exhibited a picture of his trip to the Landes.[3] Art historians often note Clague's aesthetic affinities to the Barbizon, citing the common compositional devices, shared color schemes and strong emphasis on the qualities of light that Clague gleaned from Barbizon paintings. Although some scholars have alluded to deeper connections between American and Barbizon landscape painting—referencing, for instance, a shared "persuasively mysterious sentiment"[4] and reliance on "muddy tonal colors"—Clague's depictions of Louisiana offer new ways of understanding the Barbizon, as well as its influence in the United States more generally.[5]

The idea of a Barbizon "school" was first formulated by Alfred Sensier, biographer, critic, and chief supporter of a number of the French artists within the group.[6] Intended as a way to create identity and increase the value of their artworks, the term collapses a number of artists with distinct aesthetic practices into a single term, despite the fact that many of them actively resisted being understood as part of any coherent school of painting during their own lifetimes. Art historians often retrospectively frame Barbizon art around an embrace of untamed nature, but such categorizations ignore the ways in which these paintings reflect an emerging environmental awareness, and how many of the landscapes these artists painted were under environmental threat.[7] For the subject of so many "Barbizon" paintings —the forest—was undergoing drastic reform just as many of these artists began achieving prominence, making their primary subject a particularly fraught site for representation.

Barbizon paintings pictured a landscape in the midst of major environmental reform. Far from simply capturing an untamed, untouched nature, they often explicitly responded to ongoing political and ecological conflicts regarding land use and water management. In the same decades that the village of Barbizon became an increasingly popular destination

**Fig. 2**
Théodore Rousseau, *The Forest in Winter at Sunset*, circa 1846-67, Oil on canvas, 64 x 102 3/8 inches, Metropolitan Museum of Art, Gift of P.A.B. Widener, 1911, 11.4, Image © The Metropolitan Museum of Art. Image Source: Art Resource, NY.

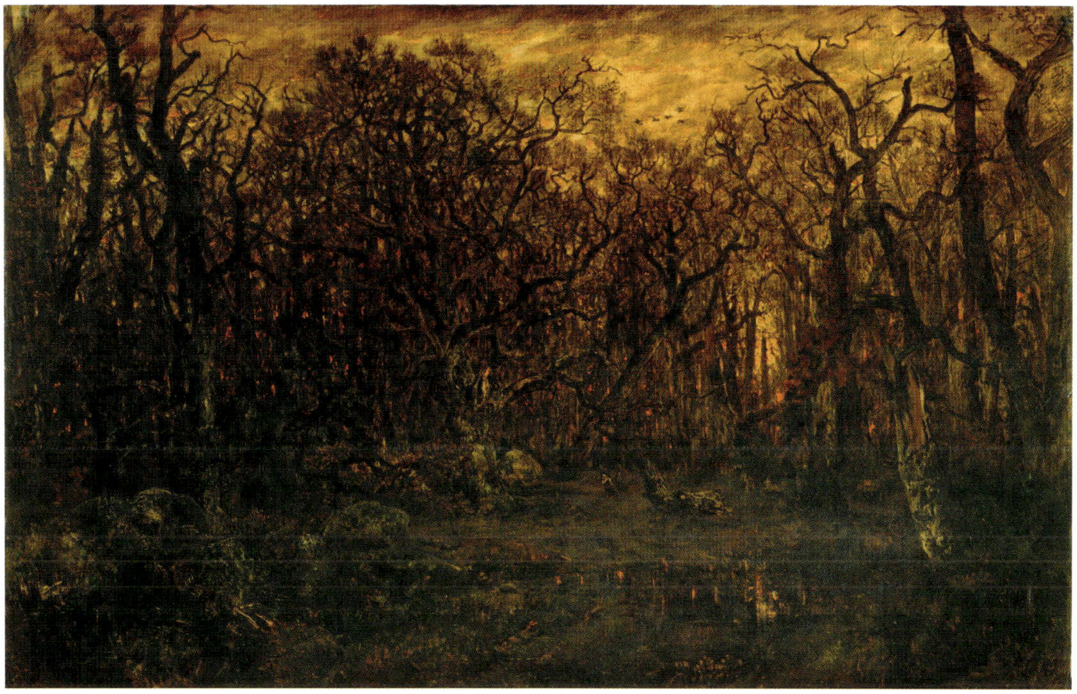

for artists, the French government embarked on a sweeping system of environmental reforms that created conflicts in the Fontainebleau forest between centralized administration and local residents, public good and private interest, and common rights and individual landholdings.[8] The artists at Barbizon—working and living in the landscape they were depicting—witnessed these conflicts firsthand. Their keen attention to the landscape's aesthetics led to a keen understanding of its attendant social and political struggles, which they often chronicled in their work. The small figures who often populate Barbizon forest scenes, for instance, are typically peasants whose very existence depended on forest access. We see two such peasants at the center of Rousseau's monumental *The Forest In Winter at Sunset* (circa 1846-67; Fig. 2), so called faggot-gatherers, traditionally permitted to collect deadwood to heat their homes, whose rights to do so were being increasingly curtailed and ultimately eliminated by the new forestry codes. Although crucial to the social character of the image, the figures are so small they might be overlooked, establishing the vast scale of the woods but at the same time grounding any sublime reverie the trees might trigger back into questions of sustenance. These peasants—frequently tucked into Barbizon scenes from this period—stage a confrontation not just between man and nature, as is often described by art historians, but also between different constituencies and competing ideologies about land, resource, and state.

When Clague arrived in Louisiana, it was this merger of aesthetics and politics that he brought into his Louisiana scenes. In Louisiana, Clague found an immediate visual anchor to the Barbizon in the many live oak trees that define Louisiana's landscapes. An extant series of pencil and ink sketches of live oaks, created between 1857 and 1868, show Clague applying Barbizon aesthetic strategies to Louisiana. Such tree studies are often considered the first step in a traditional landscape artist's training, but for Barbizon artists, trees often formed an important subject in their own right.[9] Clague composed his tree sketches with a sensitivity

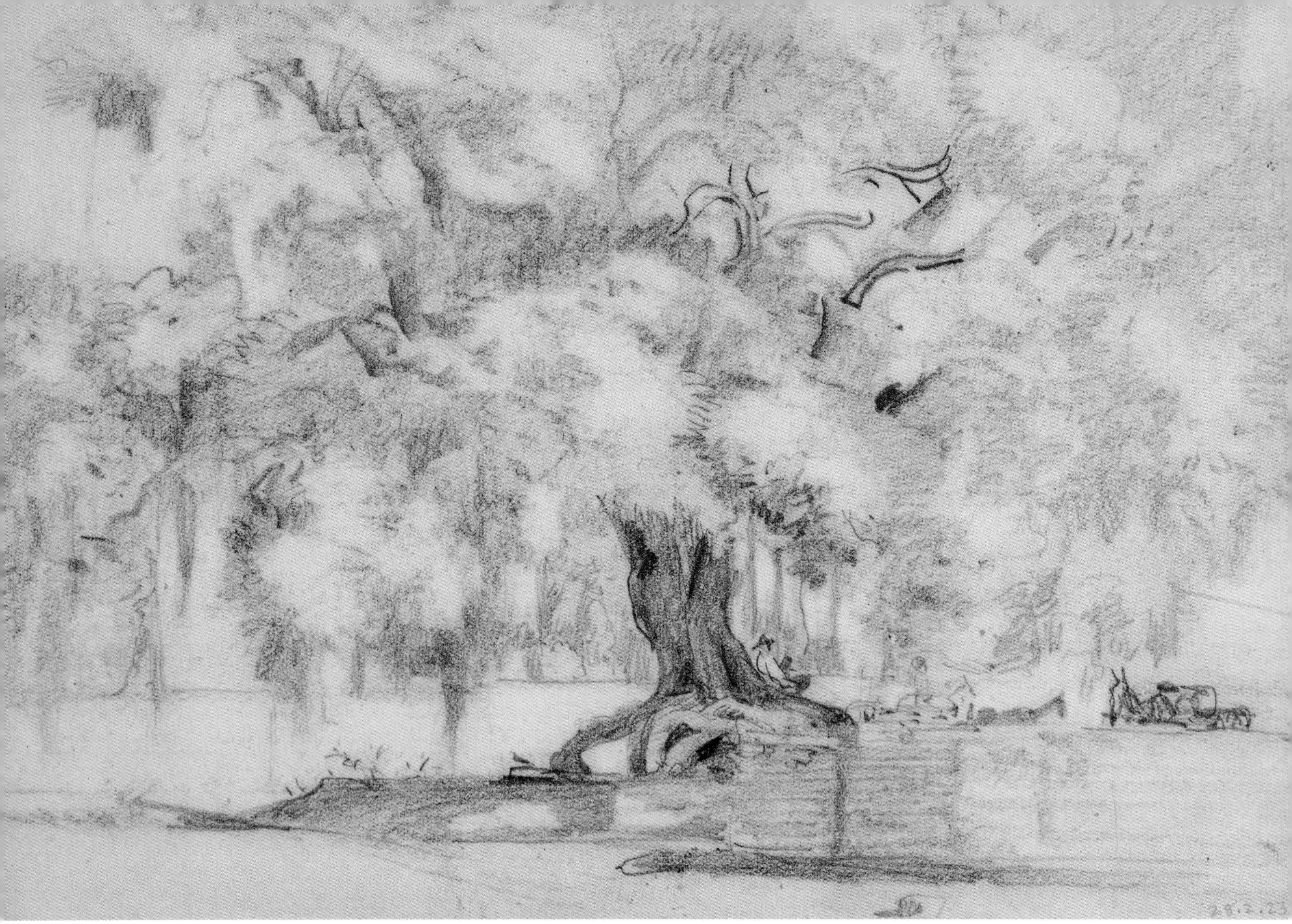

to light and shadows gleaned from Barbizon art. In his close studies of live oaks (circa 1857-1868; Fig. 3), Clague demonstrates a particular ability to create nuanced tones with his pencil, moving between strong outline and subtle shading. A figure reclines between the water and a live oak, which Clague sets, as he so often does, right at the water's edge. Horizontal bands of shading and a hint of brushy growth along the bank marks the distinction between water and land, and the tree fans out across the page, filling the composition with Spanish moss entangled within the oaks. Adept at capturing these tangles of branches, leaves and draping moss, he often reserved areas of the blank page to suggest the lighter tone of the draping fauna, offset by sharply delineated branches and softly rendered leaves.

Clague's sketches reveal a shared working method with artists like Rousseau. Both exhibit the rapidity of work made on site, within the landscape, as well as careful attention to the unique features and formations of individual trees.[10] Rousseau often developed his tree studies into canvases that challenged the notion of a "finished" artwork, as in *Groupe de chênes* (1852; Fig. 4), a cluster of oaks of varying ages that celebrates their unique forms. In this painting, the intricacy of the trees' branches, echoed by their carefully traced shadows on the ground, underscores the particularity of these specific trees, which are rendered almost as portraits. Centrally placed, without accessory framing elements, *Groupe de chênes* follows no predetermined compositional format, further emphasizing its locality and connection to the landscape's organic growth.

**Fig. 3**
Richard Clague, *Untitled*, circa 1857-1868, Pencil and ink on paper, 12 x 15 inches (framed), New Orleans Museum of Art: Gift of S. A. Trufant, 28.2.23. Photography by Roman Alokhin.

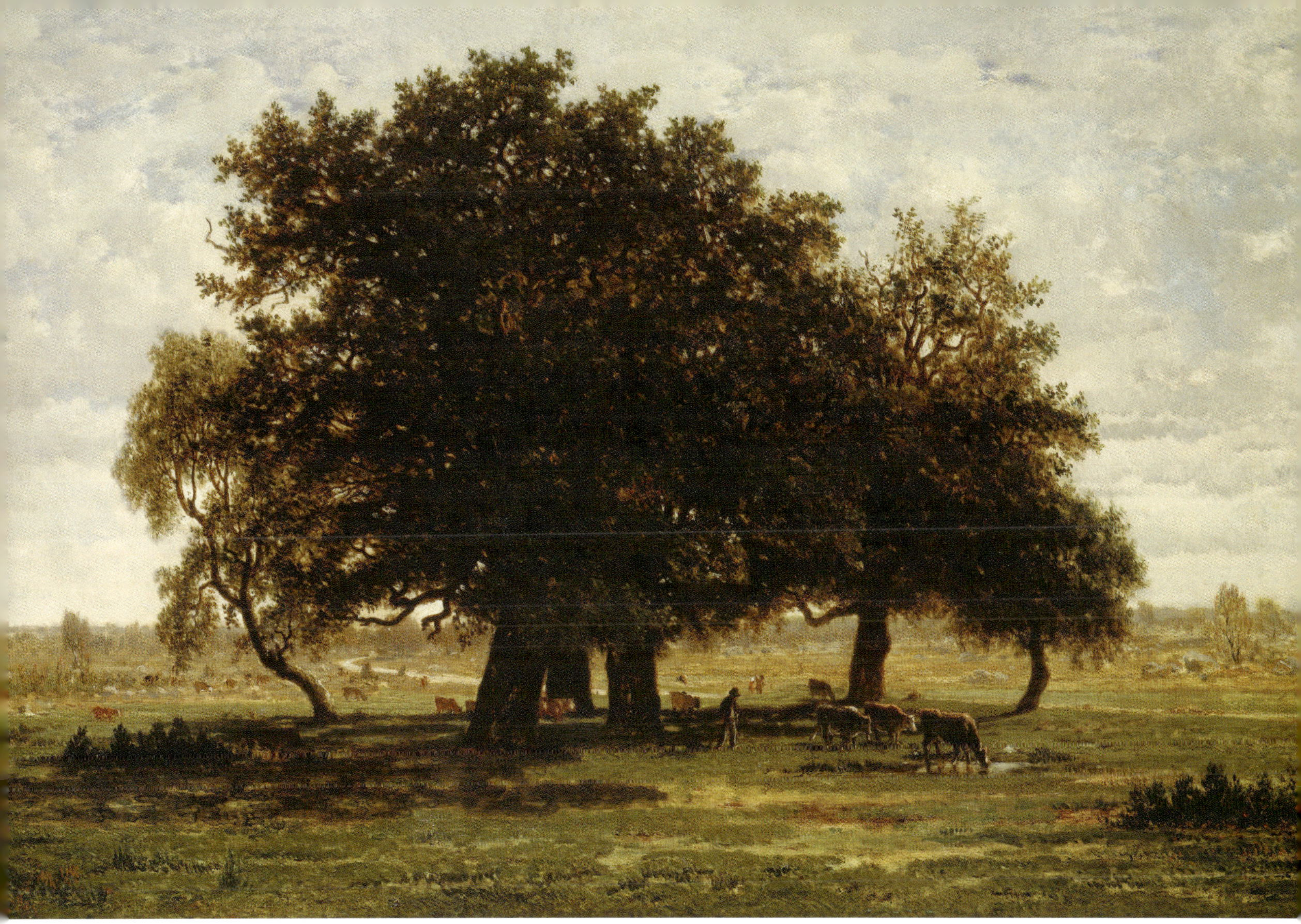

**Fig. 4**
Théodore Rousseau, *Groupe de chênes*, 1852, Oil on canvas, 25 ¼ x 39 ½ inches, Musée du Louvre ©RMN-Grand Palais / Art Resource, NY

Rousseau and other Barbizon artists' devotion to oak trees was not just about aesthetic appreciation, but also a way to emphasize a tree species that was falling increasingly under threat. As part of ongoing French forestry reforms, new scientific silvicultural methods meant administrators increasingly preferred forests to be grids of orderly trees, generally pines. The knotty particularity of oaks Rousseau celebrated in his work was ill-suited to this more regimented vision for the woods.[11] Many Barbizon artists intervened directly in this struggle, filing an 1852 petition to prevent the state from converting oak forests to faster growing, more easily harvested pine. Rousseau is generally assumed to be one of the authors of the petition, and elsewhere he poetically proclaimed that the oaks were a public cause:

> *Until now, it has been the state which has preserved the sacred tree, symbolizing the force and persistence of the soil; that national tree which formerly served as the natural cathedral for the celebration of the mysteries of our ancestors. If the state destroys them, it is up to public opinion to protect their remaining descendants.*[12]

In these public statements, Rousseau questioned the environmental implications of such policies. His paintings, too, advocated for the oaks, and were intended to promote their preservation.[13] *Groupe de chênes*, for instance, was officially connected to this preservationist effort, being purchased by the duc de Morny, who presented the artists'

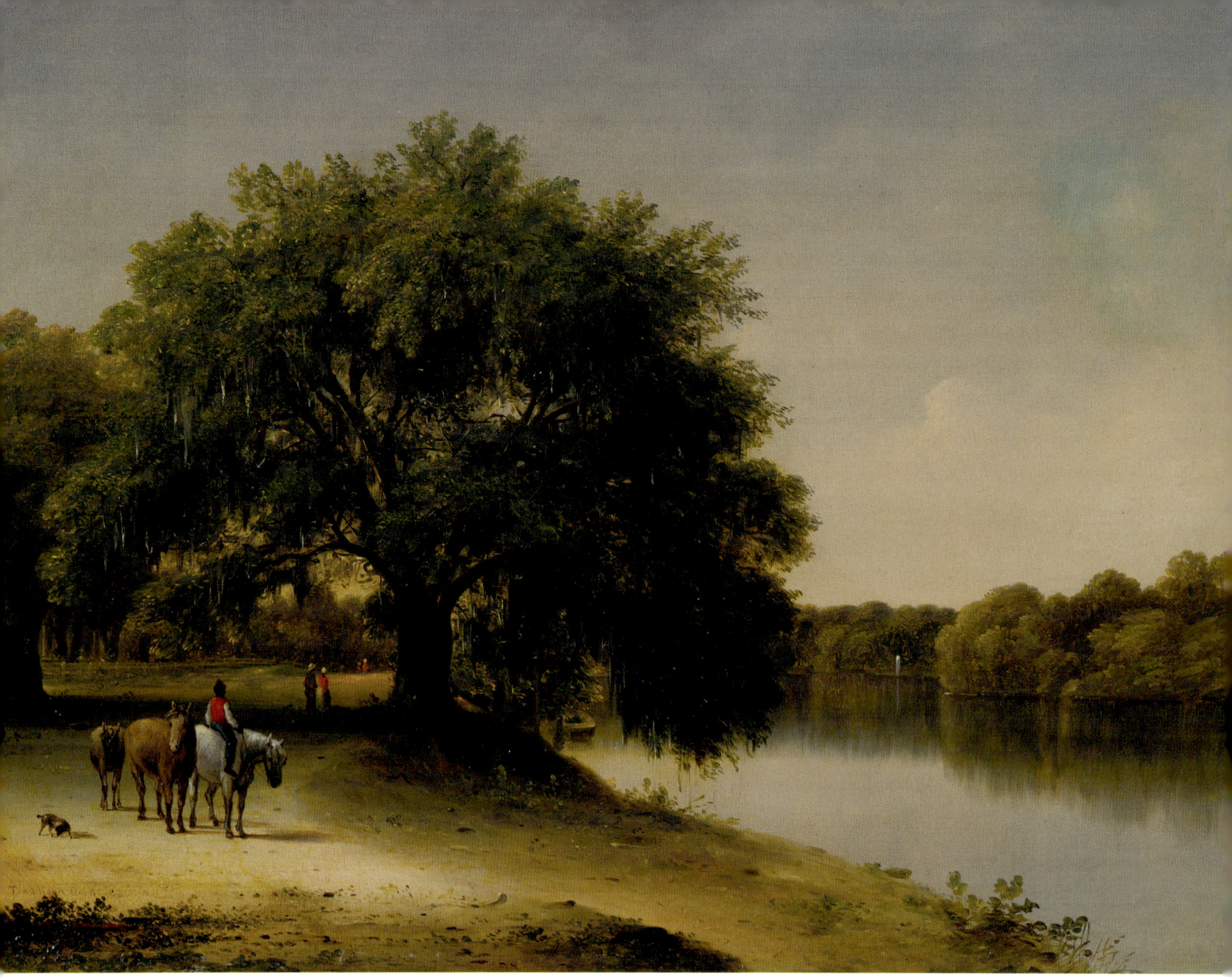

petition to preserve Fontainebleau to his half-brother, the Emperor Napoleon III.[14] As a result of this petition—and the widespread discussion their paintings and public statements evoked—the old oak section of Fontainebleau became France's first officially protected landscape in 1861, demonstrating landscape painting's ability to impact public policy regarding land use and preservation.

**Fig. 5**
Thomas Addison Richards, *River Plantation*, 1855-1859, Oil on canvas, 16 7/16 x 22 5/16 inches, Morris Museum of Art, Augusta, Georgia.

During this period, Louisiana was also undergoing similar land reforms that likewise had strong ecological and environmental consequences. In the Swamp Land Acts of 1849 and 1850, the United States government pushed responsibility for managing Louisiana's wetlands from the federal government back to individual states, with the express directive that they be drained and reclaimed.[15] While the French oak was closely tied to national identity, Louisiana's live oaks signaled something particularly local, almost foreign. They were closely connected to a region of the United States—the South—that was then undergoing its own identity crisis. In his survey of Southern landscapes, British-born artist Thomas Addison Richards identified the live oak as the southern counterpart to the New England elm, but was often caught between appreciating the oak's exoticism and his interest in tying it to a more universal landscape vision. In a series published in

*Harper's Bazaar* in the 1850s, in which he regretted the lack of attention given to Southern landscapes, Richards wrote: "Of all the trees of the South, the live oak is perhaps the most remarkable, leading the arborous beauty of the country no less universally, and even more charmingly, than the elm of the New England landscape, and with the additional value of perpetual freshness."[16]

Richards' own paintings of the South often try to fit the Southern landscape into pre-established models of the "picturesque." The idea of the picturesque, developed in England, had an immense impact on the production and reception of landscape representation in the nineteenth century. Defined first by the English artist and Anglican cleric William Gilpin as "that kind of beauty which is agreeable in a picture,"[17] the picturesque came to signify pleasingly composed views with gentle transitions between foreground, midground, and background. To achieve a picturesque view, artists structured the gaze through the careful placement of trunks of trees and figures, but these were ultimately seen as accessories to the landscape, and subordinate to overall compositional effect. Guiding the viewer's eye, the picturesque artist reproduces the effect of gazing upon a landscape over which one has ownership, and the power to look, untroubled, across orderly swathes of terrain.

Richards, like many artists of the period, created harmonious compositions that naturalized both the social conditions and the environmental hazards of Southern landscapes, aligning them with conventional modes of European and American landscape representation rather than appreciating their unique characteristics or highlighting their political struggles. Richards's *River Plantation* (1855-59; Fig. 5), painted near the Savannah River in Augusta, Georgia relies on a gentle recession of depth of field, suggested by both the diminishing *staffage* figures—including an enslaved person, waiting in the foreground with several horses—and the diagonal perspective of the river.[18] These two lines of recession dramatically converge on a majestic live oak, whose draping presence mitigates the sharpness of the perspectival angle. In the painting, Richards notably maintains a clear boundary within the image between water and land. The edge of the river is a neat line, its bank solid—a strong visual denial of the often unstable and shifting nature of landscapes placed, like this one, on the border between water and land.

In contrast to artists like Richards, Clague's Louisiana landscapes were emphatically attentive to the aesthetic and political particularities of the wetlands, and as such resisted assimilating Louisiana into more universal conceptions of the "picturesque." Clague's work, instead, chronicled the interaction between water and land in Louisiana, and his paintings showed how these landscapes forcibly denied the easy gaze of the picturesque. The flooded ground in paintings like *Rural Louisiana Farm Scene* (circa 1850; Fig. 6) highlights the particularly unstable mélange of wet and dry that constitutes Louisiana's terrain. The sharp line of the characteristic pieux fence creates a boundary between the houses to the left of the canvas and the marshy ground to the right; cattle hover undecidedly between the two zones. The fence cuts through the scene so sharply that it at once announces its presence and highlights its ultimate futility, should the water ever rise. The fence, further, does not lead our eye toward a point of interest in the background of the scene, but instead

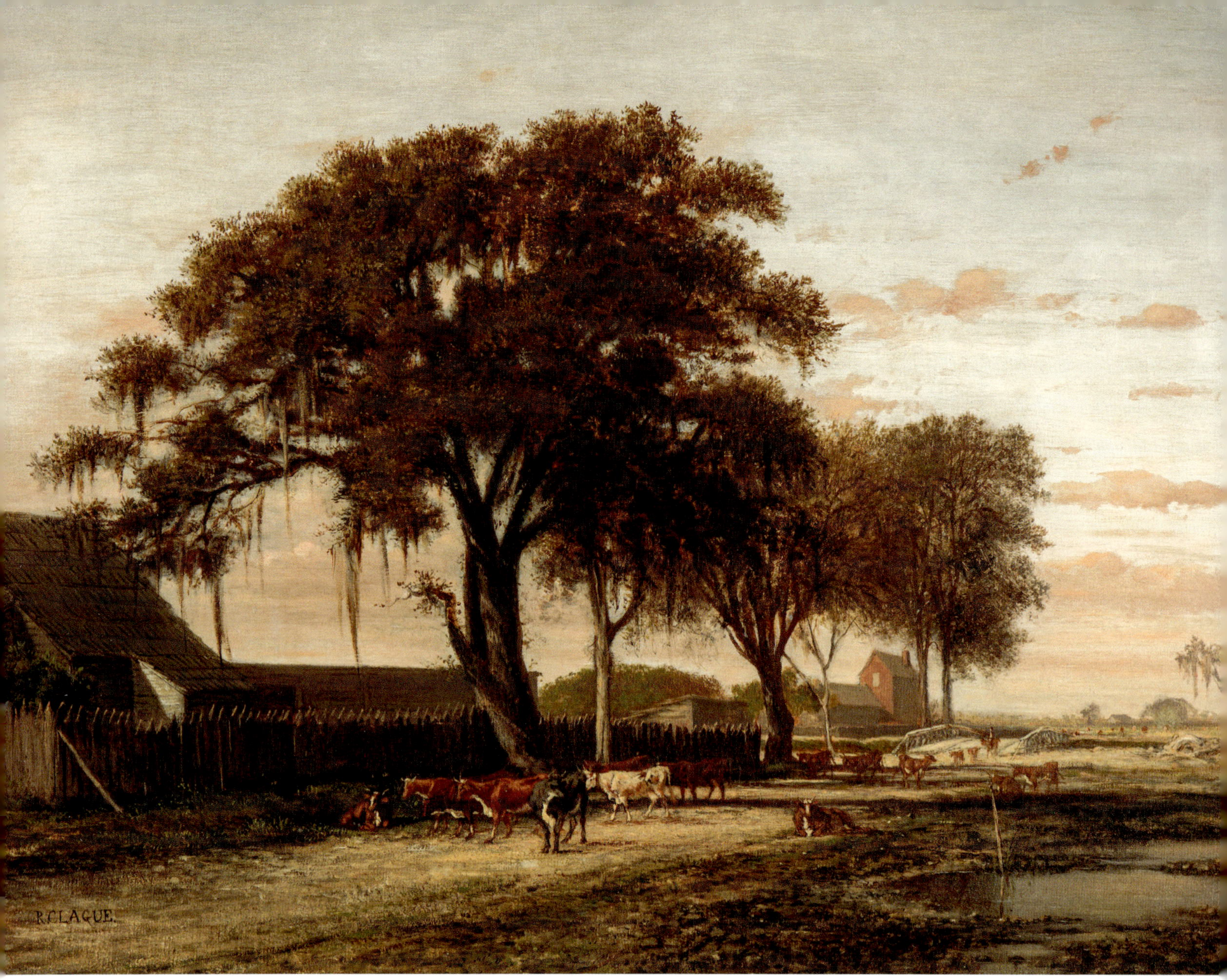


serves to close off our view, deliberately frustrating conventions of classical landscape representation. Such paintings resonate strongly with Barbizon work like Rousseau's *The Farm (Cottage at the Edge of the Marsh*) (circa 1860; Fig. 7), an image that similarly features flooded ground and an open, ill-defined foreground. Rousseau and Clague both highlight the flatness of wetland terrain, the way it levels the field of vision, such that there is, frustratingly, no singular point of emphasis. While Rousseau included only a small house in the midground of his painting to create focus, Clague's scene insists on a more prominent engagement with the inhabitants of the landscape, pointing towards the unique politics of land use in Louisiana during this period.

In choosing to represent wetlands at all, artists on both sides of the Atlantic went against the prevailing sentiment that they were areas of insalubrious, unwelcome waste. Geographer William Darby wrote of the Atchafalaya Basin in 1816, "To have an idea of the dead silence, the awful lonesomeness, and dreary aspect of this region, it is necessary to visit the spot. Animated nature is banished; scarce a bird flits along to enliven the scenery."[19] Even the astute observer of American nature John James Audubon had to agree, lamenting "those sultry days which render the atmosphere of the Louisiana swamps pregnant with baneful

**Fig. 6**
Richard Clague, *Rural Louisiana Farm Scene*, circa 1850, Oil on canvas, 23 ¼ x 31 ¾ inches, Collection of Michael and Virginia White. Photography by Roman Alokhin.

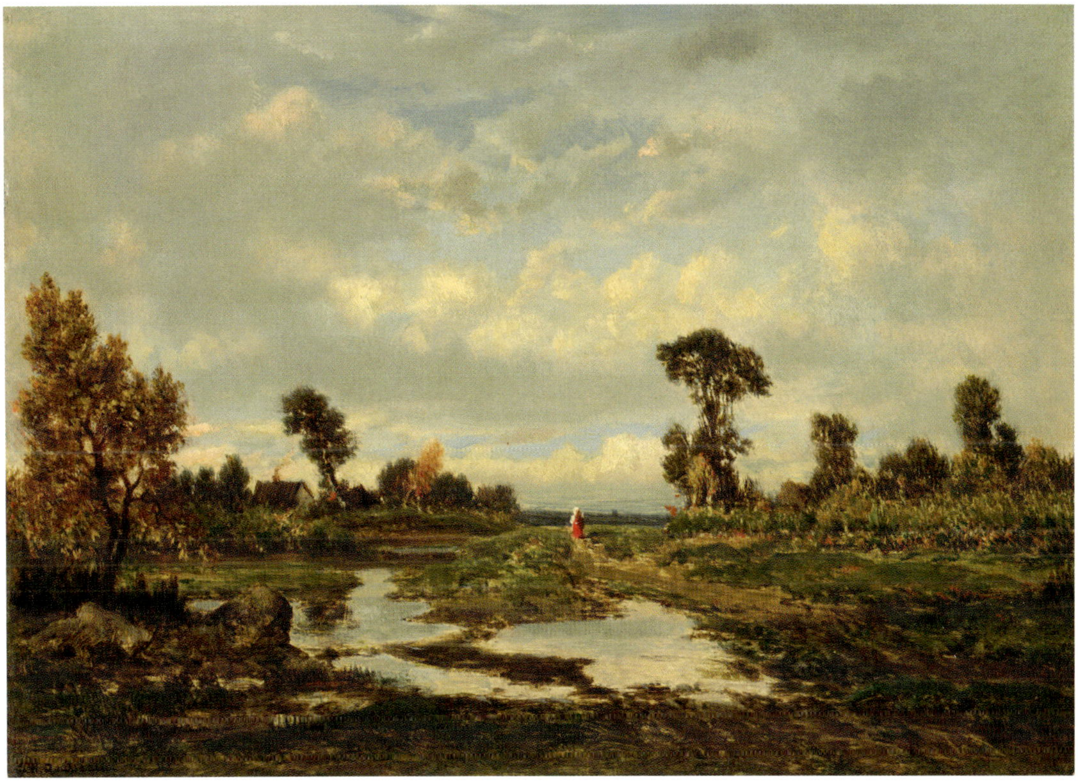

Fig. 7
Théodore Rousseau, *The Farm (Cottage at the Edge of the Marsh)*, circa 1860, Oil on panel, 8 9/16 x 11 1/2 inches, The Clark, Acquired by Sterling and Francine Clark before 1955, 1955.849, Image courtesy Clark Art Institute. clarkart.edu

effluvia."[20] Beyond their supposedly repugnant characteristics, wetlands were actually hard to see in ways that posed both aesthetic and practical challenges for artists. With ground constantly shifting between water and land, wetlands defied the clear boundaries or rational order that defines most landscape representation. As Darby observed, "the rivers, bayous, and lakes are so mingled, [and] intersect each other in such intricate mazes, that no absolute certainty can be attained."[21] The Lower Mississippi Basin was not properly surveyed until 1850, when Congress finally apportioned $50,000 for a topographical and hydrographical survey of the region. The solution, evident to Darby already in 1816, was drainage; he saw it as a matter of the very "justice and humanity of the nation."[22]

Underscoring these philosophies was a profound need to separate land and water, a separation that ran counter to the river's natural propensity to change course. This division was enacted primarily through levees placing an artificial constraint around the river, holding it, unnaturally, in place. These levees created a buildup of pressure that was understood, even in the nineteenth century, to be dangerous and unsustainable. Charles Ellet warned in 1853 that the progressive construction of levees, "by means of which the water that was formerly allowed to spread over many thousands of low lands, is becoming more and more confined to the immediate channel of the river, and is, therefore, compelled to rise higher and flow faster, until, under the increased power of the current, it may have time to excavate a wider and deeper trench to give vent to the increased volume which it conveys."[23] This enforced division between land and water led to catastrophic floods in 1849, 1858, 1927, and, of course, 2005.[24] The Civil War, further, left many of the levees that held back the river devastated, but persistent racial violence in the 1870s was used as a pretext for the federal government to withhold aid.[25]

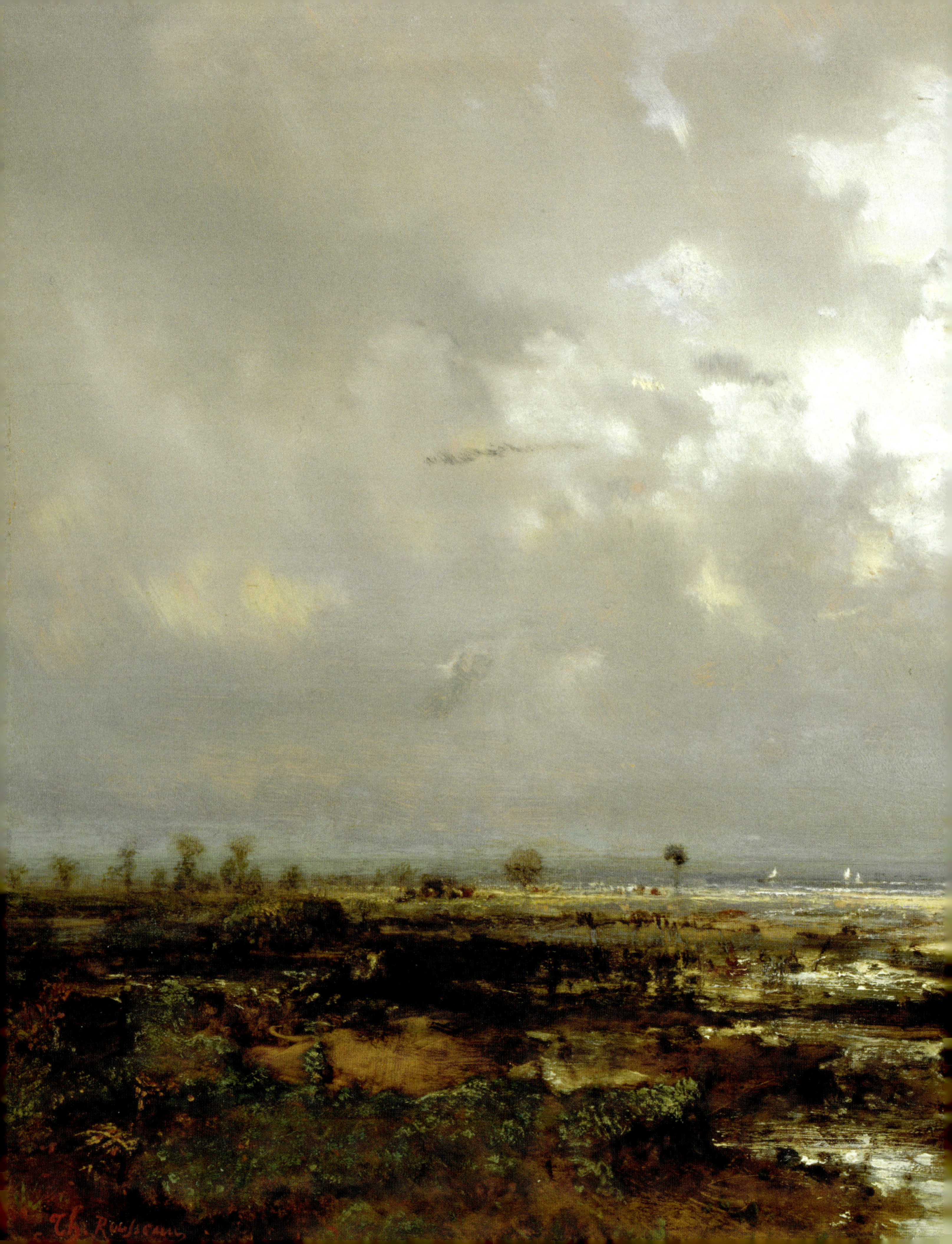

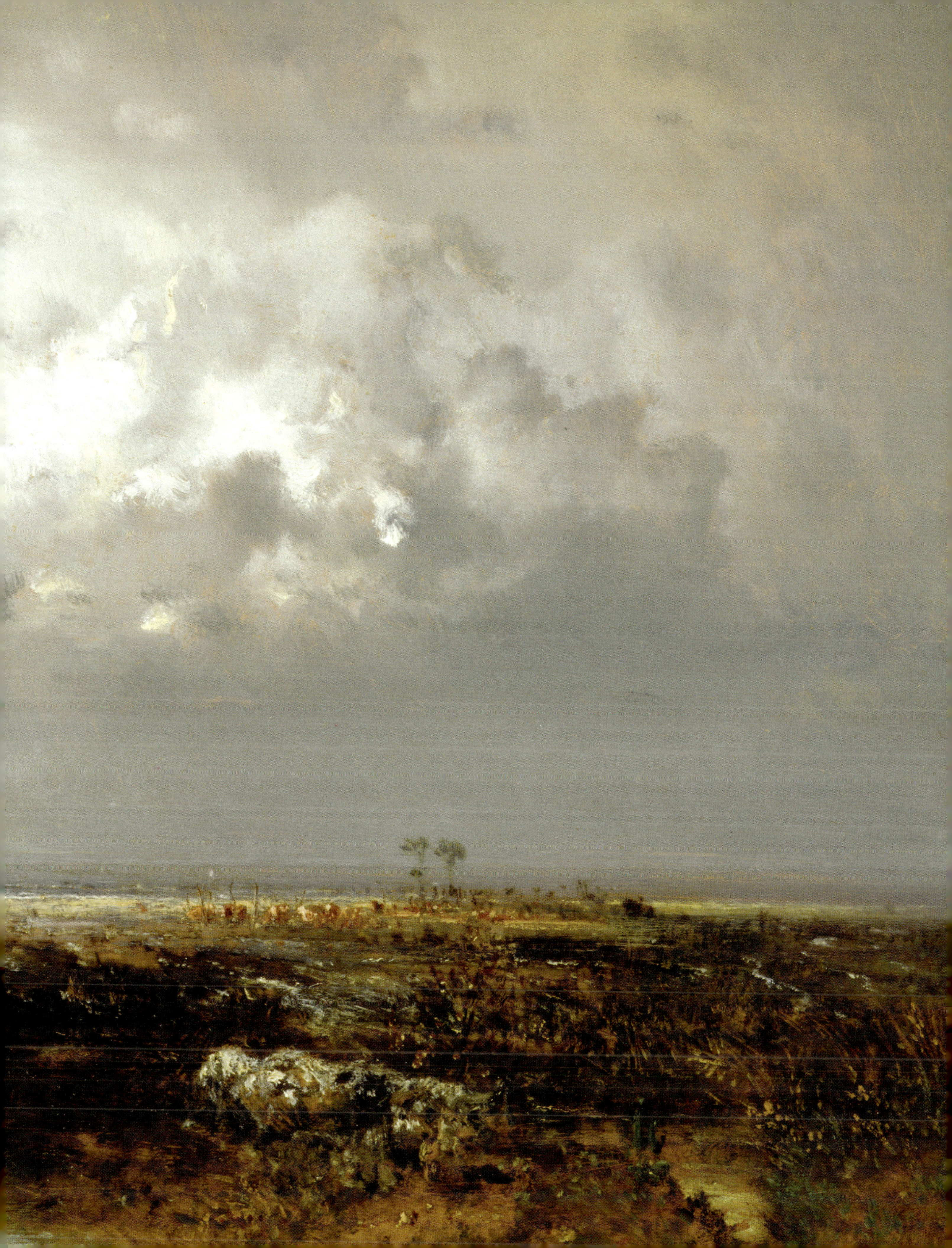

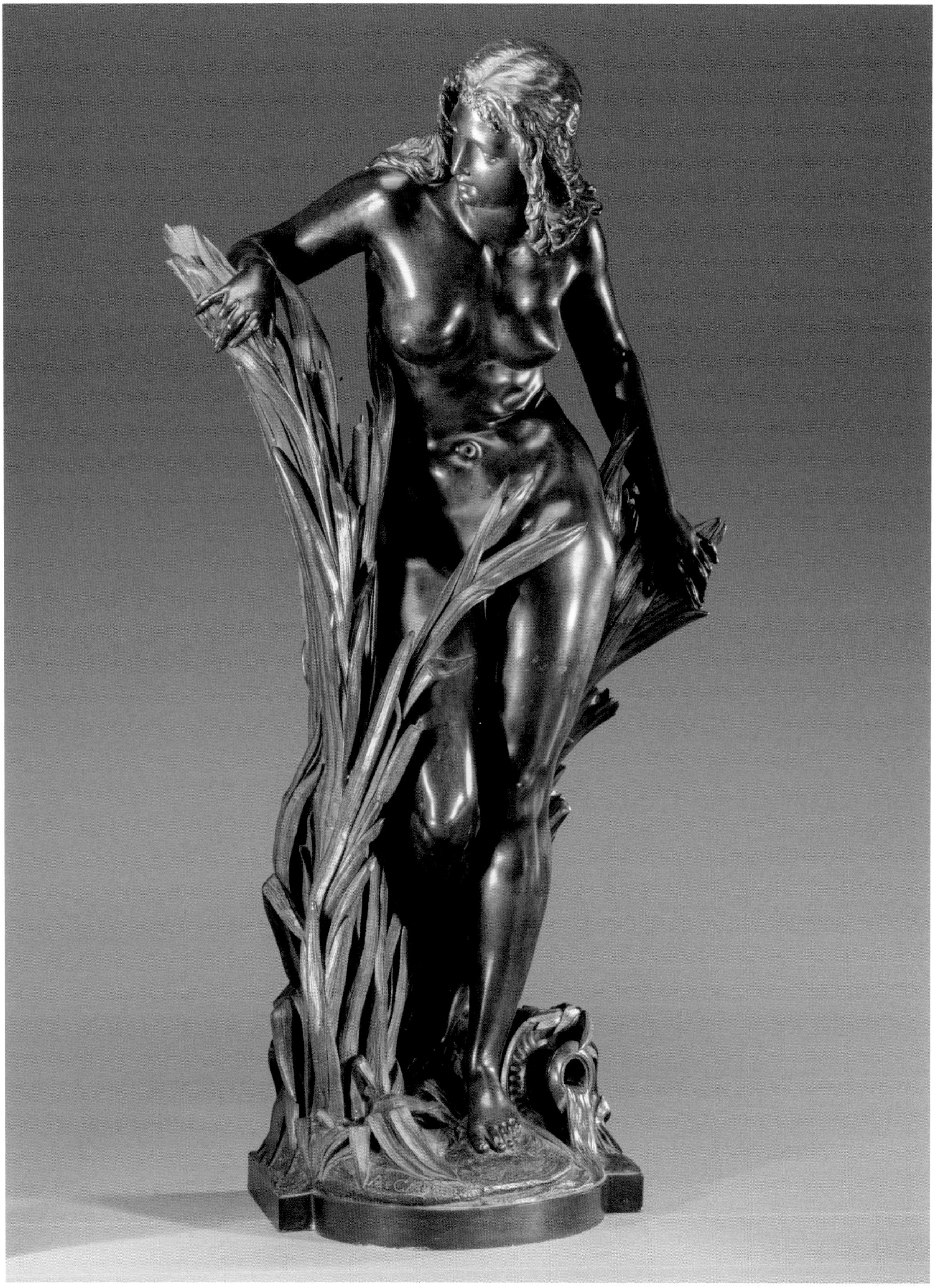

**Fig. 8 (pp. 68-69)**
Théodore Rousseau, *A Swamp in the Landes*, after 1844, Oil on panel, 16 7/16 x 22 5/16 inches (framed) The Walters Art Museum, Baltimore, 37.991.

**Fig. 9 (left)**
Albert-Erneste Carrier-Belleuse, *Woman in Reeds (Undine)*, circa 1865, Bronze with green and gold patination, 30 x 18 x 9 1/2 inches, New Orleans Museum of Art, Gift of John G. Agar in memory of his father, William Agar, 15.51. Photography by Judy Cooper.

**Fig. 10 (below)**
Jean-Auguste-Dominique Ingres, *The Spring (La Source)*, 1820-1856, Oil on canvas, 64 x 31 1/2 inches, Musée d'Orsay, 1986, deposited at the Musée d'Orsay, Paris, by the Louvre Museum, Paris, RF 219. ©RMN-Grand Palais (Musée d'Orsay) / Thierry Le Mage.

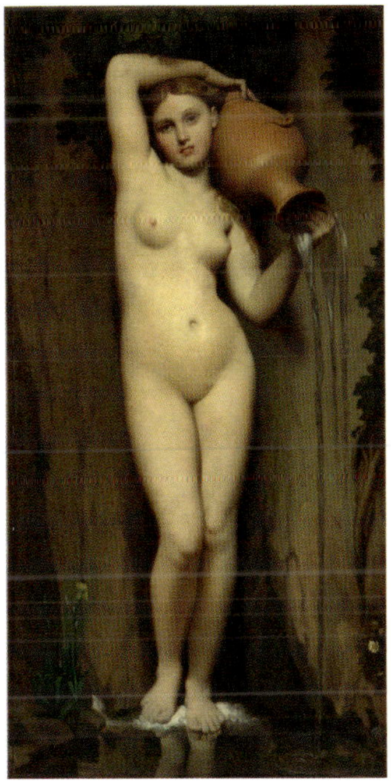

In France, discussions of draining the Landes date to the eighteenth century, but only in the nineteenth was there enough administrative centralization and technological advancement to make actual progress. Rousseau and Dupré decided to visit the region as drainage projects were on the horizon, and debates about the status of wetlands were occupying French national consciousness. When they arrived in the Landes in 1844, however, both Rousseau and Dupré struggled to adapt the techniques of representation they had developed in the forest of Fontainebleau to the wetland landscape of Landes. While trees had provided both subject matter and powerful compositional structure in the Fontainebleau works, the low brushy ground of the Landes offered no such focus. The region was comprised of extensive marshes, vast open areas without topographic relief. As Alfred Sensier records, Dupré lamented: "What man can touch he can master, but this sky without clouds, these wells of light, are a problem as discouraging for the painter as they are impossible to measure."[26]

Rousseau similarly found himself overwhelmed by the region's topography, and Sensier remarked that he was drawn to the blue of the sky but found it "evasive."[27] Rousseau responded to the vast openness of the landscape with an equally open canvas. Though Rousseau initially struggled, working, as Sensier tells us, only in a monochrome palette, when he returned to Paris he painted *A Swamp in the Landes* (after 1842; Fig. 8), a luminous image with an expansive view across a flooded plain. The fullness clustered at the center of *Groupe de chênes* has been completely emptied out. Two-thirds of the canvas is devoted to the sky, but it is a sky in an intense dialogue with the ground below, picking up on the waterways that crisscross the scene, and creating parallel streams of light and dark above. There are no foreground framing elements; on the contrary, the foreground seems to dissolve hazily into midground and distance without clear delineation. The scene has regional details: the scrawny Atlantic pine, a loosely penned-in area with what appear to be cattle, and in the far distance sails, extending our gaze all the way to the sea. It is difficult to measure or grasp the distance covered: the details serve not to establish scale but instead to open up the image outwards. Rousseau's water is ethereal. Silvery white brushstrokes glance over the ground of the image without gathering into any defined area. Dragging a thinly loaded brush horizontally across the canvas in short strokes, he evoked the sparse, fleeting sensations of this liminal region. This scene celebrates the potential of the wetland region to provide new painterly possibilities, and an aesthetic openness that accorded with a political desire to preserve a landscape in a state of flux.

Rousseau actively protested landscape interventions into the French countryside, but there were other French artists who were much more supportive of territorial reforms. The members of the so-called Bordeaux school quickly replaced France's sacred oak—made famous in Barbizon paintings—with the more orderly pine trees that grow across France's southwest region.[28] The sculptor Albert-Erneste Carrier-Belleuse similarly registered a shift from the embrace of wild nature, to acceptance—and even celebration—of civilization's efforts to control nature, and harness its power. Carrier-Belleuse's allegorical sculpture *Woman in Reeds (Undine)* (circa 1865; Fig. 9)—which had been in a New Orleans private collection likely since at least the turn of the century—marks a departure from similar

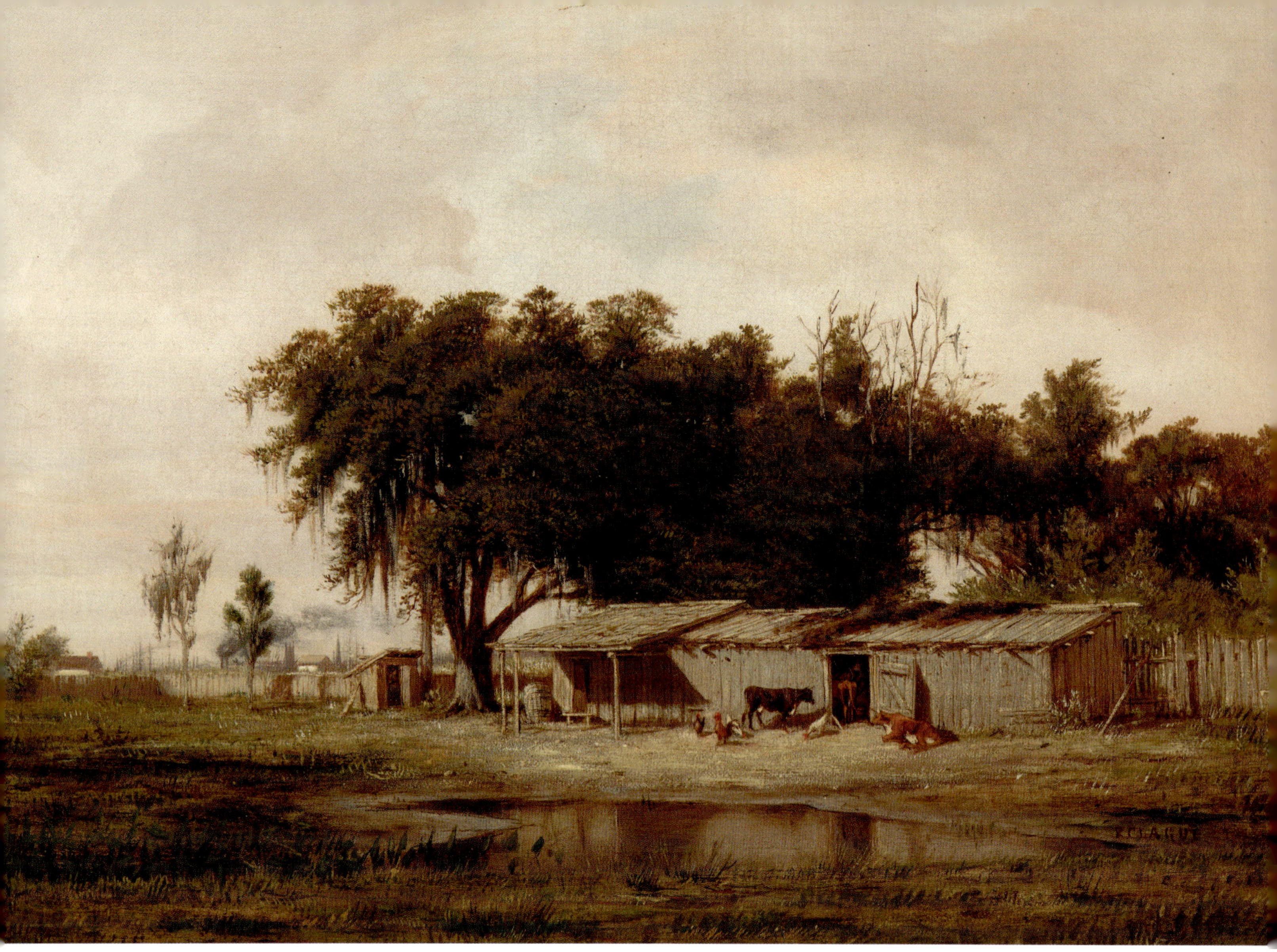

**Fig. 11**
Richard Clague, *Back of Algiers*, circa 1870-1873, Oil on canvas, 21 x 27 1/4 x 2 1/2 inches (framed), New Orleans Museum of Art, Gift of Eugenia Uhlhorn Harrod in memory of her husband, Major Benjamin Morgan Harrod, 13.5. Photography by Roman Alokhin.

**Fig. 12 (opposite)**
Richard Clague, *Scene in Algiers*, n.d., Oil on canvas, measurements not available, Lent anonymously for the 1974 Richard Clague exhibition at the New Orleans Museum of Art, Photograph by Betsy Swanson.

representations of water produced just a few decades earlier, like Jean-August-Dominique Ingres' painting *The Spring (La Source)* (1820-1856; Fig. 10).[29] While Ingres' image was intended as a metaphor, and the woman meant to be a nereid or water spirit, the more literal title of Carrier-Belleuse's work reflects a move away from mythology and towards naturalism: a naturalism that registers and responds to France's changing relationship with water, through new water policies and increasing water control. In Ingres' painting, the nereid holds a decorative vase in her hand that has, in Carrier-Belleuse's sculpture, fallen to the ground, where its rounded mouth reads not as an allegorical urn, but as a water pipe. Divorced from mythological symbolism, the vase becomes something else: an artificial water conduit. Water flows from the vase to wrap in a tight loop around the sculpture's base, an emblem of humanity's control over the ways of water. The tension within the sculpture between naturalism and mechanical control, between water as a metaphor and water as a real resource to be controlled and managed, echoes larger questions surrounding France and Louisiana's relationship to water management, and control over their wetlands. Perhaps this is why Carrier-Belleuse's sculpture would have so appealed to an art collector in New Orleans.

In contrast to the tightly orchestrated circuit of Carrier-Belleuse's water system, Clague's compositions evoke an alternative environmental politics: a refusal to control water or land. As Clague developed a new mode of painting for Louisiana's wetlands, he expanded on

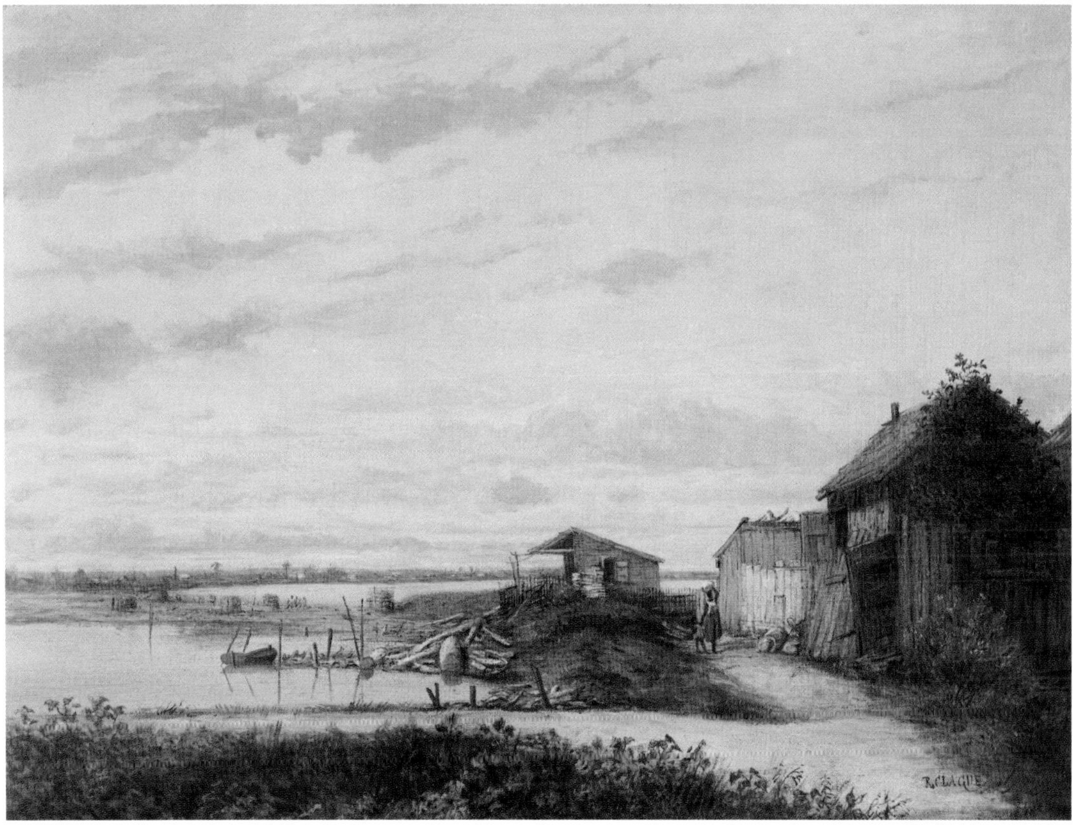


Rousseau's exploration of wetland terrain, which eventually became codified by his students as the "Bayou School." Creating a new form of composition suited to the low, undulating waterways of New Orleans' backwaters, Clague rarely depicted the dark, mysterious swamp that many associate with Louisiana landscape painting, nor the clearly defined Mississippi River. He was drawn instead to sites in a constant state of flux between wet and dry, often depicting Algiers, a poor area across the river from the city, where he eventually settled in 1873.[30] While Algiers Point, on the bend of the Mississippi, offered high ground, the further one got from the river the lower the land sank. We see this low lying, inundated ground in Clague's *Back of Algiers* (circa 1870-73; Fig. 11), a painting in which muddy ground coalesces into a dark puddle in the foreground, with blurred edges that suggest a landscape in constant flux. *Scene in Algiers* (n.d.; Fig. 12) is similarly set on the edge of a backwater, separated from the river by a meager bank along which driftwood gathers.

The art historian Estill Curtis Pennington described *Back of Algiers* as "a squalid scene of decay, with derelict structures set in a landscape of ruin."[31] The poverty of the scene—a small barn, a scattering of animals—contrasts with the beckoning church spires of the city glimpsed along the painting's horizon. This work's very title conveys the social status of its site: as environmental historian Lawrence Powell claims, "the back of town" is what "New Orleans's netherworld of poverty and poor drainage has always been called."[32] Powell links "poverty" and "poor drainage" as a matter of course, a persistent bias that determined water management policy in greater New Orleans. Neither fully swamp nor productive land, interstitial spaces like the *Back of Algiers* were first deliberately neglected, and later intentionally eradicated, within our vision of Louisiana's landscapes. Indeed the author of

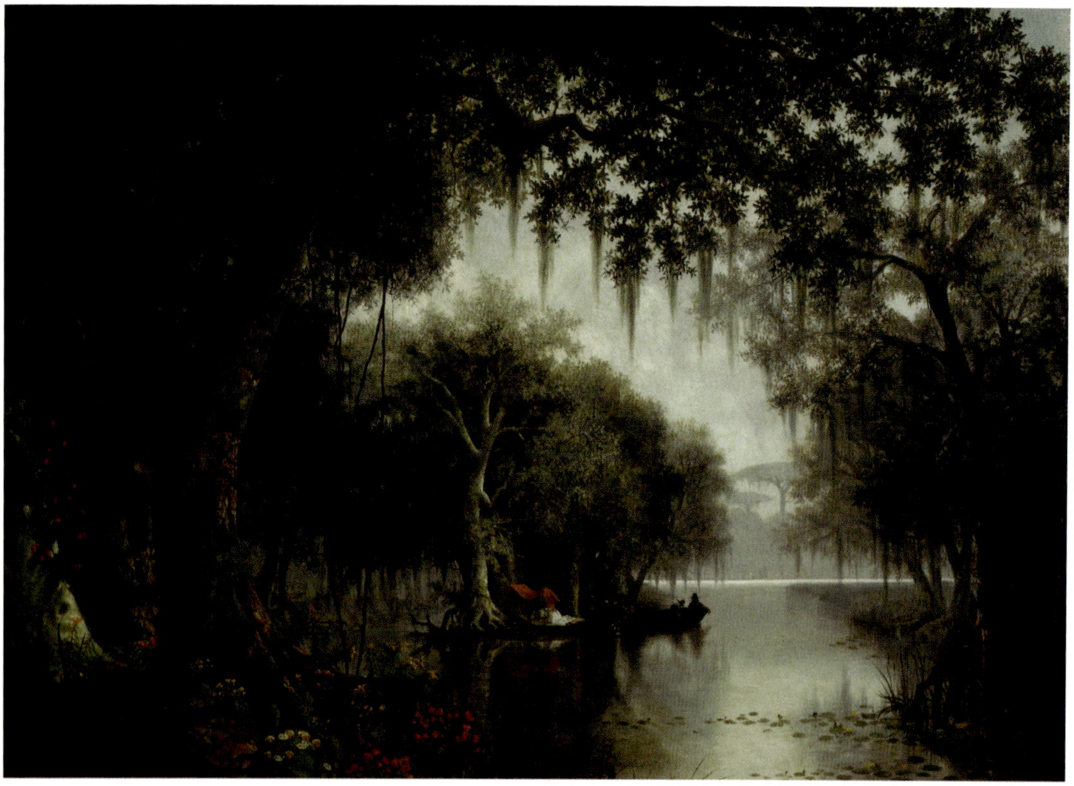

**Fig. 13**
Joseph Rusling Meeker, *The Land of Evangeline*, 1874, Oil on canvas, 40 ½ x 52 ⅝ inches (framed), Saint Louis Art Museum, Gift of Mrs. Wright Prescott Edgerton in memory of Dr. and Mrs. W. T. Helmuth by exchange 163:1946. Image courtesy Saint Louis Art Museum.

**Fig. 14 (opposite)**
Richard Clague, *Untitled (Korosko, Egypt)*, March 25, 1857, Pencil and ink on paper, 12 x 15 inches (framed), New Orleans Museum of Art, Gift of S. A. Trufant, 28.2.45. Photography by Roman Alokhin.

the only catalogue of Clague's work, Roulhac Toledano, laments that he chose to depict these tame sites when so much "truly wild" scenery was on offer.[33] In her preference for the darker recesses of cypress-filled swamps, Toledano may have been thinking about an image like Joseph Rusling Meeker's *The Land of Evangeline* (1874; Fig. 13).[34]

Meeker participated in what the Americanist David Miller has characterized as nineteenth-century America's fascination with the romantic associations of swamplands, often called a "Dark Eden." Clague's landscapes, however, have yet to be adequately defined, much less mythologized.[35] Rather than romanticizing his landscapes to poetic effect, Clague chose instead to be responsive to the lived realities of inhabiting Louisiana's river delta. He remained highly attuned to the particularities of his chosen site, showing the realities of living within them by constantly witnessing and recording the ground's passage from wet to dry, and back again. While Louisiana's water management policy depended on clarifying the separation between water and land, Clague instead pointed attention to their interdependence across all of his paintings. Clague was likely more aware than many artists of the intricacies of the Louisiana water system, the process of fill and drainage, and the importance of areas of marsh and overflow to relieve the pressure of the massive river. From December of 1856 to March of 1857, Clague traveled with Ferdinand de Lesseps's expedition to investigate the source of the Nile River, producing a group of extant sketches that show his efforts to capture the river's topography, and the ways in which people lived with the water (1857; Fig. 14). Clague would have been in the company of knowledgeable hydrologists and hydrographers and been expected to produce official documentation, as understanding the Egyptian water system was considered crucial to France's colonial interests.[36] Clague himself may have been chosen for the expedition thanks to his exposure

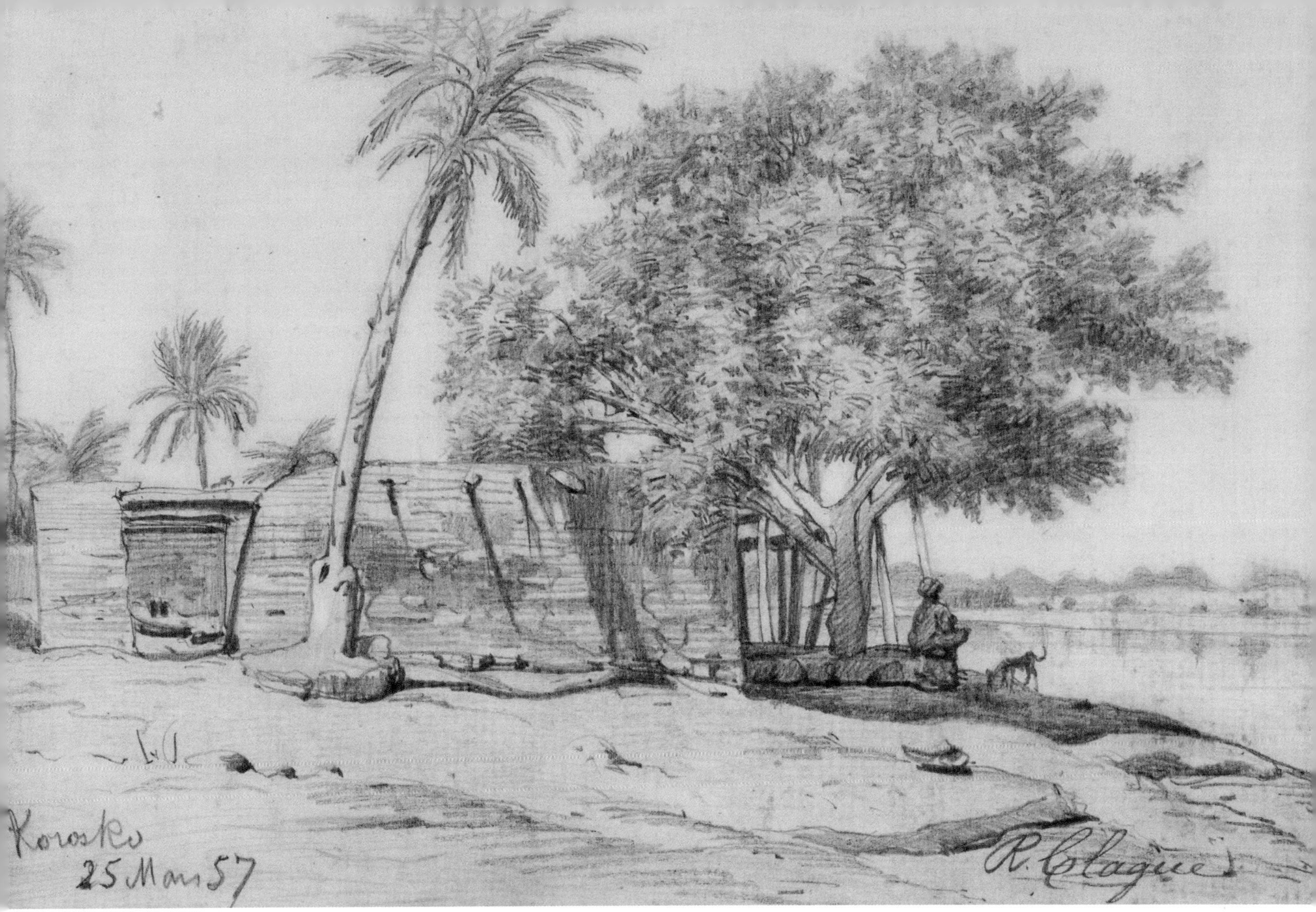


to the Mississippi, which was often compared to the Nile—Cairo and New Orleans lie on approximately the same line of latitude and the similarities between the rivers have been extensively documented and observed since the nineteenth century.[37]

In Clague's *Fisherman's Camp* (n.d.; Fig. 15) the uncertain bounds of the region's water systems are left deliberately unresolved. Set on the swampy ground near Lake Pontchartrain, the view, as in Rousseau's *Swamp,* is open and expansive. In a seeming nod to the French artist's work, the landscape stretches into the distance to reveal a glimpse of passing sails on Lake Pontchartrain.[38] Clague's obituary describes his struggle with "the difficulties of perspective in a level country"—the same low, flat emptiness Rousseau and Dupré struggled with in the Landes—but, in *Fisherman's Camp,* this feature becomes an opportunity to explore atmospheric effects.[39] Pinkish hues ground Clague's dramatic sky in a deliberate temporality, and only the thinnest margin of land separates the dark waters of the foreground from the strip of clearer blue lake along the horizon, recalling Darby's "intricate maze" of waterways. The painting only gradually reveals the distinction between the glimmering, reflective water and more solid land, as Clague builds up richly pigmented, deeply opaque strokes of tan paint to create an only somewhat solid surface for the fisherman's shack to sit. The rendering of that bank—its emergent quality—reminds us that New Orleans owes its very existence to natural levees created out of millennia of sedimentary deposits from the Mississippi, a fundamental interdependence of land and water that continues to determine the region's topography. The pigment that rendered

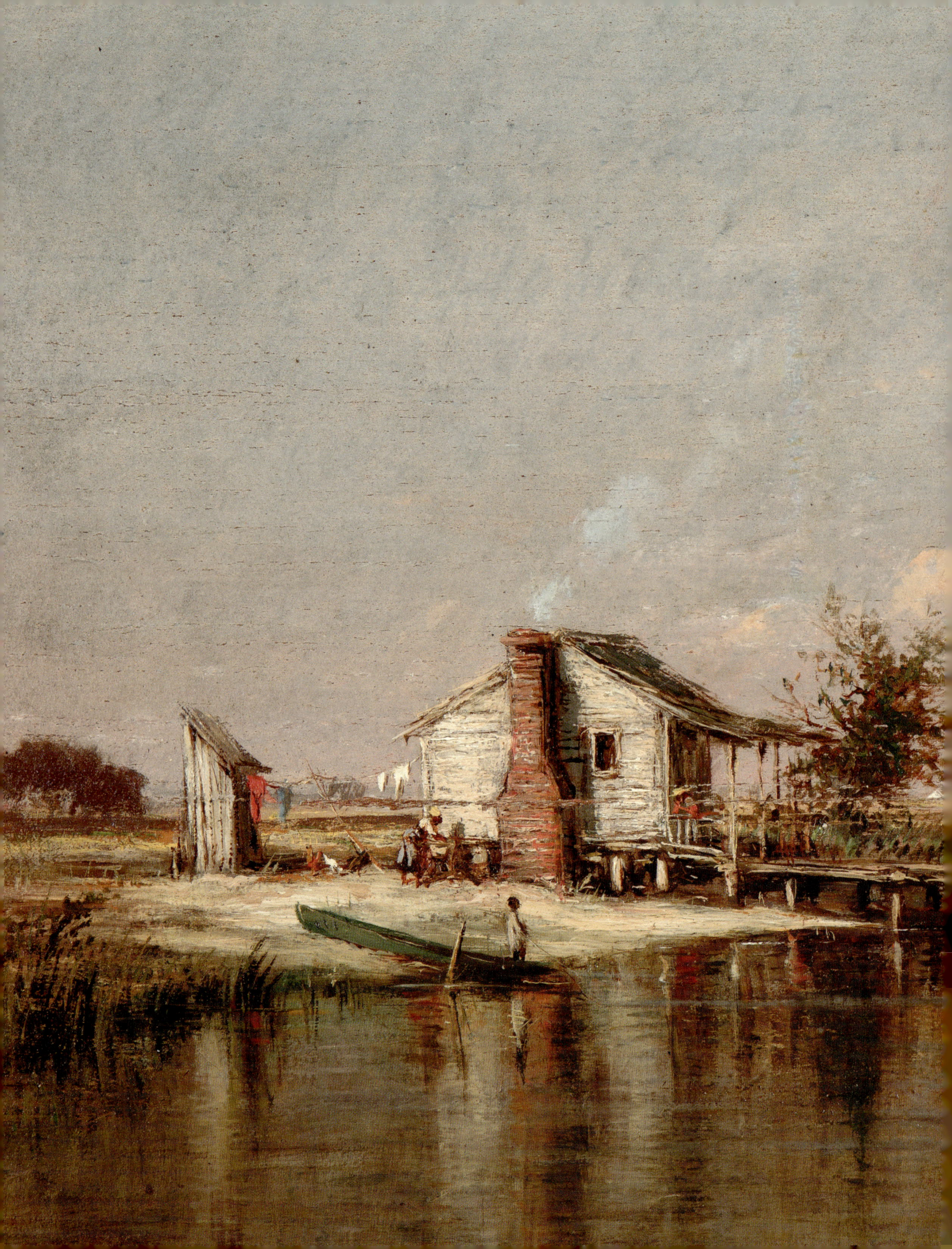

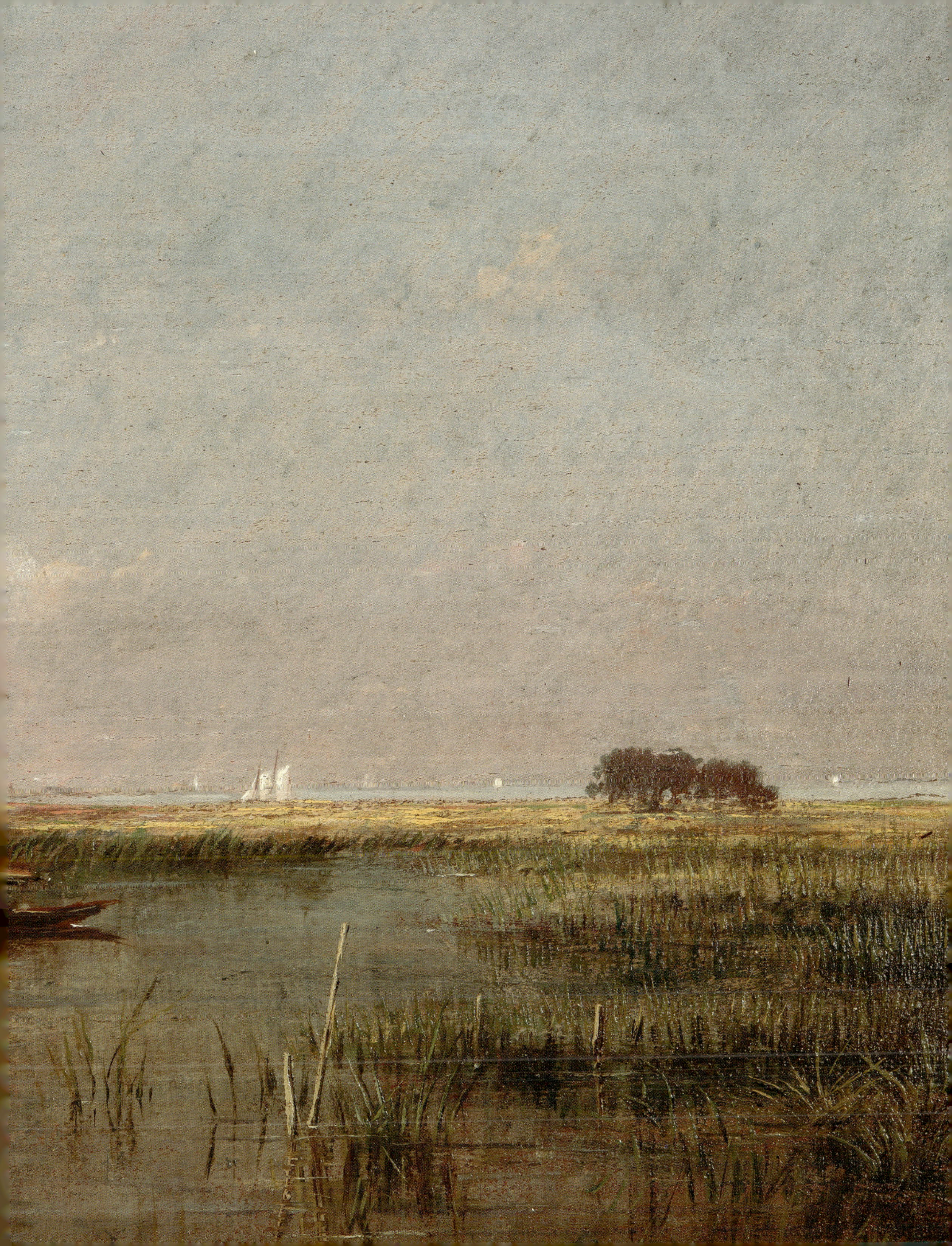

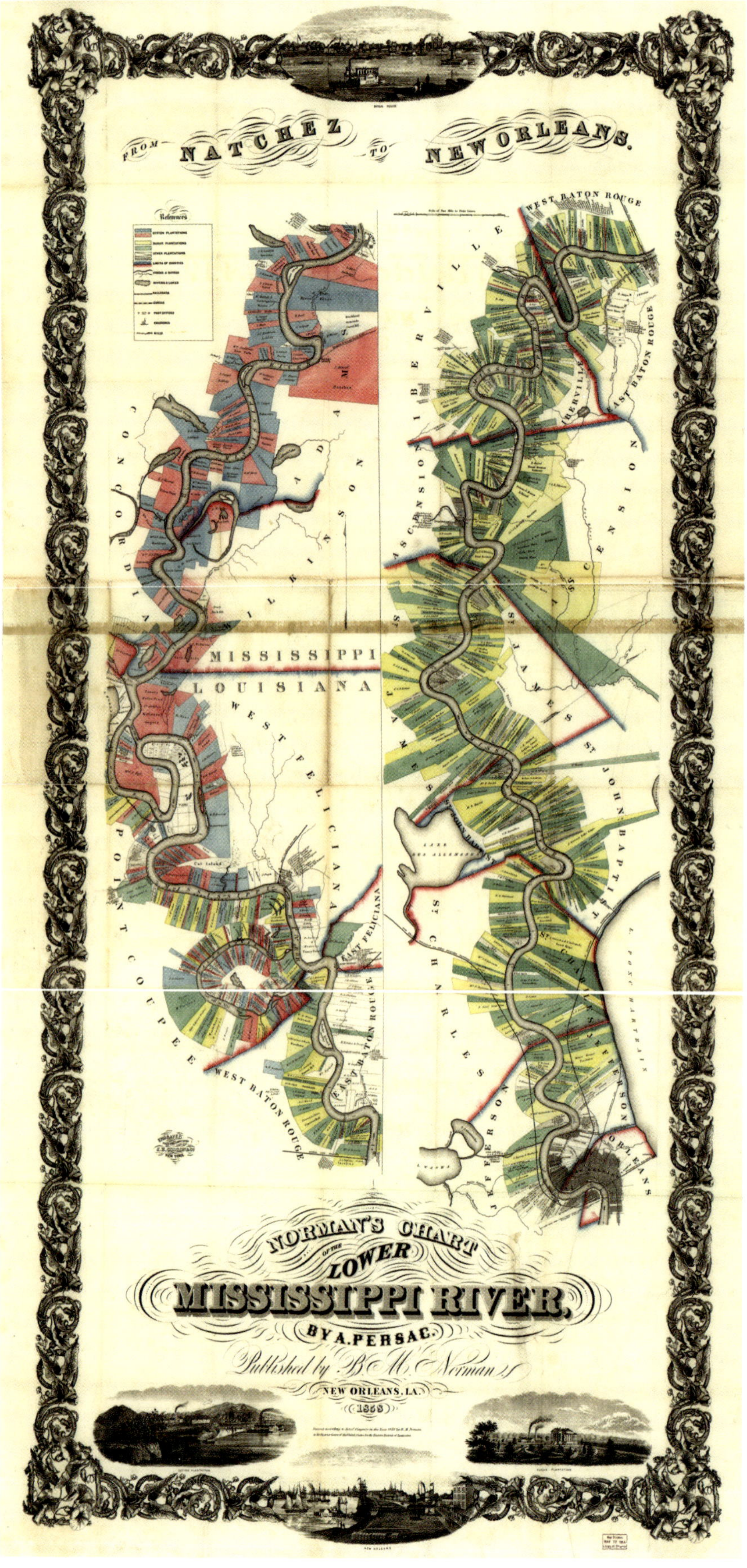
FROM NATCHEZ TO NEW ORLEANS.
MISSISSIPPI
LOUISIANA
CONCORDIA
WILKINSON
WEST FELICIANA
EAST FELICIANA
POINT COUPEE
WEST BATON ROUGE
EAST BATON ROUGE
IBERVILLE
ASCENSION
ST. JAMES
ST. JOHN BAPTIST
ST. CHARLES
JEFFERSON
ORLEANS
NORMAN'S CHART OF THE LOWER MISSISSIPPI RIVER,
BY A. PERSAC.
Published by B. M. Norman
NEW ORLEANS, LA.
1858

Fig. 15 (pp. 78-79)
Richard Clague, *Fisherman's Camp*, n.d., Oil on wood panel, 18 3/4 x 22 3/4 inches (framed), New Orleans Museum of Art, Gift of Mrs. Benjamin M. Harrod, 13.6. Photgraphy by Roman Alokhin.

Fig. 16 (opposite)
B.M. Norman and Marie Adrien Persac, *Norman's Chart of the Lower Mississippi River*, 1858, Engraving on paper, 63 x 29 1/2 inches, Library of Congress, Geography and Map Division.

Clague's paints opaque is, in his method of painting, akin to the sediment the river brought from the Rocky and Allegheny mountains and deposited along its ever-growing banks.

The Mississippi is "muddy" because of this sediment; Clague's aforementioned "muddy tonal colors," then, are not just an aesthetic choice borrowed from Barbizon but an astute observation on New Orleans's material connection to greater America. Mark Twain, for instance, described New Orleans as a "town being built upon 'made' ground," formed from sediment brought south by the flow of water. This consciousness of the land as having been "made" by water generated, in turn, anxiety about the land's potential *unmaking*. An 1851 text described the "liquid wall that surrounds the city" and says, "I am certain there are few nervous ladies and gentlemen, who, if they *could* be induced to make a short ascent in a balloon from any portion of New Orleans, and so take a bird's eye view of its situation, would consent to inhabit its precincts without the preparation of a life-boat in their garrets or at least the latest improvement of a life-preserver in their pockets."[40]

The levees that fought to hold back this "liquid wall" were, for most of the nineteenth century, the responsibility of property owners, resulting in the particular settlement pattern visible in "Norman's Chart" (1858; Fig. 16). Compiled and illustrated by Marie Adrien Persac, a Frenchman trained in engineering in Lyon, and named for its publisher, Norman's Chart is five feet long and accompanied by four illustrations by Persac of typical cotton and sugar plantations with bustling harbors and well-maintained banks. In the chart, the Mississippi River is tightly bound, held in place by radiating plots of land that are marked with individual landowners' names. This radiating pattern dates to the French period, when land was allocated such that each settler would have some river access, some arable land on the high natural levee close to the river, and some lower lying backswamp. The government accorded land on the condition that property owners maintained their own levees, though regulation, oversight and standardization were limited for most of the nineteenth century.[41] The names listed, then, stand for both ownership and responsibility: any weak link and the levee system would collapse.

After completing the survey, Persac capitalized on plantation owners' desire to record their domains, setting up shop as a sort of documentarian and producing highly detailed gouache studies of plantation landscapes like *Bois de Flêche* (1861; Plate 19) —with, notably, no water in sight. The highly ordered, regimented ground of *Bois de Flêche* corresponds to the plantation owner's dominion over both land and people. What we do not see in Norman's Chart or Persac's views are the low lying areas just behind the neatly defined, color-coded parcels: the flood zones that are the exact focus of Clague's oeuvre. While Norman's Chart would suggest that these areas are uninhabited, Clague instead reveals ways of inhabiting this tenuous landscape: the most obvious difference between his *Fisherman's Shack* and Rousseau's *Swamp* is the titular shack that interrupts the view. In Clague's paintings, trapper's cabins and shanties all constantly underscore the presence of the people who lived in these regions. Clague's landscapes were frequently populated, likely for this reason, and his oeuvre features a range of vernacular architecture, again to reinforce the lived realities of these uncertain landscapes. These were mostly palmetto and cypress shacks that were deliberately temporary: a material acknowledgement of the constant threat of flood in backwater areas.[42]

While Toledano attributes Clague's interest in the "domesticated landscape" to his European sensibility, Clague is also responding to a particularly American dynamic, a segregation of the landscape based on race and class.[43] The swamps of Louisiana had long been home to Acadian communities, and we often see figures—likely from those communities—in paintings like *Trapper's Cabin, Manchac.*[44] Several of Clague's paintings also include black figures, who are shown in ways we rarely see in the art of the South.[45] In *Fisherman's Camp,* Clague included two small figures, a man fishing and a woman washing clothes, and a possible third figure leans over the porch rail, seemingly in conversation with the titular fisherman, though the sketchiness of Clague's brushwork here makes it hard to be certain.[46] *Scene in Algiers* similarly includes two black figures: a woman carrying a bundle atop her head and a small child. These figures do not appear in the preparatory sketch for the painting, suggesting Clague intentionally added them to underscore the scene's social politics. It would be easy to dismiss these figures as no more than a "picturesque" accent, or, worse, a deliberate smoothing over of racial conflict by painting these figures into a scene of relative domestic ease. Clague's personal background certainly supports such a reading: much of his wealth came from his father's involvement in the slave trade, and he himself had enlisted in the Confederate army. But it's also possible that Clague was showing how these figures had created a space for themselves within a broader social and political landscape that was largely inhospitable, and often violently exclusionary.

Clague's paintings picture a reality in which the very indeterminacy of these landscapes made them available to marginalized communities in a way that more clearly defined—and safer—spaces within the city were not. Clague's *Batture Shanty* (1870; Fig. 17) even more explicitly charts this complex alignment between unfixed environments and available social spaces. The "batture" is a bank between the river and the levee that is covered when the river is high, and exposed when it is low. While the river itself was maintained as public property, and all arable land was sold as private asset, responsibility for—and access to—the batture remained largely undefined.[47] Clague's image of a "batture shanty" then, shows the possibility for settlers to take up these ill-defined zones, and to create structures, however precarious, within them. Clague's willingness to see and to picture uncertain hydrological zones, in this way, led to his unexpected awareness of similarly uncertain social zones: areas at the margins of the city that provided shelter for the rural poor, black and white. In this way, Clague's work makes visible another kind of engagement with the land, offering an alternative to the rigid order and carefully controlled waterways of Norman's Chart, focusing instead on how this indeterminate ground opened up new environmental and social possibilities that were foreclosed by a levees-only policy.

By 1879, after much debate, the federal government was finally persuaded to take responsibility for the Mississippi floodplain, relieving private owners and local governments of responsibility for the levees by establishing the Mississippi River Commission and appointing the US Army Corps of Engineers to lead levee construction. A consequence of the construction of more effective levees was the elimination of large swaths of the backwater areas—the batture and the inland marshes—that Clague painted. This deprived the river of natural outlets and forced many settlers out of their homes. Louisiana's

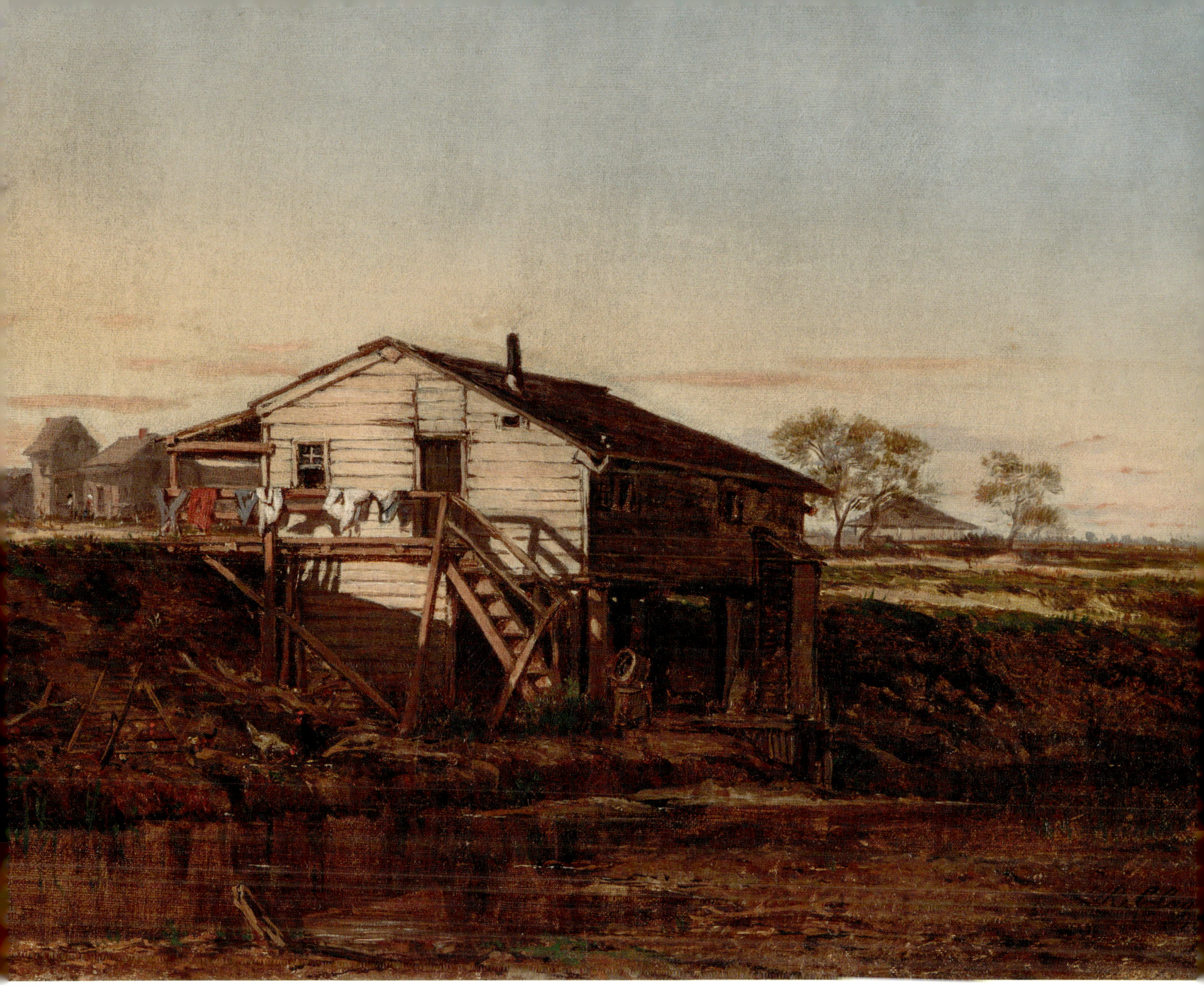

**Fig. 17**
Richard Clague, *Batture Shanty*, 1870, Oil on canvas, 22 x 26 1/8 x 3 1/4 inches (framed), New Orleans Museum of Art, Museum Purchase through the Ella West Freeman Foundation Matching Fund, 71.3. Photography by Roman Alokhin.

landscapes were thrust into a polarizing dynamic: either drained, ordered, and habitable, or flooded, uncontrolled, and abandoned. As environmental historian Christopher Morris has described, "Levees led ultimately to the destruction of the edges, enabling cotton fields to consume what remained of the forest and wetland. With no place left to hide, hunt, and fish, laborers had to work on the plantations."[48] By the late 1880s, according to Morris, most African American men worked on someone else's land. In this way, water management became a way of securing both environmental and social boundaries. By adapting Barbizon artists' willingness to make their landscapes political, and finding inventive ways to represent unfamiliar terrain, Clague's work offered a new way of envisioning the possibilities for wetlands—and the people that inhabited them. Highlighting the wetlands aesthetic and social possibilities, Clague's paintings spoke to questions of water management, property, and settlement in ways that were remarkably ahead of his time. Returning to Clague's work now offers an opportunity to reflect on past and current environmental policy, and look towards ways we once lived with water.

1 While Roulhac Toledano acknowledges the impact of Rousseau's Berry landscapes on Clague—"There can be no doubt that Clague saw paintings by Rousseau from the Berry period"—she does not mention the Landes work, a testament to the lack of attention these landscapes have received in scholarship. Roulhac Toledano, *Richard Clague, 1821-1873, exh. cat.* (New Orleans, LA: New Orleans Museum of Art, 1974), 18.

2 Biographical information on Clague is taken from Toledano, *Clague*.

3 Rousseau exhibited *A Marsh in Les Landes* at the 1853 Salon. Scott Allan, ed. *Unruly Nature: The Landscapes of Théodore Rousseau* (Los Angeles, CA: Getty Publications, 2016), 37.

4 Joshua Taylor uses this phrase to describe what American artists drew from Barbizon Art in his preface to Peter Bermingham, ed. *American Art in the Barbizon Mood* (Chicago, IL: University of Chicago Press,1976), 10.

5 Estill C. Pennington, *Downriver: Currents of Style in Louisiana Painting, 1800-1950* (Gretna, LA: Pelican, 1991), 90.

6 Alfred Sensier, *Souvenirs sur Théodore Rousseau* (Paris: Léon Techener, 1872) and Alfred Sensier, *La vie et l'oeuvre de J.-F. Millet* (Paris: A. Quantin, 1881).

7 Many such scholarly efforts seek to cast Barbizon as the foundation for Impressionism. This position is expressed most succinctly in the title to Steven Adams, *The Barbizon School and the Origin of Impressionism* (London: Phaidon, 1997).

8 For a discussion of French forest politics, see Tamara Whited, *Forests and Peasant Politics in Modern France* (New Haven, CT: Yale University Press, 2001).

9 The study of landscape was codified in the early nineteenth century by Pierre-Henri de Valenciennes in his treatise, *Elémens de perspective pratique* (Paris, 1800).

10 For a detailed analysis of Rousseau's painterly practice, see Scott Allan, "'A Method Matters Little': Rousseau's Working Procedures as a Painter," in Allan, *Unruly Nature*, 23-43.

11 Andrée Corvol has extensively studied the changes to the French woods and leads a *Groupe d'Histoire des Forêts Françaises* (GHFF); see Andrée Corvol, *L'homme aux bois: histoire des relations de l'homme et de la forêt* (Paris: Fayard, 1987).

12 Théodore Rousseau, in conversation with Théophile Thoré, "Par Monts et par bois," *le Constitutionnel* 27 and 28 November 1847, cited in Albert Boime, *Art in an Age of Counterrevolution* (Chicago, IL: University of Chicago Press, 2004), 510.

13 Art historian Greg Thomas has identified *Groupe de chênes* as explicitly intended to promote preservation of the trees. See Greg Thomas, *Art and Ecology in Nineteenth-Century France: The Landscapes of Théodore Rousseau* (Princeton, NJ: Princeton University Press, 2000), 59.

14 Thomas, *Art and Ecology,* 109.

15 Ralph W. Tiner, *In Search of Swampland: A Wetland Sourcebook and Field Guide* (New Brunswick, NJ: Rutgers University Press, 2005).

16 T. Addison Richards, "The Rice Lands of the South," *Harper's New Monthly Magazine* (November 1859).

17 William Gilpin, An *Essay on Prints* (London, 1768).

18 Christopher Hanlon has identified the figure as an enslaved person. Christopher Hanlon, *America's England: Antebellum Literature and Atlantic Sectionalism* (New York, NY: Oxford University Press, 2016), 106.

19 William Darby, *A Geographical Description of the State of Louisiana* (Philadelphia, PA, 1816), 69.

20 John James Audubon, *Ornithological Biography* (Edinburgh, 1834), 2-27; This passage is found in the section on "The Runaway," in which Audubon records his encounter with an enslaved person attempting to escape a plantation. The role of swamps as affording potential cover for those seeking escape was famously chronicled in Harriet Beecher Stowe's *Dred: A Tale of the Great Dismal Swamp* (New York, NY: Sully and Kleinteich, 1856); the trope appears again in David Hunter Strother's, "The Dismal Swamp," *Harper's Monthly* (1856), which is accompanied by a sketch; it also features in Henry Wadsworth Longfellow's poem, "The Slave in the Dismal Swamp," (1855); the theme was painted by Thomas Moran, *Slaves Escaping Through the Swamp* (1865). However, as I will show, the kind of wetlands pictured by Clague differed in both environmental and social terms from the swamp imagined in these narratives.

21 Darby, *A Geographical Description*, 224.

22 Darby, *A Geographical Description*, 270.

23 Charles Ellet, *The Mississippi and Ohio Rivers: Containing Plans for the Protection of the Delta from Inundation*s (Philadelphia, PA: Lippincott, Grambo, and Co., 1853), 17.

24 A recent NPR story reported "Levees Make Mississippi Floods Worse, But We Keep Building Them," *All Things Considered*, NPR, May 21, 2018, 11:15am, https://www.npr.org/2018/05/21/610945127/levees-make-mississippi-river-floods-worse-but-we-keep-building-them.

25 Christopher Morris, *The Big Muddy: An Environmental History* (Oxford: Oxford University Press, 2012), 160.

26 Sensier, *Souvenirs*, 146.

27 Sensier, *Souvenirs*, 146.

28 Bruno Foucart, Preface to *Art et bourgeoisie: La Société des Amis des arts de Bordeaux (1851-1939),* by Dominique Dussol,(Bordeaux: Atelier du CERCAM/Le Festin, 1997).

29 This sculpture was donated to the New Orleans Museum of Art in 1915, by the son of William Agar, an art collector in the city who was actively collecting European and American art from the mid-nineteenth century

onward. While records of purchase are not available, it is likely that the sculpture has been in the city since at least the late-nineteenth century.

30 Pennington associates Clague's move to Algiers with his eventual death from hepatitis, reaffirming associations between wetlands and disease. Pennington, *Downriver*, 79.

31 Pennington, *Downriver*, 80.

32 Lawrence Powell, *The Accidental City: Improvising New Orleans* (Cambridge, MA: Harvard University Press, 2012), 99.

33 Toledano describes Clague's "rejection of the mysterious, romantic quality of the lowland swamps" as a product of his quest for a "customary concept" or an "ideal image of a European domesticated landscape"; an interpretation with which I disagree here, as the landscape he highlights is far from a European ideal and are only "domesticated" in a way that would be problematic in the social context of postbellum New Orleans, as I discuss further below. Toledano, *Clague*, 22.

34 The painting depicts a scene from Henry Wadsworth Longfellow's poem 'Evangeline, A Tale of Acadie' (1847).

35 Miller likens appreciation for the swamp to new mental processes on the part of Americans for whom an expansionist narrative no longer functioned. David Miller, *Dark Eden: The Swamp in Nineteenth-Century American Culture* (Cambridge, MA: Cambridge University Press, 2010).

36 Former NOMA director E. John Bullard suggested such official drawings exist, but have yet to be found, in his preface to Toledano, *Clague*, 10.

37 Thomas Ruys Smith expounds on this similarity, and its relationship to narratives of slavery, in his *River of Dreams: Imagining the Mississippi before Mark Twain* (Baton Rouge, LA: Louisiana State University Press, 2007), 1-12.

38 Toledano identifies the location. Toledano, *Clague*, 38.

39 *New Orleans Bee*, November 30, 1872, cited in Toledano, *Clague*, 26.

40 A. Oakey Hall, *The Manhattaner in New Orleans; or Phases of 'Crescent City' Life* (New Orleans, LA, 1851), 120.

41 The specifications for levee maintenance are described in Jesse Poesch and Barbara SoRelle Bacot, eds. *Louisiana Buildings 1720-1940* (Baton Rouge, LA: Louisiana State University Press, 1997), 129.

42 Martin Reuss describes the temporary condition of architecture designed to withstand seasonal fluctuation in his *Designing the Bayous: The Control of Water in the Atchafalaya Basin, 1800-1995* (College Station, TX: A&M University Press, 2014), 21.

43 Toledano, *Clague*, 22.

44 Vaughn Baker, "In and Out of the Mainstream: The Acadians in Antebellum Louisiana" in *The Cajuns: Essays on Their History and Culture*, ed. Glenn R. Conrad (Lafayette, LA: Center for Louisiana Studies, 1983) and Carl Brasseaux, *Acadian to Cajun: Transformation of a People, 1803-1877* (Jackson, MS: University of Mississippi Press, 1992).

45 Charles Giroux, whose work remains very little studied, seems also to be recording these spaces on the edge, ways of living along the bayou, with works populated by African American settlers, fishermen, and hunters. Giroux does not share, however, Clague's interest in an indeterminate ground, offering instead clear bounds between water and land.

46 *Fisherman's Camp* is indexed in *The Image of the Black in Western Art* (IBWA) (Harvard University) on Artstor.

47 Oliver A. Houck, *Down on the Batture* (Jackson, MS: University Press of Mississippi, 2010).

48 Morris, *The Big Muddy*, 161.

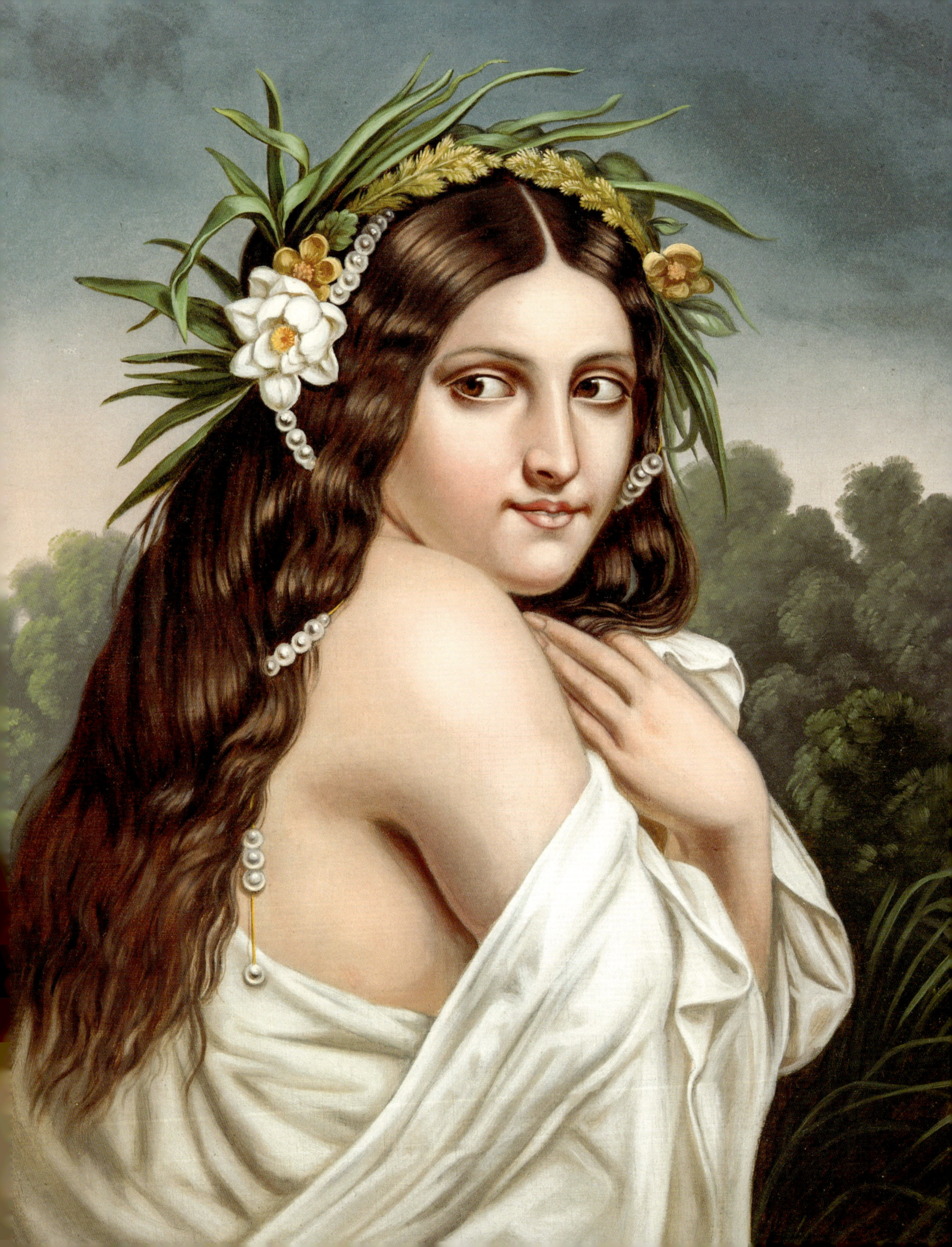

# The Spirit of Louisiana: Painting Racialised Geographies in the Slave-Holding Atlantic

Anna Arabindan-Kesson and Mia L. Bagneris

In 1863, as the United States, never more divided, was rent by war, Henry David Thoreau imagined the possibility of a unified America, one extending from sea to shining sea and brought together by shared cultural values that transcended region. Significantly, this vision explicitly excluded the South: "Our sympathies in Massachusetts," Thoreau wrote, "are not confined to New England: though we may be estranged from the South, we sympathize with the West."[1] Art historian Angela Miller identifies a similar logic in the development of nineteenth-century American landscape painting, demonstrating how the pastoral and transcendent landscapes of New England and the majestic vistas of the Western frontier came to stand for the nation. Such images worked to produce an image of the United States that corresponded to a particular set of "American" cultural values, which associated "nature with virtue, purity, and uncomplicated harmony, as well as with national unity, pride of place, and a unique identity distinct from that of Europe."[2] These pictures of New England—symbolic of the nation's past—and of the West—the promise of its future—were fundamentally less about land than about the supposedly "national" values, ideologies, and narratives associated with it.

Nowhere in this ostensibly national vision, however, was there a place for the South. Pictures of the South, and specifically of Louisiana, rarely conform to the canonical nineteenth-century American landscape conventions that developed around the images of the East and the West, and their difference from these popular visions of America positioned the region outside dominant narratives of nationhood. This exclusion set "America" apart from "the Americas" and ultimately emphasized the country's differences from its neighbors in the slaveholding Atlantic. In shifting our gaze to the South, specifically to nineteenth-century artist imaginings of Louisiana, this study puts the view of American painting into a broader hemispheric geography—what scholar Joseph Roach defines as the Circum-Atlantic.[3] Because of the state's unique liminal geographic and cultural location, looking to Louisiana emphasizes a transnational view of America that connects it to histories of colonialism and slavery across the Atlantic world.[4]

Considering Louisiana landscape painting during the long nineteenth century from multiple perspectives—local, national, and greater Atlantic—shows how representations of land created racially encoded geographies and supported racialized dynamics of power. This essay explores two contested sites in Louisiana landscape painting—the plantation and the

**Fig. 1**
George David Coulon, *Spirit of Louisiana*, 1894, Oil on canvas, 33 ¼ x 28 ¼ x 3 inches (framed), New Orleans Museum of Art, Gift of the Fine Arts Club of New Orleans on the occasion of their 60th Anniversary, 76.69.

female body—to show how these representations helped claim Louisiana's land for its white settlers, both materially and metaphorically. Considering these two modes of representing Louisiana demonstrates how visions of the state were informed by its place within a greater Atlantic context and implicates American painting in the construction of the same sorts of racialized geographies that undergirded all slaveholding societies. This essay shows how Louisiana landscapes helped produce a racialized politics of place that asserted, both implicitly and explicitly, who had the right to claim the worlds they portrayed.

## Impenetrable Country That Would Be Easy to Clear: The Plantation in the New World Colonial Imagination

From the moment of their first encounter with the majesty and wild abundance of Louisiana's Mississippi River Valley, Europeans described the territory in terms that simultaneously praised its untamed abundance and emphasized how readily that bounty might be brought under their control and exploited. In the chronicles of his early eighteenth-century exploration of the Lower Mississippi River Valley, André Penicault described the incredulity with which he and his fellow crew members viewed the territory, "We regarded this beautiful river with admiration…The country, on its banks, appeared to be everywhere covered with splendid trees of every description, such as oak, ash, elm, and many others, the names of which we did not know." Likewise, recording his impressions of Louisiana in a journal he kept during one of three reconnaissance expeditions he led up and down the Mississippi River to explore the territory for France, Pierre LeMoyne d'Iberville observed, "Both banks of the river, almost the entire distance above the sea, are so thickly covered with canes of every size…that one cannot walk through them. *It is impenetrable country, which would be easy to clear.*"[5] The irony inherent in Iberville's vision of Louisiana—its simultaneously impenetrable fecundity and unencumbered accessibility—exemplifies the promise of the so-called New World in the colonialist imagination and positions Louisiana within a wider Caribbean discourse.[6] Such thinking framed these lands as places that "required" precisely the type of disciplined management that the colonial project could provide, in order to transform their providential surplus into productive supply.[7]

Edenic New World landscapes visualized the paradox inherent in Iberville's observations of Louisiana. Typically revolving around an ideal of the wild, untouched natural world, they also implicitly showcased its potential for cultivation. Artists embraced the conventions of the picturesque, a European aesthetic pioneered by Claude Lorrain and Salvator Rosa, to materially effect this sort of speculation. Describing both an intention to see the natural world as a picture and a set of conventions mobilized to create this visual transformation, the picturesque reshaped human relationships to the natural environment, bringing it, if not under control, at least under the guise of some kind of order. As European artists traveled to the New World, so too did these frames and terms of reference, where they were mobilized as a way of managing the inherent contradictions of representing plantation landscapes.[8]

The mobility of this picturesque aesthetic mode made unfamiliar lands recognizable, knowable, and ultimately possessable. In the Caribbean, the picturesque was bound up

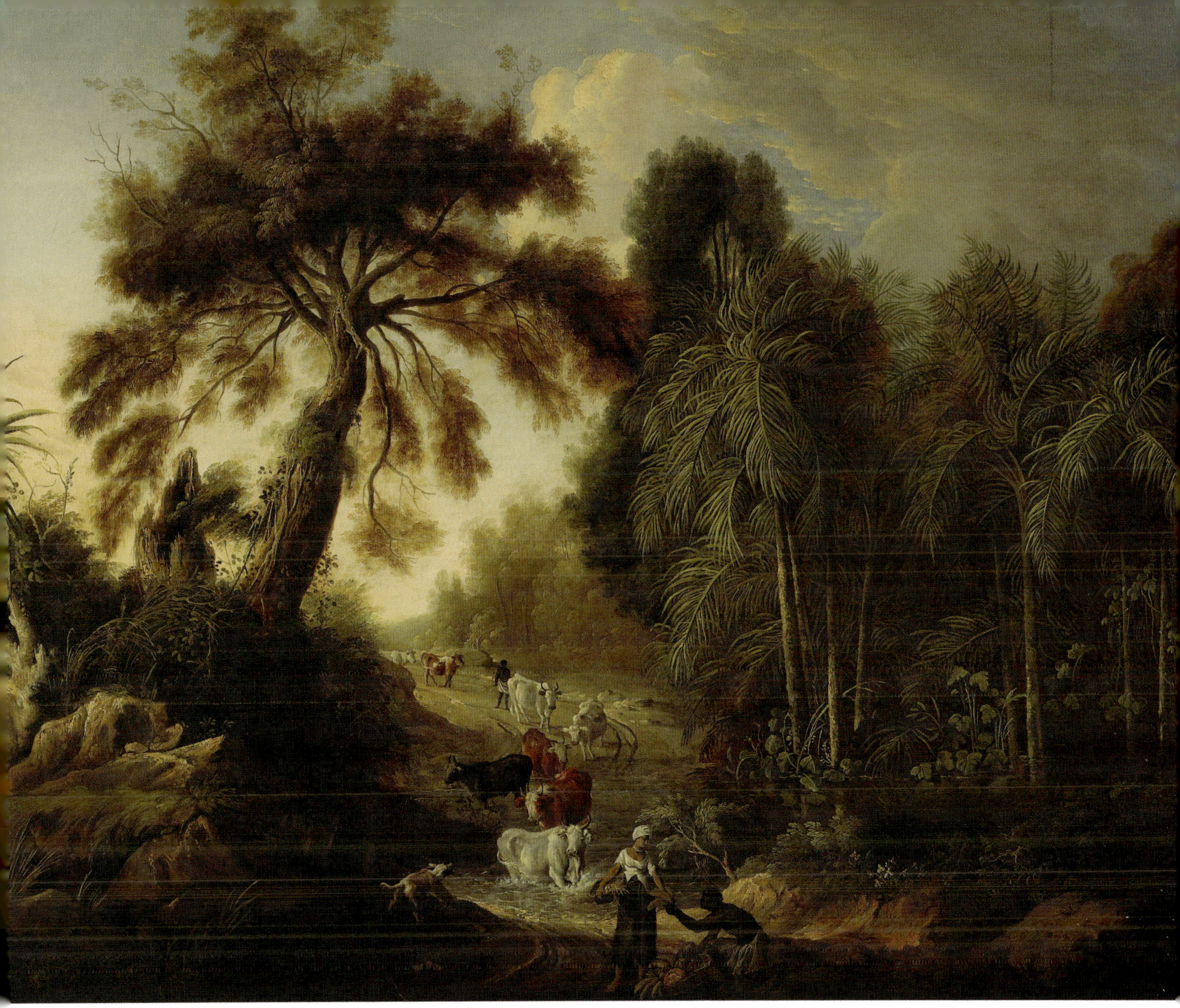

Fig. 2
George Robertson, *Spring Head of the Roaring River*, 1775, Oil on canvas, Wallace Campbell Collections, Kingston, Jamaica. Photo: Franz Marzouca, courtesy of Wallace Campbell Collections.

with the economics of colonial expansion—specifically slavery and the plantation complex. It enabled a form of commodification by which land was transformed into an object to be consumed and nature ordered into a potential center of resource extraction.[9] This visual possession belied the literal material one, constructing the illusion of "an island Eden untouched by the evils of capitalist greed" that obscured the exploitation of land and of labor that lay at the crux of the plantation economy.[10] Plantation pictures provide insight into how colonists and planters developed fundamentally New World identities, across the Americas, refracting their experiences of a changing social milieu through picturesque visualizations of nature and the human relationship to it.

The work of George Robertson exemplifies this New World iteration of the picturesque. Arriving in Jamaica in 1773 under the patronage of William Beckford of Somerly, Robertson created several picturesque plantation landscapes, later circulated as engravings, that depict the planter's impressive holdings, constructing scenes of visual pleasure that arrange the natural features of the Jamaican landscape to underscore its providential bounty.[11] In *Spring Head of*

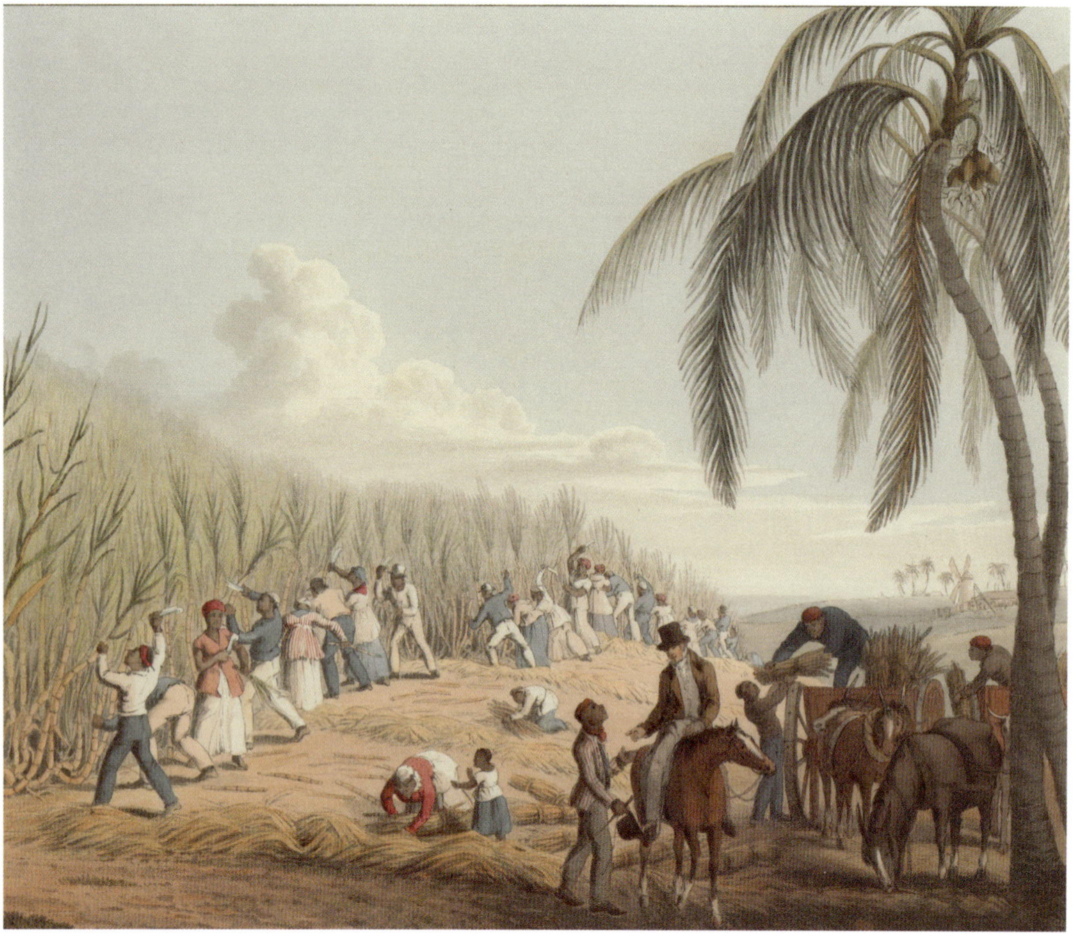

Fig. 3
William Clark, *Ten Views in the Island of Antigua, Cutting the Sugar Cane*, [London], Thomas Clay, 1823. Hand-colored aquatint, 14 x 18 ½ inches, Yale Center for British Art, Paul Mellon Collection.

*the Roaring River* (1775; Fig. 2), the painter uses contrasts of light and shadow to emphasize the lush vegetation of the island. Looming over the dimly lit foreground dense with foliage, tall leafy trees form a dark enclosure on the right side of the picture space. Meanwhile, on the left, Robertson stocks the tableau with the telltale features of the picturesque—the framing *repoussoir* and the blasted tree trunk. This symbolic tree trunk, with its evocation of the cyclical temporality of nature, or something more foreboding, often works to disrupt the pastoral idyll, but here it merely enhances the rustic nature of the scene. Half hidden by the rust-colored leaves of the neighboring tree, both features direct the viewer's gaze toward the gloriously lit midsection of the canvas where a tiny black figure drives a herd of cattle through a stream bisecting a lush island forest. In the foreground, a brown-skinned woman, simply dressed save for a glimmering choker of beads at her neck, holds a basket of produce at her hip, emphasizing the curve of her body and that she, too, is there for the viewer's visual consumption and pleasure.[12] She offers a morsel to a black man kneeling at her feet. Another basket, teeming with the abundant gifts of the land, rests between them and confirms the status of the island as a tropical Arcadia.

Through this picturesque lens, Robertson renders Beckford's sugar plantation—in truth the epitome of unfeeling commercial ventures and the site of brutalizing forced labor—as an unspoiled island Eden. This requires the erasure of any evidence of the coercive labor of the plantation machine; however, Robertson manages to accomplish this without erasing the

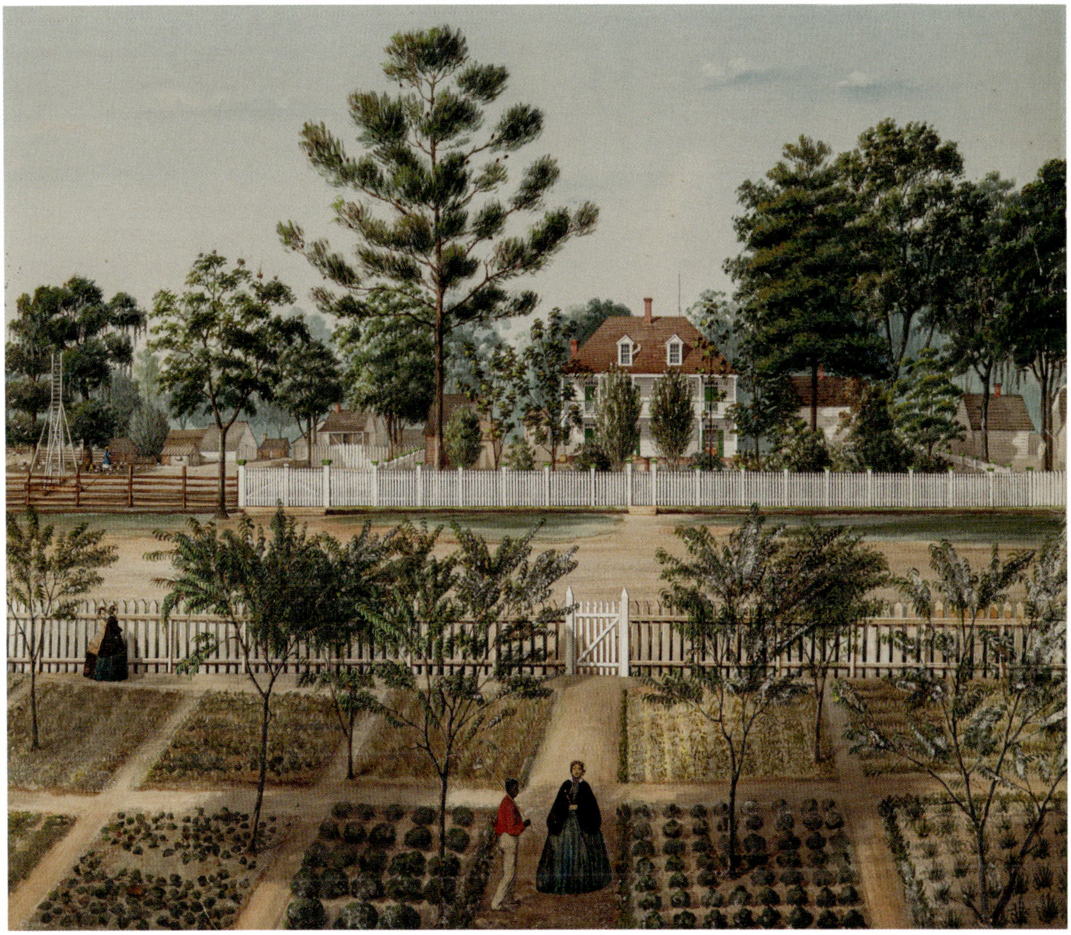

**Fig. 4**
Marie Adrien Persac, *Bois de Fleche Plantation*, 1861, Gouache and collage on paper, 16 x 22 ½ inches, Louisiana State Museum, Gift of Mrs. Olga Delomme Wagner, 1990.049.1. Photography by Roman Alokhin.

evidence of colonial power, i.e. the African body. William Clark's *Ten Views in the Island of Antigua, Cutting the Sugar Cane* (1823; see Fig. 3 for an example) depicts the colonial reality of land and labor in the British Caribbean more accurately. Invited to the island by planters, Clark recorded the key stages in sugar production; but, although detailed and based on his in-person observations, even these are idealized as the artist tempers the reality of the extraction of human labor as resource by offering the viewer a rustic image of compliant workers.[13]

Robertson's use of black figures in the mode of conventional pastoral staffage marks Jamaica as a quintessentially colonial space, one in which colonial power—like the presence of Africans on the island—seems natural and inevitable such that it (and its inevitable partner, slavery) becomes an institution that has seemingly existed since time immemorial, a system so organic that it eludes representation. The uncultivated magnificence of Robertson's vistas make it easy to forget that they represent Beckford of Somerly's extensive plantations. Yet, that they do so is the only reason why they are recorded; this simultaneous forgetting and remembering is precisely the point of their existence.

Robertson's pictures exemplify the work of artists painting in the West Indies whose colonialist visions of Edenic island Arcadias excised any explicit acknowledgment of the institutional presence of the plantation. Painters of Louisiana plantation pictures, however, typically worked in modes quite distinct from their Caribbean counterparts. Although

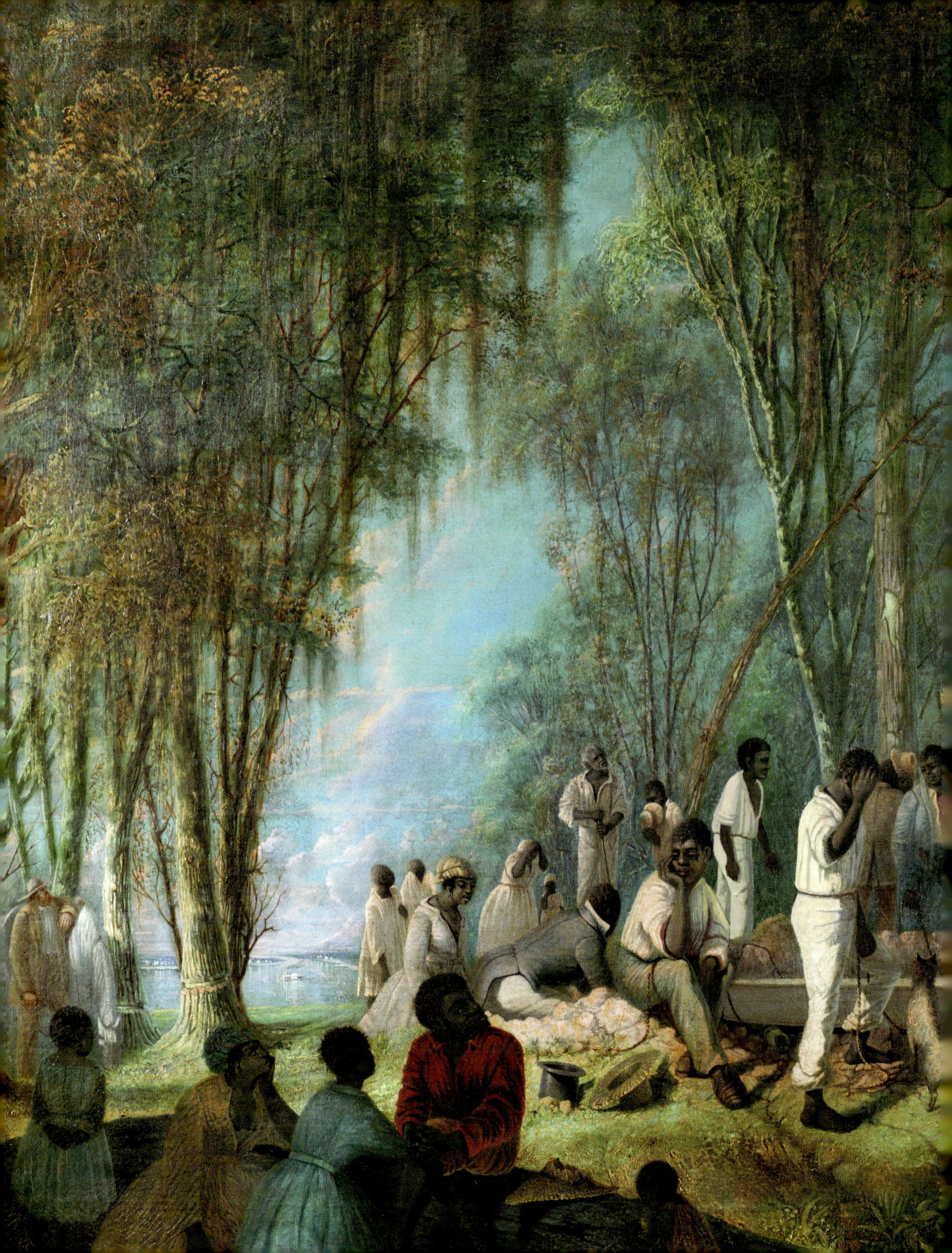

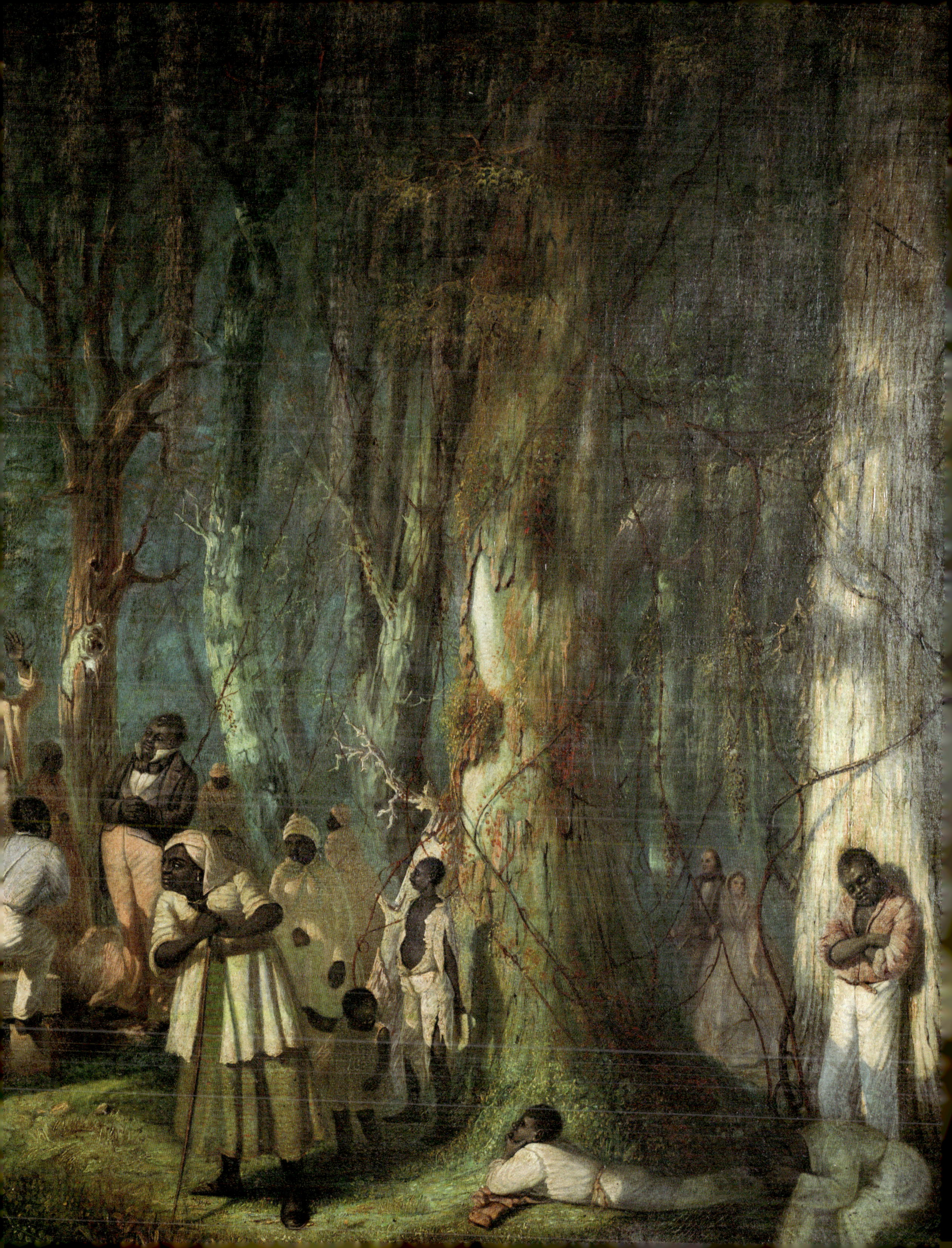

general landscape representations of Louisiana did engage picturesque conventions, when painting plantation views, antebellum Louisiana artists often embraced an aesthetic that Iberville's blunt statement about the ease of clearing Louisiana for cultivation and settlement had foreshadowed, emphasizing the plantation space as a pristine "colonial garden", a site of precise colonial—that is white—management and control.[14] Importantly, both of these iterations of the plantation picture ultimately represented the colonial landscape relative to the white gaze. Even when black bodies are featured, the space—whether as a site of untamed abundance ripe for consumption or one of carefully managed cultivation—exists relative to white colonial power.

## New World Order: Persac's Precise and Peaceful Plantations

Painters of Louisiana's landscape developed their own "bayou picturesque" conventions, which drew upon, but were in many ways distinct from, the example set by their Caribbean counterparts. By the mid-nineteenth century, when landscape became a serious occupation among American artists, painters like Joseph Rusling Meeker and William Henry Buck had devised a very place-specific visual vocabulary for the region—majestic oaks dripping with Spanish moss, "sleepy bayous, swamps teeming with wildlife, lakes dotted with cypress knees"—to produce the image of Louisiana as a place of romantic wildness much like the island Edens of the Caribbean.[15] Initially, these works were produced as part of scenic panoramas that offered paying viewers the opportunity to survey the region, or formed the painted backdrops for theatrical productions.[16] Picturesque images celebrated the untamed Louisiana landscape—its wild swamps and thick, entangled growth, described in 1871 by journalist Alfred R. Waud as a "lush mystery of vegetation."[17] These sites of foreboding overgrowth might have expressed something of nature's dark side, but their lush and fecund beauty also suggested something Edenic.[18]

However, in contrast to paintings of the Caribbean, rarely was this bayou picturesque explicitly a *plantation* picturesque.[19] Louisiana planters, like those of the U.S. South more generally, preferred images of their holdings that, rather than showcasing the splendor of uncultivated abundance, highlighted the proper harnessing of such natural gifts.[20] The plantation landscapes of Marie Adrien Persac reflect the tastes and aspirations of the Louisiana planters who commissioned them, offering an idealized and pristine vision of the plantation as a space of serenity and gentility.[21] Persac transforms Robertson's romantic wilderness into a carefully cultivated, ordered landscape of working fields, quaint outbuildings, and stately plantation homes. In the watercolor *Bois de Fleche Plantation* (1861; Fig. 4), for example, Persac presents the viewer with a painstakingly ordered space, the various features of the plantation complex organized into a rigid geometry according to function. The pronounced verticals of white picket fences contrast sharply with the unfinished horizontal slats of more rustic enclosures, both serving to divide—along with a road that bisects the picture space laterally—the various plantation spaces from one another; manor house, outbuildings, cotton press, gardens: a place for everything, and everything in its place.[22] The plantation's vegetable gardens in the foreground—with their meticulously

**Fig. 5 (pp. 92-93)**
John Antrobus, *A Plantation Burial*, 1860, Oil on canvas, 52 ¾ x 81 5/16 inches, The Historic New Orleans Collection, 1960.46.

mapped rectangular beds and cleared, straight paths—function as a synecdoche for the whole picture, reproducing, within the picture itself, its well-ordered logic on a smaller scale.

Persac presents a cropped view of the beds, with the foreground painted right to the very edge of the picture space, as though the well-dressed white lady walking up the garden's center path has come to welcome us as visitors, yet the scene is remarkably empty. Conspicuously missing are the enslaved black people whose labor actually creates all that the viewer sees. Persac does not absent them entirely; their presence is necessary to explicitly mark the site as a plantation space. The picture requires their presence, but it also requires the absence of the brutal forces that assure this presence and compels their labor. As in Clark's series of lithographs, Persac's rare black laborers function as rustic additions that reinforce the scene's sense of order.

Enslaved people were viewed as a form of raw material. Their management, as Caitlin Rosenthal has shown, was aimed at their transformation into productive and profitable property.[23] The horrifying beauty of Persac's plantation landscapes emerges from the dissonance between what is pictured and the picture itself. What is being pictured is the regulation of black lives, the brutalization of black bodies, and the theft of black labor for white profit. What we see, however, is something entirely different; Persac seamlessly integrates black figures into the order of his picture, arranging them to accentuate the idealization of its perfectly mapped space. In both the Caribbean and in Louisiana, whether through the picturesque of Robertson's island Edens or the eerie serenity of Persac's precisely managed estates, plantation pictures revolved around the careful positioning of black figures who not only signal the transformation taking place—i.e. the imposition of colonial power on land and people—but who also embody this transformation.

## Reframing the Plantation Picturesque in Louisiana: John Antrobus and Robert S. Duncanson

In light of the Louisiana plantocracy's preference for pictures that highlighted the precise management of their properties—both terrestrial and human—over the untamed Edens of the plantation picturesque employed in the Caribbean, the exceptional works that do apply picturesque conventions to Louisiana plantations are significant, particularly in the way that they engage with the plantation as a racialized space. Not only was the picturesque geographically mobile, it was politically pliant, and these works reveal the flexibility of the picturesque to accommodate diverse attitudes about race, space, and power through the representations of human beings in nature.

In *A Plantation Burial* (1860; Fig. 5), John Antrobus adapts picturesque conventions to depict a scene on the Louisiana plantation of the late-governor Tilghman Tucker. The artist, who had spent time on Tucker's plantation, presumably knew the estate well and made his sketches from life, later revising these impressions into a pleasing finished composition in the studio.[24] Cosseted in a woodland cove on the property, a group of enslaved African Americans conduct a funeral for one of their deceased. Put to a very different use, the triangular arrangement of figures at the center of the scene recalls the configuration often used for published illustrations of slave auctions in newspapers like *Harpers Weekly*, but Antrobus also draws on the bayou picturesque—its conventional contrasts of color, evocative framing devices, and unique vernacular visual vocabulary—to structure the work. Soaring above the congregation of mourners, tall, moss-laden trees—ubiquitous features of this regional iteration of the picturesque—frame the scene and establish the confines of the space. Entangled with vines that creep up their trunks, they, along with the verdant ground cover, suggest the Arcadian fertility of the land. Recalling the incandescent treatment of light at the center of Robertson's *Spring Head of the Roaring River*, the thicket of trees forms a visual contrast with the calm body of water in the distance, its glassy surface reflecting the glowing sunset in shades of pastel pink.

Using the sunset to create a spotlight on the group in the center of the painting, Antrobus constructs the scene like a stage set, presenting a diverse cast of characters in the funeral-goers who evince a range of emotions from grief to boredom.[25] The artist offers a glimpse of the generally unseen lives of enslaved African Americans on the plantation; however, he pairs his attention to the various emotions captured on their faces with his focus on the overgrown, uncontrolled natural world. The opposite of Persac's picture of precise plantation management, the domain of the plantation associated with blackness appears unmanaged (although, of course, it is carefully constructed to look this way) and perhaps even unmanageable. Yet despite—or perhaps because of—the wild landscape of Antrobus's picturesque, the artist subtly frames the scene with figures of white control. Relatively isolated on the left margin of the picture, a red-bearded white overseer observes the enslaved people's activities while, on the opposite side of the work, a finely dressed couple, undoubtedly the owners of the plantation—and, of course, of the bodies whose activities they surveil—also watch the funeral activities unfold. Their presence underscores that, despite initial appearances, all is in order, and everything is under [white] control.

Although Antrobus's painting uniquely recognizes the independent life and culture of enslaved African Americans, it also spectacularizes their emotional lives – what historian Daina Ramey Berry might call their "soul value" or the value of human lived experience beyond the logic of profit.[26] However, while black life is both codified and commodified into spectacle, *A Plantation Burial*, in bringing the interior lives of enslaved African Americans and the reality of white control into the same space, also suggests the contestations within the idealized imagery of the plantation itself. In other words, the picturesque transformation of the natural world is unable to fully materialize black life as *merely* resource.

Exploiting such tensions and filtering his vision through the lens of popular fiction, in *Uncle Tom and Little Eva* (1853; Fig. 6), Robert S. Duncanson uses the plantation picturesque to radically different effect, working to upend the naturalization of the racialized dynamics of power that supported slavery and arguably using it to suggest the possibility of a new national narrative. Commissioned by abolitionist Reverend James Frances Conover, the painting represents an episode taken from Harriet Beecher Stowe's recently published, international bestseller, *Uncle's Tom's Cabin* (1852), in which Eva interrupts her lesson teaching Tom to read the Bible and gestures toward a glowing sunset, foreshadowing her own death. Drawn from a description in the novel and set just outside New Orleans on the

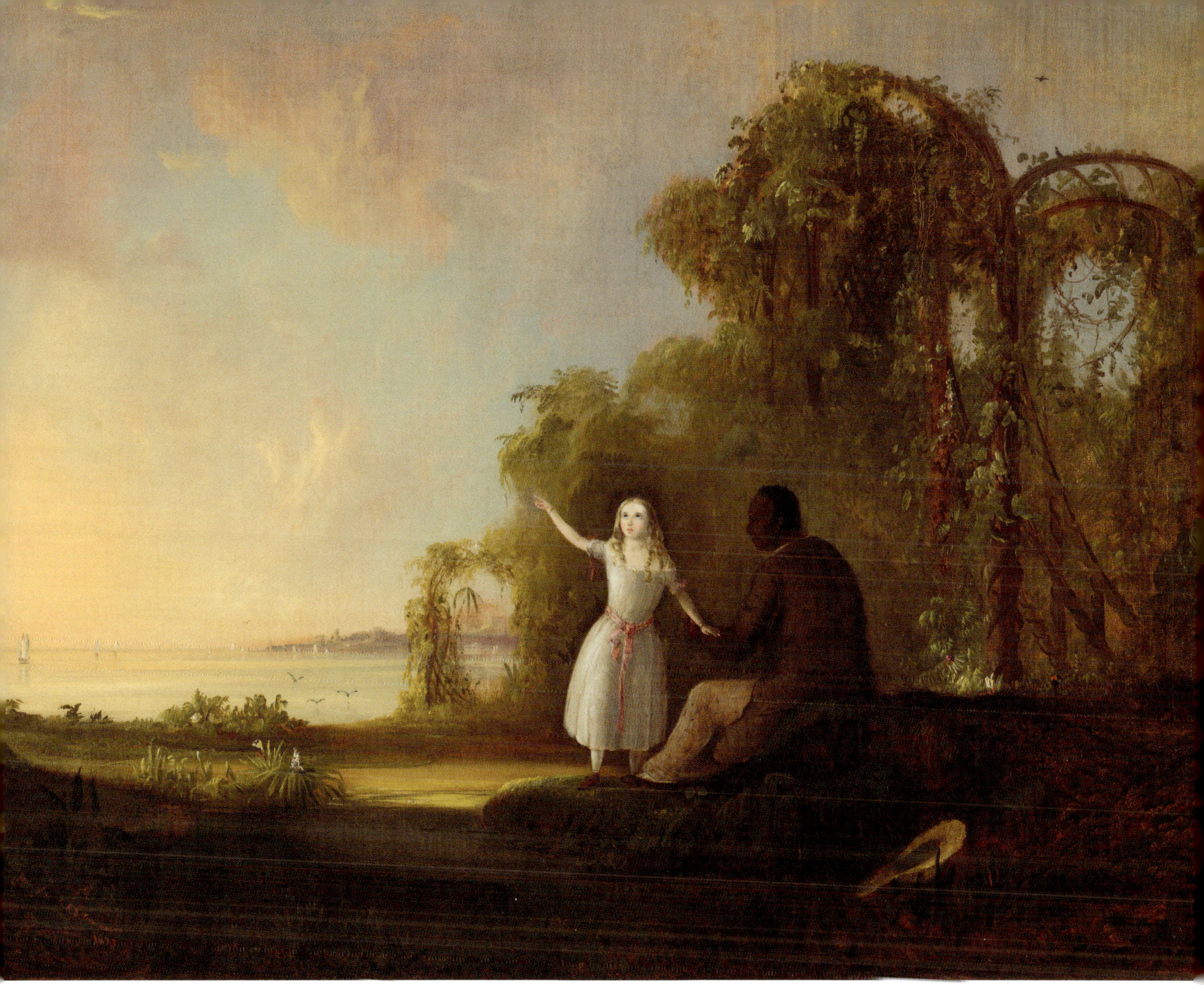

Fig. 6
Robert S. Duncanson, *Uncle Tom and Little Eva*, 1853, Oil on canvas, 27 1/4 x 38 1/4 inches, Detroit Institute of Arts, Gift of Mrs. Jefferson Butler and Miss Grace R. Conover, 49.498

St. Clare family plantation on Lake Pontchartrain, the painting features Tom sitting on a low earthen bank and holding Eva's hand as she points to the luminous sky. The villa—formed from bamboo-work, fragrant with tropical plants and flowers, filled with light—drips with Edenic beauty precisely as Stowe describes it.

Embracing all the hallmarks of the Louisiana picturesque, Duncanson frames the figures with trees draped with flowers and Spanish moss and sets the tableau's lush vegetation against the calm waters of the lake. Here, Louisiana, a center of the slave trade, becomes the site of transformation as Eva's spiritual prophecy is linked to Tom's metamorphosis, and both foretell a kind of redemption. Although sentimental and patronizing figures who, in the novel, are developed to evoke sympathy for the abolitionist cause, in Duncanson's painting Eva and Tom also signify the possibility of a national redemption from the institution of slavery. Significantly, the recognizable landscape of Louisiana, depicted as a lost Eden, serves as the site for this redemptive possibility. Duncanson's canvas radiates with glowing light, from the glassy water to the golden sky, coupling his interest in literary allusions with his mastery of lighting to imagine this landscape as a site of racial reconciliation. Moreover, in doing so,

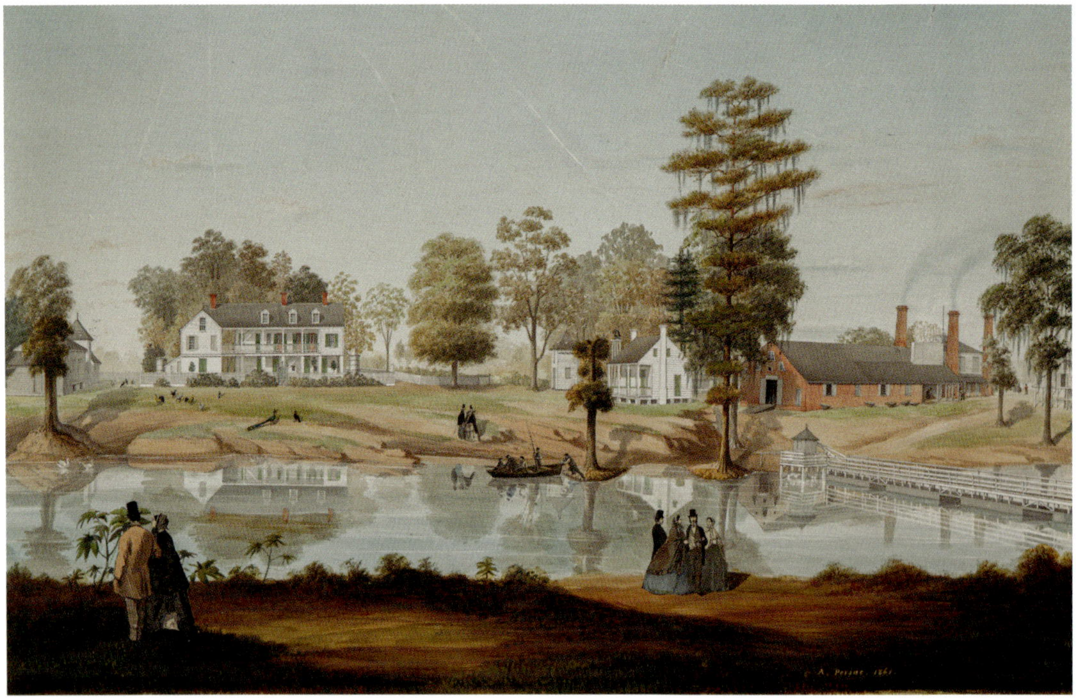

Fig. 7
Marie Adrien Persac, *Olivier Plantation, Orange Grove*, 1861, Gouache and collage on paper, 18 ⅛ x 23 ¾ inches, Louisiana State Museum, Loan of Mrs. Rene T. Beauregard, 07155. Photography by Roman Alokhin.

the painter gestures toward another kind of transformative experience: one that would take place within the hearts and minds of the painting's viewers who are compelled to consider how black experience and black life lay beyond the racialization of space embedded in the conventions of plantation painting.

## Bodies in Space: Female Figures and Racially Encoded Geographies

Whether depicting New World Edens, meticulously managed estates, sites of the surveillance and spectacularization of black life, or imagined landscapes of racial reconciliation, plantation paintings presented racially encoded geographies to their viewers. With the obvious exception of Duncanson's abolitionist scene of interracial cooperation, these works employ specific pictorial devices to compose and aestheticize nature in order to suggest white settlers as the rightful possessors of the natural resources of the New World (including the black bodies whose transplantation they often obscure). However, as these pictures already suggest, it was not only through the depiction of nature itself that landscape paintings racially marked space for their viewers. Contrasting two pictures with somewhat similar compositions, Persac's *Olivier Plantation, Orange Grove* (1861; Fig. 7) and Agostino Brunias's *View on the River Roseau, Dominica* (circa 1770; Fig. 8), demonstrates the different ways that the inclusion of human figures racially encoded these landscapes. Both works depict New World landscapes (Louisiana and Dominica, respectively) that feature a few human-made structures and a central body of water, and both artists populate the scene with tiny human figures, albeit to quite different effect.

Emphasizing the plantation as the domain of white gentility, Persac sparsely peoples the serene space with a few groups of elegantly attired white figures. The artist's rendering of the plantation's crystal waters and stately trees brings some attention to the providential gift of its natural beauty; however, his primary pictorial focus is on all that the planter has made of it. Placed

Fig. 8 (pp. 98-99)
Agostino Brunias, *View on the River Roseau, Dominica*, circa 1770-80, Oil on canvas, 33 ⅛ x 62 $^{3}/_{16}$ inches, Art Institute of Chicago, Gift of Emily Crane Chadbourne, 1953.14

at an oblique angle in the right margin of the picture, the precisely engineered bridge invites the viewer's gaze across the water to celebrate the planter's achievements exemplified by the manor house with its many outbuildings and the orderly division of its fenced-off spaces. Indeed, Persac reiterates these achievements through their literal repetition, turning the calm surface of the central body of water into a reflective mirror that doubles the scene. Despite the artist's concentration on these elements, the tiny white figures are more than insignificant afterthoughts. They perform no labor (with the possible exception of the group in the boat), but their leisure defines the space. Their task is simply to enjoy it, encoding the landscape as a site—and a sight—meant for white pleasure.

Brunias's tableau works in a very different way. The artist crowds the scene with a motley assortment of brown and black figures—mostly women of various shades and statuses—engaged in a variety of activities that register both leisure and labor. Finely dressed women with parasols in their hands and tall, elegant headwraps, hats, or bonnets atop their heads stroll at the waters edge. A few stop to chat. One negotiates a purchase from a dark-skinned female huckster with a basket of fruit. In the water, a party of mixed-race women bathe nude under the shade of a tree near the left edge of the picture space. Their obvious leisure contrasts with the work of others with whom they share the stream. At the opposite end of the canvas, a number of topless washerwomen beat laundry against the river rocks. Between the two groups, a lone woman, also topless, fords the water using a walking stick to balance the weight of the heavy bundle she carries on her shoulder, and two other female figures lift their skirts above their knees in order to wade across the water. In contrast to the manor house in Persac's picture, in Brunias's work the rustic structures fade into the landscape, blending almost seamlessly into the excessively verdant space—more island Eden than cultivated plantation. As in other West Indian pictures, including Robertson's aforementioned picture of the Beckford plantation, Brunias's use of black and brown bodies identifies the space as the colonial Caribbean. On the one hand, their presence *a priori* suggests the white colonial and plantocratic power for which Brunias worked. However, as recent scholarship on the artist's work has demonstrated, Brunias's pictures often left room for alternative, more complicated and arguably subversive interpretations, and, with no evident features of white authority or surveillance, the brown and black figures here seem very much in possession of the world being depicted.[27]

Artists aiming to express the racial dynamics of power in the New World also used less literal mobilizations of the human figure, deploying more symbolic depictions of female bodies to represent actual terrestrial ones. Considering examples from across the slaveholding Atlantic of the use of female bodies to racially encode physical geographies demonstrates how artists adapted this convention in ways that reflected the particular political concerns and ideologies of their time and place. Dating to the very beginning of the sixteenth century, for example, allegories of the continents used female bodies to represent terrestrial ones. In the traditional assignment of symbols and accouterments to each figure, continental allegories inevitably reinforced racial stereotypes and hierarchies, for example, presenting Europe as refined and civilized compared to Asia, Africa, and America, her supposedly less advanced sisters. However, few portrayed the racial aspect of colonial power

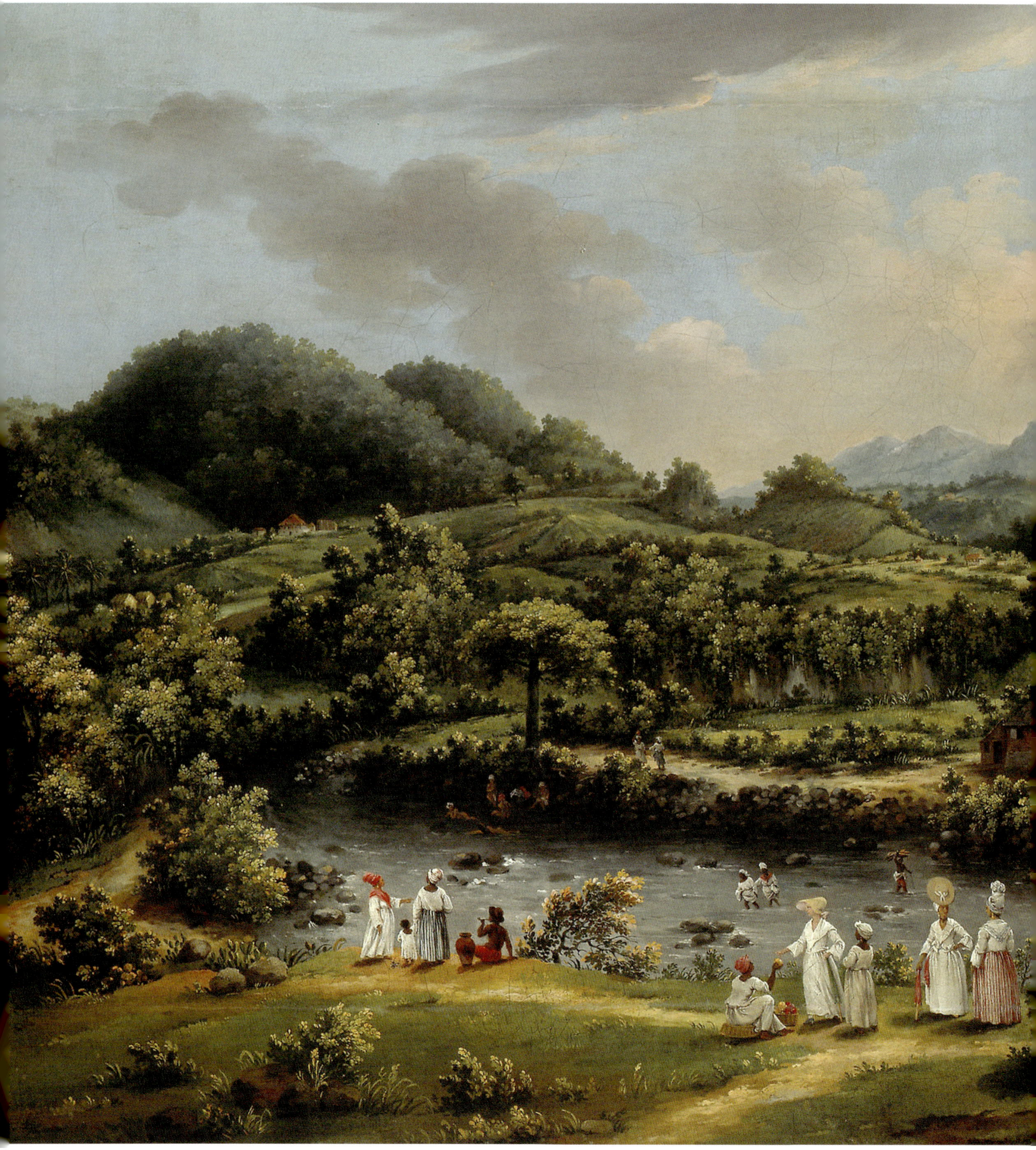

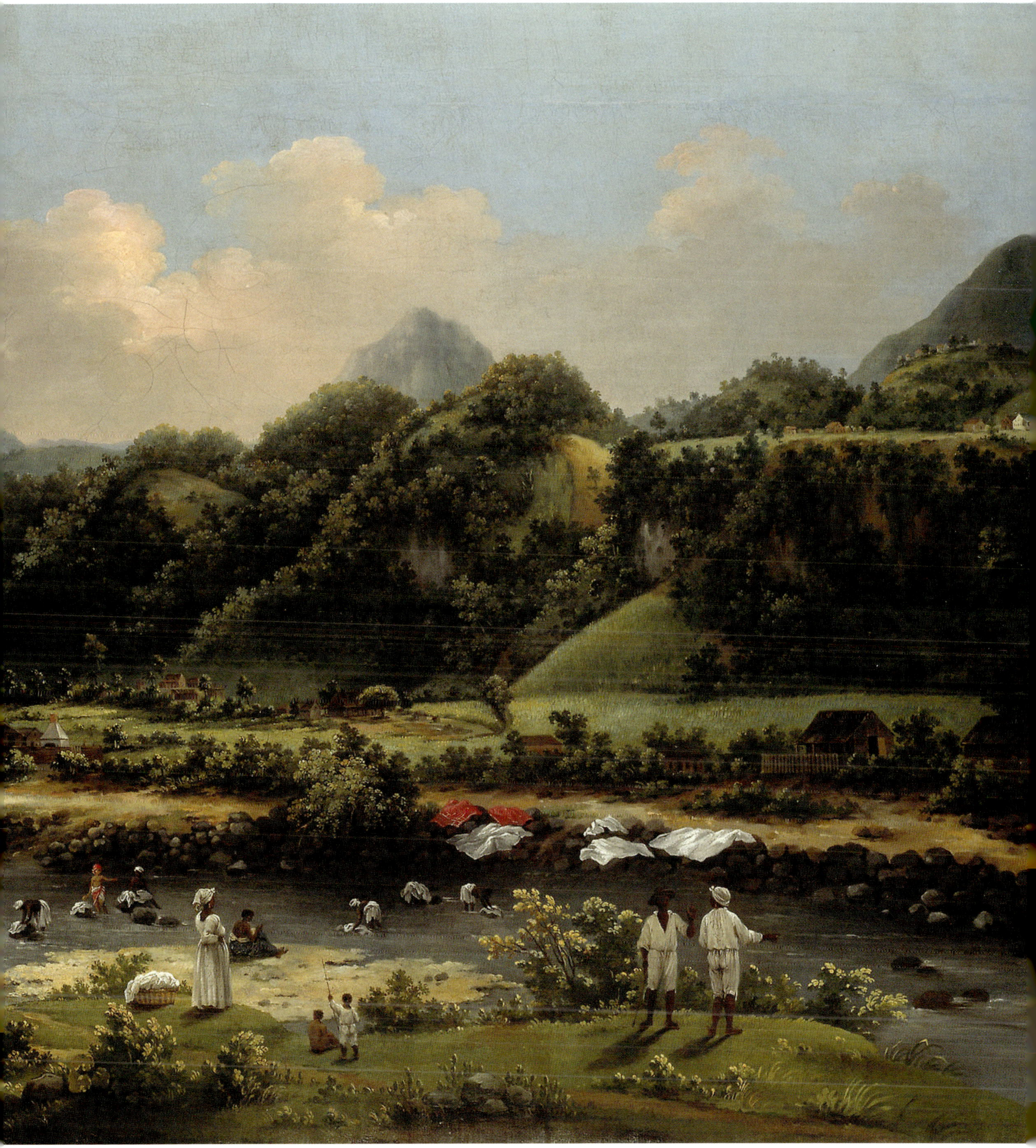

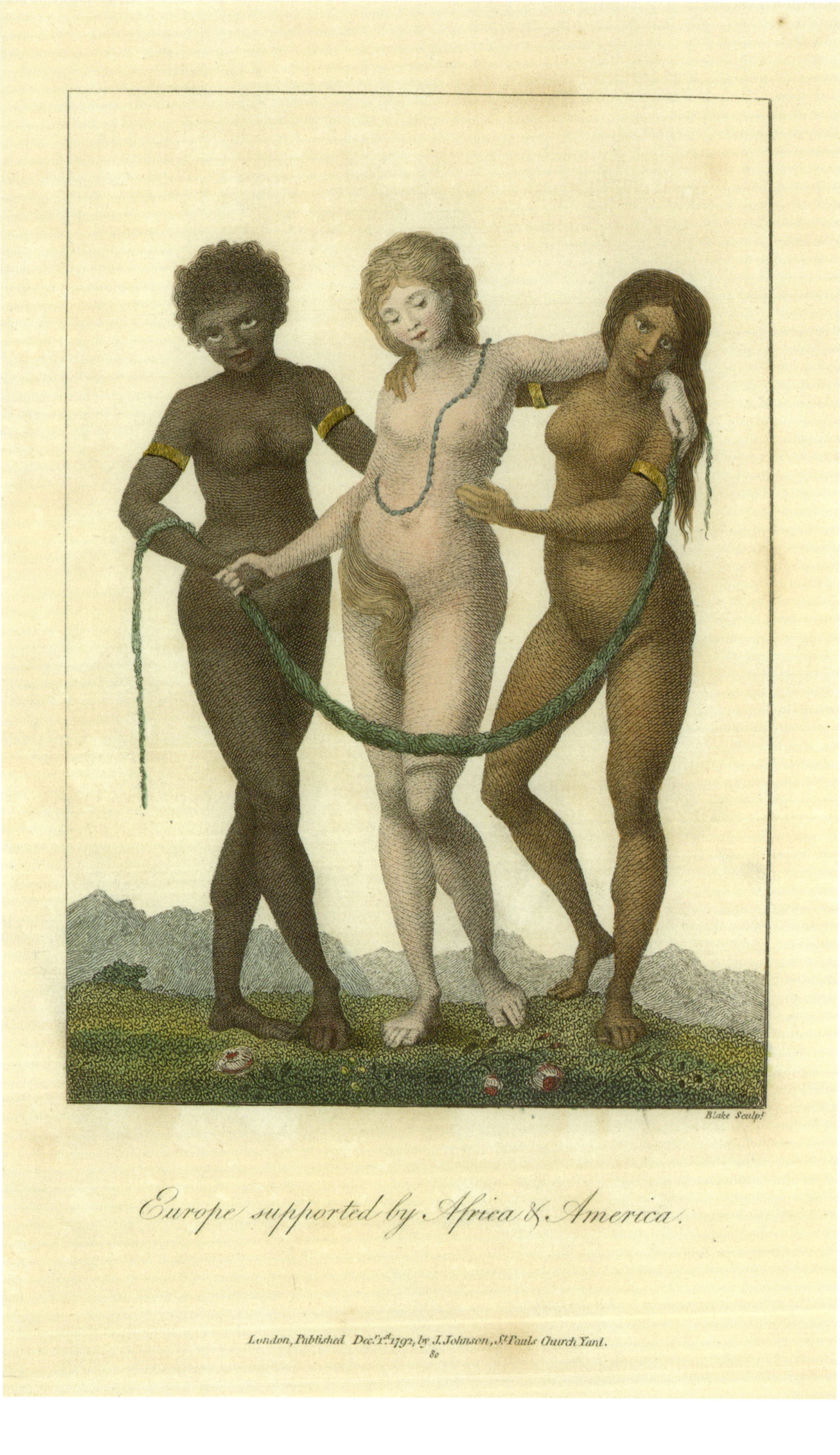


**Fig. 9 (left)**
William Blake, *Europe Supported by Africa and America*, 1792, Engraving with hand coloring, 7 x 5 inches, Courtesy of the John Carter Brown Library.

**Fig. 10 (right)**
Agostino Brunias, *Mulatresses and Negro Woman Bathing*, mid-late 18th century, Gift of Harvard College Library, 1975, Courtesy of the Peabody Museum of Archeology and Ethnology, Harvard University, PM975-5-30/9416d

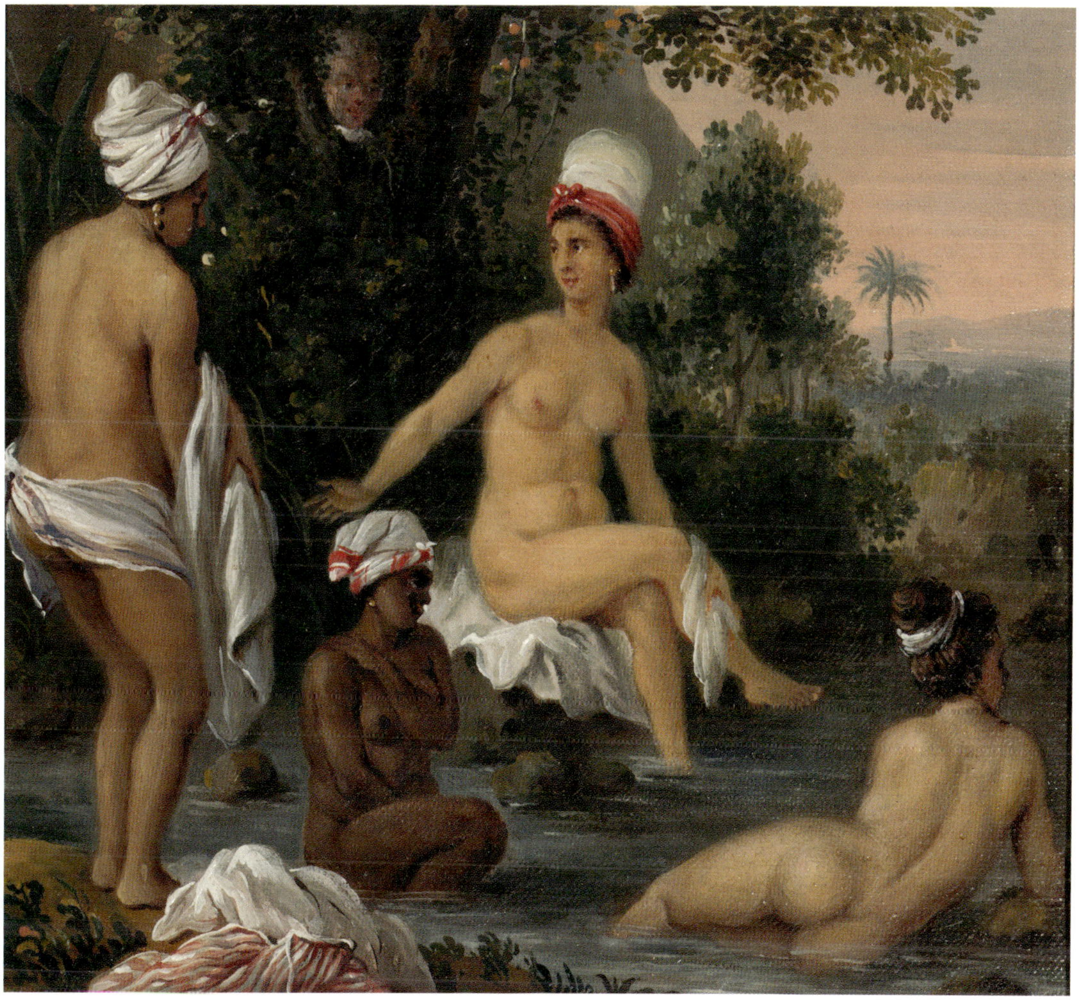

as explicitly as William Blake's unquestionably imperialist and unequivocally erotic continental allegory *Europe Supported by Africa and America* (1792; Fig. 9).[28]

In Blake's image, a fair Europe stands between a beautiful, dark-skinned Africa and an equally lovely, tawny America. Europe clasps her African companion's hand and lazily rests her pale arm around the shoulder of her American counterpart, their bodies forming a human chain of comeliness echoed by the verdant garland draped in front of them. However, not all of the lovely links in this chain are equal; Africa and America wear gold bands around their upper arms, indicating that their bonds to Europe are not ones of sisterhood but of servitude. The placement of one of each of the darker figure's arms around Europe's body underscores this relationship; just as Europe built her great empire on a foundation of brown and black land and labor, their dark bodies constitute the pillars that support the fairest of them all. While the arm bracelets worn by Africa and America underscore their service to Europe, the long string of beads Europe wears like a sash from shoulder to hip suggests the treasures that this service yields. Moreover, the harmony among the three figures implies Europe's entitlement to these rewards. Although all three of the figures are nude, with similarly womanly bodies and full, round, perky breasts, Europe's demure downcast gaze works to temper her nudity with a sign of modest femininity. Africa's and America's eyes, on the other hand, brazenly engage with the viewer, a suggestive gesture that invites him—and it's always a him, for despite the identity of the actual viewer, these images are constructed for a heterosexual male gaze—to visually consume their nakedness. Positing an implicit analogy between female flesh and physical geography, Blake's allegory suggests that both are equally available to Europeans for the taking.

Artists painting in the slaveholding Atlantic often mobilized black and brown female bodies as surrogates for land that Europeans might conquer or as a way of advertising the riches and resources that such lands offered for exploitation (which included the women themselves). In images like Brunias's *Mulatresses and Negro Woman Bathing* (mid-late eighteenth century; Fig. 10), popular perceptions of black and brown women of African descent as hyperfertile and innately over-sexual supported direct visual analogies between their bodies and the lush tropical landscape and its natural bounty.[29] Ultimately, female bodies of color became the quintessential figures associated with the New World, and the availability of their bodies coded these lands as sites meant for white exploitation.[30] However, early colonial tropes that used Indigenous, black, and especially mixed-race female bodies as visual surrogates for lands elsewhere in the slaveholding Atlantic could not be transferred wholesale to the American South and were revised to suit local sensibilities.

## Imbibing White Supremacy like Mother's Milk: Dominico Canova's *Mother Louisiana*

Within the context of contentious debates about slavery that culminated in the Civil War and postbellum struggles regarding Reconstruction and Redemption, artists painting Louisiana in the second half of the nineteenth century were challenged to adapt these modes of representation to respond to American national and, especially, Southern regional political realities. Working for patrons who almost without exception would have endorsed plantocracy and white supremacy, these artists revised popular tropes that had conventionally featured women of color, replacing them with white female figures that coded Louisiana as a white space. Moreover, deploying white female bodies in the form of timeless allegories to stand for Louisiana, these works posited the image of a white Louisiana that had existed since time immemorial.

Although obviously taking formal inspiration from the Renaissance *disegno* of his native Italy, in *Mother Louisiana* (circa 1850; Fig. 11), Dominico Canova firmly roots the allegorical subject of the painting's title in a local landscape. Canova's crisp line work and handling of Mother Louisiana's weighty drapery mark the contours of her hefty figure as she sits, as though on a throne, against a verdant setting. The canopy of a thick palm tree, surrounded by a tangled assortment of Indigenous flora, rises above her lovely white face, forming the back of her queenly seat. The wide stance of the figure's parted knees amplifies the stability of the picture's pyramidal composition and also expands the capacity of the stately mother's lap. This is certainly a necessity given her caretaking responsibilities. As she lifts her breast—its pink nipple visible between her fingers—and offers it to the waiting blonde babe in her arms, five additional naked white nurslings await their turn to suckle. Canova certainly draws upon centuries of traditional Marian iconography which, as a decorative and mural painter who completed a number of church commissions during his period of activity in New Orleans, he undoubtedly knew well.

However, *Mother Louisiana* also evokes an eerie resonance with an iconic representation of

**Fig. 11**
Dominico Canova, *Mother Louisiana*, circa 1850, Oil on canvas, 56 x 48 inches, Roger Houston Ogden Collection, Courtesy of Ogden Museum of Southern Art. Photographed by Patrick Barnes.

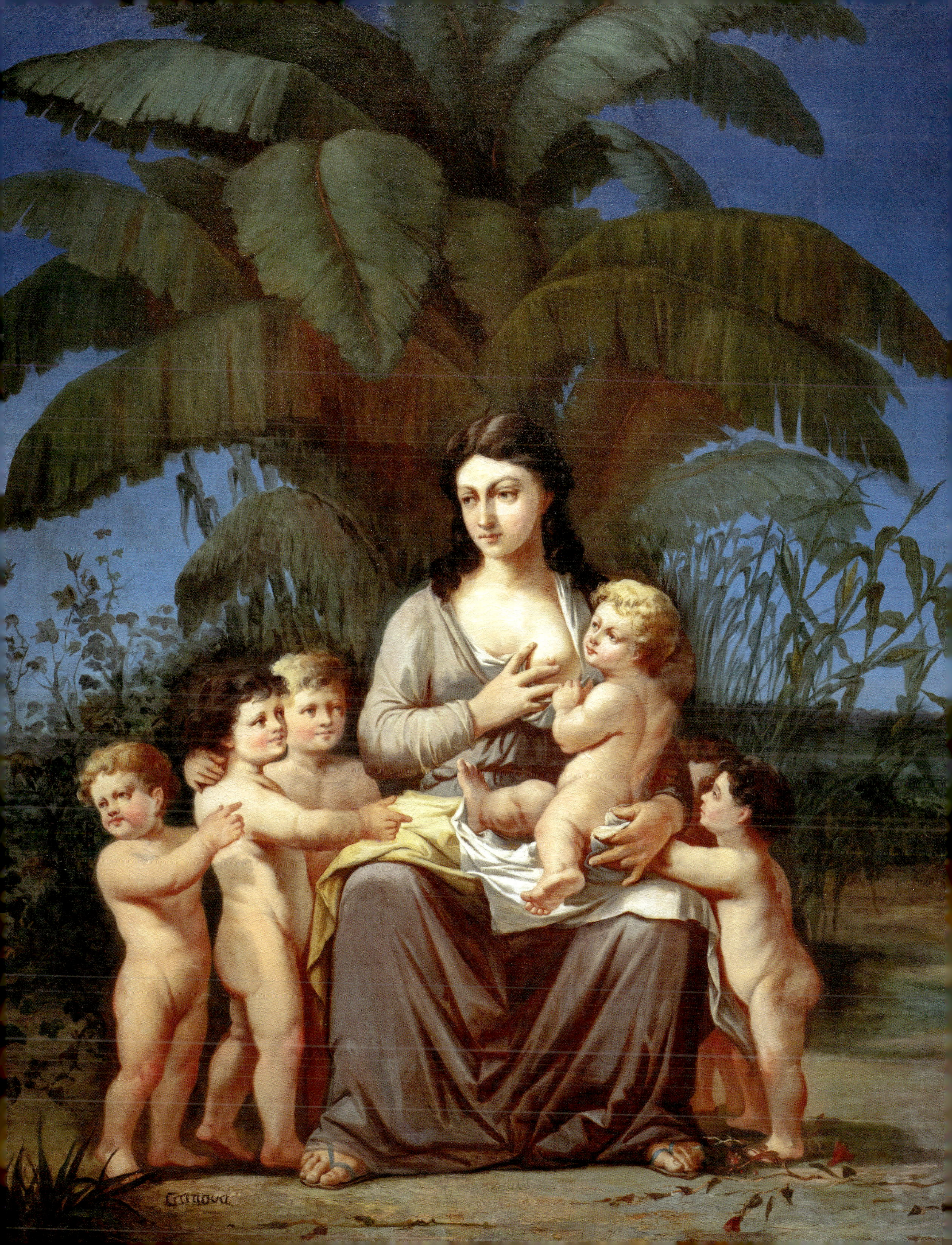

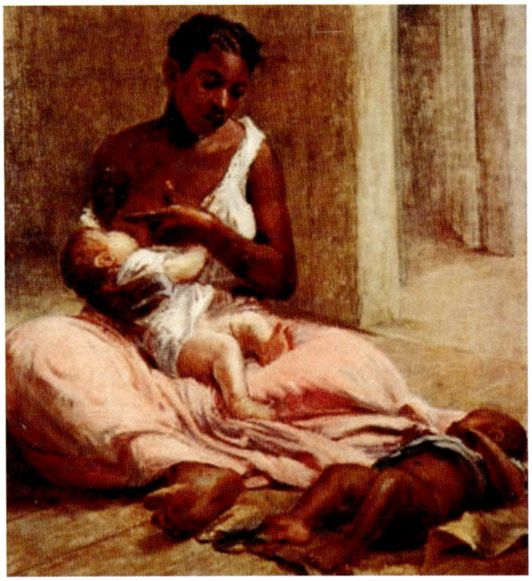

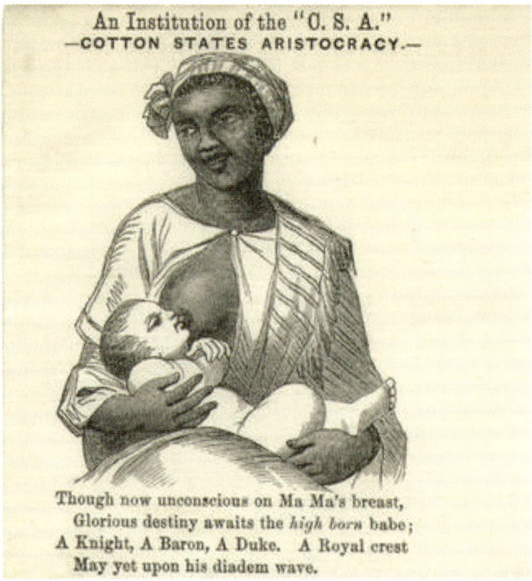


**Fig. 12 (left)**
Lucílio de Albuquerque, *Mãe Preta*, 1912, Oil on canvas, 71 x 51 inches, Bahía Museum of Art/ Wikimedia Commons

**Fig. 13 (right)**
Unidentified Artist, *Envelope with Enslaved Woman Nursing White Baby*, 1861-65, Ink on paper, 3 x 3 ½ inches, Library Company of Philadelphia.

breastfeeding unique to the slaveholding Atlantic, that of the *Mãe Preta*, or Black Mother (see, for example, Figure 12, Lucílio de Albuquerque's early twentieth-century rendition, probably the most well known painting of the popular image).[31] Generally depicted as an enslaved black woman nursing the white infant of a slaveholder at the expense of her own child (often pictured, sometimes left out of the frame), the enslaved black wet nurse is so well-known and enduring an icon in Brazil that her name is synonymous with a popular brand of dark beer.[32] Canova may or may not have been familiar with the specific iconography of the *Mãe Preta*, but American iterations of the image did exist and were even reproduced on a series of envelopes during the Civil War (Fig. 13). Moreover, recent scholarship by Emily West and R.L. Knight indicates that wet-nursing by enslaved women in the antebellum South—once thought to be relatively "uncommon" in that only about one-fifth of white mothers were believed to have depended on enslaved women to breastfeed their children—was far more pervasive than was previously speculated.[33] Therefore, Canova's image is more than just an innocuous allegory that incidentally figures Louisiana as a white woman; it constitutes a pictorial erasure of an important antebellum reality. *Mother Louisiana* denies the actuality of forced labor by enslaved black women by replacing it with an idealized image of white motherhood. Moreover, the allegorical nature of *Mother Louisiana* and its Edenic landscape setting extend that erasure, making Louisiana's whiteness appear natural and timeless, as though since the beginning of time, Louisiana had sustained itself on the natural resources of whiteness rather than the usurpation of Indigenous American land and the exploitation of black labor.

## Race-ing a New World Flora: George Coulon's *Spirit of Louisiana* and Albert Eckhout's *Mameluca*

Producing a similar effect, George David Coulon's post-Reconstruction *Spirit of Louisiana* (1894; Fig. 1) features a pale-skinned female figure as an allegorical personification of the state. Loosely wrapped in white drapery, she evokes a classical goddess, appearing to the viewer as a bayou iteration of Flora, the Roman goddess of flowers, spring, and fertility. Cascading down her back, the figure's long, wavy chestnut tresses are interlaced with pearls and crowned with a headband of Indigenous flowers and plant life. Coulon sets the gleaming figure against a rather nondescript but verdant landscape background, her white face rising above even the trees as the pink cast of the sky echoes her blushing cheeks. The artist's painterly treatment of the background's generalized greenery contrasts with the geographical specificity suggested by the more naturalistically rendered *magnolia grandiflora*, yellow evening primrose, and spiky swamp grass of the figure's floral crown. Rather than depicting actual trees, the loose, gestural brushwork of the arboreal backdrop offers the suggestion of trees, conveying a sense of abundance but also demonstrating that the actual land is not the focus here; the idea of it is. Indeed, adorned with native flora and presented essentially *au naturel*, the figure of Louisiana is depicted almost as a landscape feature herself, and her white presence constitutes the picture's most important geographical signifier. As rendered by Coulon's brush, post-Reconstruction Louisiana is unmistakably white.

However, while *Spirit of Louisiana* obviously draws on the iconography of Flora in Western painting as well as the general conventions of geographic allegorical representation, the picture must also be considered in light of visual culture tropes, dating to at least the seventeenth century, that employ these conventions to associate the bodies of women of color—and especially mixed-race women of color—with the fecundity of colonized territories in the Circum-Atlantic. The classicized women of color displayed in a landscape setting in Agostino Brunias's *Mulatresses and Negro Woman Bathing* (mid-late eighteenth century; Fig. 10) offers a prime example:

> *Like a trio of Eves before the fall, the brown beauties in* Mulatresses and Negro Woman Bathing *unabashedly lay their bodies bare, each figure posed and positioned in a different way so as to display the female form from a variety of perspectives....A verdant landscape of tall grasses and leafy foliage painted in array of rich greens ranging from emerald to forest dominates the painting, extending to three of the four corners and conveying, along with the bountiful shade tree, the fecundity of the land...Indeed, the women themselves appear to rise organically from the landscape, particularly the reclining mulatress and the crouching negress—their bodies sunk low in the water as if rooted in the sandy bottom of the shallow stream. Given the depiction of four nude figures, the presence of only a single discarded dress underscores this notion, as if the women, themselves the lush fruit of the New World, have emerged* au naturel *from the land.*[34]

Moreover, the particular Caribbean-ness of these brown Venuses—highlighted by Brunias's depiction of them as rising organically from the tropical landscape—results in a visual analogy that relates the women to the land itself. Brunias suggests their bodies, ripe with organic sexuality, as another type of exotic fruit indicative of the variety and bounty to be enjoyed in the colonized islands, and the white face of a peeping tom hidden in the branches underscores that such tantalizing fruits exist for his pleasure.[35] Of course, such depictions would not have served the interests of postbellum Louisianans who had a vested interest in distancing the state from its popular association with widespread miscegenation.

Then again, nineteenth-century white female sexuality certainly could not be presented in such an overtly sexualized way, and Coulon could not simply exchange brown and black women's bodies for white ones.

Instead, Coulon's *Spirit of Louisiana* deliberately toes the line between a kind of coquettishness and demure modesty. Rendered in profile, the body of the three-quarter length figure turns away from the viewer, but Coulon's loose arrangement of the drapery treats her audience to a significant revelation of shoulder and the side of her breast, her blue veins, like branches of the Mississippi River, traceable beneath her pearly skin. Moreover, she anxiously gathers the fabric around her with a protective gesture emphasized by the awkwardly painted hand holding the loose garment together at her chest. Choosing a position somewhere between the demurely dropped gaze of Blake's Europe and the brazen engagement of his Africa and America, Coulon's Louisiana cocks her head to the side, glancing over her bare shoulder to allow viewers a glimpse of her full face, but her sidelong gaze refuses to address them directly.[36]

Albert Eckhout's *Mameluca* (1641; Fig. 14), one of a series of eight "ethnographic portraits" the artist made of people of color during an expedition to Brazil as a painter for the Dutch court, works in a similar way to Brunias's *Mulatresses and Negro Woman Bathing* but bears an even stronger compositional resemblance to Coulon's picture. If Coulon's *Spirit of Louisiana* registers as a Louisianan Flora, Eckhout's *Mameluca* presents her Brazilian counterpart.[37] Like the figure in Coulon's painting, the brown-skinned woman (who is meant to portray a person of mixed Indigenous and European descent) wears a long, white, draped garment and a floral tiara set off by strands of semi-precious jewelry, including, a string of tiny pearls in her hair. However, as in Brunias's picture, Eckhout's seventeenth-century depiction of a woman of color reflects the raced and gendered dynamics of its colonial time and place, and his New World Flora displays an explicit sexuality that Coulon's cannot. The boughs of the cashew tree, heavy with its fruit, and the guinea pigs at her feet—which seventeenth-century European viewers understood as the New World equivalent of rabbits—indicate the fertility of the woman and the land she represents. The flowers in her headdress identify her with the floral bounty that overflows the basket she presents in her right palm. Moreover, her gaze—in addition to the wide swath of décolletage revealed at her neckline, the peek of calf on display as she holds her gown, and her very existence as the progeny of interracial sexual relations—suggests that her body, like the produce of the land she stands on, is on offer. Eckhout's Brazilian images circulated widely as prints, and it is possible that Coulon knew the image.[38] However, whether Coulon was familiar with this particular Eckhout image or not, he would certainly have been invested in undoing the associations between the bodies of women of color, fertility, interracial sexuality, and New World lands that pictures like Brunias's and Eckhout's imply.

Of course there are important distinctions here as Coulon adapts the content and composition to reflect the reality of his own time and place. Eckhout offers a pulled back view of the landscape and the woman, showcasing all the bounty ripe for the taking by colonial power. In contrast, Coulon's close-up represents the aftermath of such consumption, an attempt to re-brand the land itself—presented in the form of a white woman—as so fundamentally white that the figure's insistent whiteness—her skin, her pearls, her drapery—overtakes the landscape itself.

**Fig. 14 (right)**
Albert Eckhout, *Mameluca*, 1641, Oil on canvas, 106 ½ x 67 inches, National Museum of Denmark, Donated as a gift to Frederick III in 1654 by Johan Maurits of Nassau-Siegen, General Governor of the Dutch Colony of Brazil, Photography by John Lee

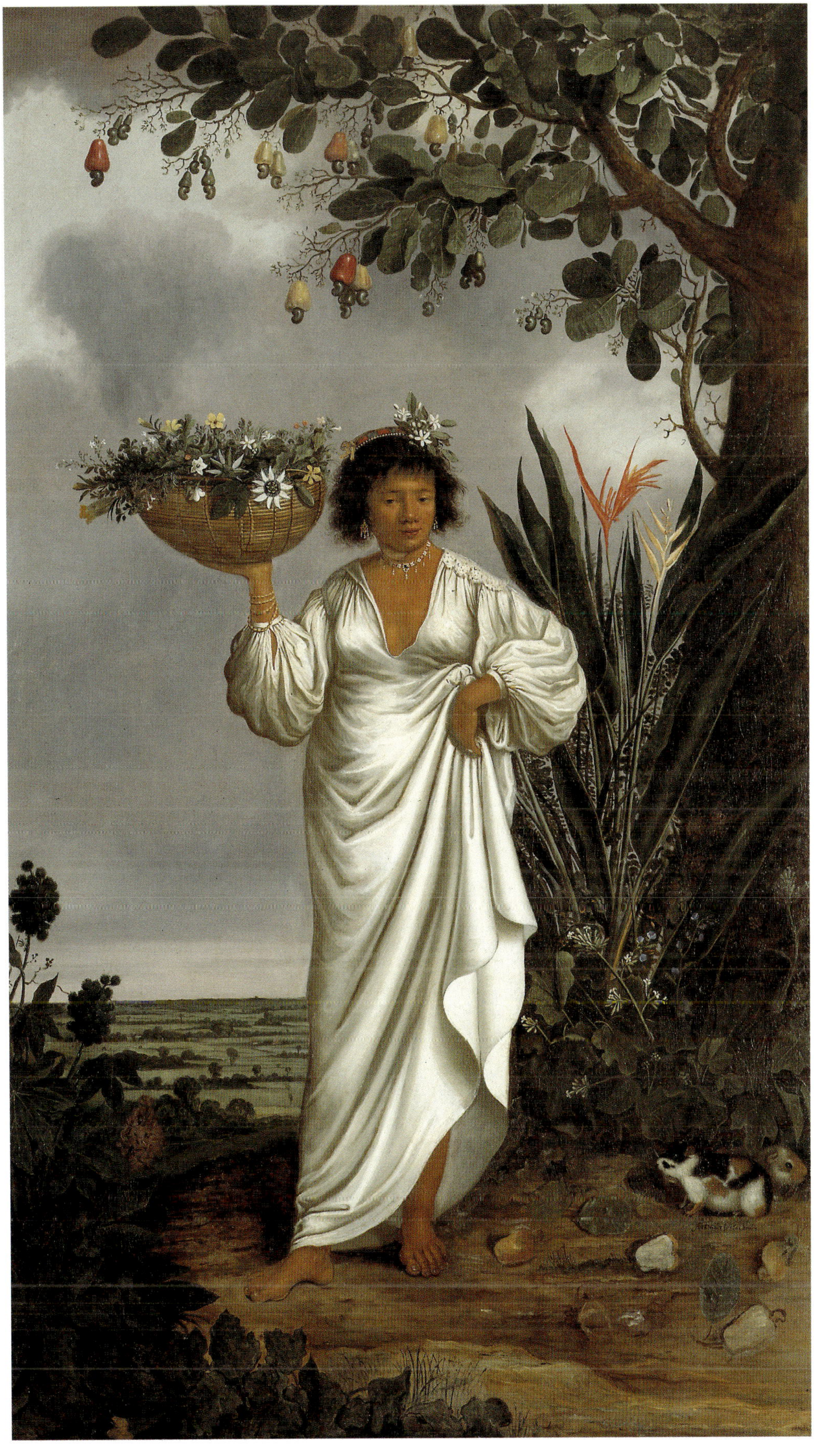

## Louisiana is a White Woman: Visualizing Louisiana in the Post-Reconstruction Poetic Imagination of Mary Ashley Townsend

The visual rhetoric of Coulon's *Spirit of Louisiana* echoes that voiced in the poem by Mary Ashley Townsend that was performed at the opening of the the New Orleans World Cotton Centennial Exposition (also called The World's Industrial and Cotton Centennial Exposition) held in New Orleans from 1884-1885.[39] The resonance makes sense given the fact that Townsend and Coulon were both founding members of the Southern Art Union, actively involved in the arts in New Orleans, and certainly knew each other's work.[40] Ostensibly aiming to strike a balance between the universal appeal necessary for an international event and the regional pride of hosting it, Townsend's poem imagines Louisiana as the embodiment of white femininity while expressing a curious and somewhat confusing combination of provincial chauvinism, global exoticism, and American national mythologies that expands the racial implications of that vision beyond the borders of the state.

With glowing references to the men who claimed and explored the Louisiana territory for European powers, Townsend offers her audience some historical context before describing a vision of personified Louisiana that conforms to Coulon's portrayal of white female beauty and confirms white colonial power:

*My gaze I lift about these palaced plains,*
*Where Peace her proudest victory maintains,*
*Remember those we never may forget,*
*And so the eye empyrean gains,*
*De Soto smiles and Joliet and Marquette;*

*And brave LaSalle, and Iberville are there,*
*This consummation of their dreams to share;*
*They, with Bienville greet us from on high,*
*To all the honors of this day co-heir—*
*Such names, such deed, such heroes never die.*

*Here smiles their fair-faced Louisiana, lo!...*
*With lips that with their gladness overflow,*
*And welcomes for the world in her sweet hands!*

*The blood of Spain is warm in upon her cheek,*
*The fire of France is sparkling in her eye,*
*And Creole graces sit upon her brow,*
*And tune the witching cadence of her voice…*[41]

Moreover, with verses like "Her opulent magnolia, year by year/Rebuilds its ivory village," Townsend goes on to link this vision directly to the Louisiana landscape in ways that rhetorically reiterate its whiteness, culminating in the description of "that white blessing which God gave the world,/The bounteous cotton, in ripened grace,/[which] O'er regal acres spreads its frostless snow." In these passages, Townsend casts her vision of Louisianan whiteness in decidedly local terms, but elsewhere she uses the occasion of the Cotton Centennial Exposition to present this Louisiana on a global stage and in terms that can be understood as simultaneously international and, importantly given the post-Civil War context, distinctly American.

Weaving references to such exotic images as "the turbaned brows of Pharaohs" and the watchful "Hindu…Beside the Brahmin temple's sacred calms" throughout the poem, Townsend makes "Cotton, that ruler of each hemisphere," the connective thread that binds the world together as it's cultivation expands:

*With steady step it went,*
*Creeping, creeping,*
*While the world was sleeping,*
*Like to some conscious blessing sent from God,*
*Gently across the hemisphere it trod,*
*Until it passed*
*To Freedom's all embracing arms at last…*
*Sweep o'er the lands and seas,—*
*And from earth's battlements*
*While all the world assents,*
*Hangs its white banner—over the Continents.*[42]

In her poetic imagination, this global empire of cotton is defined by both the crop's material whiteness and by the divinely ordained blessings of white supremacy it spreads across the globe through colonialism as it "Hangs its white banner—over the Continents." Under this banner of whiteness, the figure of Louisiana both reigns over and stands in for this global cotton kingdom. Verbally invoking the allegorical goddess that Coulon depicts, Townsend's "radiant Louisiana—peerless queen—/Crowned in all her loveliest array,/In roses sandaled—robed in living green, A smile on her red mouth,—She stands for North and South,—/She stands for West and East,—" relies on the universalizing aspect of allegory to help make the miraculous local/global double duty of this whiteness seem possible.[43]

## Cicum-Navigating this Argument: Race-ing Louisiana, Race-ing the Nation

In addition to its local/global implications, this last cadence regarding our fair Louisiana—her ability to stand for North and South, West and East—can also be understood in a national context, returning this discussion to where it started. Henry David Thoreau imagined an America in which Northeast and West, to the explicit exclusion of the South, stood for the nation, but Townsend envisions Louisiana, embodiment of the South, standing for all. In this postbellum moment, Louisiana's gleaming white image could represent the reunion of the nation so recently rent by war. Not coincidentally, Townsend opens her poem with an invocation to "…Freedom!, gentle mother of us all" and also alludes to "Sweet Liberty! thy blazing torch afar," an obvious reference to the Statue of Liberty.[44] Although the monument would not be installed until almost a year and half after the close of the Cotton Centennial Exposition, it had been planned for over a decade; its design, patented in 1879, was well known; and the completed arm and torch were displayed at the Centennial Exposition in Philadelphia in 1876 (and remained on display in the U.S. until 1882).

Significantly, the Statue of Liberty signified more than just America's dedication to liberty and the ideals of democracy. Originally proposed by Édouard René Lefèbvre de Laboulaye, president of the French Anti-Slavery Society, the Statue of Liberty also ostensibly commemorated the recent abolition of slavery as a demonstration of American commitment to these ideals, a fact signaled by the broken shackles under Lady Liberty's feet. However, this event finds no place in Townsend's poem, which conjures nostalgic images of slavery as "shouts of exultation/Now from the old plantation" accompany "the music of the clicking of the hoes…of the merry cotton picking in the rows."[45] Moreover, as an American symbol, the allegorical figure of Lady Liberty, typically embodied in a white female form, repeats the pattern of white female figures displacing women of color as terrestrial surrogates that reify racially encoded geographies. Pre-colonization images of the Americas as embodied by a powerful Native American queen gave way, during the colonial period, to a less mighty but still brown American Indian princess imagined as the daughter of Britannia, but both of these were, in the end, replaced by white, neoclassical figures exemplified by the Statue of Liberty.[46]

Sculptor Edmonia Lewis's *The Marriage of Hiawatha* (1874; Fig. 15) represents an important interjection within this iconographical shift, and its display at the Cotton Centennial Exposition in New Orleans clearly positions it in dialogue with the tropes discussed in this essay that helped reify the racialization of space.[47] One of at least four works Lewis made in response to Henry Longfellow's romantic epic, *The Song of Hiawatha* (1855), the sculpture depicts a scene from the poem in which the main character, the Ojibwe warrior Hiawatha, marries Minnehaha, a Dakota woman, thereby sealing a union between their two warring peoples. Lewis strategically highlighted both her own African American and Ojibwe ancestry as necessary to promote her career, but, as Kirsten Pai Buick has shown, her neoclassical sculptures also deliberately disavowed easy correlations with her biography, challenging circulating stereotypes around race and gender.[48]

On the one hand, Lewis's *The Marriage of Hiawatha*, like Longfellow's poem, clearly reflected sentimental perceptions of Indigenous Americans through the stereotype of the Noble Savage. Moreover, interpreting Lewis's sculpture as unequivocally resistant is difficult given its connections to Longfellow's poem that, in addition to presenting the inter-ethnic marriage of Hiawatha and Minnehaha, also arguably portrays Hiawatha as unifying their two peoples in order to prepare them to accept white colonization. However, on the other hand, Lewis is in fact deploying marble, the very material used to form whiteness as the ideal, to depict a female figure who viewers would certainly have understood as brown. Here, rather than simply reproducing a neoclassical ideal of feminine beauty (understood almost exclusively as European), the superficially incongruous use of white marble underscores Minnehaha's racial and ethnic difference while arguably including

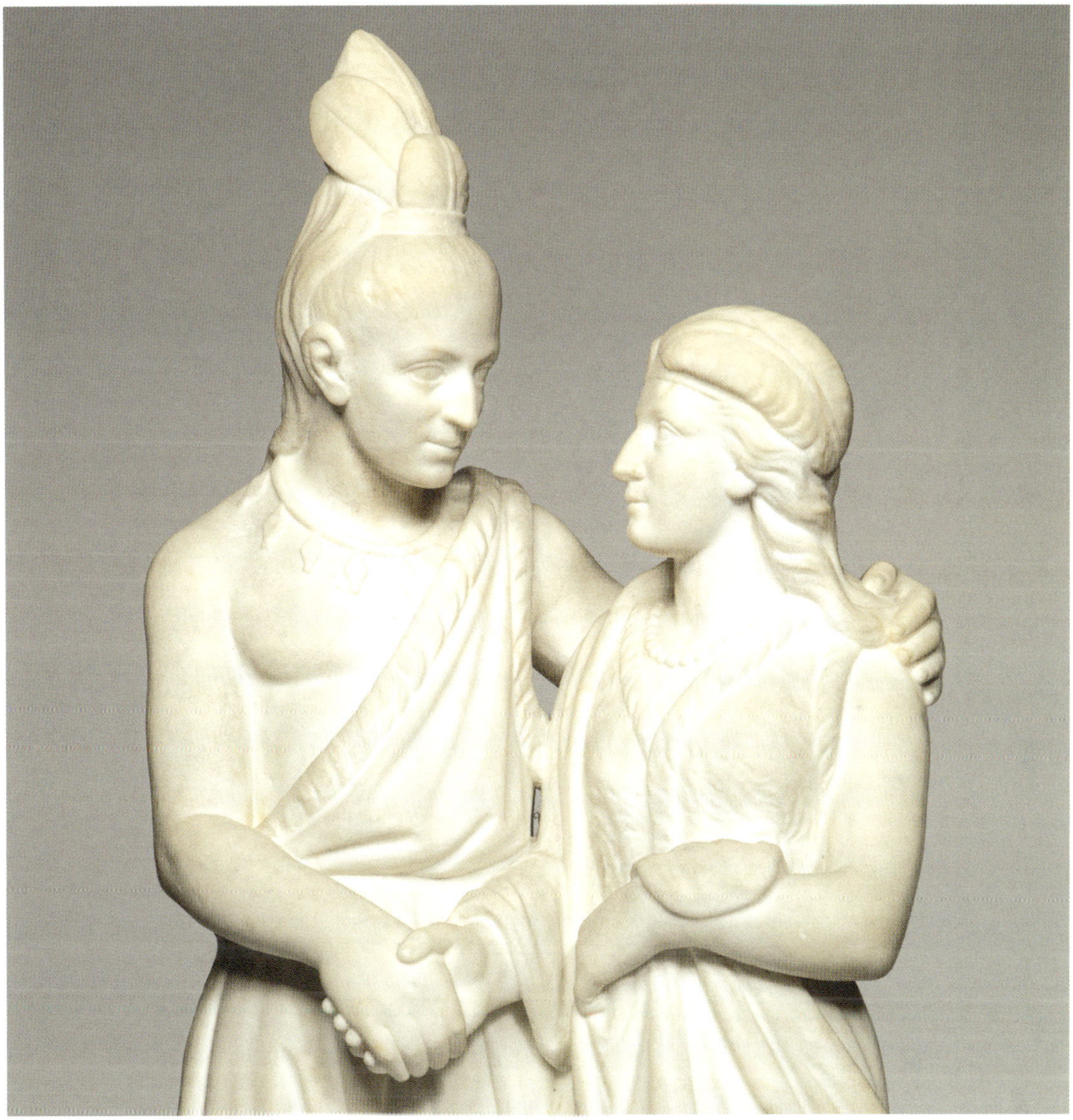

**Fig. 15**
Edmonia Lewis, *The Marriage of Hiawatha*, 1874, White marble, 31 ½ inches, Walter O. Evans Collection of African American Art

her within the realm of that ideal. Lewis's *The Marriage of Hiawatha*, therefore, can be understood as subtly recoding the symbolism of neoclassical sculpture and its marble materiality, revealing whiteness itself to be a construction—a material and aesthetic process—used to extend the racialized geography of American nation-building.

It is tempting to imagine Lewis's sculpture standing in silent opposition to works at the Cotton Centennial Exposition that, like Townsend's poem, promoted a white-supremacist vision of the United States. However, exhibited in the Exposition's "Colored Department", its ability to do so was ironically limited by its display in a racially segregated and circumscribed space. Considering Lewis's sculpture in the context of this discussion, however, underscores how the united America Townsend claims for the fair Louisiana in her poem does not represent liberty and justice for all; instead she recodes all America as a space of white supremacy. Moreover, in this context, with her spiky swamp grass crown that echoes Bartholdi's monument (installed in New York Harbor less than a decade before she was painted), it is hard not to see Coulon's pearly white *Spirit of Louisiana* as other than a Louisiana Lady Liberty, encoding the state—and, by extension, the nation—as a space of white supremacy.

1 Thoreau, Henry David. "Walking," in *Essays: A Fully Annotated Edition*. Jeffrey S. Cramer, ed. (New Haven: Yale University Press, 2013), 259. http://www.jstor.org/stable/j.ctt32bwkq. Accessed July 4, 2018.

2 Angela L. Miller, *The Empire of the Eye: Landscape Representation and American Cultural Politics* (Ithaca, NY: Cornell University Press, 1993), 12.

3 See Joseph Roach, *Cities of the Dead: Circum-Atlantic Performance* (New York: Columbia University Press, 1996).

4 This approach is informed by Katherine Manthorne's work on the plantation as a "distinctive New World institution". Manthorne advocates for comparative scholarship that attends to local specificity while viewing these sites through a Pan-American or hemispheric lens. Katherine Manthorne, "Plantation Pictures in the Americas, circa 1880: Land, Power, and Resistance," *Nepantla: Views from South 2*, no. 2 (Durham, NC: Duke University Press, 2001), 321-332.

5 LeMoyne D'Iberville, Pierre. *Iberville's Gulf Journals*. Richebourg Gailland McWilliams, ed. and trans., (Tuscaloosa, AL: University of Alabama Press, 1981) 56; emphasis added.

6 Perpetuated in a diverse array of sources including travel narratives, natural history texts, and poetry, the identification of the New World with prelapsarian abundance flourished in the colonialist imagination. In her analysis of Georgian poetry, Beth Fowkes Tobin observes the frequent references to tropical lands as Arcadias, suggesting them as Edenic lands "where agricultural abundance is produced without labor." See Beth Fowkes Tobin, *Colonizing Nature: The Tropics in British Arts and Letters, 1760-1820* (Philadelphia: University of Pennsylvania Press, 2005), 34. See also, Mia L. Bagneris, *Colouring the Caribbean: Race and the art of Agostino Brunias* (Manchester, UK: Manchester University Press, 2018).

7 Bagneris, 134.

8 For more discussion of the transportability of picturesque aesthetic practices, see Malcolm Andrews, *The Search for the Picturesque: Landscape Aesthetics and Tourism in Britain, 1760-1800* (Stanford, CA: Stanford University Press, 1989); Krista A Thompson, *An Eye for the Tropics: Tourism, Photography, and Framing the Caribbean Picturesque* (Durham, NC: Duke University Press, 2006); Romita Ray, *Under the Banyan Tree: Relocating the Picturesque in British India* (New Haven, CT: Yale University Press, 2012).

9 Jill H. Casid, *Sowing Empire: Landscape and Colonization* (Minneapolis, MN: University of Minnesota Press, 2005).

10 Bagneris, 105.

11 For biographical information on Beckford of Somerly, see Tim Barringer, "Picturesque Prospects and the Labor of the Enslaved," in *Art and Emancipation in Jamaica: Isaac Mendes Belisario and His Worlds*, Tim Barringer, Gillian Forrester, and Barbaro Martinez-Ruiz, eds. (New Haven, CT: Yale Center for British Art in association with Yale University Press, 2007), 42-44.

12 Timothy Barringer describes the effect of the work precisely, observing that 'Robertson's glamorous, enslaved Afro-Jamaican woman, as seen by a metropolitan audience in London, would perhaps have signified a Rousseauian figure of natural beauty.' ibid., 45.

13 For discussion of Clark, see Barringer cited above and Ann Bermingham, *Landscape and Ideology: The English Rustic Tradition, 1740-1860* (Berkeley, CA: University of California Press, 1986).

14 Manthorne makes use of the term "colonial garden" to describe the plantation more generally although she does not explicitly clarify her rationale for this precise turn of phrase. Here, we borrow the term to connote the idea of management and cultivation implicit in many Louisiana plantation landscapes.

15 Anglo-American Museum, "The Louisiana Landscape, 1800-1969" (Baton Rouge: 1969), p. 19 quoted in Estill Curtis Pennington, *Downriver: Currents of Style in Louisiana Painting 1800-1950* (Gretna: Pelican Publishing, 1991), 65.

16 Pennington, 65.

17 Alfred Waud, *Every Saturday Magazine*, July 15, 1871.

18 David Miller, *Dark Eden: The Swamp in Nineteenth-Century American Culture* (Cambridge, UK: Cambridge University Press, 1989), 47–76.

19 If we take the title at face value, Marshall J. Smith's *Bayou Plantation* (circa 1879-1890) offers a possible exception. However, the image, credited elsewhere as *Bayou Farm* (see, for example, Pennington, 81) hardly corresponds to the picture of a plantation in the popular imagination nor does it represent that type of image that most planters would have commissioned. Moreover, the post-Emancipation date assigned to the work places outside of the types of plantation images we discuss here.

20 For images of plantations elsewhere in the American South that correspond to Persac's serene "colonial garden" aesthetic, see, for example, Edward Savages images of Mount Vernon, circa 1787-1792.

21 H Parrott Bacot et al., *Marie Adrien Persac: Louisiana Artist* (Baton Rouge, LA: LSU Press, 2000).

22 These features are identified on the Louisiana State Museum's webpage for Marie Adrien Persac. See: https://www.crt.state.la.us/louisiana-state-museum/collections/visual-art/sculpture/. Accessed June 17, 2019.

23 Caitlin Rosenthal, *Accounting for Slavery: Masters and Management* (Cambridge, MA: Harvard University Press, 2018).

24 Roberta Sokolitz, "Picturing the Plantation," in *Landscape of Slavery: The Plantation in American Art*, Angela D Mack and Stephen G. Hoffus, eds. (Columbia, SC: University of South Carolina Press, 2008), 52.

25 Pennington, 111.

26 Daina Ramey Berry, *The Price for Their Pound of Flesh: The Value of the Enslaved, from Womb to Grave, in the Building of a Nation* (Boston,MA: Beacon Press, 2017).

27 Bagneris, 6-7.

28 Much of the language for this discussion is borrowed from Bagneris, 163-165.

29 See Bagneris, especially Chapter 3.

30 For more on the association of black and mixed-race women with New World land, see, for example, Bagneris's *Colouring the Caribbean*; Kay Dian Kriz, "Marketing Mulatresses in Agostino Brunias's West Indian Scenes" in *Slavery, Sugar, and the Culture of Refinement: Picturing the British West Indies, 1700-1840* (New Haven, CT: Yale University Press, 2008); and Patricia Mohammed, "Gendering the Caribbean Picturesque," *Caribbean Review of Gender Studies* 1.1 (April 2007): 1-30.

31 For a comprehensive treatment of the *Mãe Preta* in visual culture, see Kimberly Cleveland, *Black Woman Slaves Who Nourished a Nation: Artistic Renderings of Wet Nurses in Brazil*, (Amherst, NY: Cambria Press, 2019).

32 Marcus Wood, *Black Milk: Imagining Slavery in the Visual Cultures of Brazil and America* (Oxford, UK: Oxford University Press, 2013), 2.

33 Emily West with R.L. Knight, "Mothers' Milk: Slavery, Wet-Nursing, and Black and White Women in the Antebellum South," *Journal of Southern History* Vol. 83.1 (February 2017): 37-68.

34 Bagneris, 147-148.

35 ibid., 149.

36 Casting her coy gaze over a bare shoulder, *Spirit of Louisiana* is also reminiscent of Jacques Guillaume Lucien Amans's *Creole with a Red Headdress* (circa 1840), now in the Historic New Orleans Collection. Given Amans reputation and Coulon's deep and long-term involvement in establishing the New Orleans art scene in the nineteenth century, it's likely that Coulon had seen the now well-known painting of a woman of African descent in an off-the-shoulder white blouse.

37 For a comprehensive discussion of Eckhout's painting in Brazil, see Rebecca Brienen, *Visions of Savage of Paradise: Albert Eckhout, Court Painter in Colonial Dutch Brazil* (Amsterdam: Amsterdam University Press, 2006). For discussion of *Mameluca*, including its clear status as a "dusky Brazilian Flora", see pp. 162-168, from which much the information we develop in this essay was drawn.

38 It does not appear, however, that this or any other work by Albert Eckhout was the "Eckhout" singled out on April 12, 1852 by the Daily Crescent as a highlight of a current exhibition of "One of the choicest collections of oil paintings and engravings ever on exhibition in New Orleans." The free exhibition, held in the French Quarter on Common Street, was sponsored by the Southern Art Union, of which Coulon was a founding and active member, but the work on display was a copied rendition of *The Storming of Chepultepec* by a contemporary German artist also named Eckhout (See *The New Orleans Daily Crescent*, March 15, 1852 and *The Daily Union*, August 3, 1852). The authors thank Dr. Adrian Anagnost helping us to confirm this.

39 Mrs. Mary Ashley Townsend a.k.a. Xariffa, "The Centennial Poem" in Herbet S. Fairall, *The World's Industrial and Cotton Exposition, New Orleans, 1884-85* (Iowa City, IA: Republican Publishing Company, 1885): 23-28; accessed via Google Books June 08, 2019.

40 For more on Townsend, who was a something of a grand-dame of the New Orleans arts scene and a very well known and widely published poet, see Miki Pfeffer, "Exhibiting Women: Sectional Confrontation and Reconciliation in the Woman's Department at the World's Exposition, New Orleans, 1884-85" (2006). University of New Orleans Theses and Dissertations. 339; https://scholarworks.uno.edu/td/33. Accessed June 20, 2019.

41 Townsend, 24.

42 ibid., 26.

43 ibid., 25.

44 ibid., 23.

45 ibid., 26.

46 For more on this phenomenon, see E. McClung Fleming, "The American Image as Indian Princes, 1765-1783" *Winterthur Portfolio*, Vol. 2 (1965): 65-81, and Yasmin Sabina Khan, *Enlightening the World: The Creation of the Statue of Liberty* (Ithaca, NY: Cornell University Press, 2010), 93-96.

47 Deborah C. Pollack, *Visual Art and the Urban Evolution of the New South*, (Columbia, SC: University of South Carolina Press, 2015), 111-160.

48 Our brief discussion of Edmonia Lewis cannot do sufficient justice to her artistic work, nor her complicated career. For more on Edmonia Lewis, see Kirsten Pai Buick, *Child of the Fire: Mary Edmonia Lewis and the Problem of Art History's Black and Indian Subject* (Durham, NC: Duke University Press, 2010).

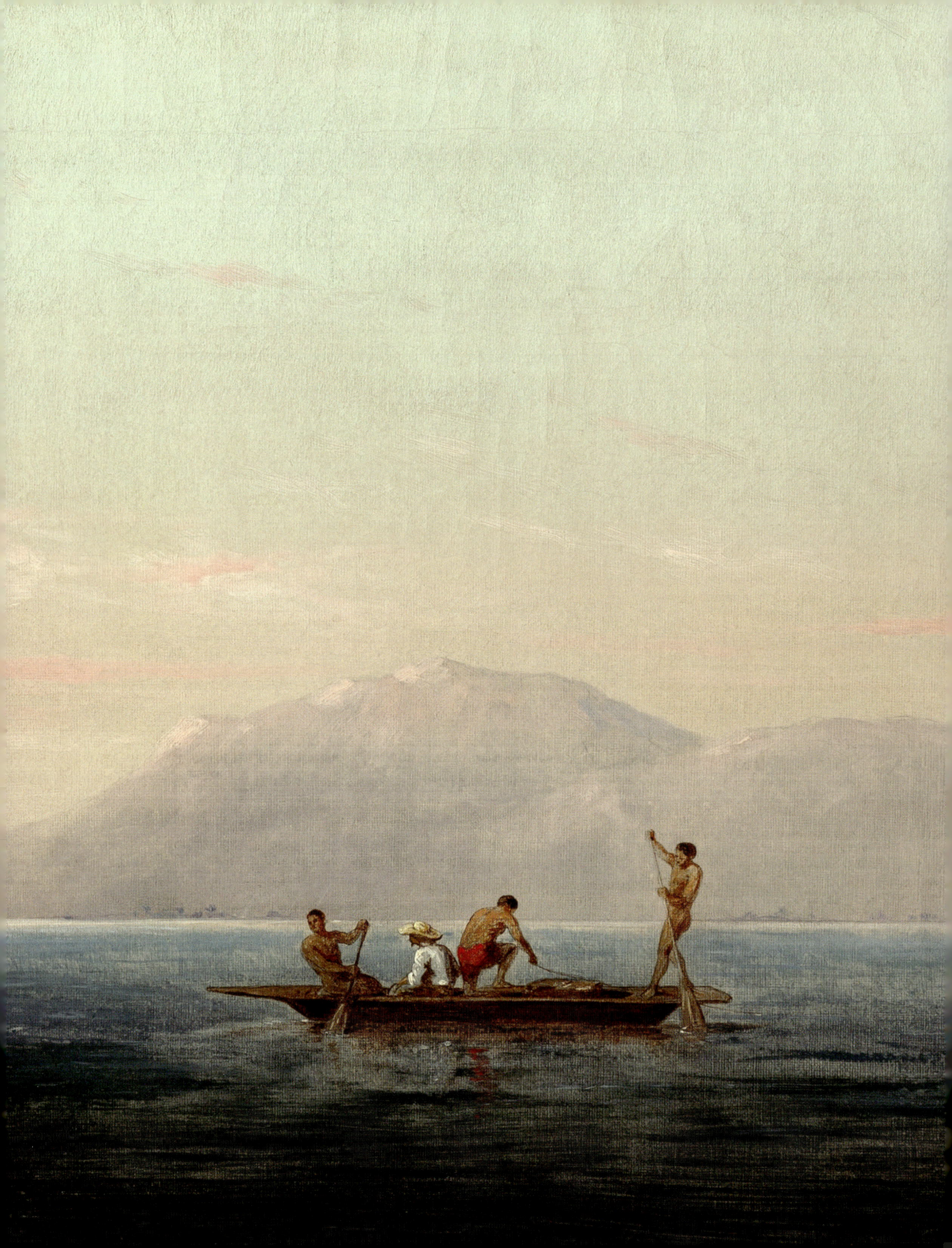

# Sister Republics: Mexico at the New Orleans World Cotton Centennial Exposition

Aurora Yaratzeth Avilés García

The 1884, New Orleans World Cotton Centennial Exposition (also called The World's Industrial and Cotton Centennial Exposition) brought together art, industry, and innovation from countries all over the world. Organized around the centennial anniversary of the first shipment of cotton from the United States to Europe, the Cotton Centennial Exposition sought to show New Orleans's continued relevance as a center for global trade in the wake of the Civil War and the aftermath of Reconstruction. According to its promotional materials, the Cotton Centennial Exposition represented "the resources, products, manufactures, arts and inventions of the New World and resuscitated South."[1] Crucial to this vision of a "resuscitated South" was repositioning New Orleans not as one of the southernmost cities in the United States—mired in the histories of slavery and the plantation economies of the past—but rather as the northernmost city in Latin America: a gateway for new cultural and economic connections between the United States and Central and South America. To achieve this goal, New Orleans turned to the Mexican government, inviting Mexico to create the largest and most elaborate art installations and agricultural and horticultural displays by any foreign nation. Highlighting the cultural and geographic connections between New Orleans and Mexico, the resultant displays emphasized the economic and political benefits of an alliance between the two places:

> *We are its nearest neighbors, more similar in governmental institutions, more sympathetic in customs and manners, and more closely identified in business interests than with any other section of the United States [...] there is every argument in favour of an entente cordiale between Mexico and New Orleans, and thence with the Mississippi Valley, that no other city or part of the country can claim [...] The cultivation of trade interests, then, with our sister Republic, is a duty of paramount importance. Mexico, Central and South America [...] by all the laws of commerce belong to us in New Orleans.*[2]

Referred to throughout promotional materials from the Cotton Centennial Exposition as "sister republics," Mexico's contributions to the fair stretched across six different buildings, and included an exhibition of Mexican paintings, displays of horticultural and mineralogical resources, and industrial displays designed to emphasize the rich resources of the country. "Mexico has sent in profusion the products of her forest, mines, waters, garden, orchards, fields and mills, in a thousand varied and beautiful forms," wrote Louisiana Governor John

**Fig. 1**
Judah LeVasseur, *Fishing on Lake Managua, Nicaragua*, circa 1840, Oil on canvas, 31 ½ x 21 ½ inches (framed), Private Collection, Image courtesy of Heritage Auctions.

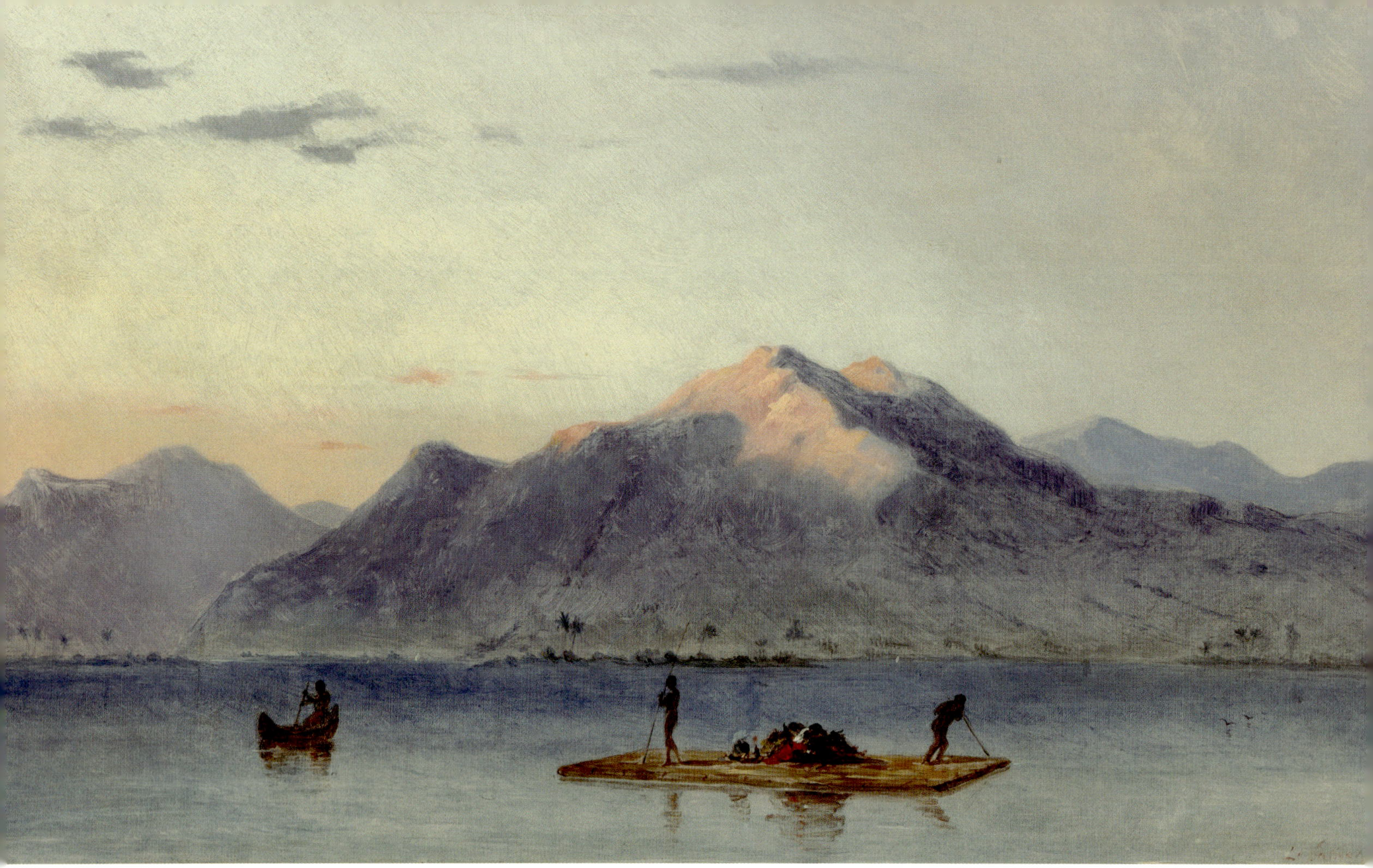

McEnery. "The results will strengthen the bonds of amity between the two republics, which have similar histories and a glorious common destiny."[3] Tying New Orleans's future to trade with Central and South America, the Cotton Centennial Exposition sought to remake the city—and reimagine its landscape—by and through these new connections to Central and South America.

While strong commercial and cultural ties between New Orleans and Central America had existed since the Spanish occupation of Louisiana's territories from 1763 to 1801, Mexico's presentation at the Cotton Centennial Exposition represented something new. While no paintings specifically of Mexico by artists living in New Orleans are known to have survived, several by artists that travelled to other parts of Central and South America—likely via Mexico—do still exist. One example is a recently rediscovered pair of paintings by the French artist Judah LeVasseur, who lived in New Orleans from 1837 to 1842. During that time, LeVasseur appears to have travelled to points throughout Central and South America, and his pendant paintings of Nicaragua [circa 1840; Figs. 1 and 2] were almost certainly painted on a voyage to Central America that he embarked on while he was living in New Orleans.[4] Among the earliest known depictions of anywhere in Central or South America made by an artist living in the United States, these works picture the region as vast, unexplored territory, and place LeVasseur—who appears to show himself being rowed into shore in one of the paintings—in a position of both visual and political mastery. It was, in part, this longstanding sense of ownership that the organizers of the Cotton Centennial Exposition drew upon in making Central and South America such a crucial element of New Orleans's future.

**Fig. 2**
Judah LeVasseur, *Fishing on Lake Managua, Nicaragua*, circa 1840, Oil on canvas, 31 ½ x 21 ½ inches (framed), Private Collection, Image courtesy of Heritage Auctions.

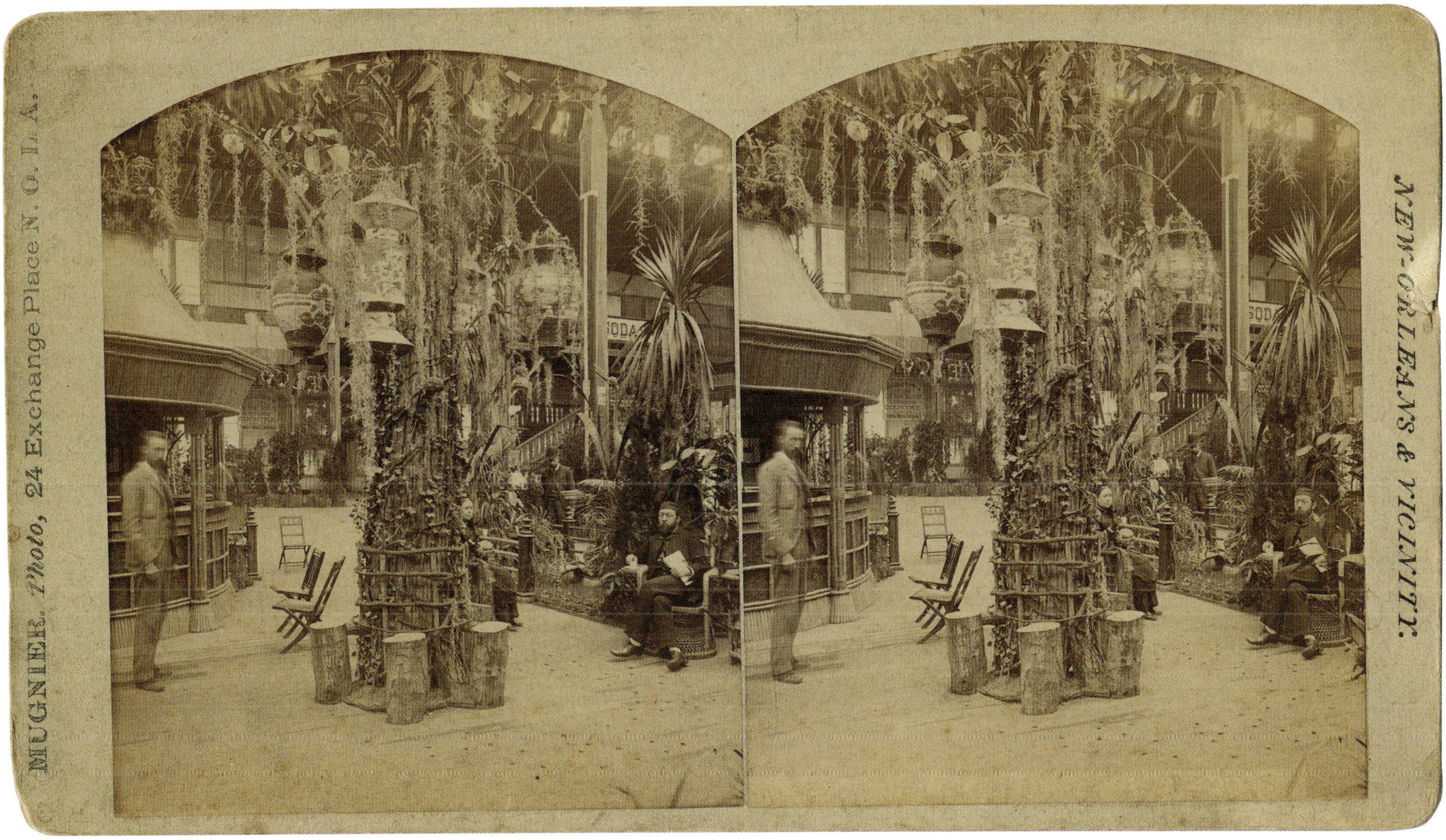


**Fig. 3**
George Francois Mugnier, *North, Central and South American Exposition*, 1884-1886, Photoprint mounted on board, 3 7/8 x 7 inches, The Historic New Orleans Collection, 1998.93.5 i, ii

New Orleans's goals for the Cotton Centennial Exposition aligned with Mexico's own objectives in participating in the fair, which was to foster new political and commercial partnerships—especially with New Orleans—and reposition itself on the world stage. On May 9th 1885, Mariano Bárcena, the representative of the Mexican chief commissioner at the Cotton Centennial Exposition, wrote a report expressing his thoughts concerning what the countries taking part in the Cotton Centennial Exposition would gain from participation in which he highlighted the "show of natural resources" as integral to Mexico's objectives:

> *A country that appears organized and which displays the results of its efforts in education and labour, deserves respect and consideration from the whole world [...] The show of its natural resources in a World Exhibition, is not only an instrument to show the elements used in its industry and other objectives, but which makes other countries interested in using the same products, thus increasing the consumption sphere and the advantages of larger production.*[5]

This emphasis on showing the country's natural resources as a way to encourage new political alliances is perhaps why geographer, geologist, and engineer Mariano Bárcena was selected by Mexico as one of the principal organizers of the Cotton Centennial Exposition. Working closely with the Mexican government, Bárcena emphasized how better knowledge of land and its elements would advance scientific progress, as well as industrial development, and serve as a basis for increasing Mexico's international commerce and trade.[6] Alongside fellow geographer Antonio García Cubas, Bárcena played an important role in the production, selection, and organization of the objects part of Mexico's installations. These installations included landscape paintings alongside maps, horticultural products, and raw materials from many different parts of the country. As demonstrated by a stereographic photograph of the North, Central, and South American exhibition within the Cotton Centennial Exposition's Horticultural Hall (1885; Fig. 3), these installations included plant species, trees, and cut timber among many other elements that tied each country's identity to the presentation of its natural resources. In service of this goal, the Mexican organizers created a large atlas specifically for the Cotton Centennial Exposition. Designed by García Cubas, the *Atlas pintoresco é histórico de los Estados Unidos Mexicanos* (*Picturesque and Historic Atlas of the Mexican United States*) presented small vignettes of natural and urban landscapes alongside maps and statistical data, offering an illustrated statistical summary of Mexico's landscape and culture. Together, the vignettes in the charts of the *Atlas pintoresco* and the data it presented linked Mexico's identity to its land and resources. The imagery also emphasized how Louisiana could connect to these landscapes through both art and trade, as part of a shared vision for a new union between both places.

## Represented by their Contents: Mapping the Mexican Landscape

Planning for Mexico's exhibitions and installations for the fair began shortly after Mexico received the invitation to participate in October 1881. From the start of planning, the Mexican Ministry understood the importance of presenting a new vision of Mexico, and began working on a book that would introduce American audiences to Mexico's history, government, flora and fauna, mining areas, transport network, education, trade, army, and navy. They worked with Antonio García Cubas to adapt his *Cuadro geográfico, estadístico, descriptivo é histórico de los Estados Unidos Mexicanos* (Geographic, Statistical, Descriptive and Historic Chart of the Mexican United States) for the Cotton Centennial Exposition.[7] The *Secretaría de Fomento* (Ministry of Development) published the book as a special edition to be shipped to New Orleans and distributed at the Cotton Centennial Exposition.[8] In 1884, the same year the *Cuadro geográfico* was published, García Cubas started working on the illustrations for the book, which became the *Atlas pintoresco*, which was published in 1885 by the printing house Debray Sucesores.[9] The volume contains thirteen chromolithographs that illustrate subjects broached by the *Cuadro geográfico.*[10] Each chart has a map at its center, with statistical data that is framed by vignettes representing landscapes, portraits, and urban scenes that illustrate the information presented in the book.

A document in the *Archivo General de la Nación* (General National Archive) confirms that, in October 1884, the publisher Debray Sucesores sent six charts from the *Atlas pintoresco, Carta de Instrucción Pública, Carta Hidrográfica, Carta Minera, Carta Orográfica, Carta Etnográfica* and *Carta Política* (Public Education Chart, Hydrographic Chart, Mining Chart, Orographic Chart, Ethnographic Chart, and Political Chart), to be put on display at the Cotton Centennial Exposition, likely the first six to be completed.[11] The chromolithographs of the *Atlas pintoresco* sent to New Orleans highlight the features Mexico seems to have most wanted to emphasize, chief among them its landscape. Porfirio Díaz, the chief commissioner in charge of managing Mexico's participation in the exhibition,

**Fig. 4 (top-left)**
Antonio García Cubas and Miguel R. Hernández or Vicente Calderón, *Carta política* (Political Chart) from Antonio García Cubas, *Atlas Pintoresco e Histórico de los Estados Unidos Mexicanos* (Mexico: Debray Sucesores Printing Press, 1885), 1885, Chromolithograph, 24 ¾ x 31 ½ inches, Library of Congress, Washington, D.C.

**Fig. 5 (top-right)**
Antonio García Cubas and Félix Parra, *Carta etnográfica* (Ethnographic Chart) from Antonio García Cubas, *Atlas Pintoresco e Histórico de los Estados Unidos Mexicanos* (Mexico: Debray Sucesores Printing Press, 1885), 1885, Chromolithograph, 24 ¾ x 31 ½ inches, Library of Congress, Washington, D.C.

**Fig. 6 (lower-left)**
Antonio García Cubas and Miguel R. Hernández or Vicente Calderón, *Carta orográfica* (Orographic Chart) from Antonio García Cubas, *Atlas Pintoresco e Histórico de los Estados Unidos Mexicanos* (Mexico: Debray Sucesores Printing Press, 1885), 1885, Chromolithograph, 24 ¾ x 31 ½ inches, Library of Congress, Washington, D.C.

**Fig. 7 (lower-right)**
Antonio García Cubas and Miguel R. Hernández or Vicente Calderón, *Carta hidrográfica* (Hydrographic Chart) from Antonio García Cubas, *Atlas Pintoresco e Histórico de los Estados Unidos Mexicanos* (Mexico: Debray Sucesores Printing Press, 1885), 1885, Chromolithograph, 24 ¾ x 31 ½ inches, Library of Congress, Washington, D.C.

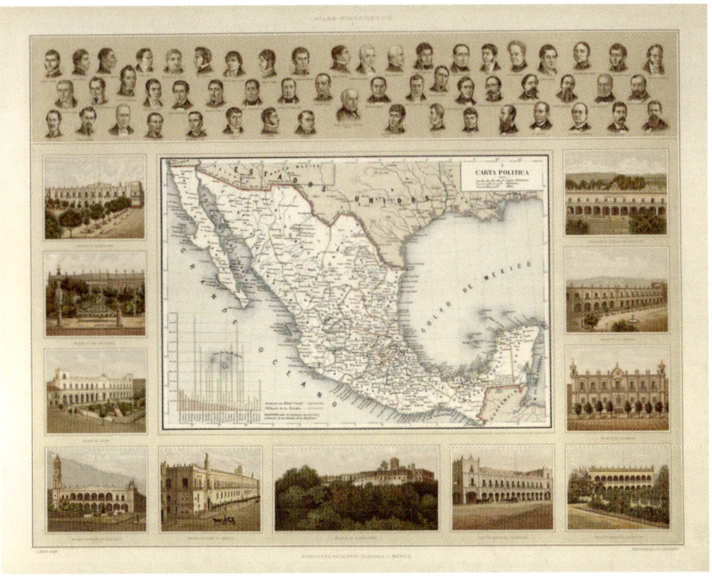

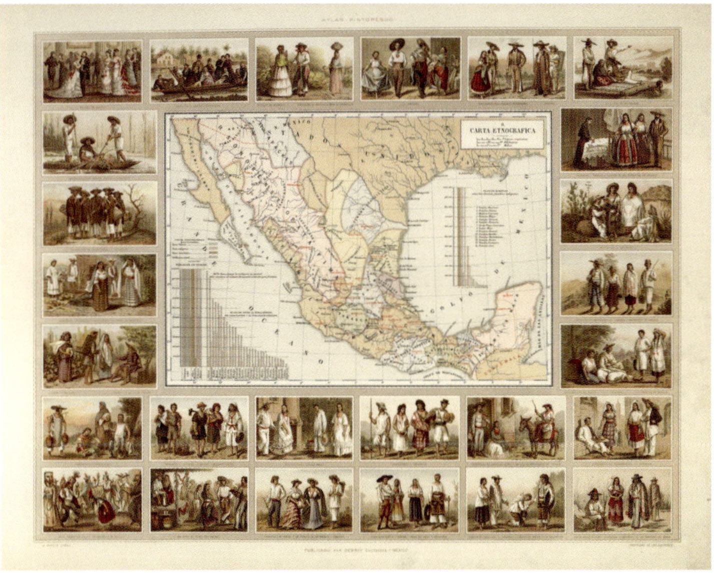

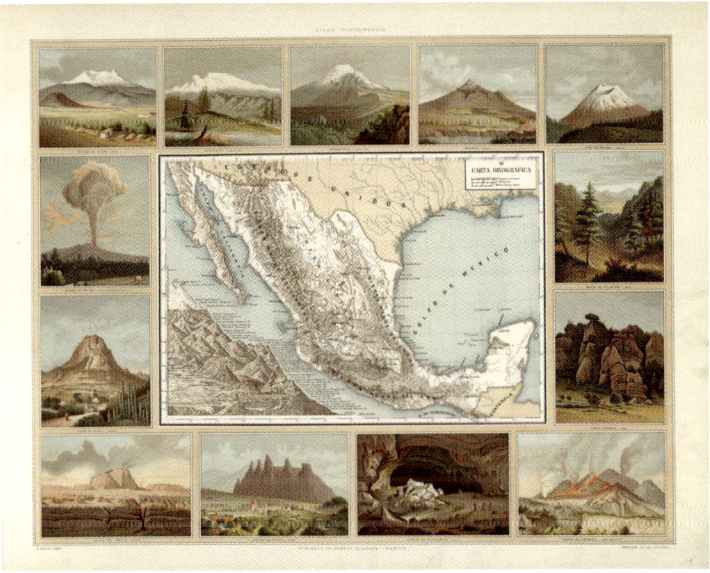

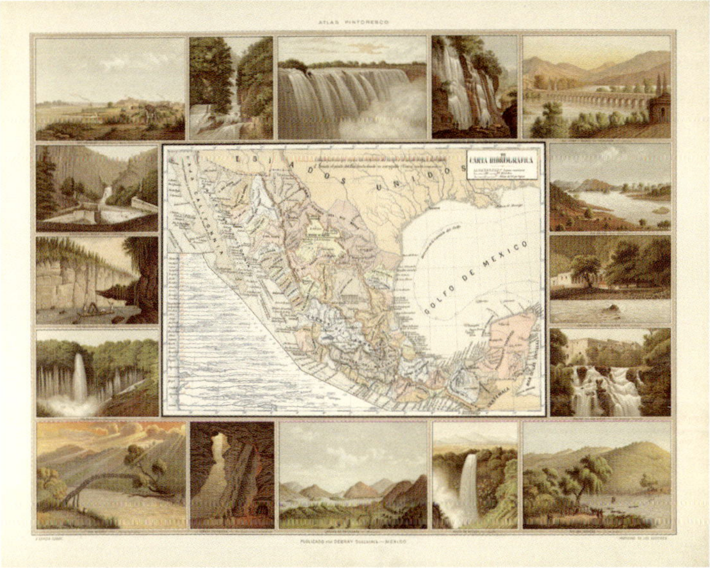

wrote of wanting to present Mexico as a modern, stable country, rich in resources. In order to showcase Mexico's great potential for development, he sought to present, "everything created by human intellect in its immense variety" in the installations and publications that accompanied the exhibition.[12] These goals were exemplified in Cubas's illustrations, such as his *Carta de Instrucción Pública* (Public Education Chart), which shows renderings of educational and arts institutions. One of these interiors portrays the gallery of modern painting at the School of Fine Arts, where works by teachers (Pelegrín Clavé, *La demencia de Isabel de Portugal*, circa 1855), as well as by the best pupils (José Obregón, *Giotto y Cimbaue*, 1857 and Joaquín Ramírez, *El cautiverio de los hebreos en Babilonia*, 1858) can be seen.[13] Other images, such as the *Carta Política* (Political Chart) (1884; Fig. 4), emphasize the stability and organization of Mexico's government and infrastructure, while still others, such as the *Carta etnográfica* (Ethnographic Chart) (1884; Fig. 5) show the different ethnic groups into which the population was divided, who are clearly ordered and classified in ways that recall the classifications of different landscape elements and minerals in subsequent

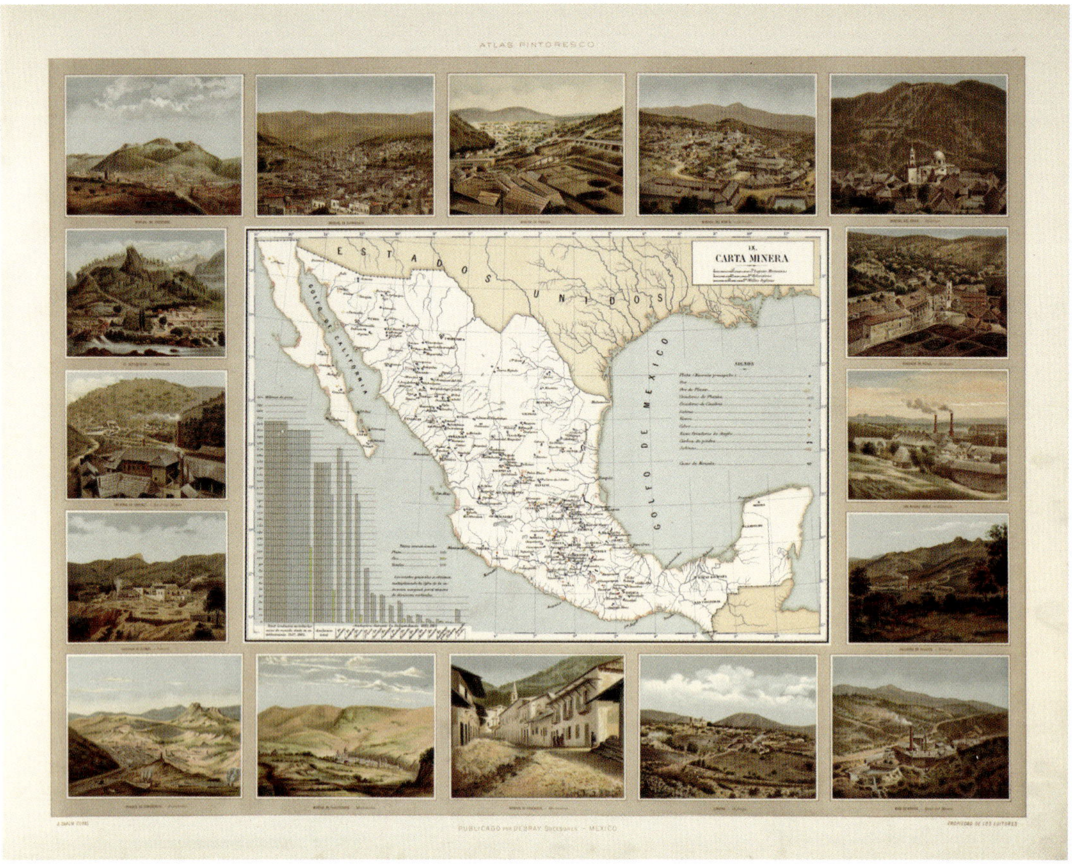


**Fig. 8**
Antonio García Cubas and Miguel R. Hernández or Vicente Calderón, *Carta minera* (Mining Chart) from Antonio García Cubas, *Atlas Pintoresco e Histórico de los Estados Unidos Mexicanos* (Mexico: Debray Sucesores Printing Press, 1885), 1885, Chromolithograph, 24 ¾ x 31 ½ inches, Library of Congress, Washington, D.C.

charts. In all of these illustrations, the maps seem to be deliberately designed so that New Orleans—and the Mississippi River, which is also clearly marked on the map—reach around the Gulf of Mexico as if to embrace—and connect—Mexico, Nicaragua, Honduras, and Guatemala with the Port of New Orleans.

Landscape, at best in the background of many of García Cubas's earlier illustrations, becomes the main feature of many of the vignettes produced for the Cotton Centennial Exposition. In the foreword to the *Atlas pintoresco*, García Cubas mentions two of the artists who made the watercolor vignettes for the Ethnographic Chart, Francisco Mendoza and Félix Parra. However, many of their watercolors were based on lithographs taken from the ethnographic chapter of García Cubas's early publication *The Republic of México in 1876.*[14] Comparing the images in the *Carta etnográfica* to these earlier illustrations, it is clear that the artists added landscape backdrops to these earlier scenes. In the vignette "*Mixtecos-Oaxaca*" for instance, the figures are presented against a background landscape typical of the Mixtec region, with cacti and maguey fields, which differs from the representation of the same figures in *The Republic of México in 1876*, in which they lack any context.

This is particularly true of the *Carta orográfica* (Orographic Chart) (1884; Fig. 6), which offers a visual description of the land and its physical features, and the *Carta hidrográfica* (Hydrographic Chart) (1884; Fig. 7), which displays the main waterways of the country. The Hydrographic Chart emphasizes examples of the infrastructure that enabled the transit of people and goods along the rivers and its potential for trade development, such as the "*Puente Grande*" in the state of Jalisco, which can be seen in the vignette "*Río Lerma y*

*Puente de Tololotlan.*" In his foreword, García Cubas also acknowledges Miguel R. Hernández and Vicente Calderón's work in creating the landscape watercolors upon which many of the vignettes in all the charts of the *Atlas* were based. These artists based their own work, in turn, on artworks by landscape painters living and working in Mexico, like the Italian painter Eugenio Landesio, who was a lecturer in landscape painting at the San Carlos Academy from 1855 to 1873, as well as José María Velasco and Luis Coto, who were both students of Landesio. Many of the landscapes in the vignettes of these charts were already connected to scientific and industrial development, and are related to drawings Velasco and Coto made for scientific and government publications. One vignette, for instance, is based off of a drawing of the Ceboruco volcano made by Velasco in 1871 as draftsman for the magazine *La Naturaleza* of the *Sociedad Mexicana de Historia Natural* (Mexican Society of Natural History), which now belongs to the *Museo Nacional de Arte* (National Museum of Art) in Mexico City. Besides being published in other scientific works, such as the *Tratado de Geología* by Mariano Bárcena in 1885, this work was reproduced in the Orographic Chart of the *Atlas*.

Other vignettes in the *Atlas* are based on drawings produced by Velasco and Coto during an expedition to Metlaltoyuca in Puebla in 1865, in which Antonio García Cubas also took part. During this trip, Velasco drew natural wonders such as the Necaxa Waterfall, which also appears in the Hydrographic Chart. In his journals, Velasco describes the waterfall as surrounded by a forest of "enormous ferns, among forests of Liquidambar trees of considerable height."[15] Unlike the drawing by Velasco published in the memoir of the expedition, the vignette in the *Atlas* offers a detailed representation of the vegetation surrounding the waterfall, which makes it possible to identify many of the species mentioned by Velasco in his memoir.[16] The vignette "*Río Necaxa,*" made after Luis Coto's drawing *Puente formado de bejucos en el río de Necaxa*, also offers a detailed representation of Mexico's landscape features and waterways, showing the great diversity of the country's landscape and vegetation, and highlighting the rivers and waterways that could enable the flow of the landscape's resources out of the country.

This idea of extraction—the movement of resources out of the landscape and into the flow of international trade—underlies many of the landscape representations in the *Atlas*, but perhaps none more than the *Carta minera* (Mining Chart) (1884; Fig. 8). Some of the vignettes even show the mining *haciendas,* or estates, probably as a reminder of the protection the federal government would grant the foreign investors, "Attention to that shall greatly increase, the spirit of enterprising will be encouraged, and those States which, through special laws have offered to protect the exploitation of the mines on their territory [...] can see that the right time has come for many of them to fulfil their legitimate wishes."[17] The vignette "*Hacienda de Regla,*" likely designed after Eugenio Landesio's 1857 painting *Patio de la Hacienda de Regla*, offers an aerial perspective or a "bird's eye view" seemingly designed to offer visual mastery of the landscape and its resources. Díaz's government did grant tax exemptions and subsidies in order to attract investment, and by the beginning of the twentieth century, North American companies ran approximately 70% of the metal industry in Mexico.[18]

Showcasing Mexico's mineral resources was so important to the organizers of the Cotton Centennial Exposition that they constructed a special building for this particular

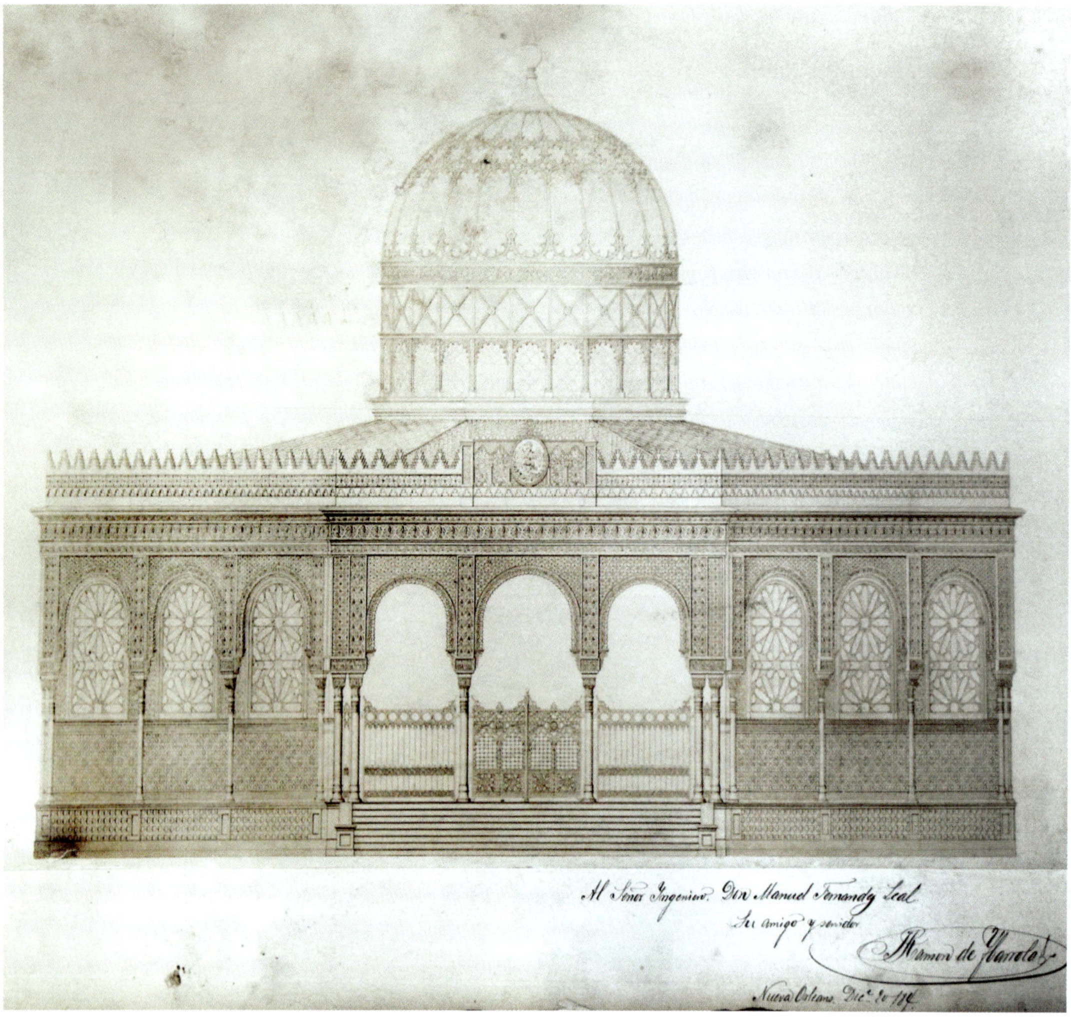

**Fig. 9**
Ramón de Ibarrola, *Kiosko Morisco*, 1884, Albumen silver print (photograph from original drawing), 17 1/3 x 21 1/4 inches, Acervo Histórico del Palacio de Minería, Fondo fotográfico Facultad de Ingeniería, Universidad Nacional Autónoma de México.

purpose, known as the *Kiosko Morisco,* or Moorish Pavilion (1884; Fig. 9), built by Ramón Ibarrola (1841-1925).[19] As Díaz himself explained, "The field of mining, rich and varied, attracts the attention of the experts in it, and the capitals from different parts of the world are getting ready to establish negotiations to move and extract the vast treasures hidden under the earth."[20] Constructed as a persuasive invitation to foreign capital interested in mining, this pavilion astonished New Orleans audiences with its elaborate decoration and mineralogical displays. One reviewer in New Orleans wrote of the "Saracenic building devoted to the display of minerology," alongside the rest of Mexico's displays, as "surpass[ing] all foreign exhibits in picturesque interest."[21] As Herbert S. Fairall described in the illustrated book he wrote about the Cotton Centennial Exposition:

> *The Octogonal Building: The Alhambra palace, under direction of Senor Giberto Crespo, a distinguished mining engineer from Mexico, was filled with minerals of rare beauty and value. Large glass cases, admirably suited for the purpose of the display, were ranged in two circles…[and] each mineral State of Mexico was represented by their contents […] In the center of the mineral palace, immediately under the dome, was built up a small pyramid of precious metals, and beneath the outer circle of cases were arrayed collections of beautiful shrubs from the tropics. The colored windows of the building showed the great display to most excellent advantage.*[22]

**Fig. 10**
Luis Coto, *Vista del Molino del Rey tomada desde Chapultepec*, 1858, Oil on canvas, 28 x 38 ½ inches, INBAL / Museo National de Arte: 1413

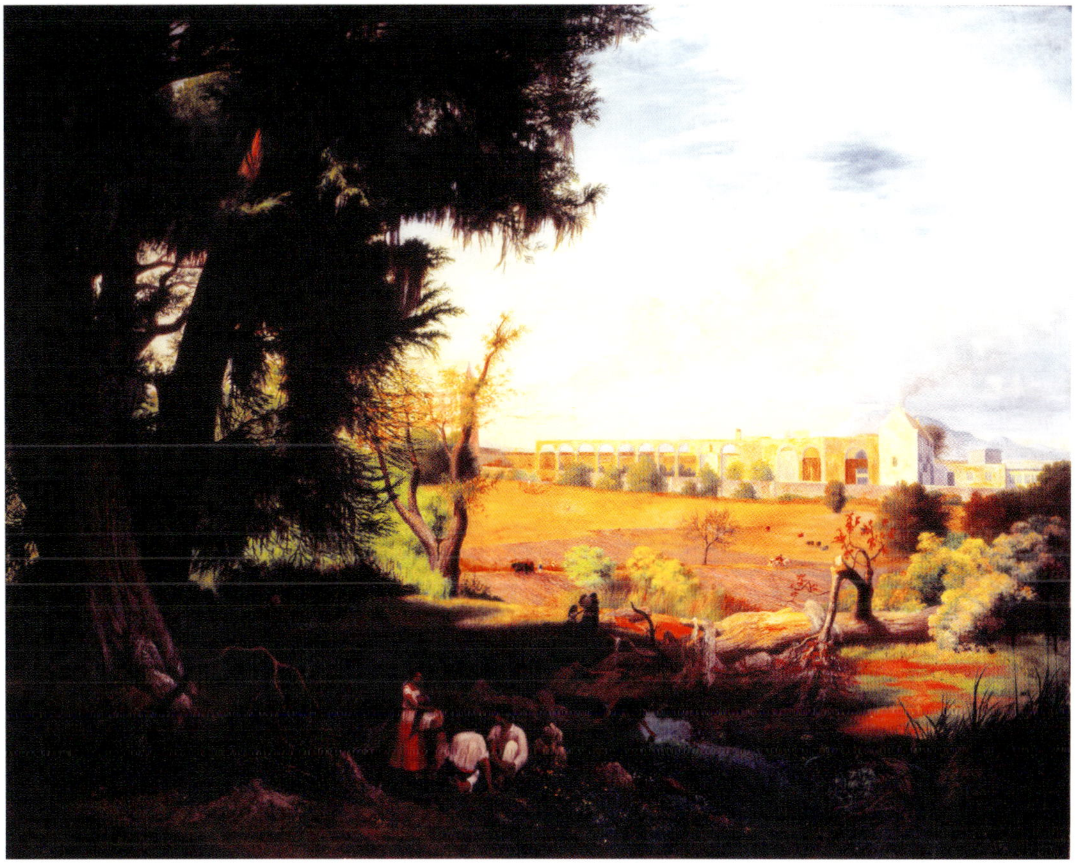

This idea that the landscapes of Mexico should be, as Fairall describes, "represented by their contents," pervaded almost all aspects of the Mexican displays at the fair. The *Kiosko Morisco*'s shaped, brightly colored windows, which, as Fairall describes, framed the surrounding landscape almost like a display case, would have drawn Louisiana's landscape into this same logic. Alongside the chromolithographs from the *Atlas,* the *Kiosko Morisco* represented the land by and through its contents, and their potential for profit. These display cases filled with minerals, and apertures from which the surrounding landscape could be viewed, worked alongside both the paintings and the framed imagery from the *Atlas* that Mexico also sent to the Cotton Centennial Exposition. The inventory of the works Debray Sucesores sent to New Orleans states that the lithographs should be framed and the others should be mounted on canvas with rods. In a letter the printing house sent to Porfirio Díaz with the shipment, it was stated that the "pictures" or frames should be covered with glass, which had not been done in advance, as it could shatter during the journey.[23] A month later García Cubas himself sent an additional shipment: "Besides the collection of Charts of the *Atlas pintoresco de la República*, sent by Debray Sucesores to be exhibited in New Orleans, I have delivered other two Collections of the same work, one for my group as exhibitor and another to decorate the Reception room that is to be established at the Exhibition palace."[24]

It is thus that three sets of these lithographs were shown among the Mexican exhibits, two in the public parts of the exhibition, and the other in the reception room, where the Mexican authorities expected to meet with foreign diplomats and potential investors. This had special importance for Mexico, whose government believed the international exhibition was an

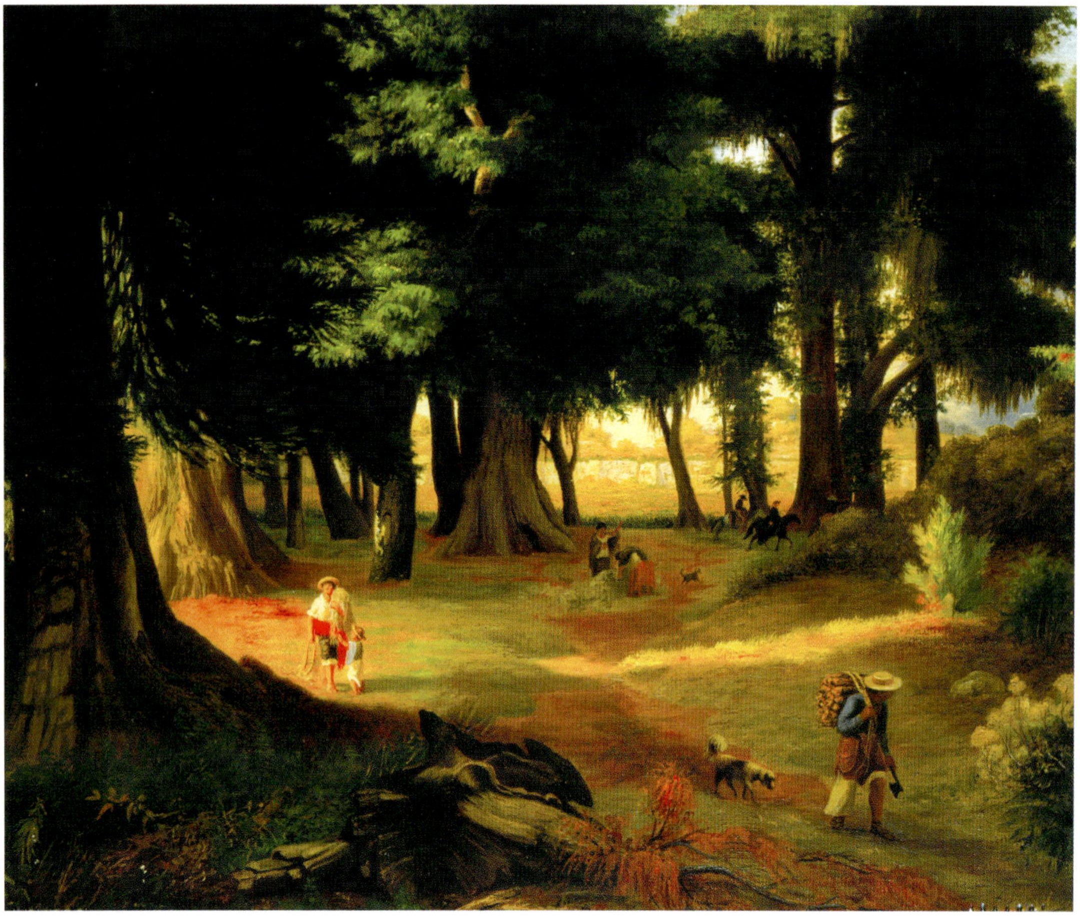

**Fig. 11**
Luis Coto, *Bosque del Colegio Militar en Chapultepec*, 1858, Oil on canvas, 28 x 38 ½ inches, INBAL / Museo National de Arte: 1518

event of "deep transcendental meaning in the effort recently started in order to move the centers of Mexican trade from London, Paris, Liverpool, Bremen, etc."[25] Throughout the Porfirian era, these efforts resulted in the exports, mostly to the United States, of mineral and agricultural products, of precious metals, oil, henequen agave, coffee, rubber, and timber.[26] It is thus that the charts in the *Atlas*, seen by politicians, businessmen, and other visitors to the Cotton Centennial Exposition, managed to convey the vastness of Mexico's territory, the richness of its natural resources, and the way in which landscape imagery could assist in this project of profiting off the land.

## Stretched to the Republics: Painting Mexico in New Orleans

Alongside these framed chromolithographs, Mexico showed nine major landscape paintings by Mexican artists at the Cotton Centennial Exposition's Fine Arts Building as part of a large display of paintings sent by the National School of Fine Arts.[27] These included five major paintings by three of Mexico's most important landscape painters of the period, José María Velasco's *Valle de México desde el cerro de Santa Isabel* (1877), Luis Coto's *Paisaje de San Cristóbal Romita* (1857), *Vista del Molino del Rey tomada desde Chapultepec* (1858) and *Bosque del Colegio Militar en Chapultepec* (1858), and Carlos Rivera's *La barranca de Metlac* (1881).[28] Seeking to show what Díaz called "the cultural stage the country has reached, which holds so many elements to awake great interest abroad," these paintings emphasized not only the bucolic nature of the Mexican territory, but also the systems already in place for harnessing its natural resources.[29] Several of

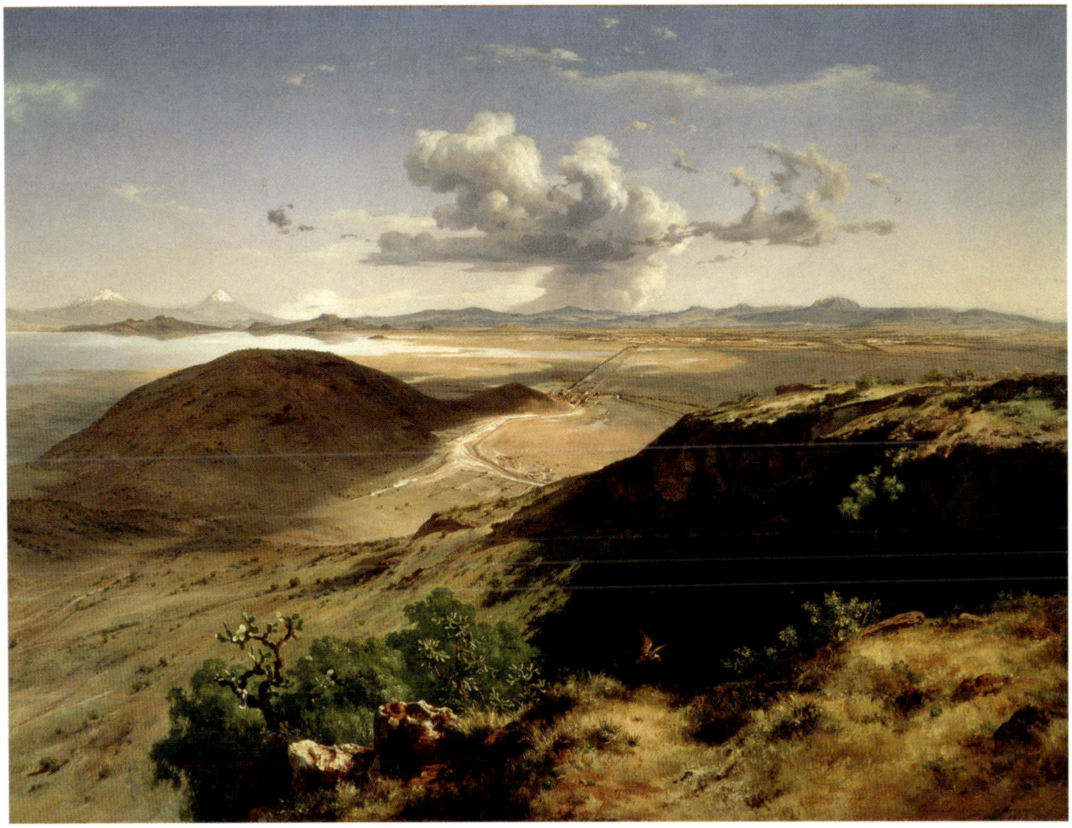

**Fig. 12**
Jose Maria Velasco, *Valle de Mexico*, 1877, Oil on canvas, 63 x 90 inches, INBAL / Museo National de Arte: 133

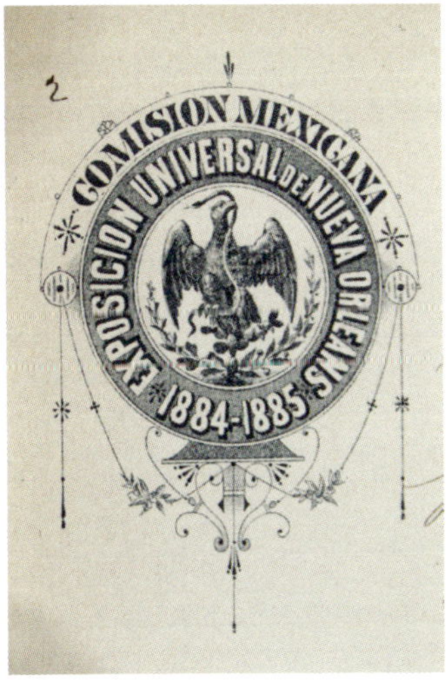


**Fig. 13**
Seal of the Comision Mexicana, Exposicion Universal de Nueva Orleans, 1884-5, Archivo General de la Nación, Photography by Huematzin Reyes Meléndez

**Fig. 14 (pp. 126-127)**
Carlos Rivera, *La barranca de Metlac*, 1881, Oil on canvas, 39 ½ x 52 inches, INBAL / Museo Nacional de Arte: 1542

the paintings chosen for the exhibition seem to have been selected to show that the obstacles to peaceful exchange between Mexico and Louisiana had ended. Two landscape works presented by Luis Coto, *Vista del Molino del Rey tomada desde Chapultepec* (1858; Fig. 10) and *Bosque del Colegio Militar en Chapultepec* (1858; Fig. 11), are seemingly peaceful landscape scenes, but just so happen to be set at sites of important battles during the Mexican-American War. Presenting a future based on peace and the verdant richness of Mexico's landscape, and a country that had moved past the violence of the recent war with the United States, the paintings show a tranquil countryside, with field workers eating, carrying wood, and laboring in the fields.[30] In both works, the *ahuehuete*, a Mexican cypress, acts as symbol of regional and historical identity.[31] In the works by Coto, these trees are not only a reference to the typical vegetation in the woods of Chapultepec, but also a symbol of memory, as witnesses of historical events from pre-Hispanic times—a resonance that might have been felt by Louisiana visitors to the fair, who shared these same associations with cypress trees from the region's swamps.

Velasco's painting *Valle de México desde el cerro de Santa Isabel* (1877; Fig.12) portrays another place central to Mexico's territorial identity, the Valley of Mexico. Painted with an aerial perspective from an adjacent peak that allowed the artist to survey the entire valley, Velasco combines careful attention to the details of the region's topography with an impression of the great expanse of the scene: the transparent atmosphere, the hills and volcanoes far away, and the depth of the central valley. The painting displays the geological structure of the terrain as well as the vegetation with such accuracy that Mexican viewers often noted the painting's resemblance to botanical illustration, with one period reviewer writing that the plants were "drawn by an artist who must be a good botanist."[32] Connecting this representation of land to Mexican national

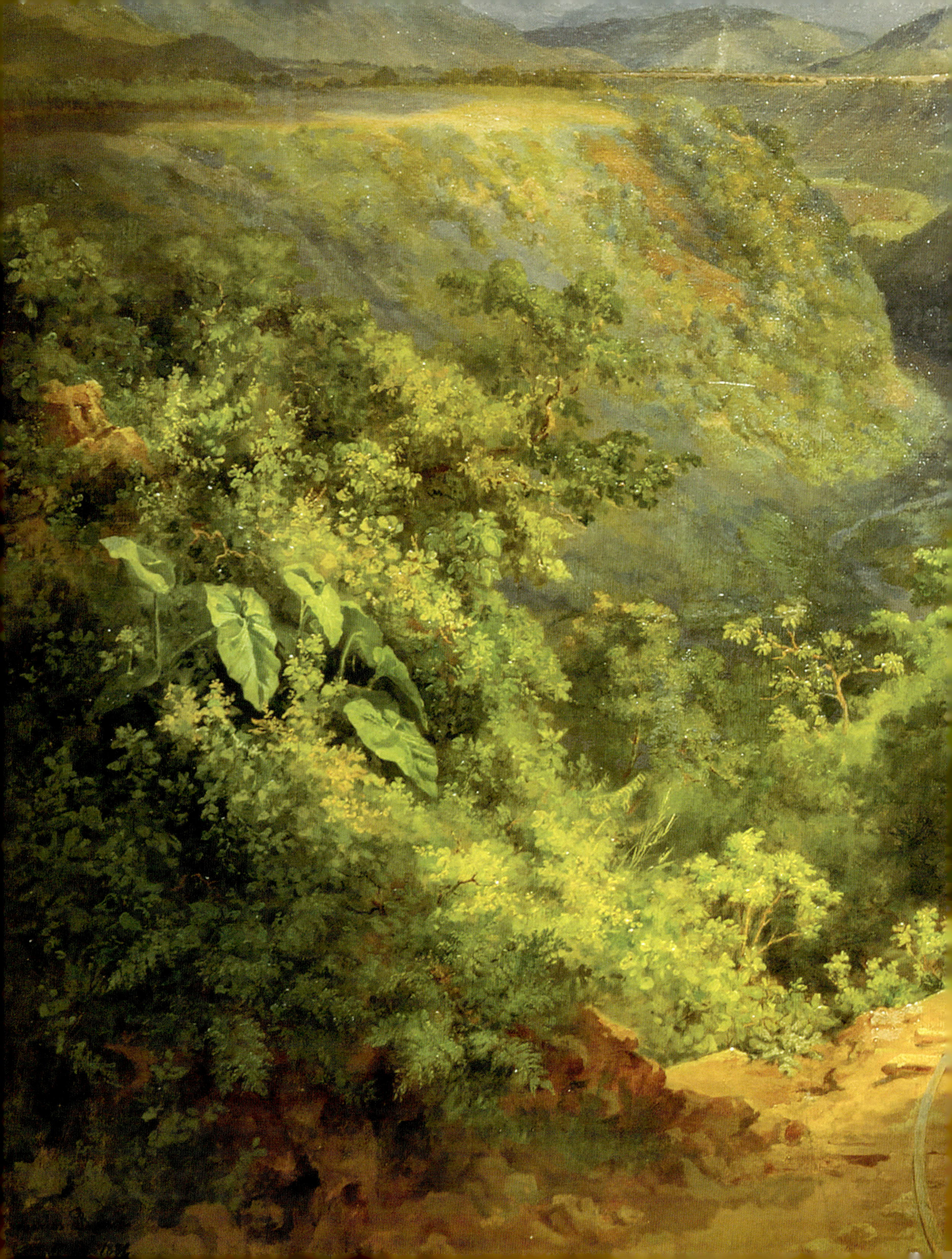

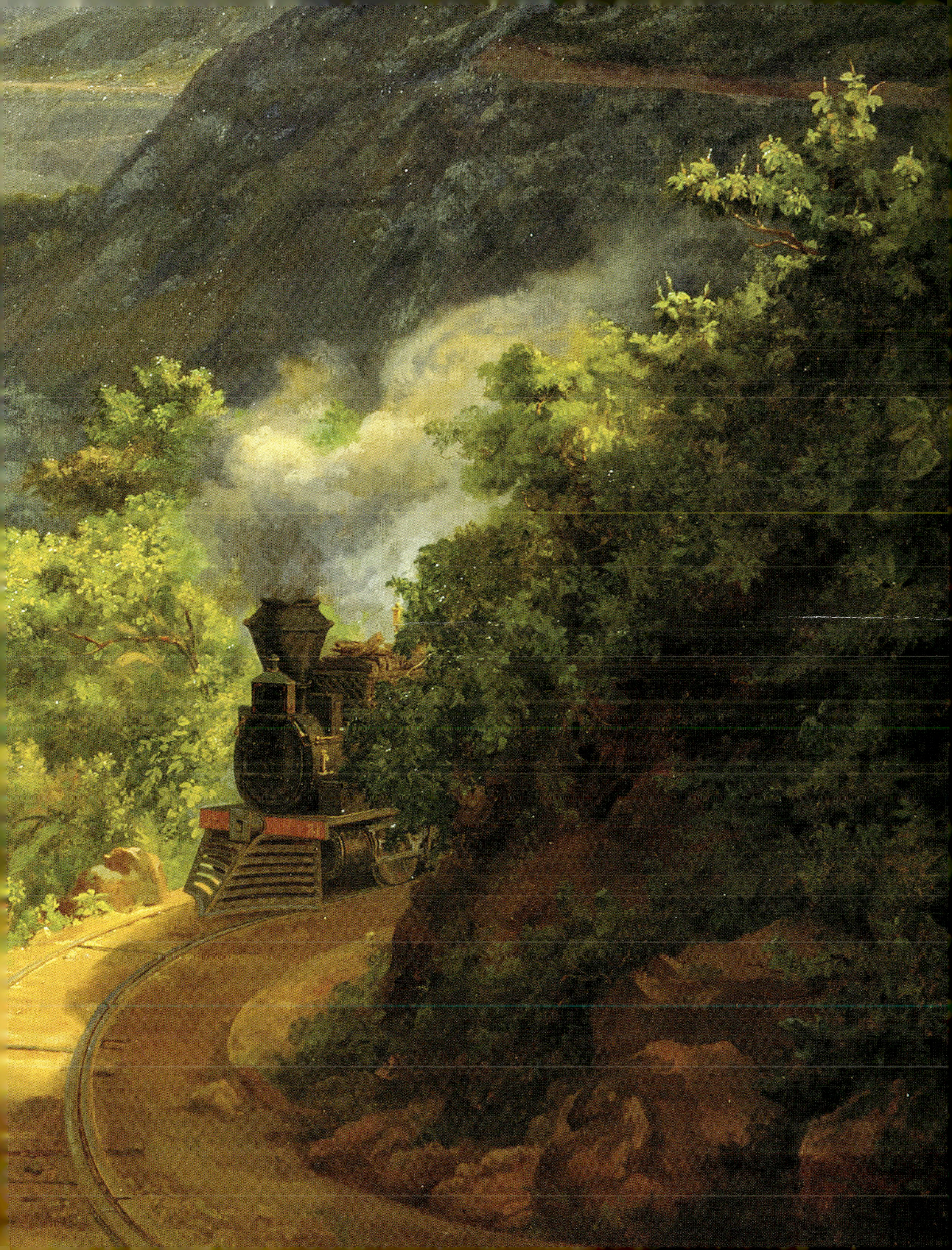

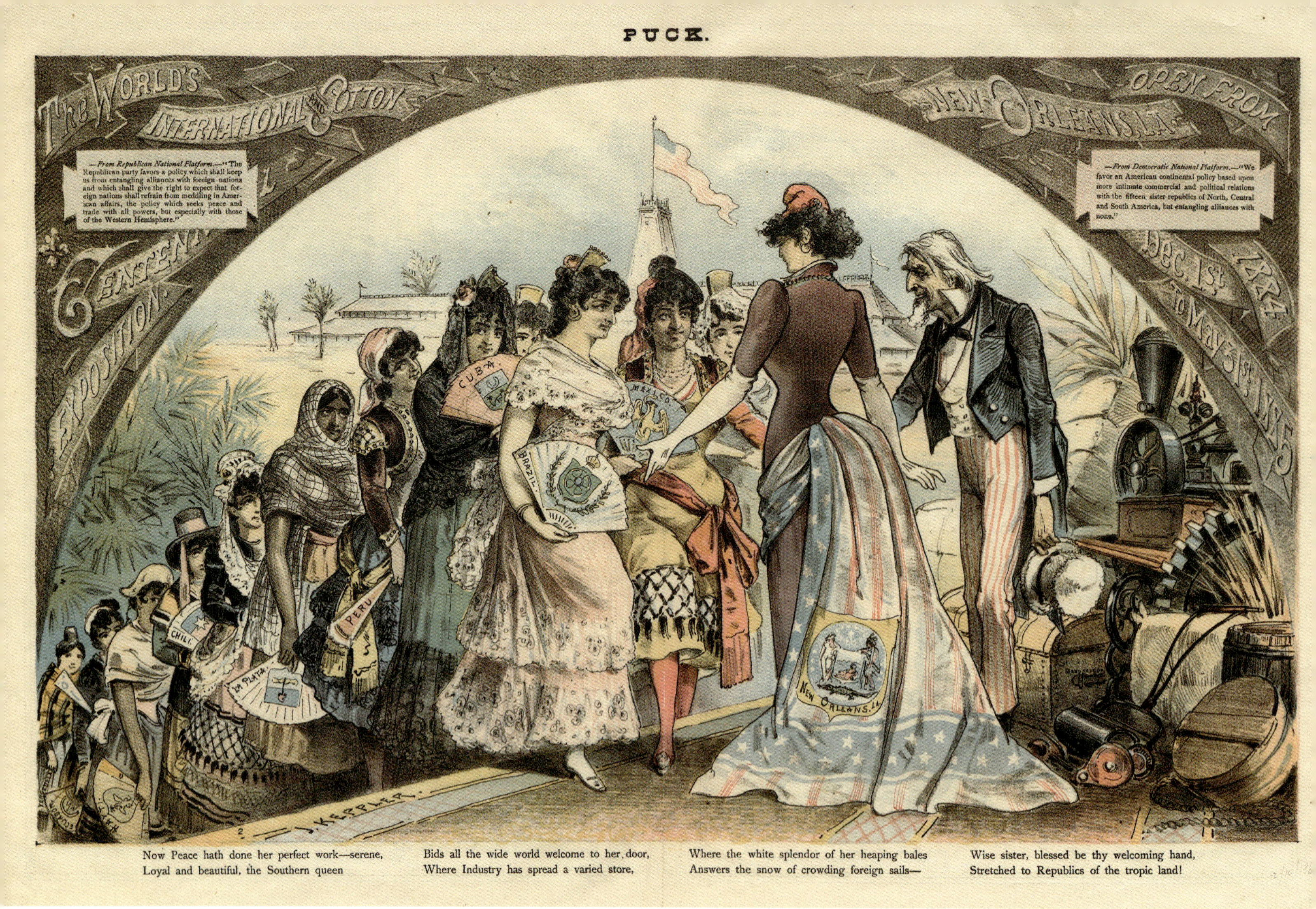


**Fig. 15**
Joseph Keppler Sr., *The World's International and Cotton Centennial Exposition, New Orleans, La.*, 1884, Color lithograph, The Historic New Orleans Collection, 1982.45

identity, the painting includes an eagle flying towards a cactus plant—a foundational symbol of Mexico's Tenochtitlan Empire, and likely also a reference to the Mexican seal—an element that the Mexican organizers also incorporated into the seal they designed for the Cotton Centennial Exposition (1882; Fig. 13).[33]

Carlos Rivera represented the impact of trade and industry on Mexico's landscapes in *La barranca de Metlac* (1881; Fig.14). Rivera, a student of Velasco's, depicts a train running through an otherwise peaceful landscape scene not unlike Velasco's *Valle de México*. In Mexican art, the train was the emblem of technical development par excellence, and Rivera's painting represents a section of the train route that runs between Mexico City and Veracruz.[34] Portraying a roaring train in harmony with nature, Rivera's painting echoes Díaz's own confidence about the spread of the railroad, "Today, when as a consequence of peace, the trains move across enormous distances of our national territory and continue expanding…is when our country is strongly impelled to come in close contact with the most enlightened nations, in order to benefit from progress together with them."[35] The Cotton Centennial Exposition opened just before the completion of new railway routes between the United States and Mexico, which was likely at the root of frequent discussions about the railroad in the popular press. As one period writer claimed, in writing about Mexico's contributions to the Cotton Centennial Exposition, "The approaching completion of the Mexican National, opening a short but very serviceable line through parts of Texas and Mexico, will place it in the power of New Orleans to gather with her own hands the trade of our sister republic, and to defy competition."[36]

**Fig. 16**
F. Arthur Callender, *New Orleans from Algiers Point*, 1893, Oil on canvas, 15 x 24 inches, Roger Houston Ogden Collection, Courtesy of Ogden Museum of Southern Art. Photography by Patrick Barnes.

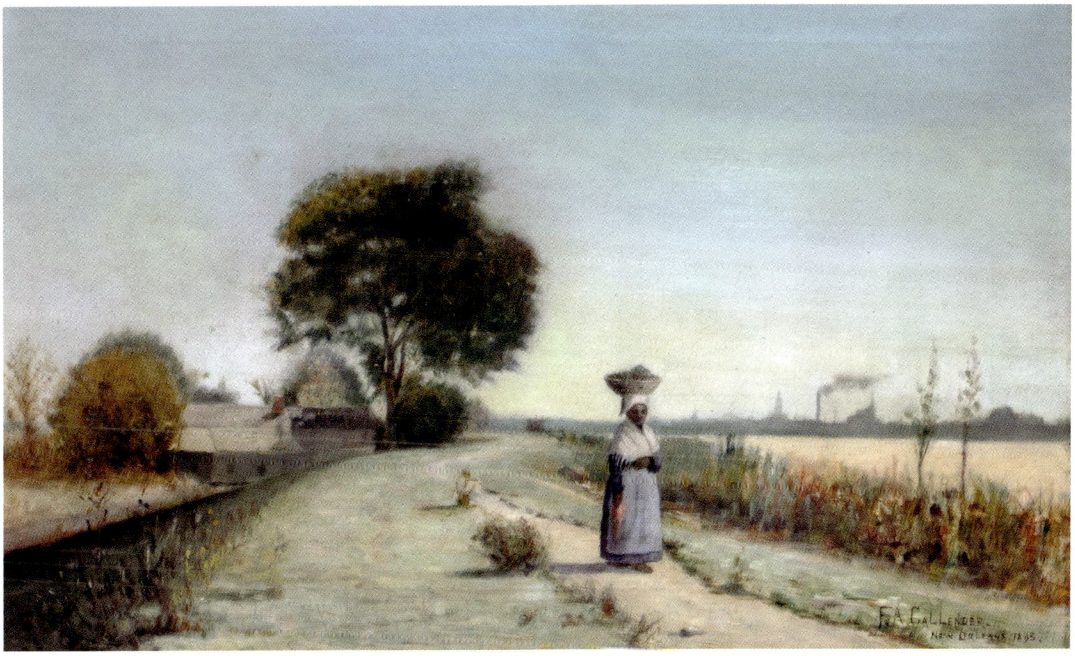

A widely distributed chromolithograph (1885; Fig. 15), published in New Orleans to advertise the Cotton Centennial Exposition, pictures New Orleans as a statuesque white woman wearing a bustle made from an American flag emblazoned with a fantastical New Orleans seal, reaching out to greet a line of fifteen women who represent, according to the chromolithograph, the "fifteen sister republics of North, Central and South America." Each of the women hold fans inscribed with various Latin American countries—Brazil, Cuba, Peru, Chile, Hayti [*sic*]—with Mexico first in line. Presenting an argument for America's—and specifically Louisiana's—expansion into Central and South America, the chromolithograph presents both the Republican and Democratic position on the matter, the Republican being to "keep us from entangling alliances with foreign nations," and the Democratic being to "favour an American continental policy based upon more intimate commercial and political relations" with the countries represented in the print. Clearly swayed towards the Democratic position, the print places an array of agricultural and industrial tools—likely meant to indicate the ways in which this increased trade could profit New Orleans and its surrounds—on the Democratic side. Along the bottom of the print runs a poem, which summarizes the Cotton Centennial Exposition's intentions:

*Now Peace hath done her perfect work—serene,*
*Loyal and beautiful, the Southern queen*
*Bids all the wide world welcome to her door,*
*Where industry has spread a varied store,*
*Where the white splendour of her heaping bales*
*Answers the snow of crowding foreign sails—*
*Wise sister, blessed be thy welcoming hand,*
*Stretched to Republics of the tropic land!*

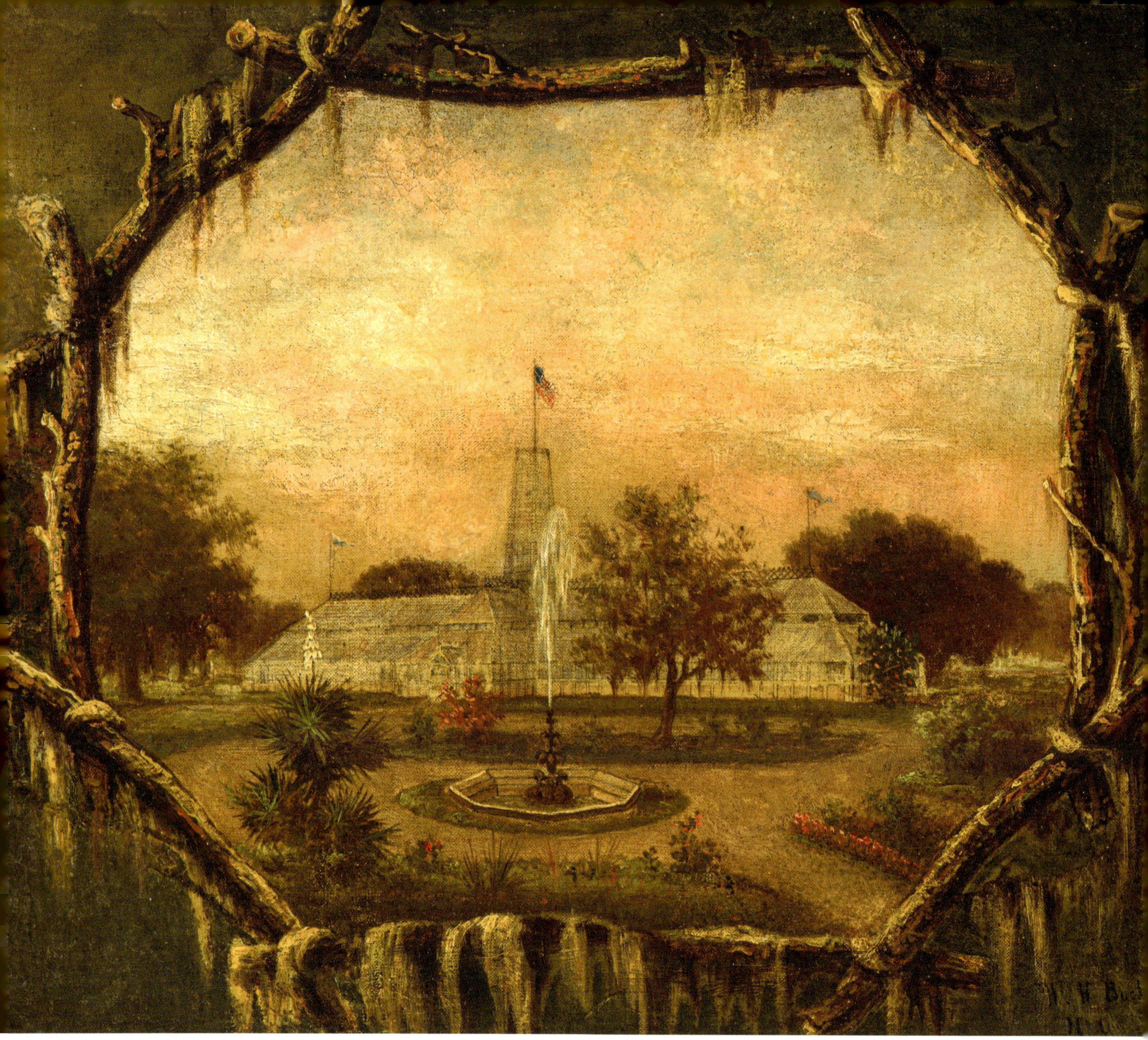

Fig. 17
William Henry Buck, *World's Industrial and Cotton Centennial Exposition (New Orleans, Louisiana World's Fair), 1885*, 1885, Oil on canvas, 23 ¾ x 27 ¾ inches (framed), New Orleans Museum of Art, Museum purchase through the Ella West Freeman Foundation Matching Fund, 71.11

In the years directly preceding and following the Cotton Centennial Exposition, Louisiana landscape paintings began more clearly registering changes to the region's landscape resulting from just the sort of increased trade and resource mining shown in the Mexican imagery from the fair. In Louisiana paintings, felled trees and railroads replace tranquil deltas, steamboats substitute for skiffs and canoes, and smokestacks begin to puff behind swamps. While no writing from Louisiana painters exists to confirm an explicit influence from the Cotton Centennial Exposition, in its wake many painters from Louisiana began to more explicitly mobilize landscape painting as a means of representing and responding to these transformations. Paintings such as F. Arthur Callender's *New Orleans from Algiers Point* (1893; Fig. 16) show artists began moving away from the lush swamp imagery so popular in the years immediately preceding the fair, and more towards representations of land that clearly showed the way that its resources were being harnessed

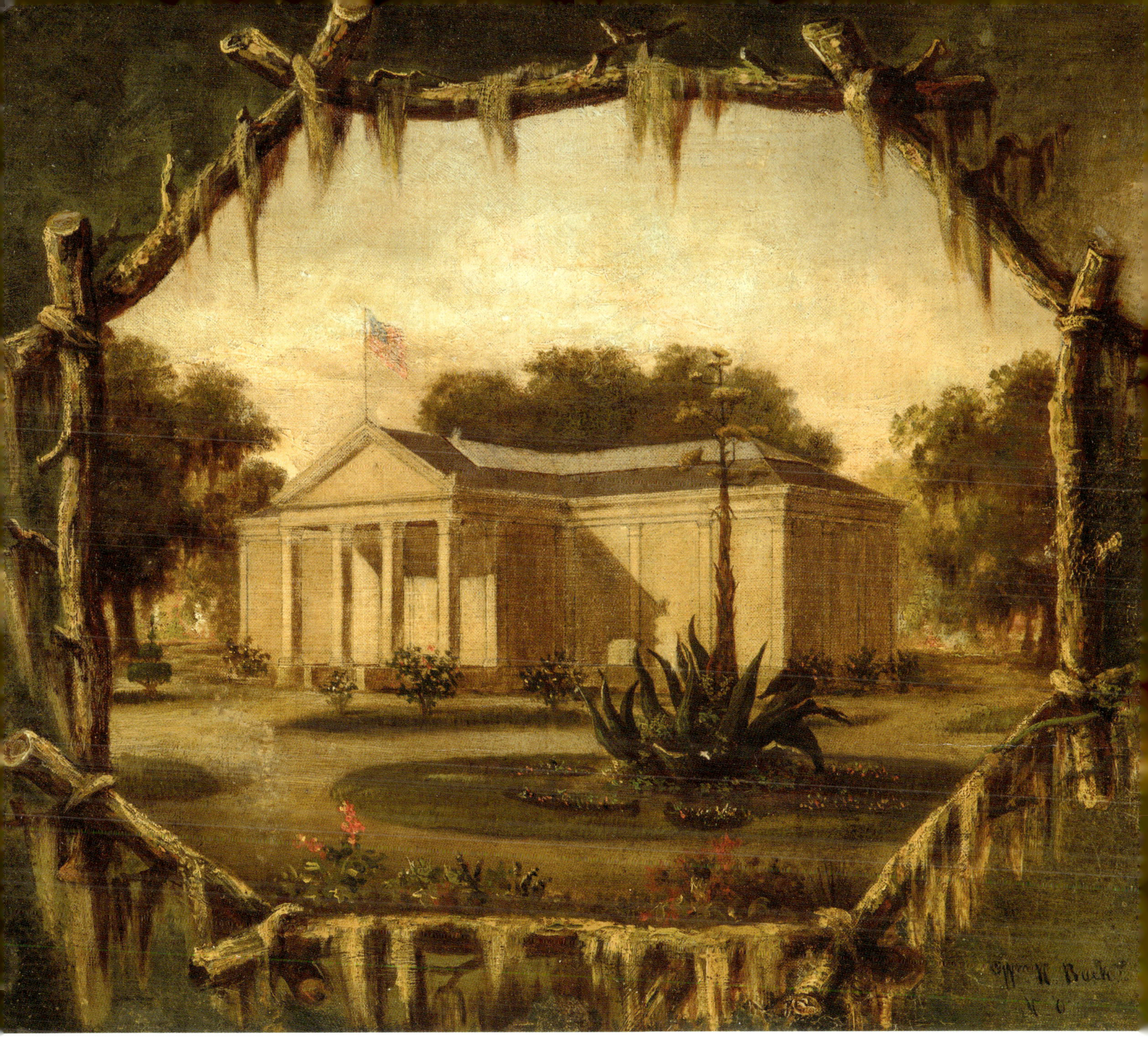

**Fig. 18**
William Henry Buck, *World's Industrial and Cotton Centennial Exposition (New Orleans, Louisiana World's Fair), 1885*, 1885, Oil on canvas, 23 ¾ x 27 ¾ inches (framed), New Orleans Museum of Art, Museum purchase through the Ella West Freeman Foundation Matching Fund, 71.10

by industry. Louisiana landscape painter William Henry Buck's paintings of the Cotton Centennial Exposition itself (1885; Figs. 17 and 18) also demonstrate something of this seeming transformation in thought. Buck made many paintings like these of the Cotton Centennial Exposition, in which he framed imagery of the fair's buildings and landscapes with rustic twigs and draped Spanish moss that recall the real scenery of his paintings such as *Louisiana Pastoral: Bayou Bridge* (1880; Plate 39) and *Swamp Scene* (1887; Fig. 19). Pulled back to reveal the crisp architecture of newly constructed buildings, with water neatly commandeered by courtyard fountains, and American flags flying high, these paintings depart in nearly all respects from the rural farm, swamp, and bayou landscapes that were the artist's signature. While there is no direct evidence that Buck was influenced by the Mexican paintings and atlases displayed within the buildings he depicted in these works, the landscape is likewise neatly ordered and framed with a logic that seems to owe something

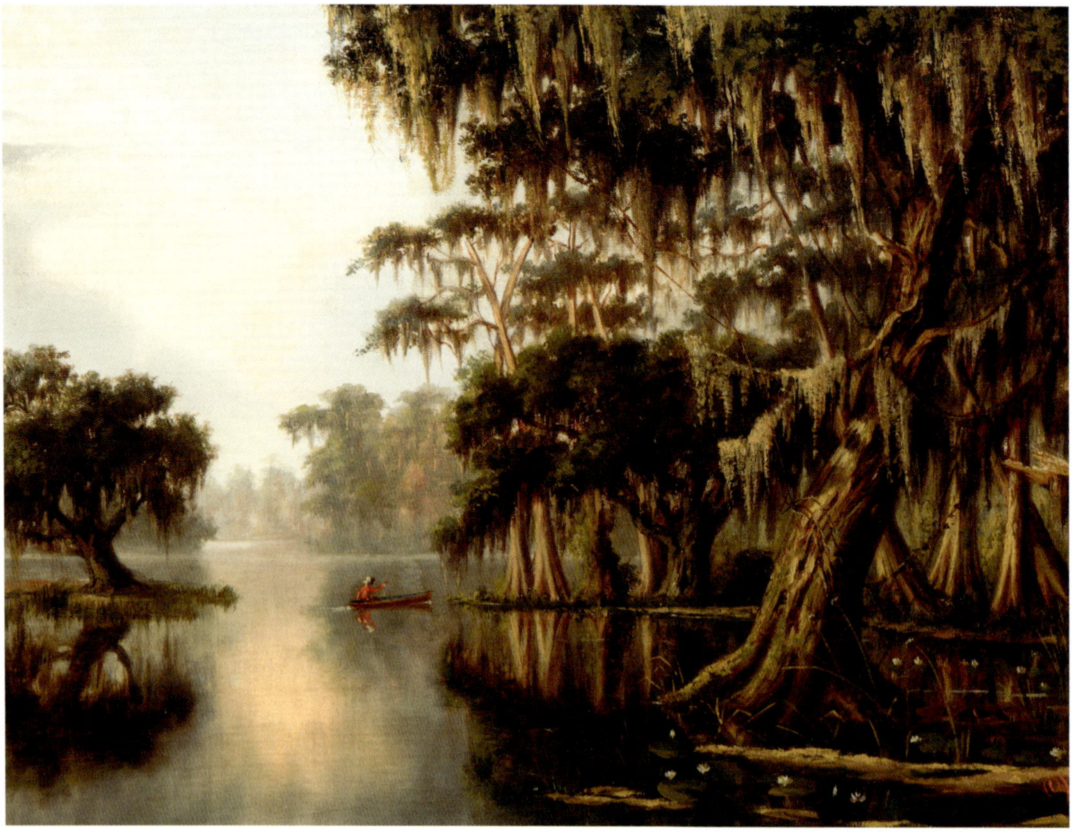

**Fig. 19**
William Henry Buck, *Swamp Scene*, 1887, Oil on canvas, 16 x 28 inches, New Orleans Museum of Art, Gift of Miss Mary Bell Swanson Mayer, 80.41

to the Mexican landscape vignettes and display cases shown at the fair—an idea perhaps most clearly insinuated by the fact that all of the frames that Buck placed around these paintings of the Cotton Centennial Exposition, like the octagonal structure of the *Kiosko Morisco*, also have eight sides.

## Landscape and Constructions of Country

Mexico's presentation at the Cotton Centennial Exposition highlighted the ways in which landscape could help convey the stakes of this economic and political expansion. Mexico's displays of landscape, through the vignettes in the charts of the *Atlas*, the paintings from the National School of Fine Arts, and the mineralogical and horticultural specimens presented in the Cotton Centennial Exposition, organized the image of a country around its natural resources, surrounding landscape vignettes with mining maps, and running trains through otherwise peaceful landscape scenes. This landscape imagery from the Cotton Centennial Exposition clearly showcased the contradictions of the period—picturing natural splendor alongside the tools for its destruction—but nonetheless served to naturalize the contradictions of modernity. To do so, the landscapes in the vignettes of the *Atlas* deployed elements drawn from Mexican landscape painting—stunning botanical details, dramatic aerial views, and representations of rich geological resources—to show the international public the splendors of a country with great potential of growth based on its mineral resources, population, history, and its technological development. Through compositional and conceptual devices common to both the vignettes and to the landscape

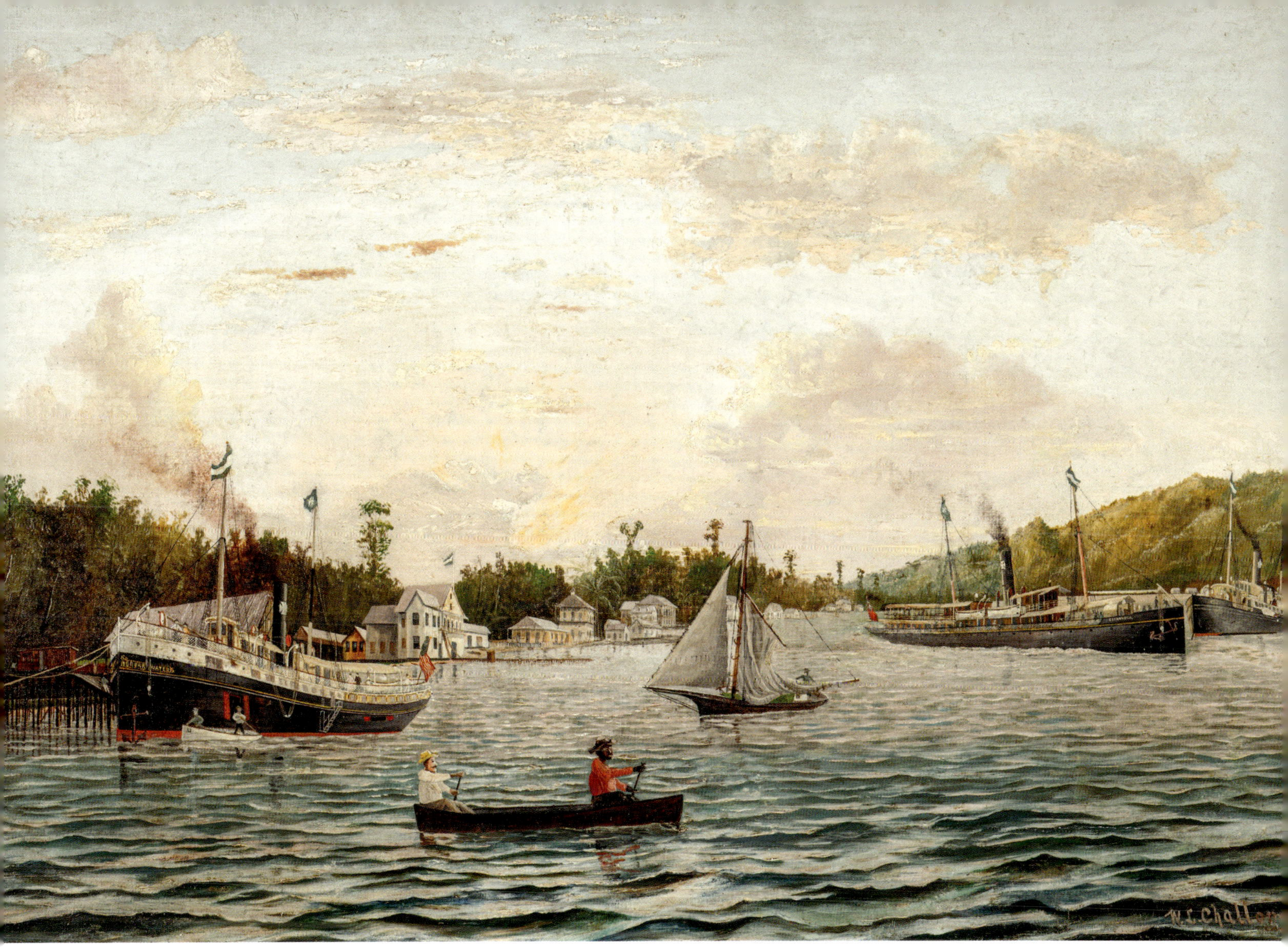

Fig. 20
Captain William Lindsay Challoner, *S.S. Breakwater, S.S. Clearwater and S.S. Wanderer in a Harbor [Honduras Port]*, 1897, Oil on canvas, 30 x 48 inches, Louisiana State Museum, XX0707, Photography by Roman Alokhin.

paintings presented at the Cotton Centennial Exposition, discursive constructions about the country were built that sought to draw together different nations, not just through shared appreciation of the land, but also shared ideas about how to mine its resources. William Lindsay Challoner's 1897 painting *S.S. Breakwater, S.S. Clearwater and S.S. Wanderer in a Harbor [Honduras Port]* (Fig. 20), painted just fifty years after LeVasseur's earlier paintings of Nicaragua, shows a transformation from the wide open vistas of LeVasseur's earlier paintings to a landscape in which a railroad—not unlike that which steams through Rivera's painting—transports goods back and forth from the port of Honduras, literalizing the relationship between New Orleans and Central and South America that the displays at the fair sought to cement, as well as the role painting had to play in both documenting and interpreting this new world order.[37]

1 "Mexico Day—Special to the Times Democrat," *The Times Democrat,* May 25, 1885.

2 ibid.

3 "Gov. McEnery's Proclamation Relative to Mexico Day," *The Daily City Item,* May 29, 1885.

4 While very little is known about LeVasseur's life and career, New Orleans City Directories list him living in the city between 1837-1842.

5 Mariano Bárcena (signed), *Informe dirigido a Alfonso Lancaster Jones, Comisionado General de México para la Exposición de Nueva Orleans (Report sent to Alfonso Lancaster Jones, Mexico's Chief Commissioner at the New Orleans Exhibition), New Orleans,* May 9, 1885, Box 76, Folder 1, Folios 14 -15, Fondo Fomento, Exposiciones Extranjeras, Archivo General de la Nación.

6 For further information, see Mireya Blanco Martínez and José Omar Moncada Maya, "*Ministerio de Fomento*, driver of the study and recognition of the Mexican territory (1877-1898)", *Investigaciones Geográficas, Boletín del Instituto de Geografía,* UNAM, 74 (2011): 74-91. http://www.scielo.org.mx/pdf/igeo/n74/n74a7.pdf.

7 See Antonio García Cubas, *El libro de mis recuerdos: Narraciones Históricas, Anecdóticas y de Costumbres Mexicanas anteriores al actual estado social* (México: Imprenta de Arturo García Cubas, Hermanos Sucesores, 1904), 452. García Cubas studied engineering and engraving at the San Carlos Academy, where he became acquainted with José María Velasco and Luis Coto. See Magali M. Carrera, Traveling from New Spain to Mexico: mapping practices of nineteenth-century Mexico (Durham, NC: Duke University Press, 2011), 144-145.

8 There were several shipments of this work to New Orleans. In a document, mention is made that 500 copies were distributed. See *"Publicaciones que la Sria de Fomento mandó imprimir á su costa y fueron repartidas en la Exposición"* in the dossier *Medallas y diplomas obtenidos por los expositores Mexicanos en la Exposición Universal de Nueva Orleans y su distribución hecha por el C. Presidente de la República,* November 12, 1885, Box 78, Folder 10, Folio 36, Fondo Fomento, Exposiciones Extranjeras, Archivo General de la Nación. In another, undated document, mention is made of 1,500 extra copies of the document. See *"Contingente de la Comisión de Publicaciones" in Correspondencia del Comisionado General.* November 5, 1884, Box 76, Folder 4, Folio 229, Fondo Fomento, Exposiciones Extranjeras, Archivo General de la Nación.

9 In *Cuadro geográfico*, under the title *"Valle de México"*, García Cubas refers the reader to a vignette in the corresponding chart of the *Atlas pintoresco,* "There is an illustration depicting the pyramids of Teotihuacán in the Archeological chart of the picturesque Atlas." Vid. *Cuadro geográfico, estadístico, descriptivo e histórico de los Estados Unidos Mexicanos* (México: Oficina tipográfica de la Secretaría de Fomento, 1884), 260.

10 The charts are divided thus: I. *Carta política*; II. *Carta etnográfica*; III. *Carta eclesiástica*; IV. *Vías de comunicación y movimiento marítimo*; V. *Instrucción pública*; VI. *Carta orográfica*; VII. *Carta hidrográfica*; VIII. *Carta agrícola*; IX. *Carta minera*; X. *Carta histórica y arqueológica*; XI. *Reyno de la Nueva España a Principios [sic] del siglo* XIX; *Valle de México*; XIII. *México y sus cercanías* (I. Political Chart; II. Ethnographic Chart; III. Ecclesiastical Chart; IV. Means of transport and sea transport Chart; V. Public Education Chart; VI. Mountain Chart; VII. River Chart; VIII. Agricultural Chart; IX. Mining Chart; X. Historic and Archaeological Chart; XI. Kingdom of New Spain at the beginning of the XIX Century; XII. Valley of Mexico; and XIII. Mexico and its environs).

11 Litografía Debray Sucesores (stamped), *Nota de los objetos que por conducto de la Comisión Mexicana remitimos a la Exposición de Nueva Orleans* (List of items sent to the New Orleans Exhibition through the Mexican Commission), México, October 21, 1884, Box 75, Folder 11, Fondo Fomento, Exposiciones Extranjeras, Archivo General de la Nación.

12 In 1884 Díaz was appointed Mexico's Chief Commissioner in charge of organizing and managing Mexico's participation in the exhibition in New Orleans. See Porfirio Díaz, *Documento dirigido al gobernador del Distrito Federal por medio del cual invita a esa entidad a participar en la Exposición de Nueva Orleans* (Letter of invitation to the Governor of the Federal District to participate in the New Orleans Exhibition), México, February 25 1884, Box 79, Folder 1, Folio 8, Fondo Fomento, Exposiciones Extranjeras, Archivo General de la Nación.

13 Pelegrín Clavé's painting is now in the collection of the *Museo Nacional de San Carlos* (National Museum of San Carlos), México City, and both Obregón and Ramírez's paintings are in the collection of the *Museo Nacional de Arte* (National Museum of Art), México City.

14 Carrera, Traveling from New Spain to Mexico, 205.

15 Elías Trabulse, *José María Velasco: Un paisaje de la ciencia en México,* (1992, rev. ed., Toluca: Instituto Mexiquense de Cultura, 2012), 140.

16 Ramón Almaraz, *Memoria acerca de los terrenos de Metlaltoyuca* (México: Imprenta Imperial, 1866).

17 Porfirio Díaz, *Documento dirigido al gobernador del Distrito Federal por medio del cual invita a esa entidad a participar en la Exposición de Nueva Orleans* (Letter of invitation to the Governor of the Federal District to participate in the New Orleans Exhibition), February 25, 1884, Box 79, Folder 1, Folio 7, Fondo Fomento, Exposiciones Extranjeras, Archivo General de la Nación.

18 Renata Keller, "US-Mexican Relations from Independence to the Present," Oxford Research Encyclopedia of American History (March 2016), 6. Consulted 9 June 2019. https://oxfordre.com/americanhistory/view/10.1093/acrefore/9780199329175.001.0001/acrefore-9780199329175-e-269.

19 Mariano Bárcena (signed), *Informe rendido por Mariano Bárcena, representante del Comisionado General de México, en la Exposición de Nueva Orleans* (Report by Mariano Bárcena, representative of Mexico's Chief Commissioner at the New Orleans Exhibition), New Orleans,

May 9, 1885, Box 76, Folder 1, Folio 32, Fondo Fomento, Exposiciones Extranjeras, Archivo General de la Nación.

20 Porfirio Díaz, *Documento dirigido al gobernador del Distrito Federal por medio del cual invita a esa entidad a participar en la Exposición de Nueva Orleans* (Letter of invitation to the Governor of the Federal District to participate in the New Orleans Exhibition), México, February 25, 1884, Box 79, Folder 1, Folio 7, Fondo Fomento, Exposiciones Extranjeras, Archivo General de la Nación.

21 Lafcadio Hearn, "Mexico at New Orleans," *Harper's Weekly*, (March 14, 1885): 167.

22 Herbert S. Fairall, *The World's Industrial and Cotton Centennial Exposition, New Orleans, 1884-85* (Iowa City, IA: Republican Publishing Company, 1885), 288-289.

23 Debray Sucesores (signed), *Carta dirigida a Porfirio Díaz acompañando el envío de trabajos litográficos a la Exposición de Nueva Orleans* (Letter to Porfirio Díaz with the shipment of lithographic works to the New Orleans Exhibition), México, October 21, 1884, Box 75, Folder 11, Fondo Fomento, Exposiciones Extranjeras, Archivo General de la Nación.

24 Antonio García Cubas (signed), *Carta dirigida al Sr. General D. Porfirio Díaz, Comisionado general de la Exposición de Nueva Orleans* (Letter to General Don Porfirio Díaz, General Commissioner of the New Orleans Exhibition), México, November 26, 1884, Fox 75,Folder 45, Fondo Fomento, Exposiciones Extranjeras, Archivo General de la Nación.

25 P. Ornelas (signed), *Acta levantada en la 1ª sesión oficial celebrada por la Comisión Mexicana en New- Orleans* (Act issued during the first official session celebrated by the Mexican Commission to New Orleans), New Orleans, December 12, 1884. Archivo General de la Nación, Fondo Fomento, Exposiciones Extranjeras, Box 73, Folder 9, Folios 4-5, Fondo Fomento, Exposiciones Extranjeras, Archivo General de la Nación.

26 Keller, "US-Mexican Relations from Independence to the Present," 6-7.

27 Mariano Bárcena (signed), *Informe acerca del estado que guardaba la Sección Mexicana de la Exposición en Nueva Orleans, á la fecha en que fue puesta bajo mi dirección así como de los trabajos emprendidos después para reformar la parte instalada de los objetos y hacer su clasificación y para organizar todas las oficinas dependientes de esta Dirección* (Report on the status of the Mexican Section of the Exhibition in New Orleans on the date it came under my supervision, as well as of the works performed in order to modify the installation of the objects, to classify them and to organize all the sections under this Department), New Orleans, March 16, 1885, Box 76, Folder 1, Folio 17, Fondo Fomento, Exposiciones Extranjeras, Archivo General de la Nación.

28 *Relación de los objetos de arte que por orden del supremo gobierno se entregan a la Comisión Mexicana para la Exposición Universal de Nueva Orleans, para su embarque y envío* (List of art works, delivered by order of the Supreme Government to the Mexican Commission at the World Exhibition in New Orleans for its packaging and shipping), México, November 10, 1884. Document 7501, Archivo de la Antigua Academia de San Carlos. Reproduced in: Eduardo Báez Macías, *Guía del Archivo de la Antigua Academia de San Carlos 1867-1907*, vol. I, (México: Universidad Nacional Autónoma de México, Instituto de Investigaciones Estéticas, 1993), 274.

29 Porfirio Díaz, *Documento dirigido al gobernador del Distrito Federal por medio del cual invita a esa entidad a participar en la Exposición de Nueva Orleans* (Letter of invitation to the Governor of the Federal District to participate in the New Orleans Exhibition), México, February 25, 1884, Box 79, Folder 1, Folio 8, Fondo Fomento, Exposiciones Extranjeras, Archivo General de la Nación.

30 Fausto Ramírez, "*Comentario a las obras Vista del Molino del Rey tomada desde Chapultepec y Bosque del Colegio Militar en Chapultepec de Luis Coto,*" *Catálogo comentado del acervo del Museo Nacional de Arte: Pintura,* Siglo XIX. vol. I (México: Museo Nacional de Arte, 2002), 173-178.

31 The Aztec emperor Moctezuma had them planted in Chapultepec. These trees are believed to have witnessed important events in Mexican history, from the time of the conquest of Mexico by Spain to the present.

32 María Elena Altamirano Piolle, *José María Velasco. Paisajes de luz, horizontes de modernidad* (México: DGE Equilibrista, 2014), 213.

33 Fausto Ramírez, "*Acotaciones iconográficas a la evolución de episodios y localidades en los paisajes de José María Velasco,*" José María Velasco: Homenaje (México: Universidad Nacional Autónoma de México, 1989), 46-47.

34 For further details of this work, see Víctor Rodríguez Rangel, "*Comentario a la obra La barranca de Metlac de Carlos Rivera,*" Catálogo comentado del acervo del Museo Nacional de Arte: Pintura, Siglo XIX, vol. II (México: Museo Nacional de Arte, 2009), 243-249.

35 Porfirio Díaz, *Documento dirigido al gobernador del Distrito Federal por medio del cual invita a esa entidad a participar en la Exposición de Nueva Orleans* (Letter of invitation to the Governor of the Federal District to participate in the New Orleans Exhibition), México, February 25, 1884, Box 79, Folder 1, Folio 7, Fondo Fomento, Exposiciones Extranjeras, Archivo General de la Nación

36 "Mexico," *The Daily Picayune*, Sunday Morning, May 24, 1885.

37 In 1880, William Lindsay Challoner emigrated from England to the Americas, first living in Argentina and then moving to New Orleans shortly thereafter. Serving as a captain for vessels bound to Jamaica, Argentina, and Honduras, he also painted many of the places he travelled, focusing on imagery of the ships, ports and harbors that were part of his trade. While many of his paintings are small and fairly hastily painted—the work of a sea captain, likely made out at sea—a painting recently discovered at the Louisiana State Museum, shows the artist's keen interest in documenting the ports and harbors throughout Central and South America that were at the root of New Orleans trade partnerships.

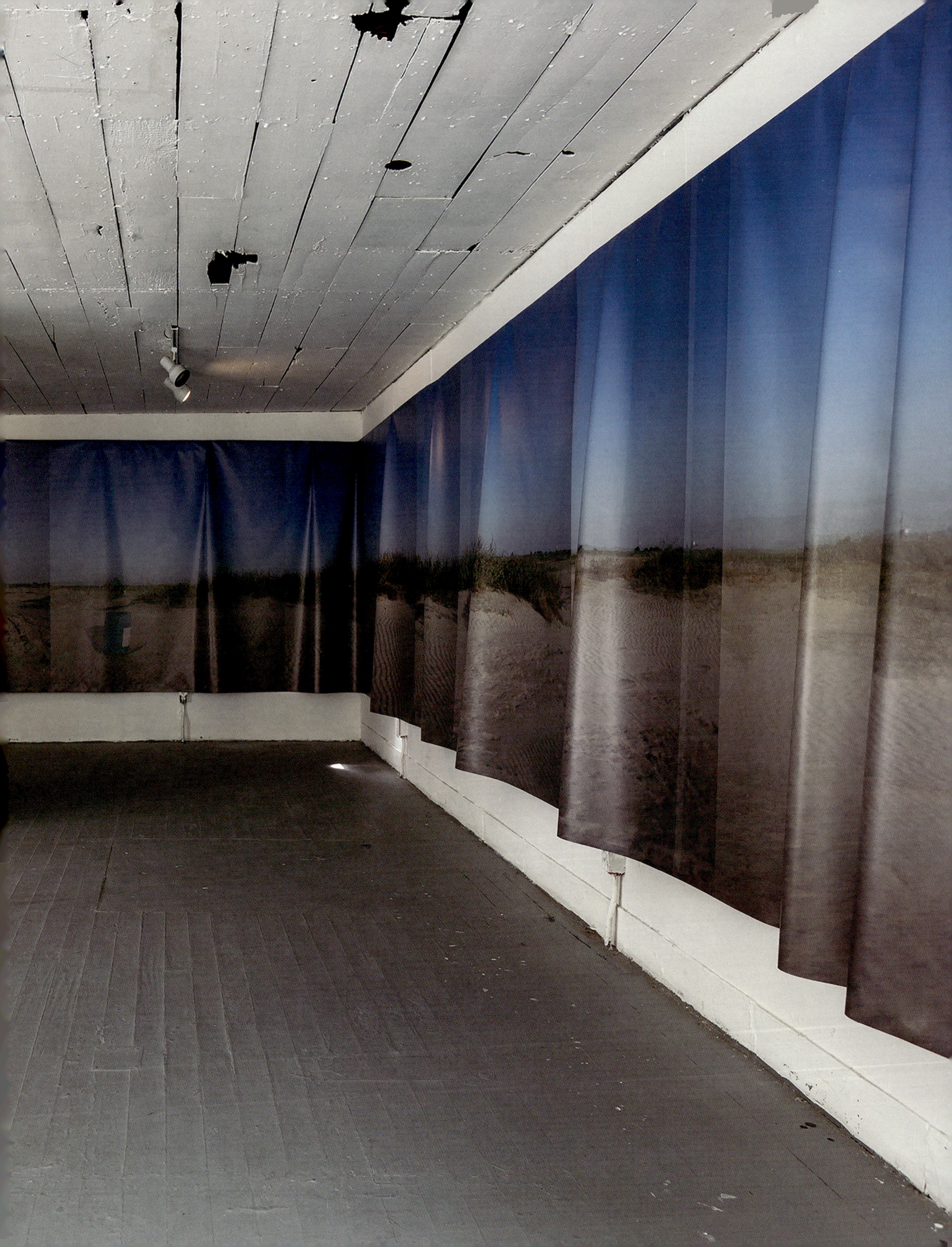

# Acadia Revisited: Regina Agu in conversation with Ryan N. Dennis

Contemporary artist Regina Agu explores how history, language and representation coalesce in contemporary ideas surrounding landscape. Her practice includes explorations of environmental justice and spatial politics, particularly as they intersect with communities of color and the artist's evolving thinking about Black Geographies—a theoretical framework that offers critical ways of understanding the intertwined geographies, histories and spaces of the African Diaspora.

As part of *Inventing Acadia: Painting and Place in Louisiana,* Agu is creating a new site-specific installation for the New Orleans Museum of Art, which will be on view at the museum from November 22, 2019 to February 10, 2020. Taking the historical representations of the Louisiana landscape in *Inventing Acadia* as a point of material and conceptual departure, Agu is creating a large-scale photographic panorama that will drape, fold and move through the museum's Great Hall. This project will combine historical reference points with contemporary landscape imagery from the region to create an immersive installation that explores the unique social and political geographies of the Gulf Coast. Drawing on her own unique relationship to the region—the artist has deep familial ties to Louisiana, and grew up between Houston, Congo, South Africa and Nigeria—Agu's project mines histories of landscape painting in search of ways we might reimagine the complex global histories and present-day

**Fig. 1 (opposite)**
Regina Agu, *Sea Change*, 2016, Vinyl print, 70 x 6 feet (approximately), Collection of the Artist, Installation view at Project Row Houses, Houston, TX. Photo credit: Alex Barber © Regina Agu 2019

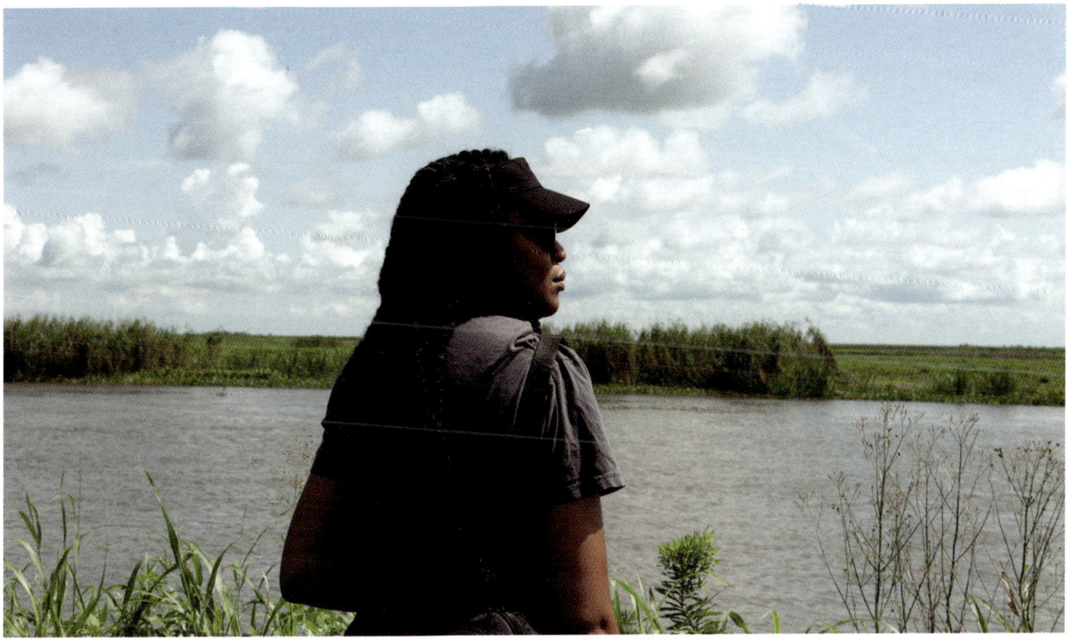

**Fig. 2**
Regina Agu at Pointe à la Hache, Louisiana, 2019, Photography by Seth Boonchai

environmental concerns that mark the landscape of the Gulf Coast.

Through a partnership between NOMA and A Studio in the Woods, an artist residency program in Louisiana focused around art and environment, Agu is revisiting many of the sites painted by artists in *Inventing Acadia* to create this new installation. Working with environmental scientists and researchers, her project considers issues ranging from land loss and environmental degradation, to the ways that these landscapes reflect histories of slavery and colonialism, exploring how such histories manifest themselves in our relationship with Louisiana's landscape today.

*In August 2019, Agu sat down with Ryan N. Dennis, Curator and Programs Director at Project Row Houses in Houston, to discuss the questions that guide her practice, and the evolution of her project for NOMA.*

**RD** How did you become interested in the history of landscape representation?

**RA** My interest in landscape began partly as a biographical exploration. I grew up between Houston, several countries in western and central Africa (including Nigeria, my paternal lineage), South Africa, and some stops in between in continental Europe. I began to understand that my family's personal history was a microcosm of larger histories of migration, and spoke to larger connections between Africa, the United States and Europe. As I moved back and forth between the Gulf of Mexico and the Gulf of Guinea, in particular, I became very aware of the shared connections of language, culture, and migration, as well as the common legacies of enslavement, colonialism, and economic ties that continue to circulate between these landscapes today.

In addition to these biographical entry points, my background and training in policy analysis continues to inform a lot of how I approach art and image making. My art practice is a deep exploration of how policy intersects with the memory and history of a community, particularly its relationship to landscape, site, and spatial politics. Being based in Houston for so many years, I became interested in Houston as an anchor city of the Gulf Coast that reflects so many of the concerns that guide my art, and began exploring the city's relationship to water, status as a port city, and connections to the petrochemical industry as a landscape of extraction.

My studies in policy analysis inform the types of questions that I ask with my work. I think that my work can ask questions that reveal both visible and invisible histories, dig deeper into the relationship between history and memory, and get at the root of many of the conversations we are having today about social and environmental policy.

**RD** How do those interests and explorations show up in your work?

**RA** Beginning with *Sea Change* (2016; Figs. 1 and 4), an installation I did at Project Row Houses in Houston in 2016, I've taken up the historical form of the panorama. This was a mode of landscape representation widely used in both painting and photography during the nineteenth century, which presented sweeping views across a wide expanse of landscape.

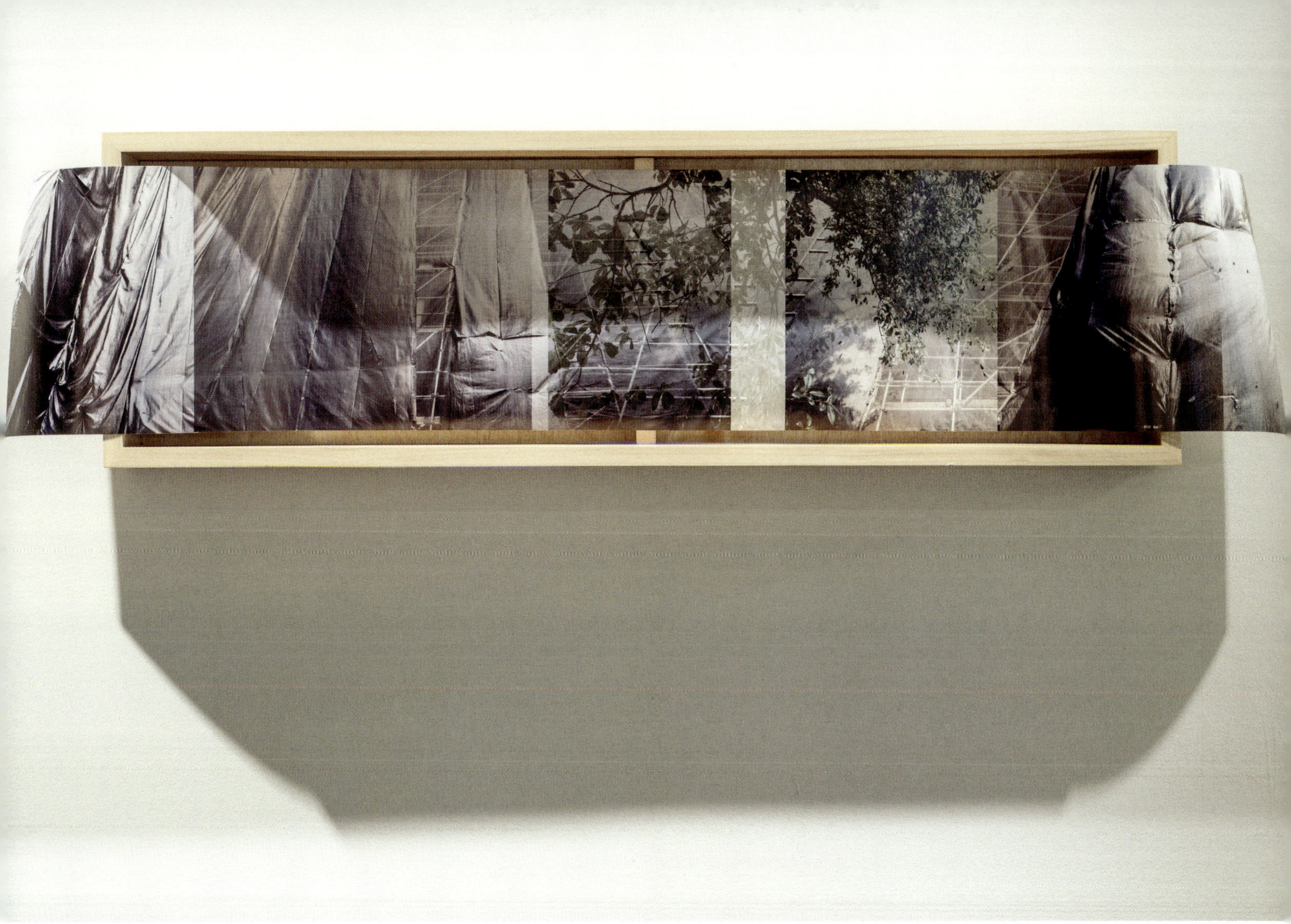

Fig. 3
Regina Agu, *Drape Panorama 02*, 2017, Digital photo print and wood, 50 ¾ x 12 1/2 x 5 1/2 inches, Collection of the Artist, Installation view at DiverseWorks, Photo credit: Paul Hester
© Regina Agu 2019

Among the most popular subjects during the period, for example, were panoramas that represented a journey up and down the entire Mississippi River, and it was a popular form in cities across the Gulf Coast as well as others across the world. Looking back to this form allows me to engage directly with the histories of landscape representation that continue to inform our relationship to land today, both materially and conceptually. As a form, the panorama is closely connected to the histories of empire, colonialism and migration I explore in my work—histories which continue to impact the geographic regions I work within today. In addition to *Sea Change*, I've also used the panorama in other bodies of work looking at the rapid real estate development cycle in Houston. For example, in works like *Drape Panorama 02* (2017; Fig. 3) I layer imagery of the changing landscape of Houston's Third Ward, the neighborhood where I lived and worked for many years, showing the way the community is changing through representations of the built environment and urban landscape.

**RD** Can you talk more about *Sea Change*? What was the impetus behind this work?

**RA** *Sea Change* was my first opportunity to create an installation at a large scale, that could spatially represent my ongoing research about the connections between the Gulf of Mexico and the Gulf of Guinea.  While living in Houston, I started researching and visiting Galveston, Texas, and became increasingly interested in the site because of its role as a important port

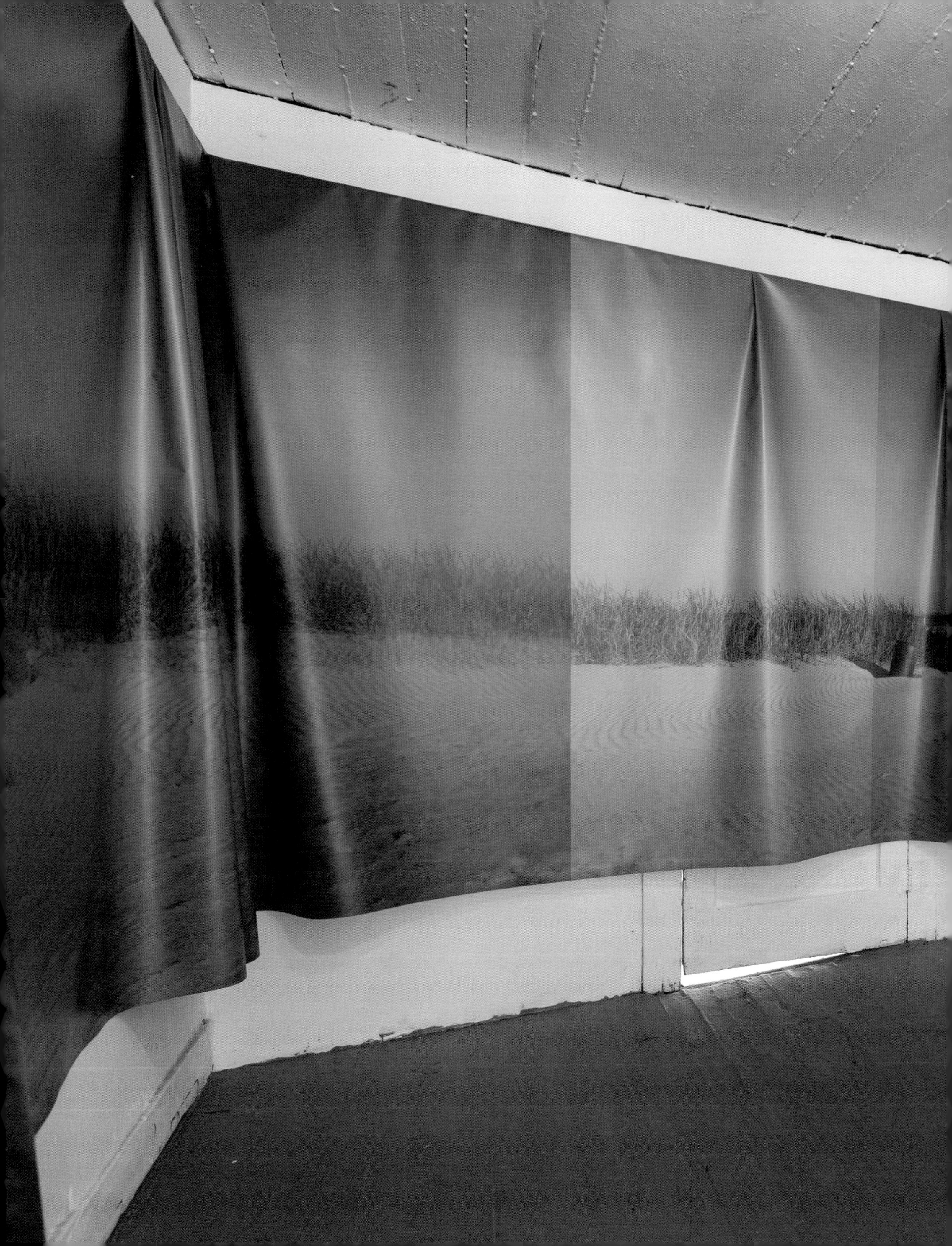

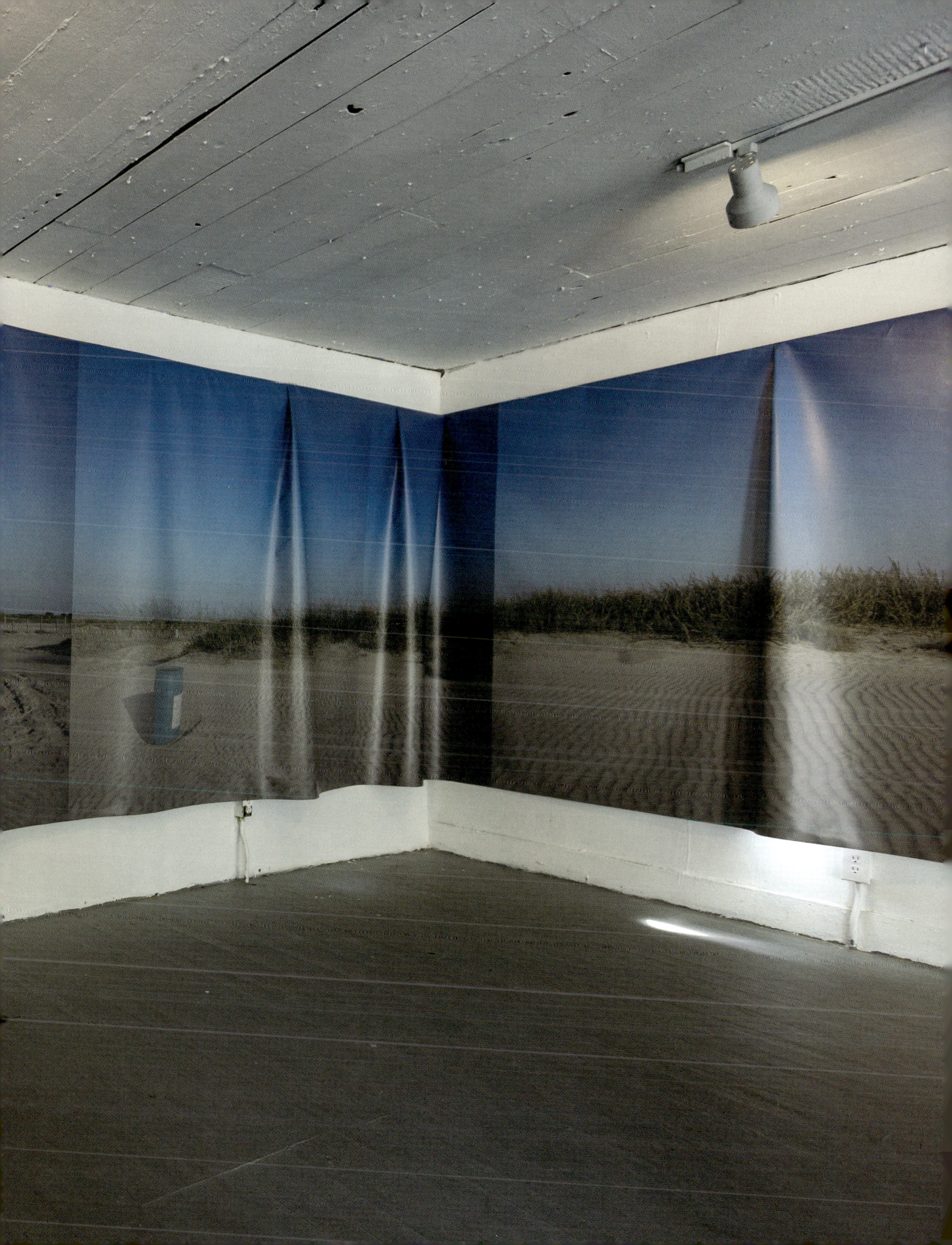

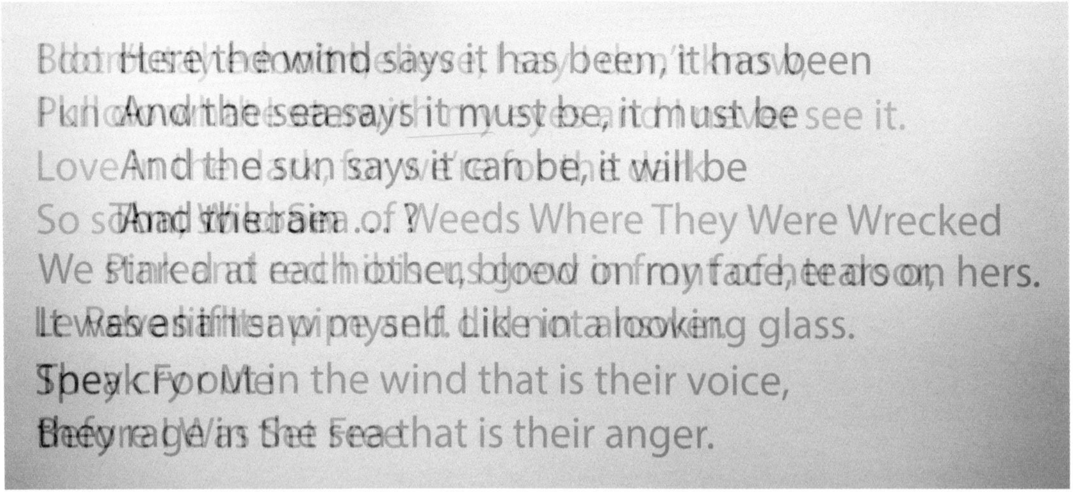


**Fig. 4 (pp.140-141)**
Regina Agu, *Sea Change*, 2016, Vinyl print, 70 x 6 feet (approximately), Collection of the Artist, Installation view at Project Row Houses, Houston, TX. Photo credit: Alex Barber © Regina Agu 2019

**Fig. 5**
Regina Agu, *Reprise*, 2017, Digitally printed vinyl, 98 x 48 inches, Collection of the Artist, Installation view at DiverseWorks, Houston, TX, Photo credit: Paul Hester © Regina Agu 2019

for the slave trade, and its connection to important historical moments like Juneteenth, a nationally celebrated day of commemoration for the end of slavery. Juneteenth marks the date in Texas when emancipation was finally enforced—and enslaved people finally freed—two full years after the official end of slavery. In visiting Galveston, I was also very interested in why these histories were largely omitted from Galveston's representation, in favor of conveying the place primarily as a regional beach destination for tourists. In 2014, I visited Galveston—as I had during so many other summers, just to enjoy the beach and take some photos—and happened to encounter the large sargassum piles that had washed up on the beach that summer, which were causing major disruptions to tourists. I was intrigued, took some photos, and didn't think too much of it until I began to pay attention to news reports about the unusual size of the seaweed piles, and realized that other coastal areas in the Caribbean and on the west coast of Africa also experienced an unusually large volume of sargassum that summer.

The geographic connection immediately caught my attention, as these are the regions that I am deeply invested in through my work. However, it was not until 2016 that I began to research sargassum and how it circulates, to try to understand the reasons behind the massive volume and atypical patterns of sargassum that summer. I reached out to two writers who had covered the 2014 incident. They connected me to a researcher based in Galveston, Dr. Tom Linton, who was researching the factors that lead to this massive sargassum invasion in 2014. Dr. Linton was very generous in introducing me to people on the Galveston Parks Board, and engineers at Texas A&M University at Galveston including Dr. Jens Figlus, who invited me to learn more about his research. He also brought me to visit the site that I ended up photographing for *Sea Change*, which was a series of dunes being constructed by Dr. Figlus and engineers at Galveston A&M to test out different methods to deal with the existing sargassum, and projected future sargassum volumes.

At the same time that I was working on this research, the novel *Wide Sargasso Sea* by Jean Rhys was reissued with a new introduction by Edwidge Danticat. For me, the novel became a text that informed the project, alongside scientific studies. I pulled out excerpts from the novel that focused around female protagonists, which described both the natural and political landscape that they confronted in the book. In addition to the large panorama installation, these texts were included in my installation at Project Row Houses as a series of layered couplets printed on transparencies pinned to the wall. I often work with text in my work in such pieces as *Reprise*, a layered text-based wall installation that I created at DiverseWorks in Houston (2017; Fig. 5).

**RD** I really enjoyed the material you chose for the installation of *Sea Change*. It allowed for so much movement that you can't get from a photograph, and created subtle but stunning performative elements as the work moved in response to its viewers. How did you choose your material?

**RA** The material I selected to print *Sea Change* (2016; Figs. 1 and 3) was very important. I chose to print the panorama on vinyl as a reference to the tourist billboards that presented Galveston as an idyllic beachfront, and the fact that I was shooting an artificial, constructed series of dunes, created to respond to sargassum's disruption of the landscape. The image itself is also a digital construction. *Sea Change* is printed as one continuous print, but the image itself consists of multiple panoramas layered on top of each other, overlapping to create disruptions and ghost images. The layering also speaks to the layered histories of that particular coastline. I installed the piece with drapes and folds to further speak to the constructed nature of the landscape, and to create a sense of physical movement.

**RD** How has *Sea Change* informed your deeper investigations of Black Geographies?

**RA** In my research for *Sea Change*, I really wanted to understand the many different frameworks and approaches we use to think about landscape in a broad sense, and the multi-faceted histories of Galveston in particular. I've been very interested in the field of geography for some time, and spent a lot of time with texts such as Paul Gilroy's *The Black Atlantic*, for example. *Sea Change* really pushed me to engage with critical geography, and Black Geographies, in particular, as a theoretical model for both my historical and contemporary explorations of the Gulf Coast. Beginning with *Sea Change*, my understanding of these theories deepened, and eventually led me to engaging with New Orleans through my participation in the Black Geographies specialty group at the Association of American Geographers annual conference in New Orleans in 2018.

**RD** You reference *Sea Change* as the starting point for many of these merging interests, but I would like you to speak about your earlier landscape studies and drawings, and how they have been part of this ongoing investigation within your practice.

**RA** *Sea Change* was definitely part of an evolving body of work—photographic landscape studies have been central to my practice for many years. One early body of work which helped me to first articulate my interest in landscape photography was developed over a period of four years, between 2011 and 2014. During this time, I began walking through Houston's Third Ward, documenting the landscape in transition—showing vanishing green

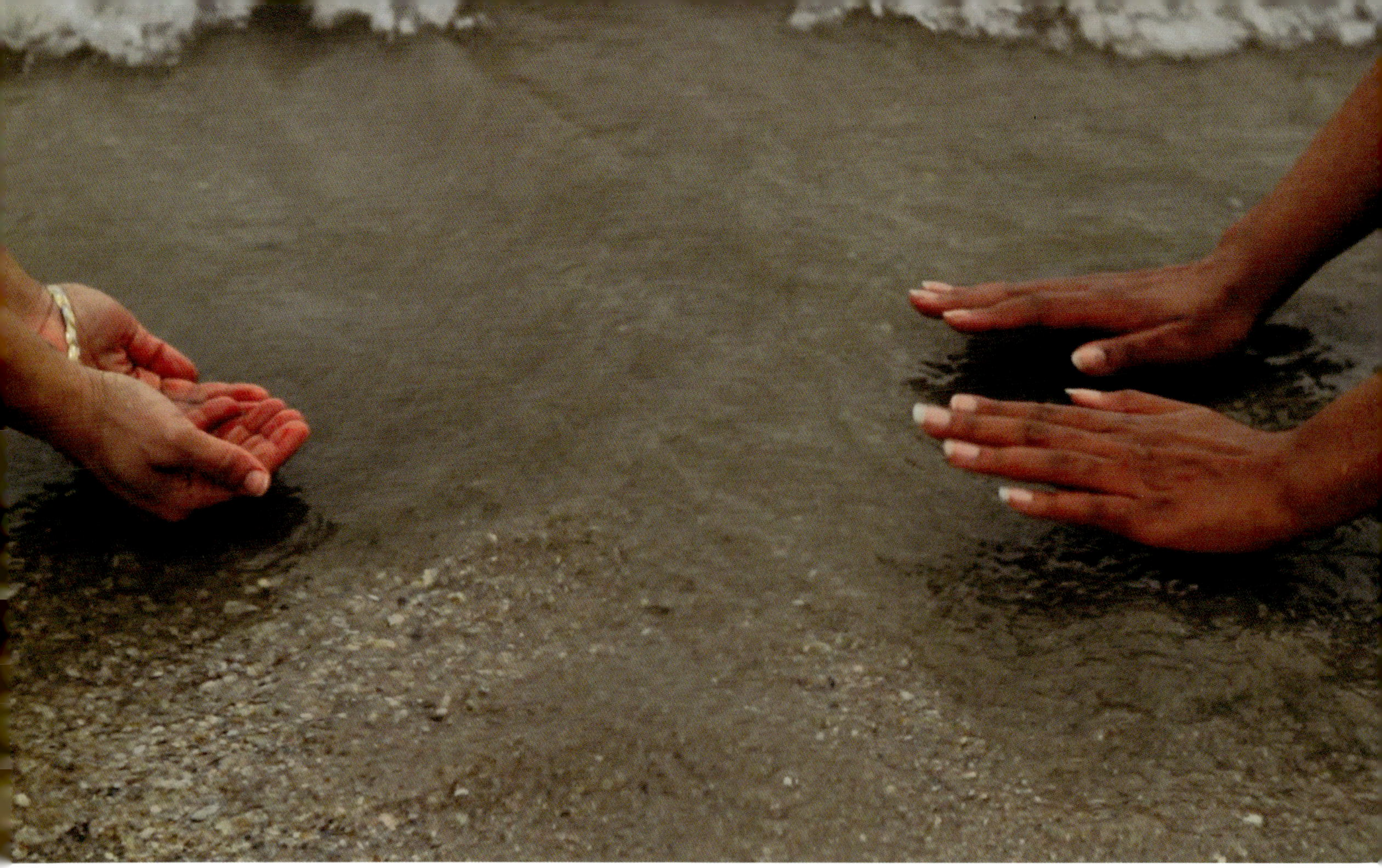

spaces, property redevelopment, foundations and floors of structures that no longer stood, and other changes. At first, I was just interested in capturing and recording the changes to my particular route over time, but when I looked back at this work, I saw that I had developed an archive of photographic studies that helped ground my research into representations of black landscapes.

In addition, my work responding to relationships between the Gulf of Mexico and the Gulf of Guinea has continued to grow. In addition to my ongoing research, and photography, I have created multiple bodies of work including drawings, installations, texts, public collaborative projects, and video. Each of these projects, and each different working method, has allowed me to take up different histories, different memories, different modes of representation. One such project is a collaborative video with Palestinian filmmaker and anthropologist Hadeel Assali, a work in progress that we are currently titling *Louisiana Water* (2019; Fig. 6). Several years ago we shot a video and series of performative actions in the Gulf off the coast of Cameron, Louisiana. We were interested in exploring performance and video as a way of speaking to some of the parallels of our families' immigration journeys into the United States through Louisiana, and the geopolitical implications of water access and water health in Palestine and Nigeria. As our practices have continued to grow, and I have returned to Louisiana, we are now revisiting this footage and planning to complete the project.

I look at *Sea Change* as the culmination of many years of work. At the same time, it brought me to a new starting place in my practice, as I began focusing on the history and potential of the panorama.

**Fig. 6**
Regina Agu and Hadeel Assali, *Still from Louisiana Water (working title)*, 2019, Digital video, Collection of the Artists © Regina Agu and Hadeel Assali 2019

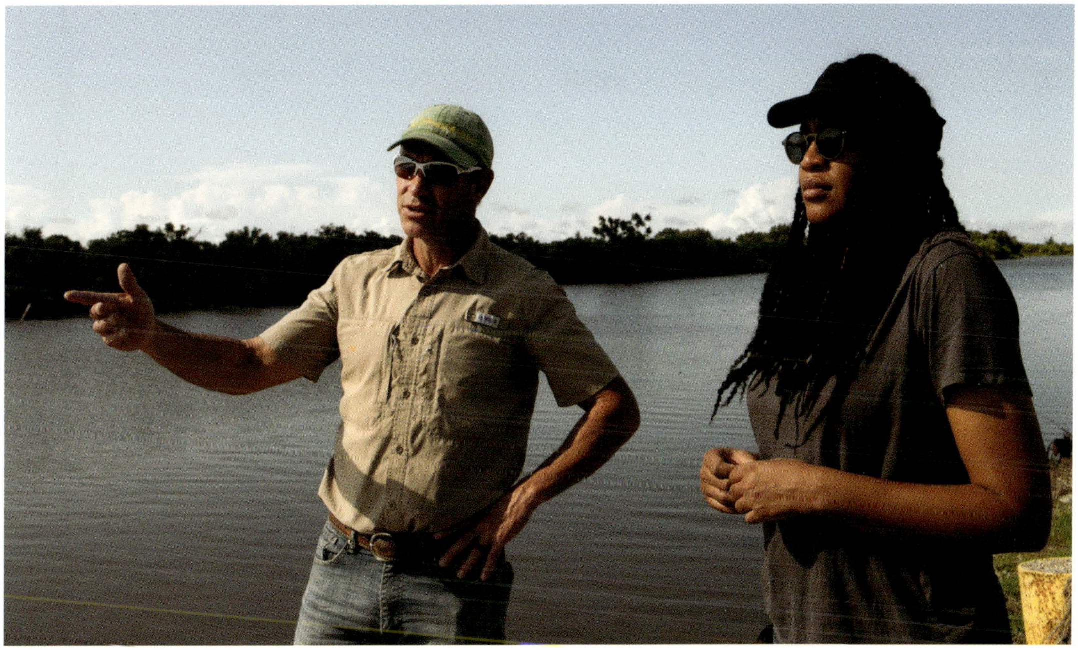

**Fig. 7**
Regina Agu with David Baker, Environmental Curator at A Studio in the Woods, at Pointe à la Hache, Louisiana, 2019, Photography by Seth Boonchai

**RD** You've been in New Orleans, developing this new project with the New Orleans Museum of Art. Can you talk about your experiences so far, and the site visits you've done during the first stages of your residency?

**RA** Through my residency with A Studio in the Woods, I am doing a series of site visits to landscapes across Louisiana in preparation for my exhibition at NOMA this November (2019; Fig. 7). I completed the first of this series of different visits with Katie Pfohl, Curator of Modern and Contemporary Art at NOMA, during the second week of August.

I knew entering my research for this project that I wanted to get to know New Orleans through its waterways. Over the course of a series of week-long visits to different places across the state, I did a series of initial site visits that gave me a kind of crash course on New Orleans' complicated relationship to water, which helped me to gain a deeper understanding of the precarity of the landscape of this particular region of the Gulf Coast. First, we visited the North Shore of Lake Pontchartrain with David Baker, the environmental curator at A Studio in the Woods, to understand the range of ecosystems in the area. I was surprised to learn about the pine forests that exist on the North Shore, which are not what I previously would have associated with this region. I was particularly interested to learn about the importance of the natural cycles of fire in the pyrogenic landscape—the role of fire in a landscape we associate so much more with water.

Next, David took us to Placquemines Parish to see the impact and effects of the levee systems, diversion pipes, and spillways, and to understand the effects of freshwater and changes in salinity in traditional oyster and crab-trapping areas. At Point à La Hache, we were lucky to come across a group of fishermen who shared openly with us about the ways they are struggling to adapt to the changing salinity of the site, caused by fresh water coming in through the Mardi Gras Pass—a natural diversion of water praised by some environmentalists, that is also drastically changing local ecosystems, and people's way of life.

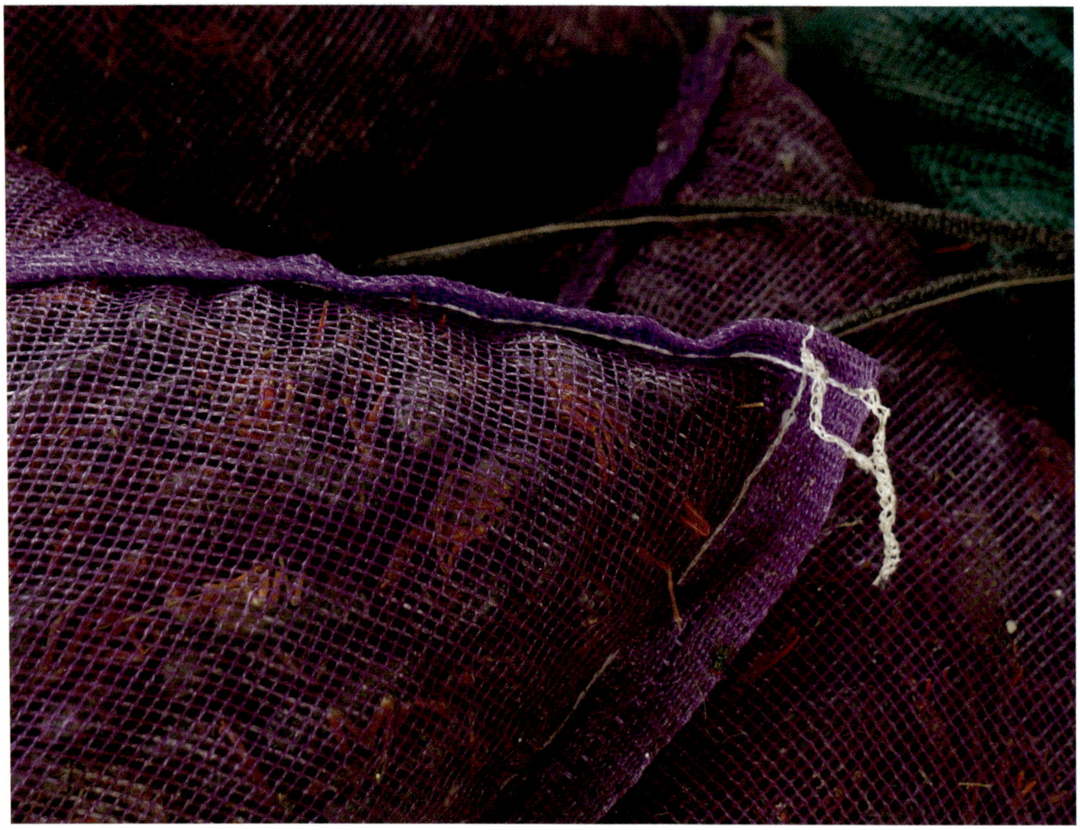

**Fig. 8**
Regina Agu, *Documentation of Site Visit to Pointe à la Hache (Crawfish Sacks)*, 2019, Digital image, Collection of the Artist © Regina Agu 2019

Some are easily adjusting their boats and gear to catch crawfish, which thrive in more fresh water, while others struggled to change (2019; Fig. 8). The men were from Plaquemines, New Iberia, and other areas close to New Orleans, and each had an intimate understanding of the changing fishing and water cycles.

Then, we went on an eight hour boat excursion into the Gulf of Mexico, the Mississippi River Delta, and the Venice Marina with Richie Blink, the Plaquemines Community Outreach Coordinator for the National Wildlife Federation (2019; Fig. 9). During this visit, I was able to see firsthand the meeting of saltwater and freshwater in the Mississippi River Delta, and the vast amounts of land loss in some areas of the Gulf of Mexico. We also saw the building of new land by the Mississippi River in areas of the delta not constrained by levees, where the natural cycle of trapping sediment was allowed to occur (2019; Fig. 10).

Then, we went on an overnight visit Turtle Cove Environmental Research Station with Dr. Robert Moreau. When we arrived, we explored part of the Manchac Pass, but had to turn back because of an incoming storm, and ended up working at Turtle Cove that day. We explored the swamp boardwalk, and Rob gave us a thorough intro into the history of the region, the impacts of logging, and the many different factors resulting in land loss in the New Orleans area. The next day, we went out on a boat ride for most of the day with Rob into Manchac Pass, Lake Maurepas, and the Tickfaw River, which is bound by protected cypress that today are just a small sliver of what used to be a richly forested region (2019; Fig. 11). I learned about the history of the cypress forests and the realities of ongoing land loss in the Lake Maurepas area.

**Fig. 9 (opposite)**
Regina Agu, *Documentation of Site Visit to the Mississippi River Delta*, 2019, Digital image, Collection of the Artist © Regina Agu 2019

**Fig. 10 (pp. 148-149)**
Regina Agu, *Documentation of Site Visit to the Mississippi River Delta (Floating Marsh)*, 2019, Digital image, Collection of the Artist © Regina Agu 2019

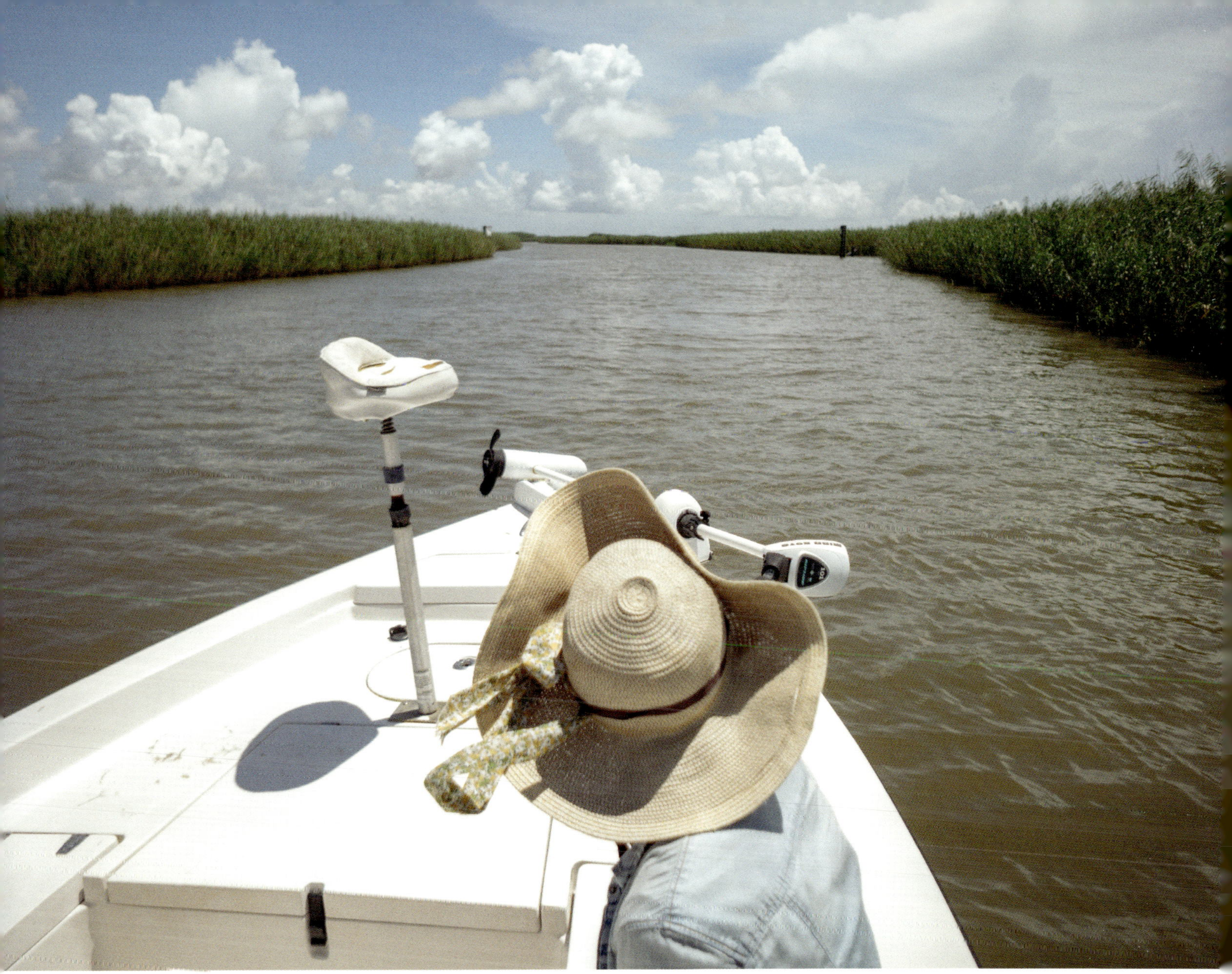

**RD** Thinking more on Black Geographies, can you speak about the role of black bodies and histories in the sites you visited? What was most striking to you? What are you hoping to investigate more deeply?

**RA** I am deeply interested in New Orleans as a Gulf Coast city, and its profound and precarious relationship to water. In my work and research, I seek to understand the history of the city and the contemporary manifestations of those histories through the lens of Black Geographies. It's easy (and deeply relevant) to focus on the events surrounding Hurricane Katrina as one entry point into the history of New Orleans. But, the impact of the storm on certain areas of the city, and the changes to the city afterwards in terms of its black population, cultural landscape, approaches to land development and infrastructure, and so many other layers were determined by a larger overarching set of policies and histories. In going on these different site visits and getting to know the lay of the land in a very direct sense, I've better understood the way that water has historically shaped New Orleans. Black Geographies are critical to understanding the contemporary and future landscape and geography of the city, and the Gulf Coast at large.

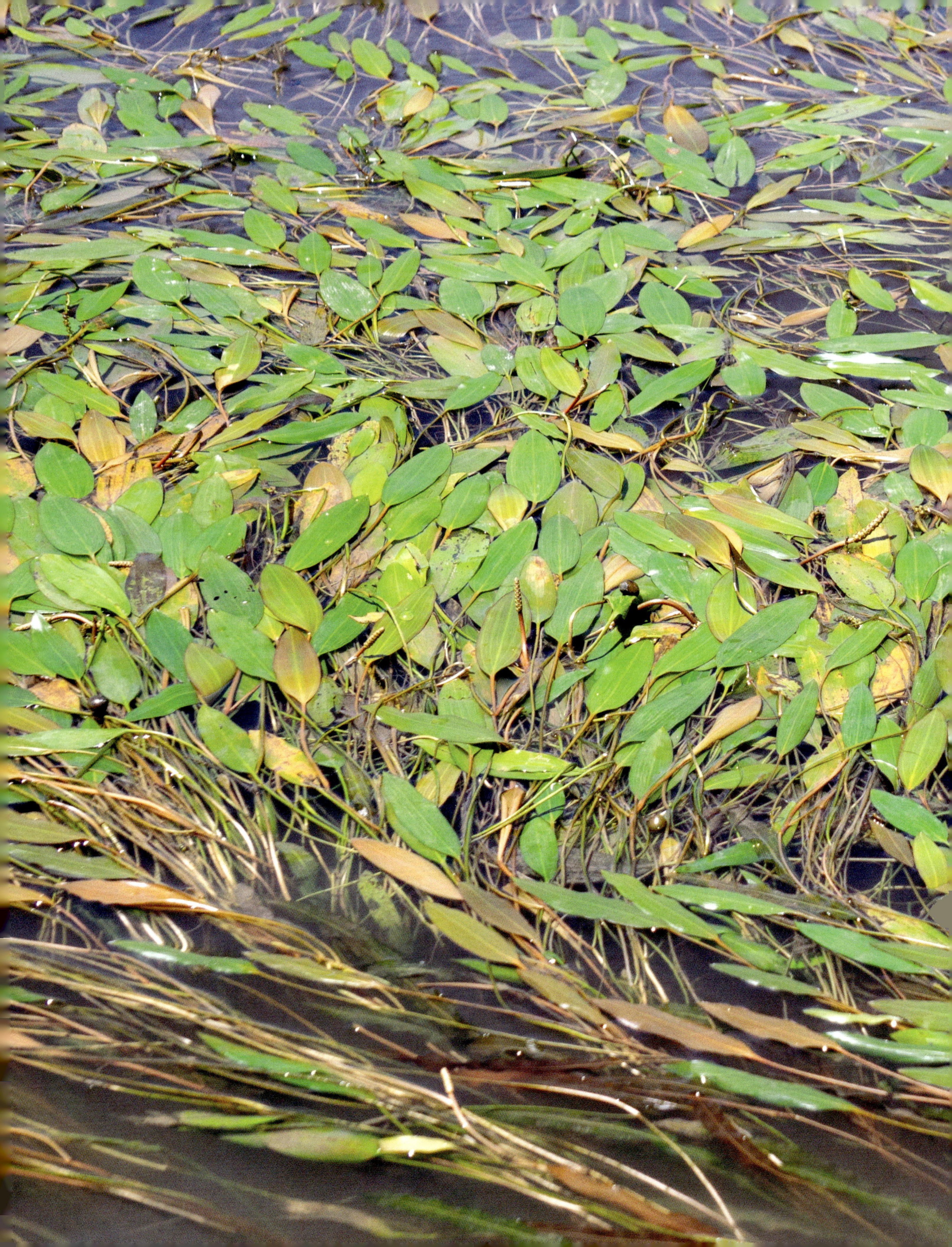

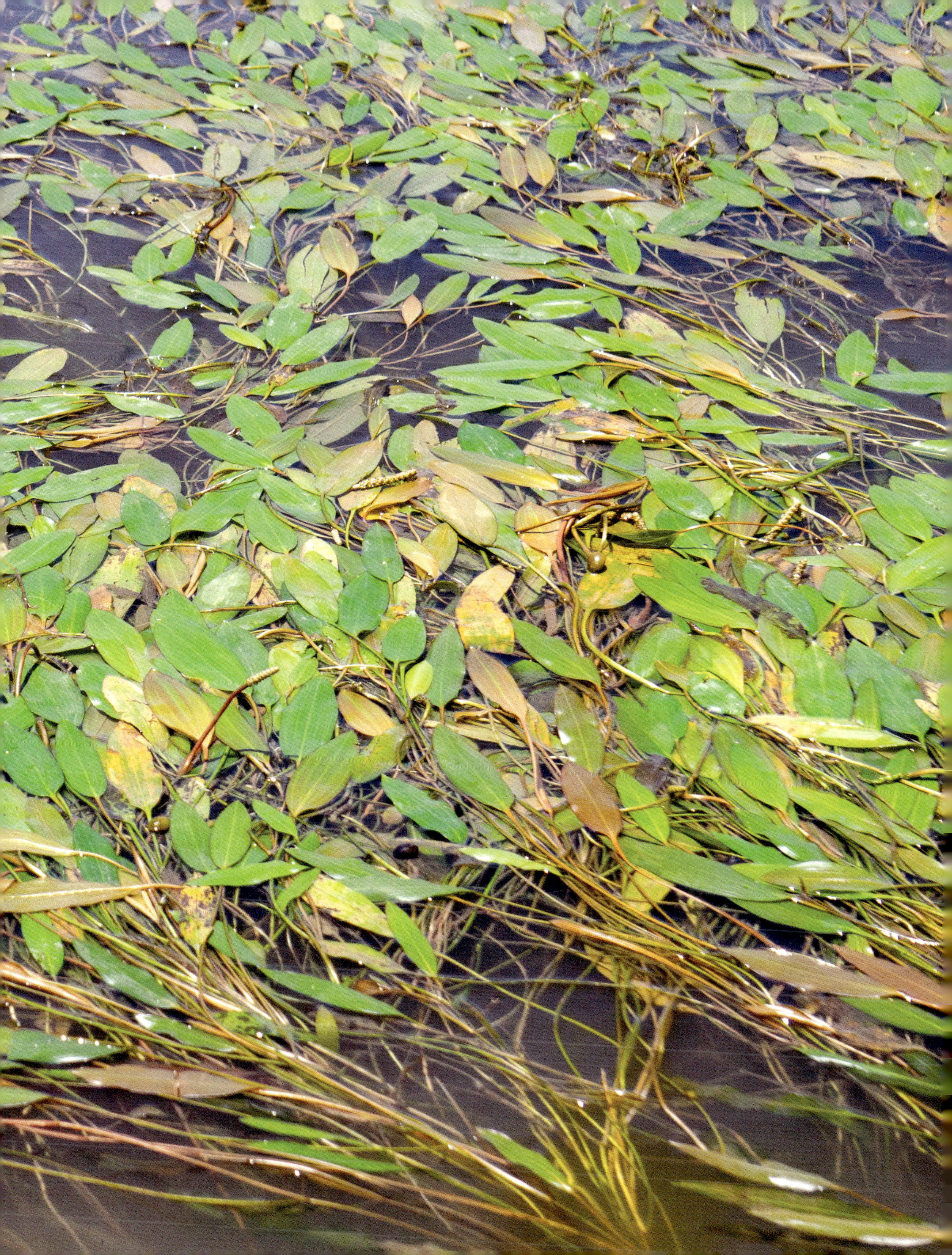

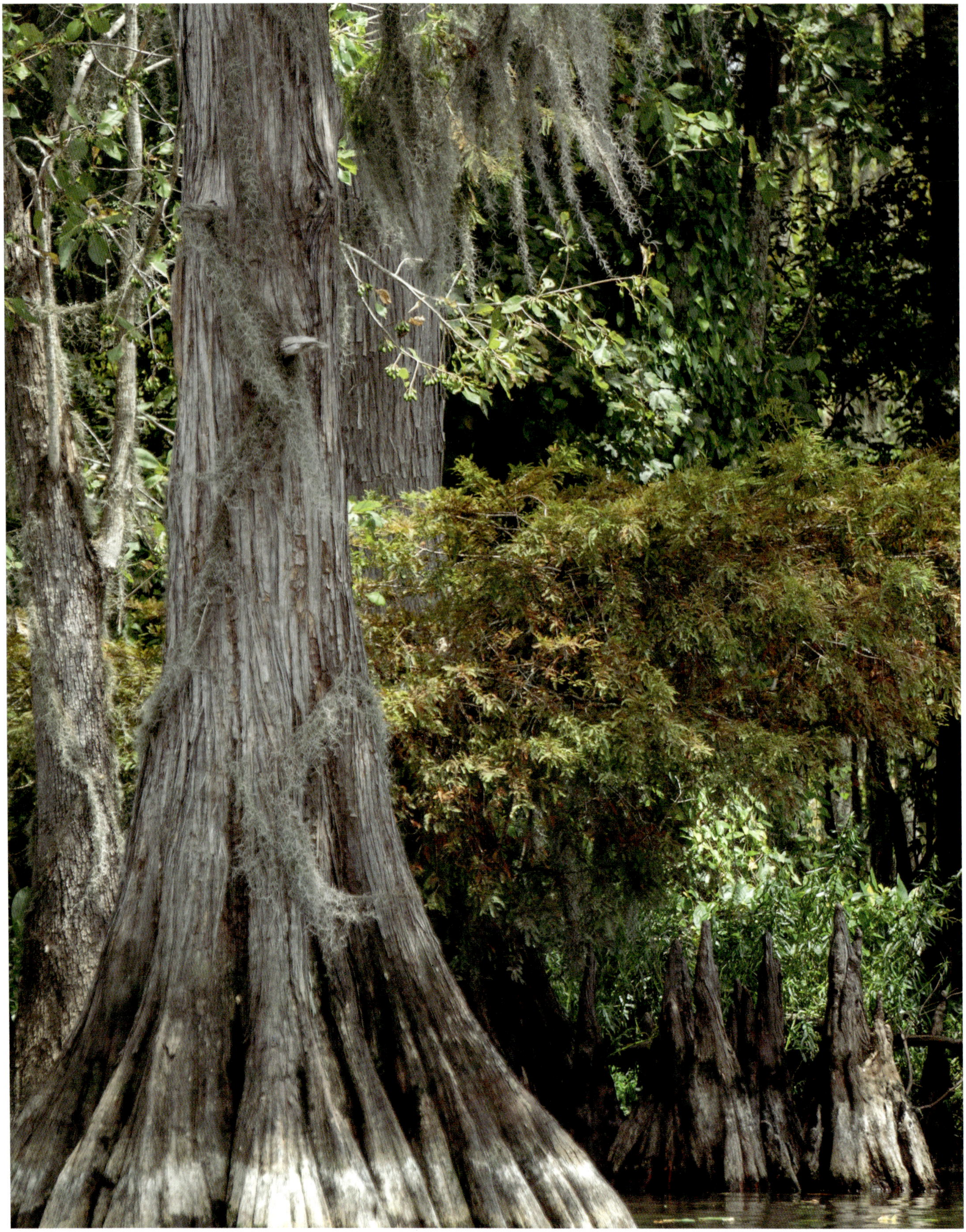

Fig. 11 (opposite)
Regina Agu, *Documentation of Site Visit to Lake Maurepas (Cypress Trees)*, 2019, Digital image, Collection of the Artist © Regina Agu 2019

**RD** Can you share more about your evolving ideas about what you will make for your project at NOMA?

**RA** For NOMA, I will create a multi-panel large scale panorama installation, photographed from the vantage point of waterways throughout and adjacent to New Orleans. This immersive, site-specific installation in the museum's Great Hall will be printed and installed with folds and drapes of fabric that reference topography and movement, in a manner similar to my prior work *Sea Change*. The panoramas will be shot during my residency at A Studio in the Woods, and will be informed by research I will conduct during that residency. Materially, the panoramas will consider the intertwined histories of landscape painting and landscape photography, and will reference sites in the *Inventing Acadia* exhibition, which will be shown concurrently at NOMA. I will research and identify contemporary sites connected to the ones represented in the historical paintings in the exhibition, focusing on our more recent relationships with these landscapes: as industrial sites, spaces for oil and natural resource extraction, places altered by changing waterways and coastlines, and landscapes marked by histories of slavery and colonial enterprises, and other geographic layers. This panorama will present multiple geographies and histories, grounded in my ongoing research into the Black Geographies, histories and spatial imaginaries of the Gulf Coast. I also hope to incorporate texts that draw from historical descriptions of the landscape, including nineteenth-century poetry, period geological and scientific texts, and other sources.

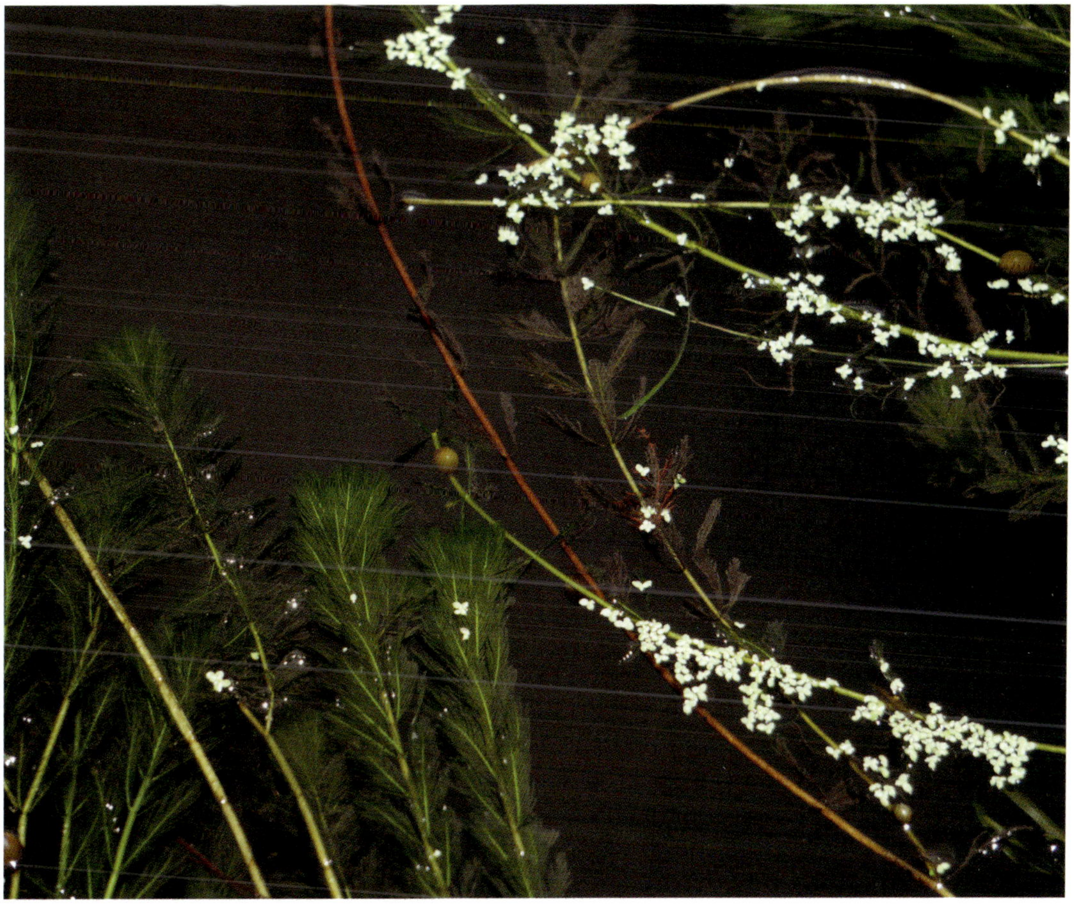

Fig. 12
Regina Agu, *Documentation of Site Visit to the Mississippi River Delta (Floating Marsh)*, 2019, Digital image, Collection of the Artist © Regina Agu 2019

# PLATES

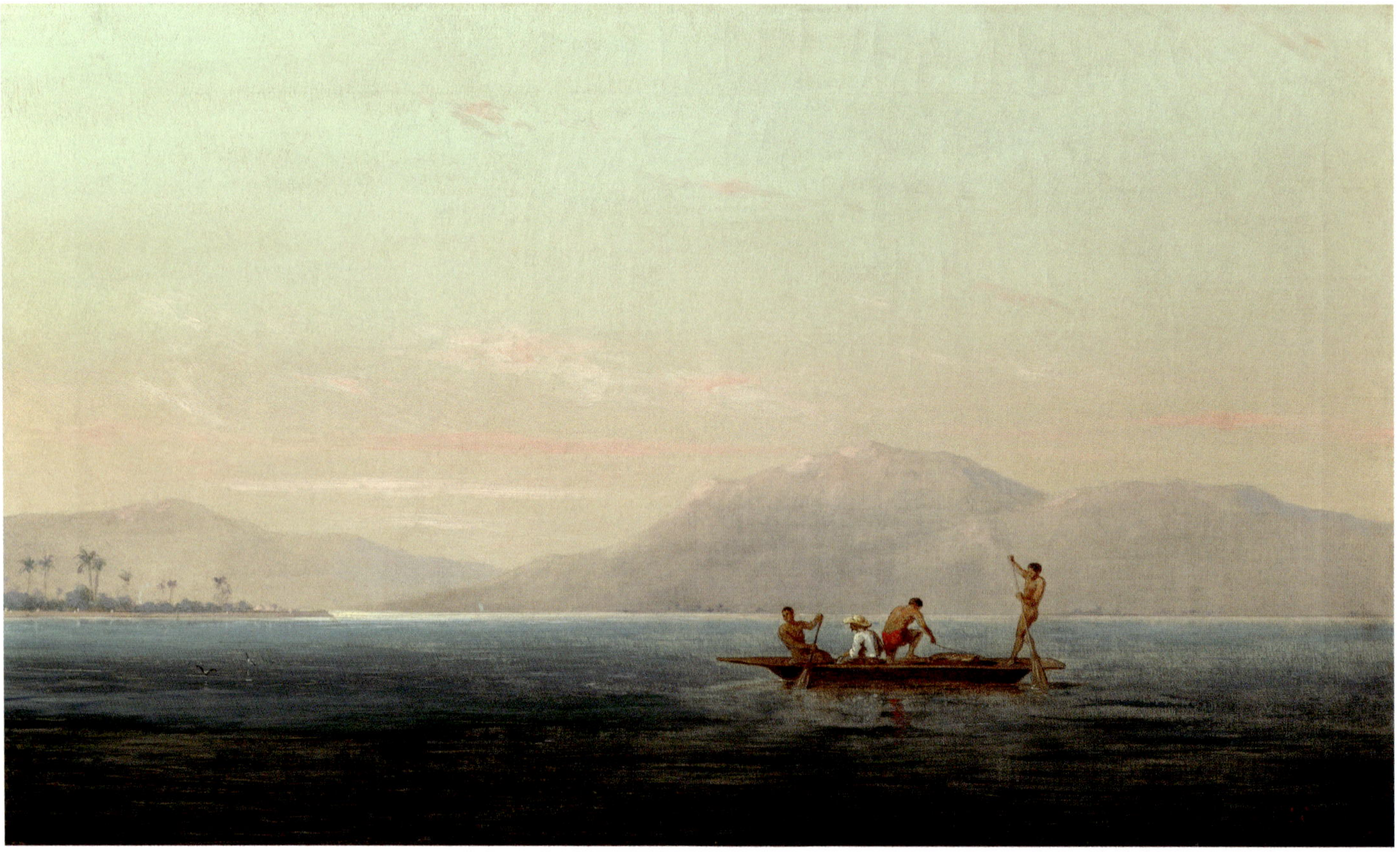

**Plate 1**
Judah LeVasseur,
*Fishing on Lake Managua, Nicaragua*, circa 1840,
Oil on canvas, 31 ½ x 21 ½ inches (framed),
Private Collection,
Image courtesy of Heritage Auctions.

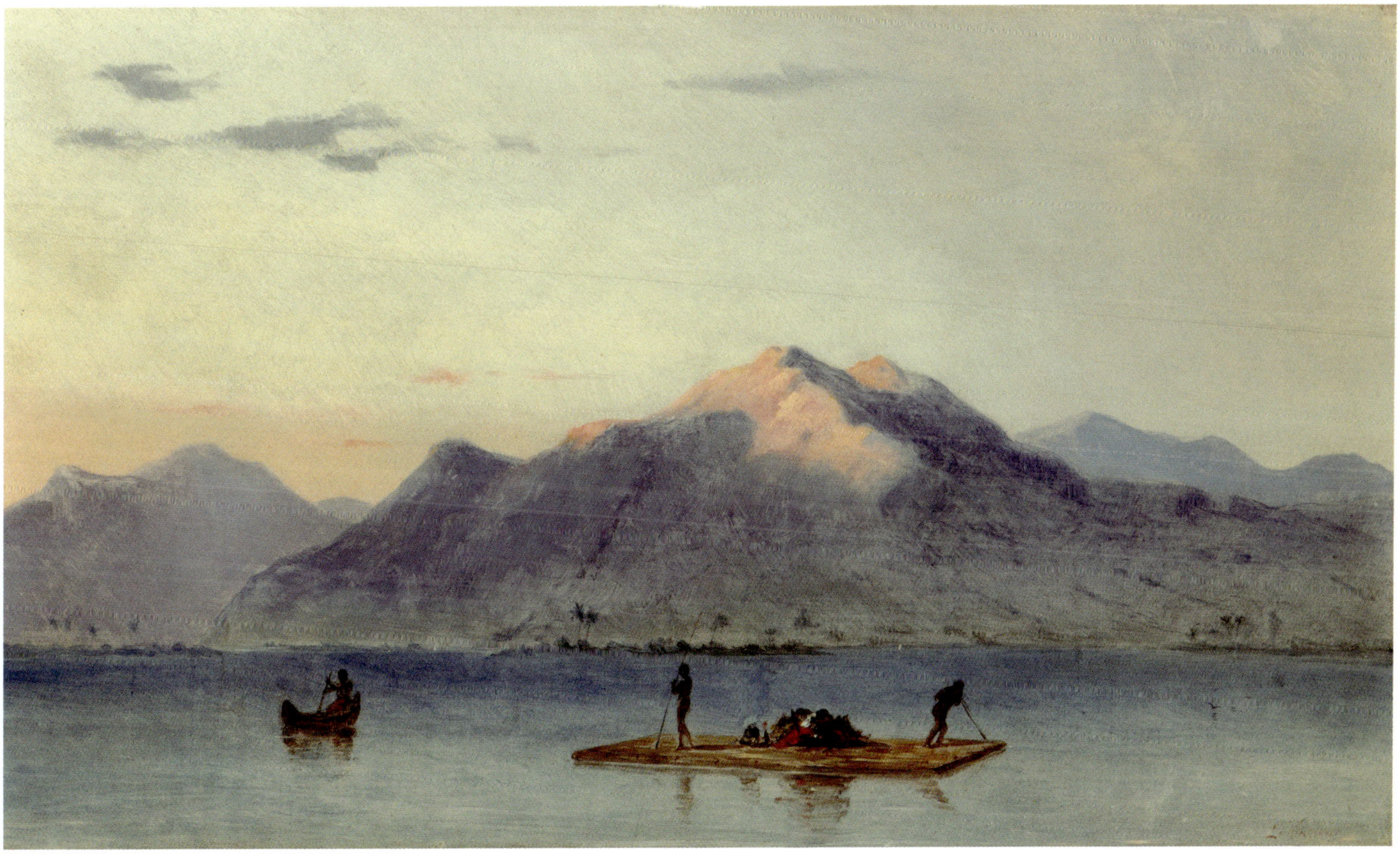

**Plate 2**
Judah LeVasseur,
*Fishing on Lake Managua, Nicaragua*, circa 1840,
Oil on canvas, 31 ½ x 21 ½ inches (framed),
Private Collection,
Image courtesy of Heritage Auctions.

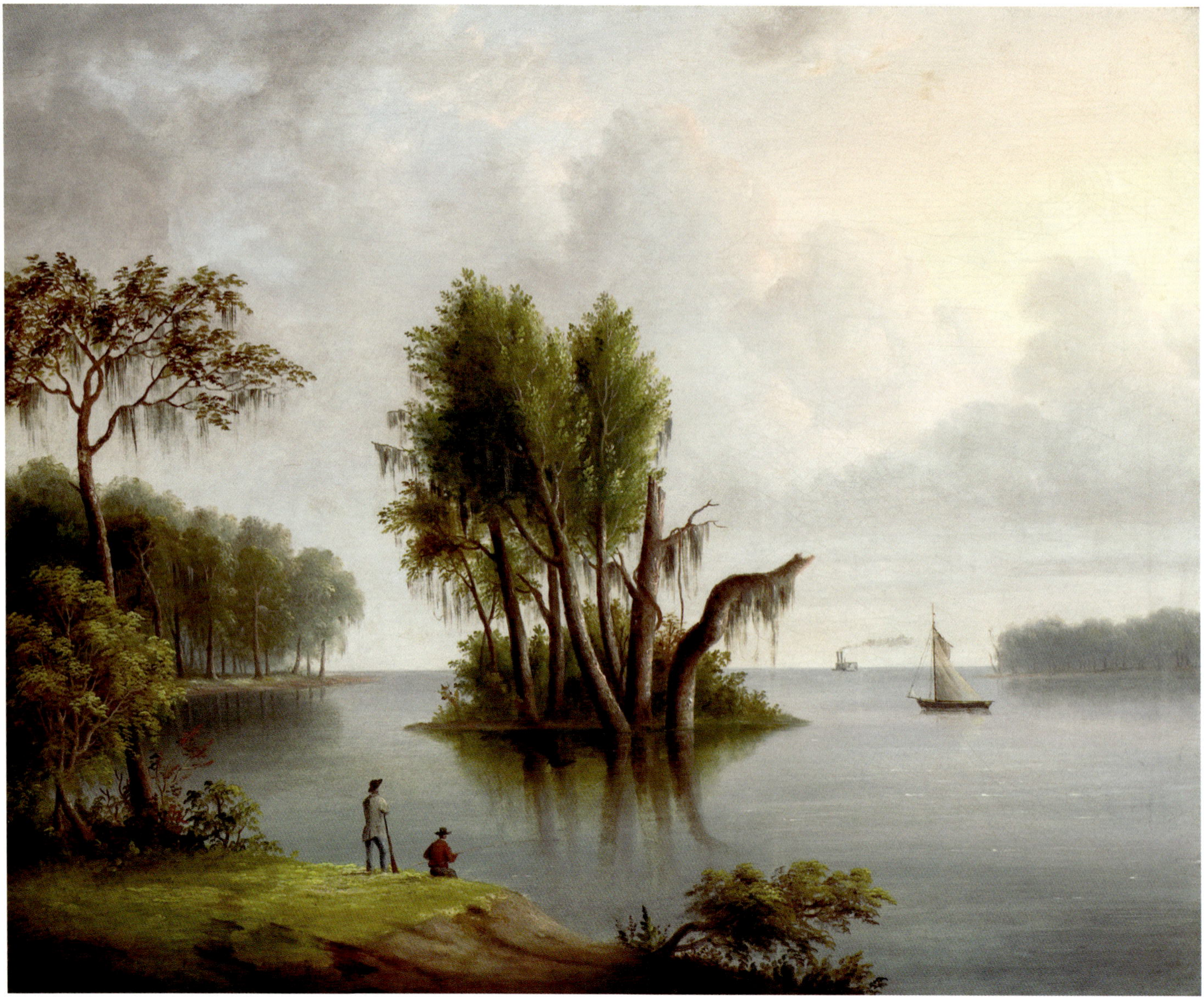

**Plate 3**
Robert Brammer,
*Mississippi Panorama*, 1842-53,
Oil on canvas, 29 x 36 inches,
Collection of Stacy and Jay Underwood.
Image courtesy of the Mississippi Museum of Art.

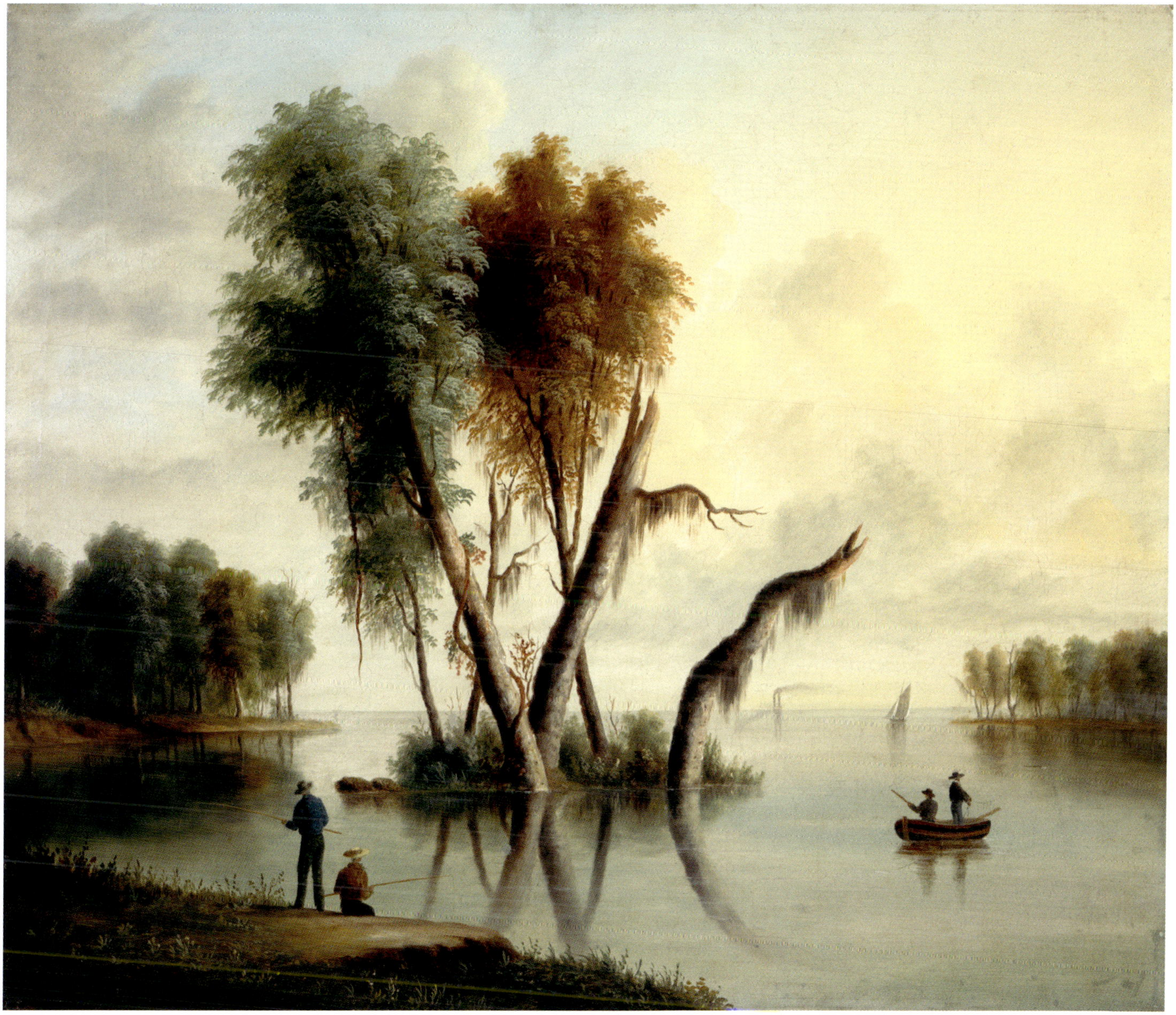

**Plate 4**
Robert Brammer,
*Mississippi Panorama*, circa 1850,
Oil on canvas, 32 x 37 inches (framed),
Ogden Museum of Southern Art.
Gift of the Roger H. Ogden Collection.
Photography by Patrick Barnes.

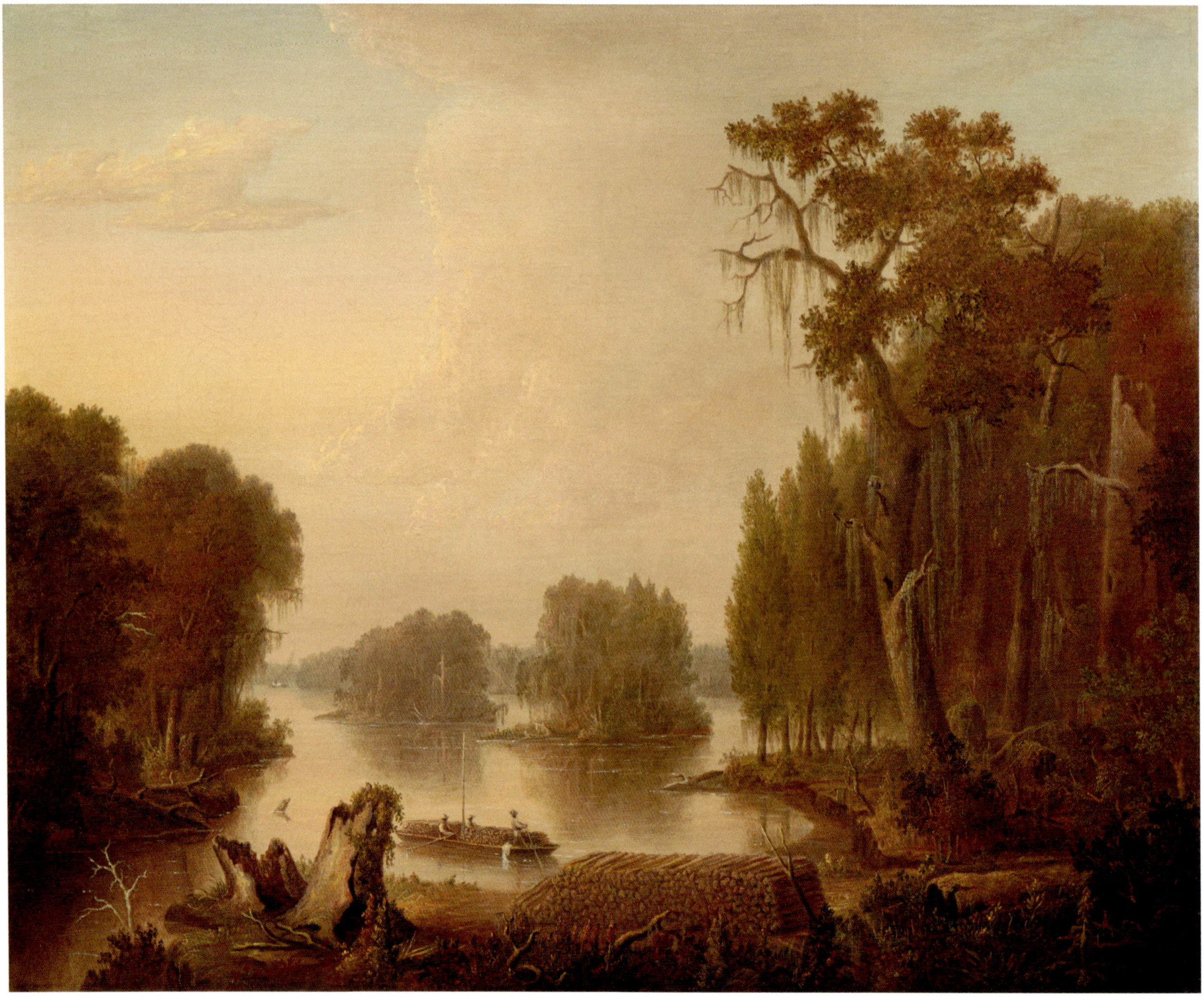

**Plate 5**
Robert Brammer,
*Wooding Up, Rodney, Mississippi*, circa 1842-53,
Oil on canvas, 41 x 48 inches (framed),
Collection of Bill Gunther,
Photography by Roman Alokhin.

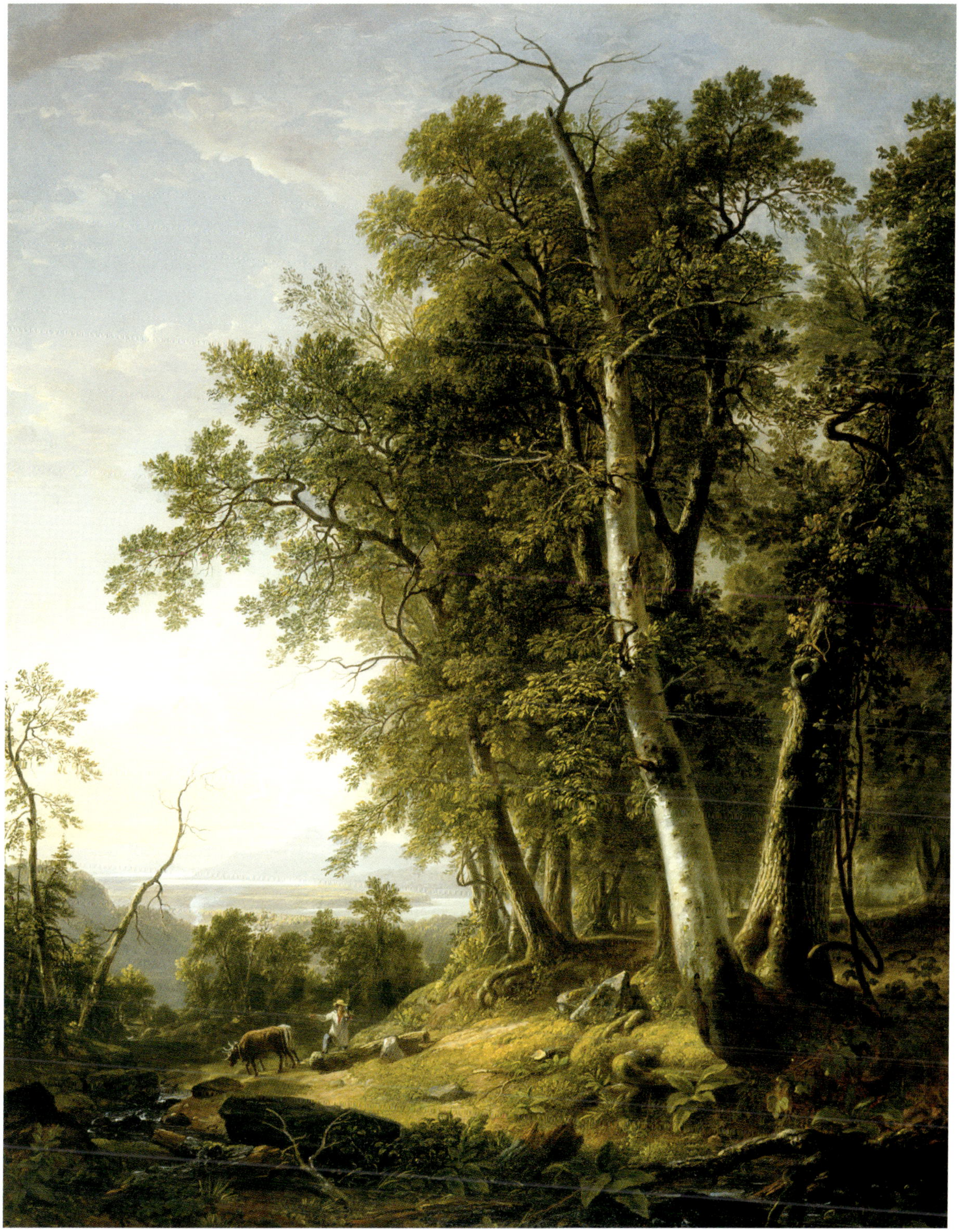

**Plate 6**
Asher Brown Durand,
*Forenoon*, 1847,
Oil on canvas, 73 ¼ x 61 ¼ x 5 ¾ inches (framed),
New Orleans Museum of Art,
Gift of the Fine Arts Club of New Orleans, 16.4

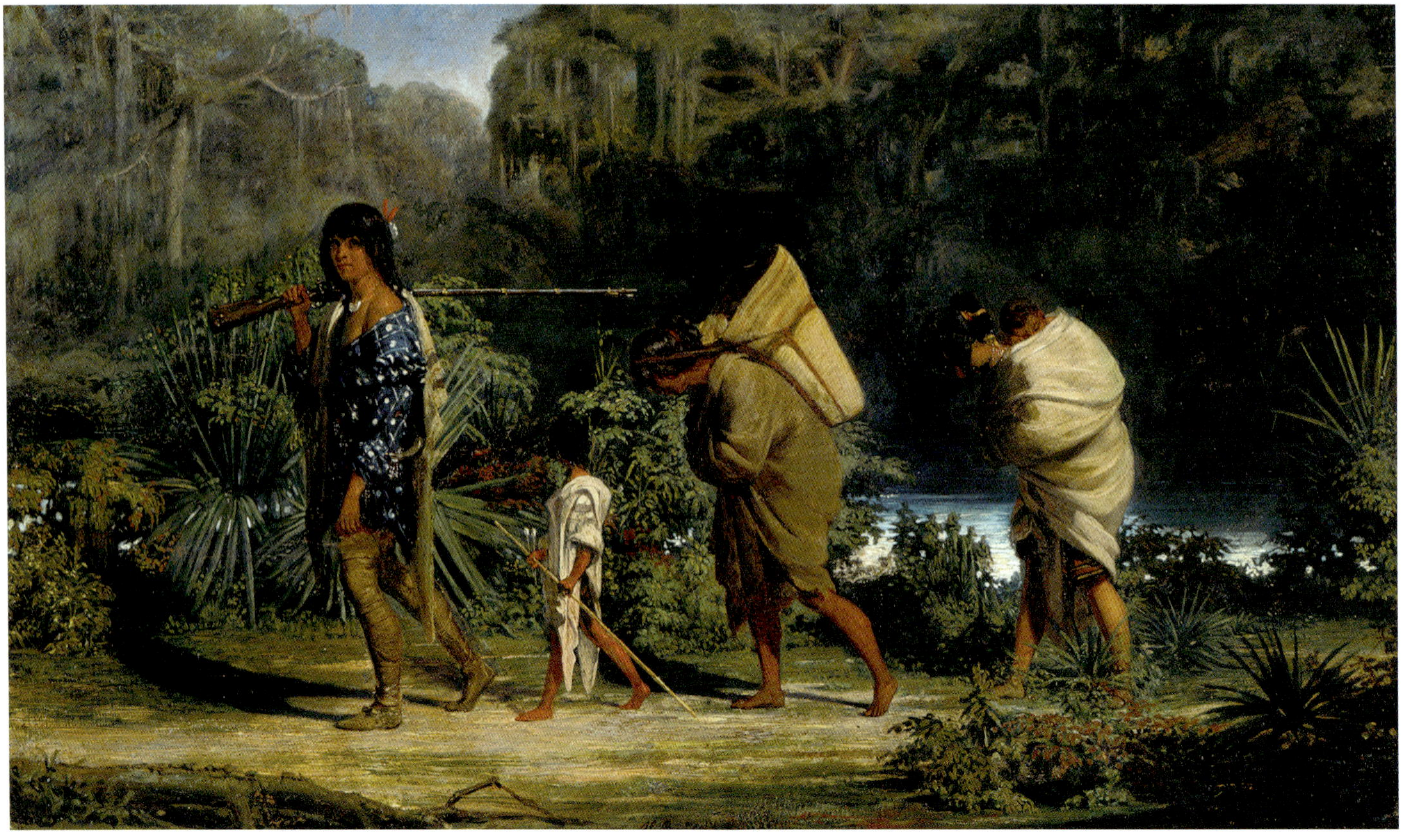

**Plate 7**
Alfred L. Boisseau,
*Marche d'Indiens de la Louisiane*
*(Louisiana Indians Walking Along a Bayou)*, 1847,
Oil on canvas, 28 1/4 x 44 3/8 x 2 inches (framed),
New Orleans Museum of Art,
Gift of William E. Groves, 56.34

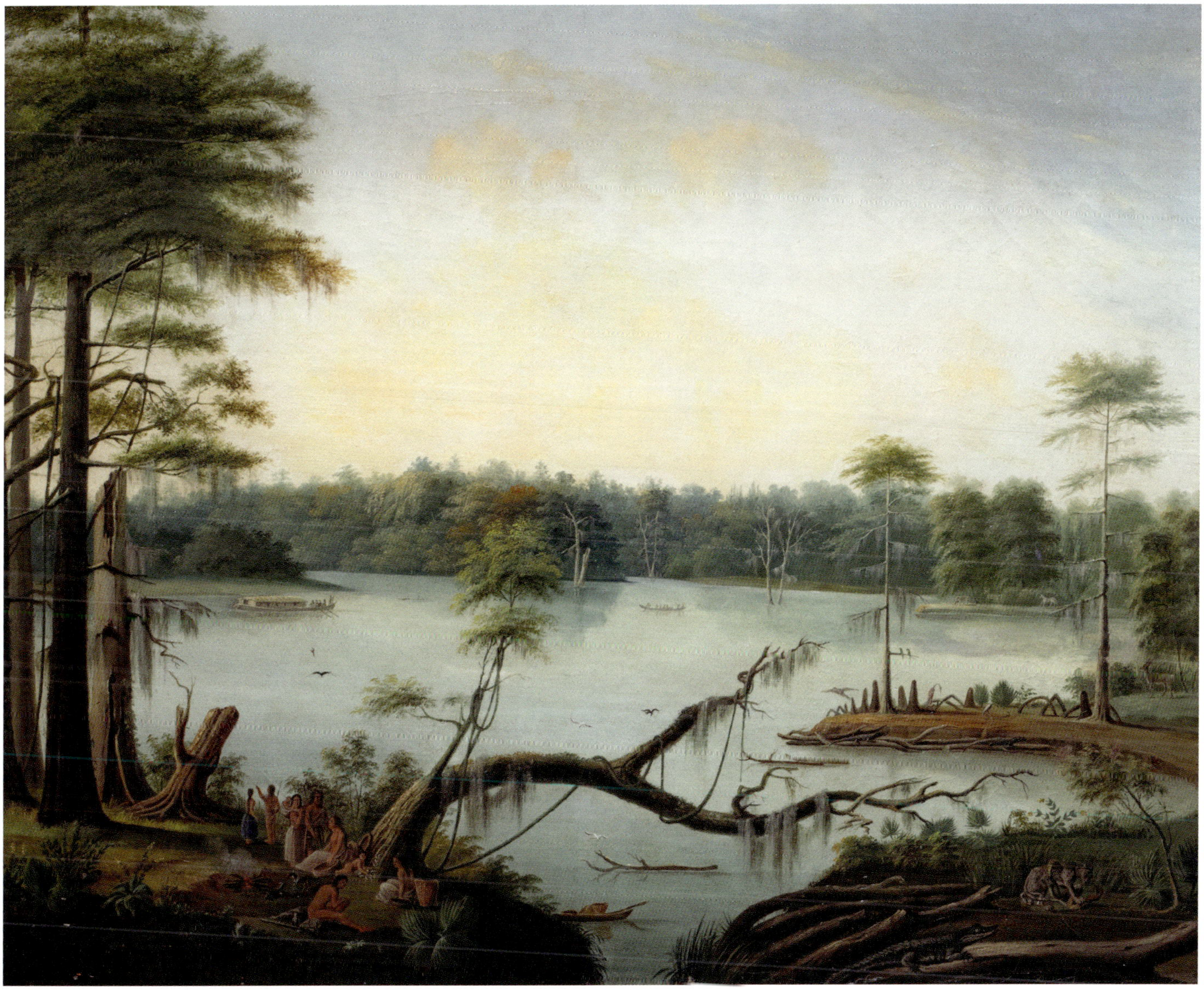

**Plate 8**

Toussaint François Bigot,
*Alchapalia, Louisiana*, 1848,
Oil on canvas, 29 ½ x 36 inches,
Roger Houston Ogden Collection,
Courtesy of Ogden Museum of Southern Art.
Photography by Patrick Barnes.

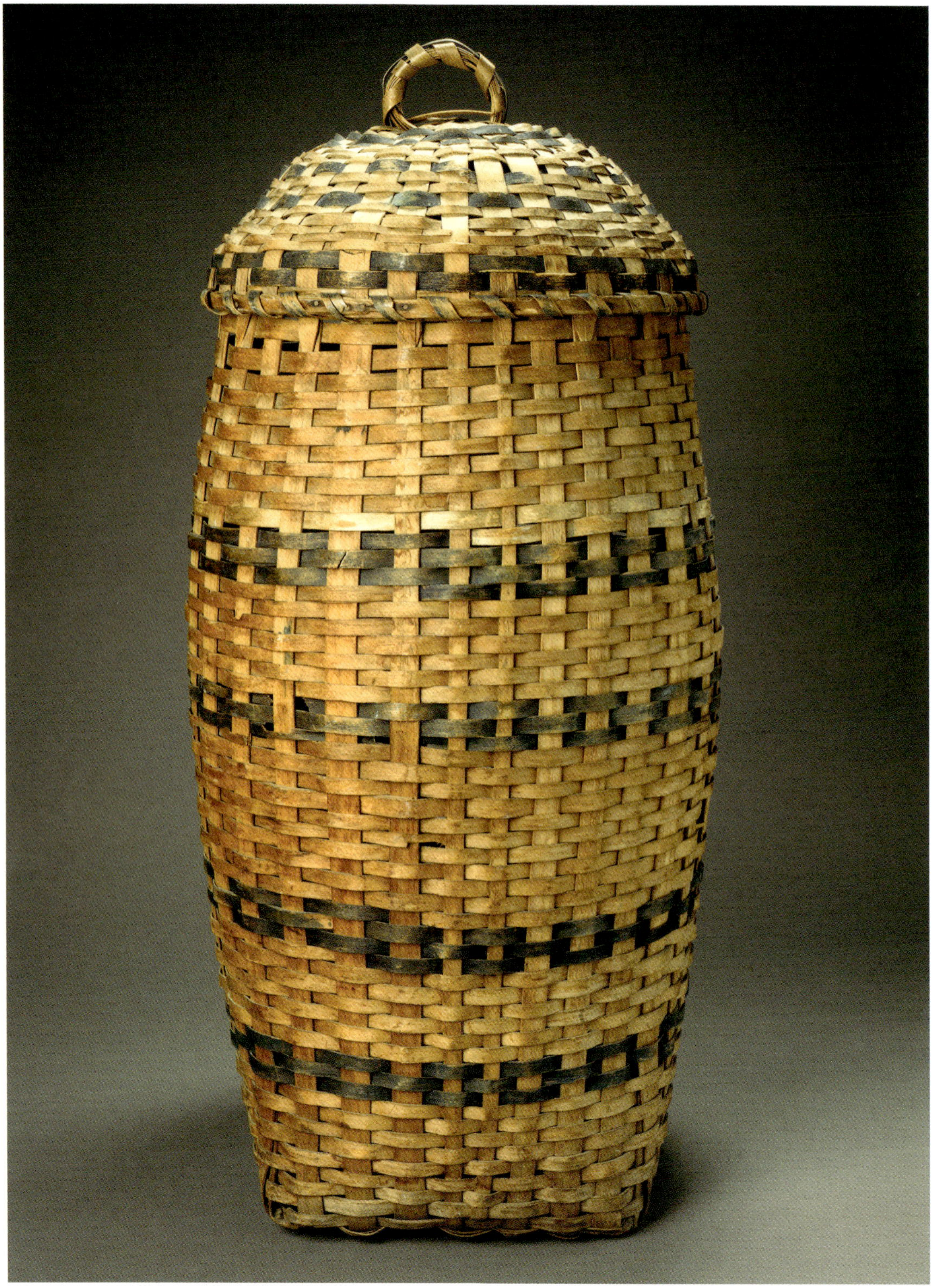

**Plate 9**
Unidentified Artist,
*Oak Basket*, circa 1900,
Natural fibers, 42 x 20 x 20 inches,
Collection of Don Fuson.
Photographed by: David Humphrey.

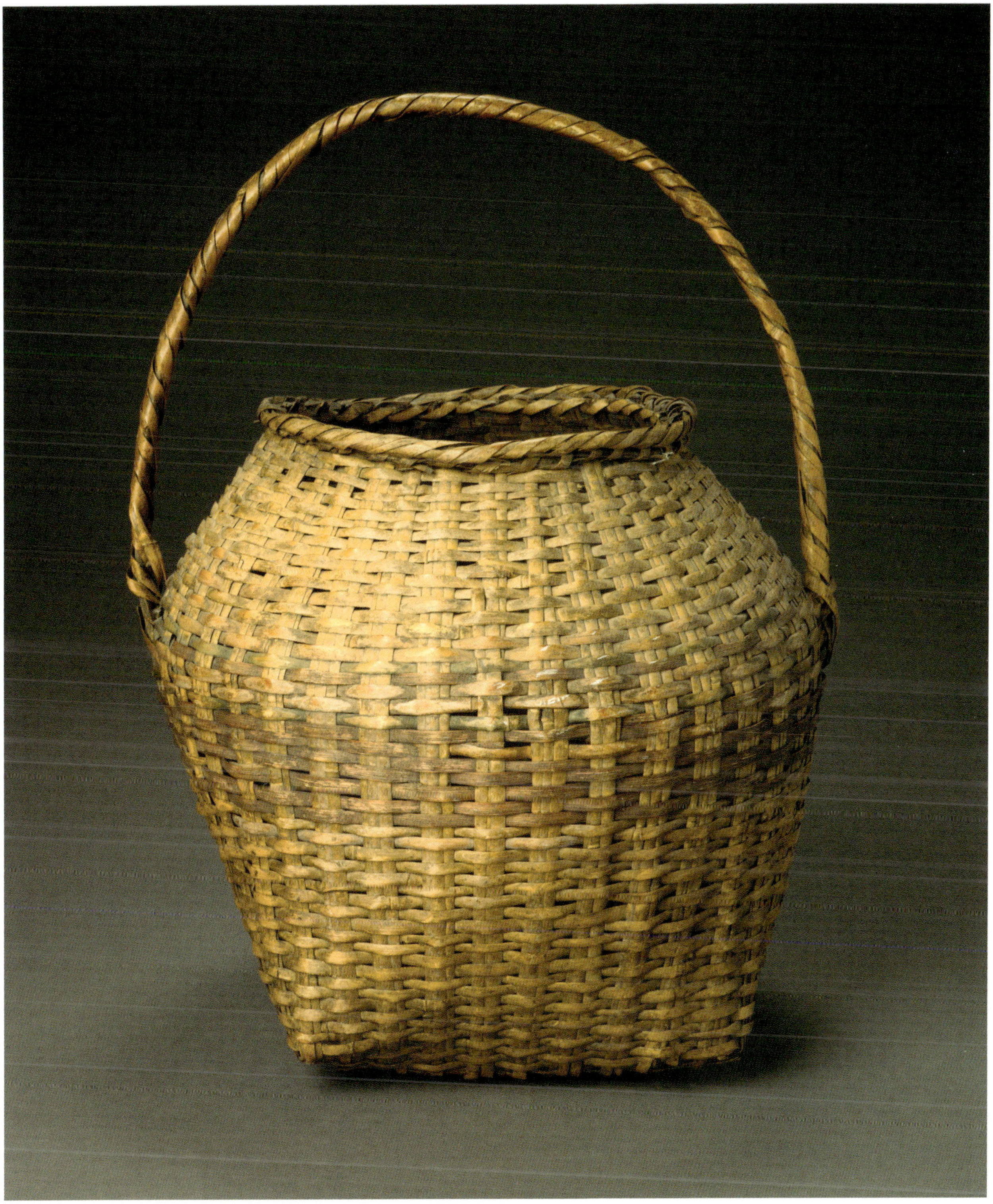

**Plate 10**
Atakapa-Ishak Peoples,
*Basket*, circa 1870,
Natural fibers, 16 x 8 x 8 inches,
Collection of Don Fuson.
Photographed by: David Humphrey.

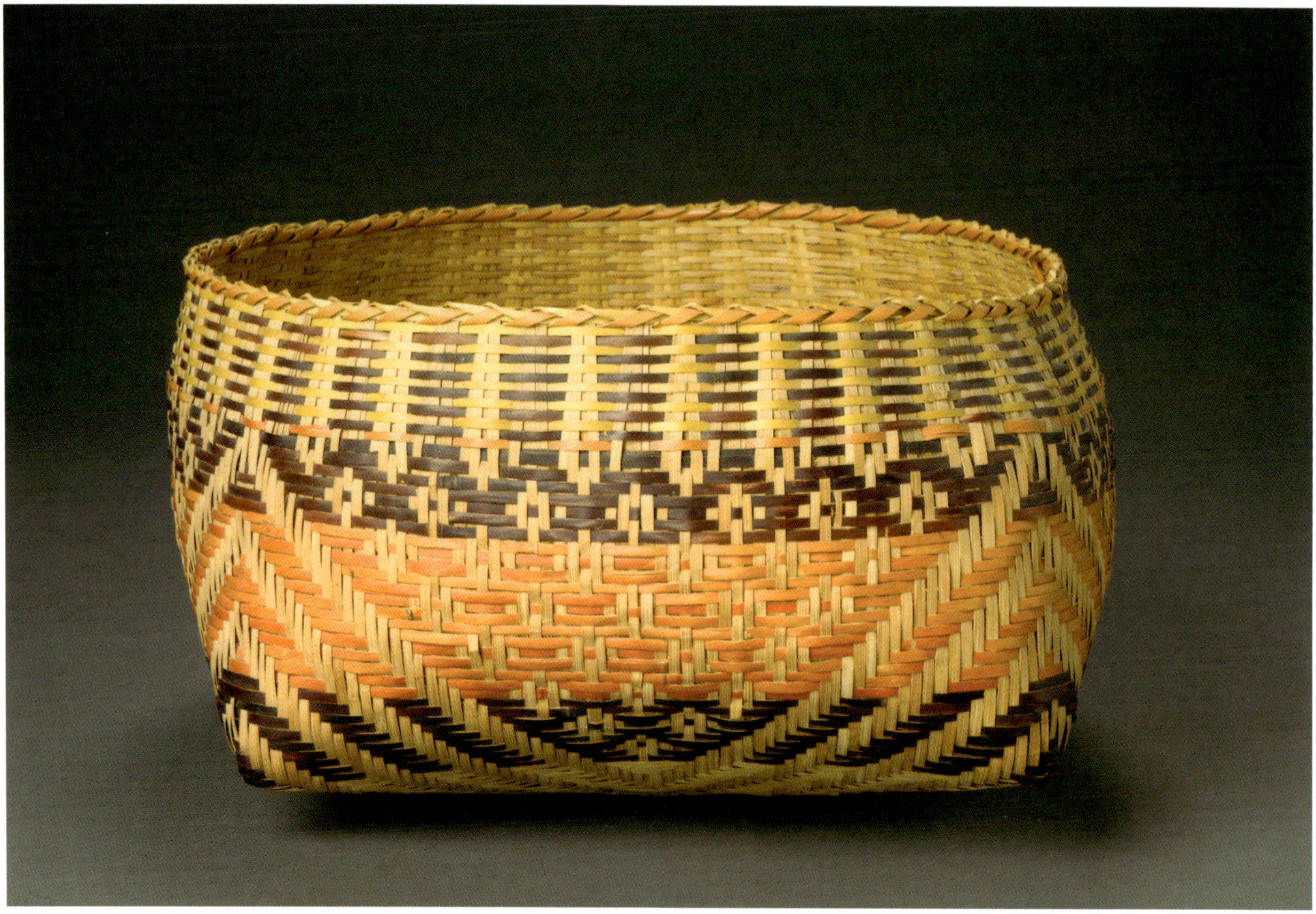

**Plate 11**
Chitimacha Peoples,
*Basket*, circa 1850-1900,
Natural fibers, 8 x 14 x 14 inches,
Collection of Don Fuson.
Photographed by: David Humphrey.

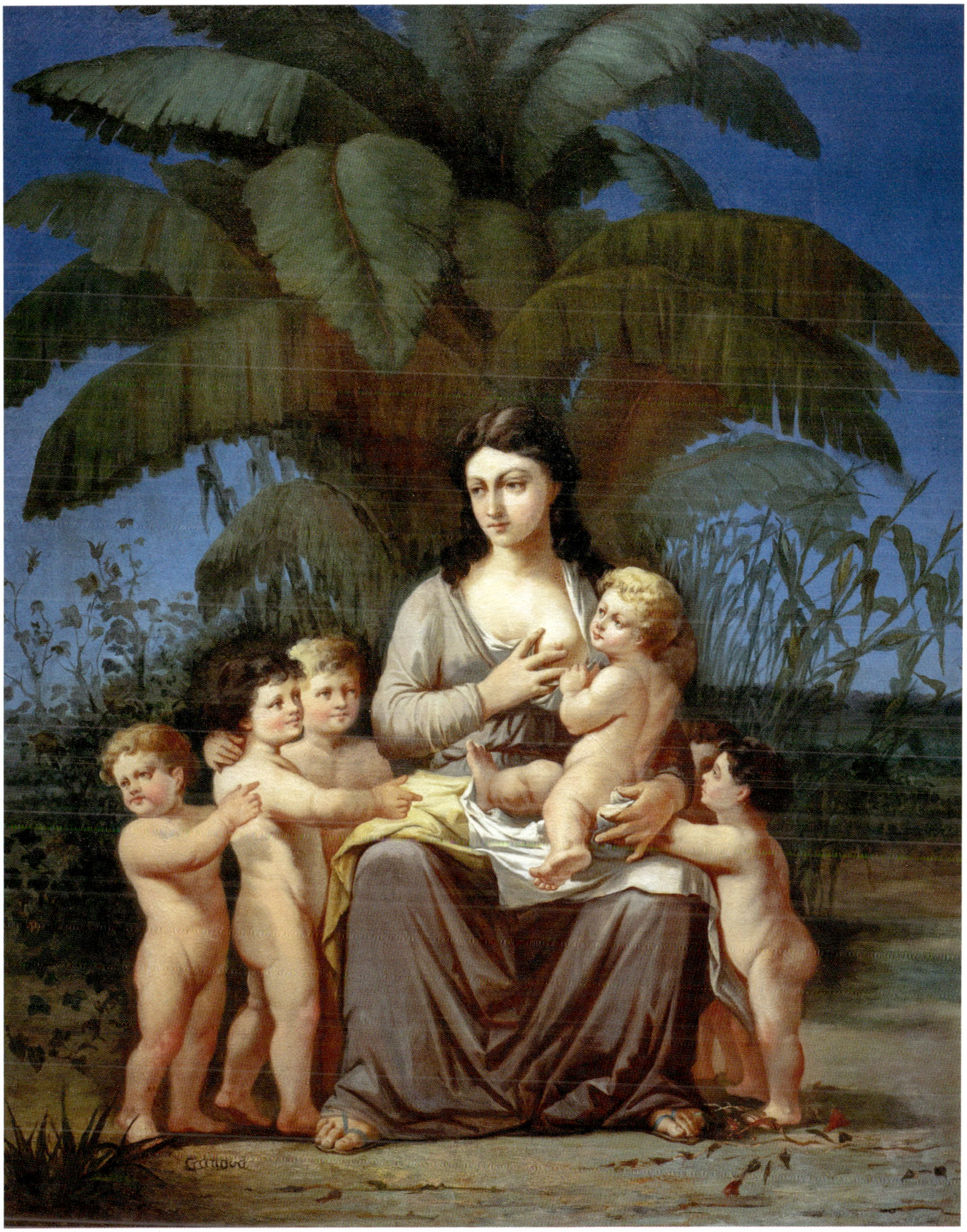

**Plate 12**

Dominico Canova,
*Mother Louisiana*, circa 1850,
Oil on canvas, 56 x 48 inches,
Roger Houston Ogden Collection,
Courtesy of Ogden Museum of Southern Art.
Photography by Patrick Barnes.

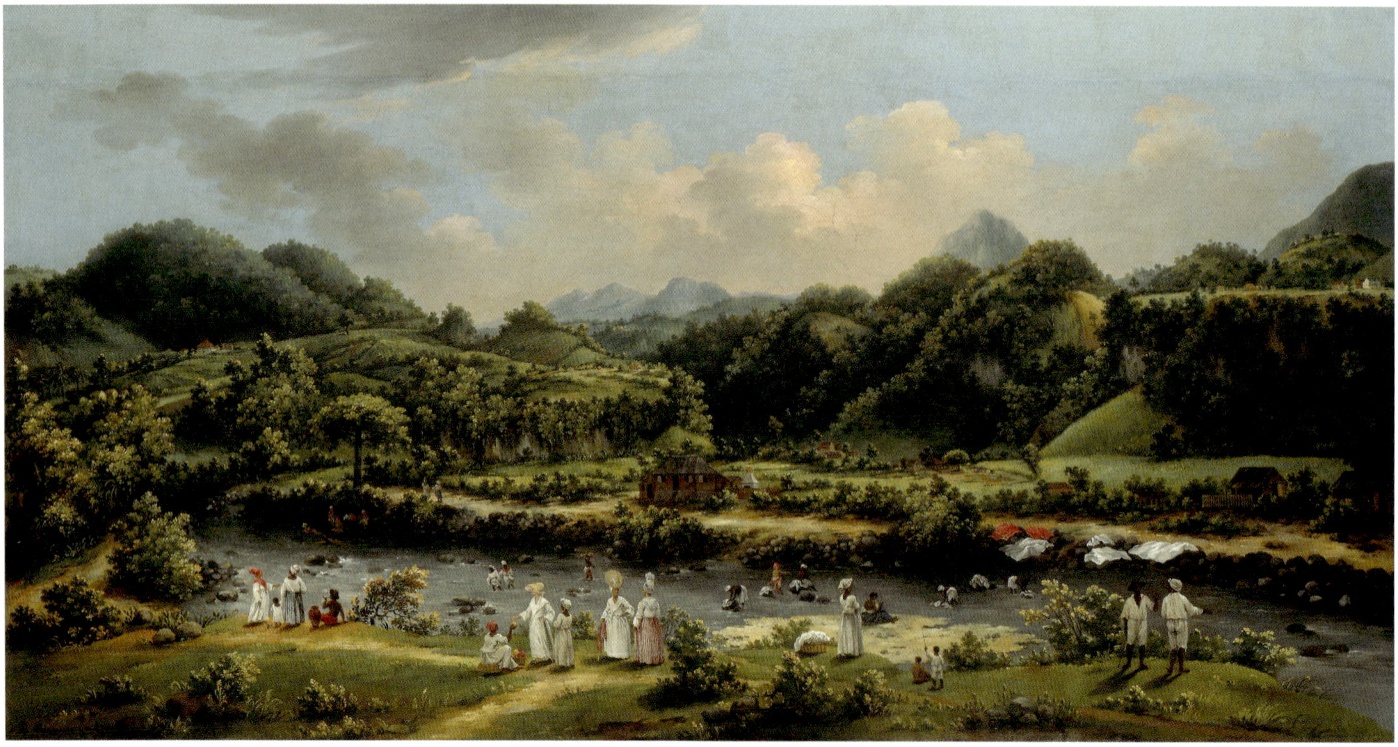

**Plate 13**
Agostino Brunias,
*View on the River Roseau, Dominica*, 1770-80,
Oil on canvas, 33 1/8 x 62 3/16 inches,
The Art Institute of Chicago,
Gift of Emily Crane Chadborne, 1953.1

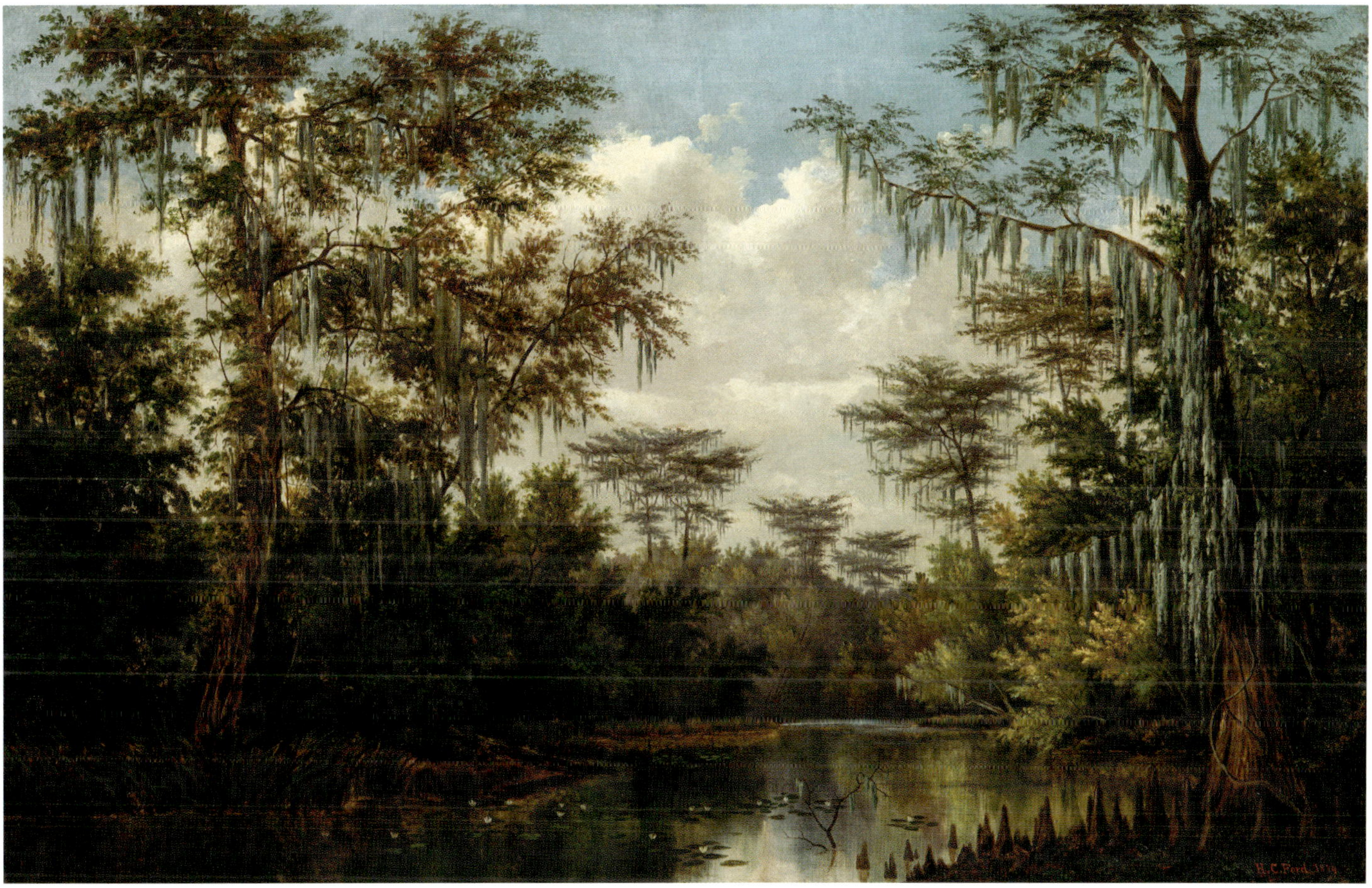

**Plate 42**
Henry Chapman Ford,
*Water Lilies and Spanish Moss*, 1874,
Oil on canvas, 30 x 48 inches,
Collection of Jennifer and Fred Heebe,
Photography by Roman Alokhin.

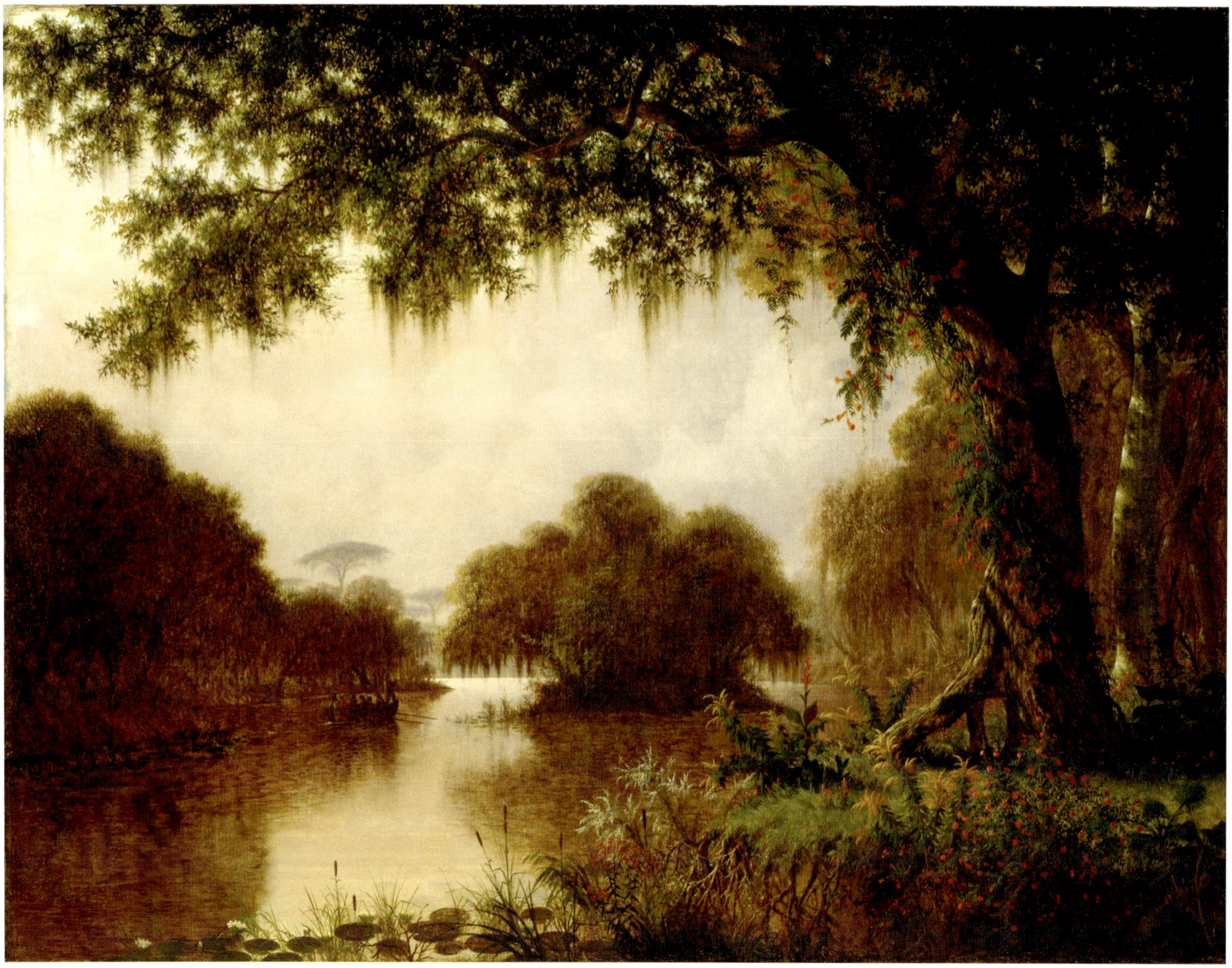

**Plate 43**
Joseph Rusling Meeker, American,
*The Acadians in the Atchafalaya, "Evangeline,"* 1871,
Oil on canvas, 32 1/8 x 42 3/16 inches (80.3 x 106.8 cm),
Brooklyn Museum,
A. Augustus Healy Fund, 50.118

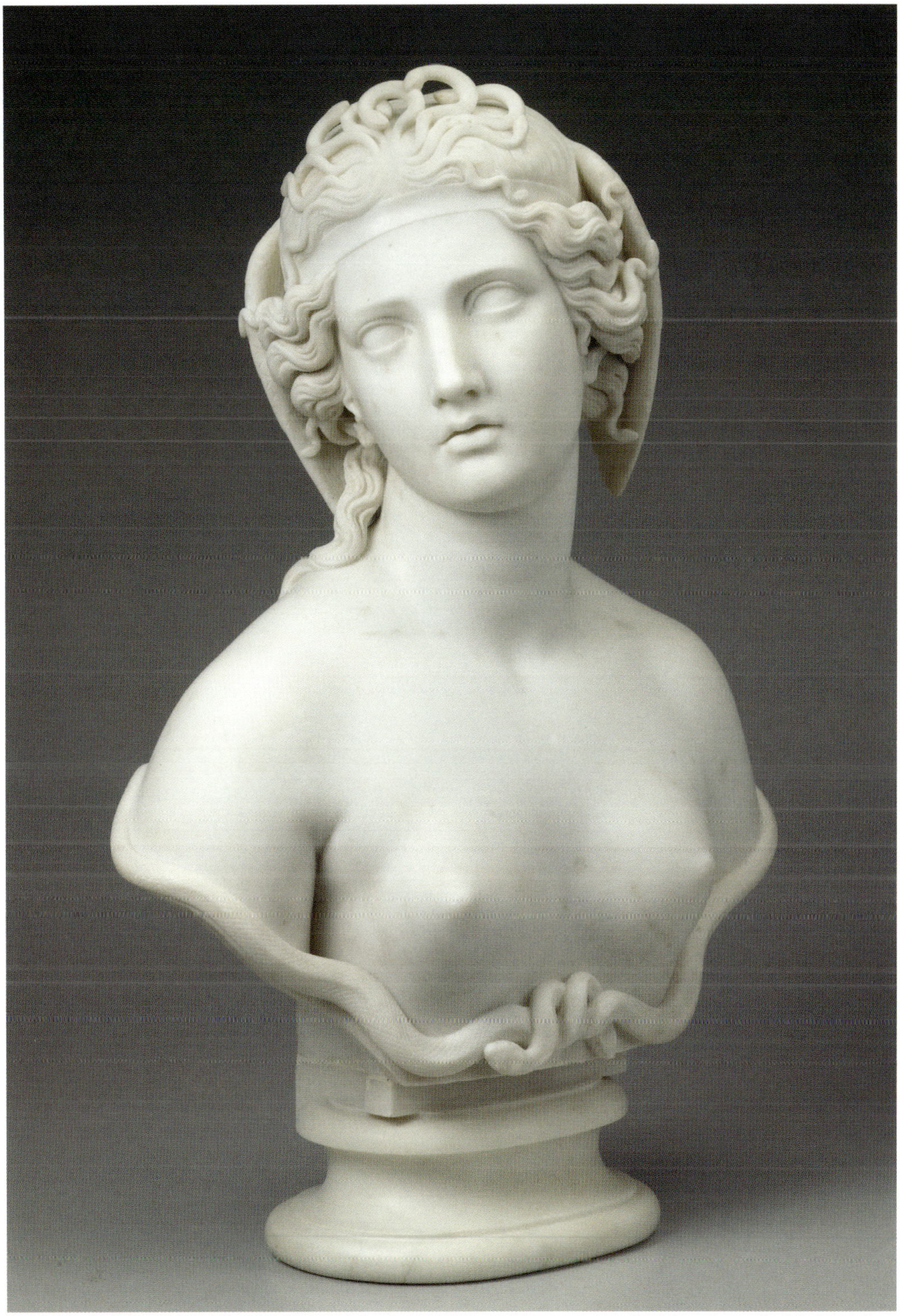

**Plate 44**
Harriet Goodhue Hosmer,
*Medusa*, circa 1854,
Marble, 27 ¼ x 21 x 9 ½ inches,
Minneapolis Institute of Art, MN, USA,
The Walter C. and Mary C. Briggs
Purchase Fund/Bridgeman Images, 2003.125

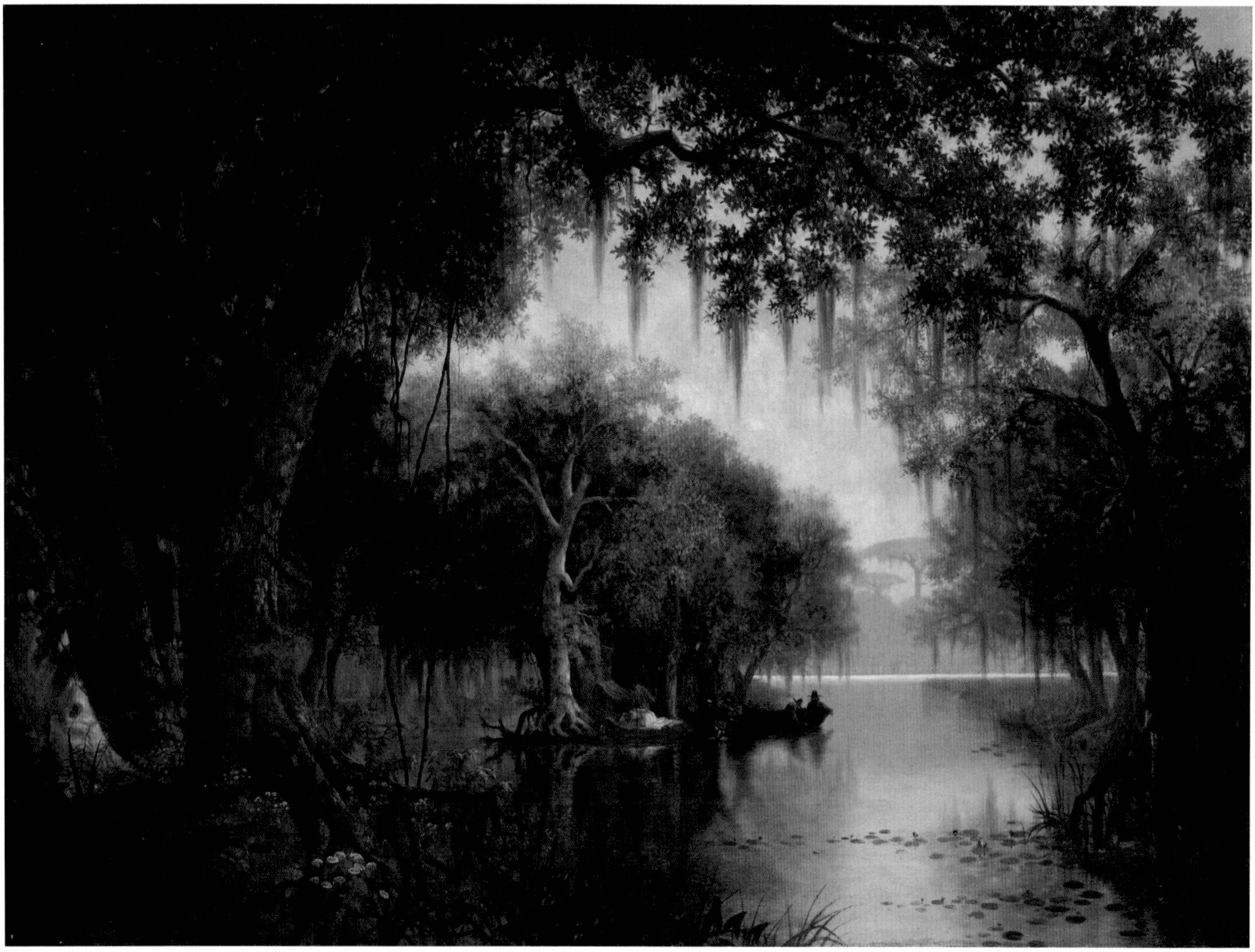

**Plate 45**
Joseph Rusling Meeker,
*The Land of Evangeline*, 1874,
Oil on canvas, 40 1/2 x 52 5/8 inches (framed),
Saint Louis Art Museum,
Gift of Mrs. Wright Prescott Edgerton in
memory of Dr. and Mrs. W.T. Helmuth
by exchange, 163:1946,
Image courtesy Saint Louis Art Museum.

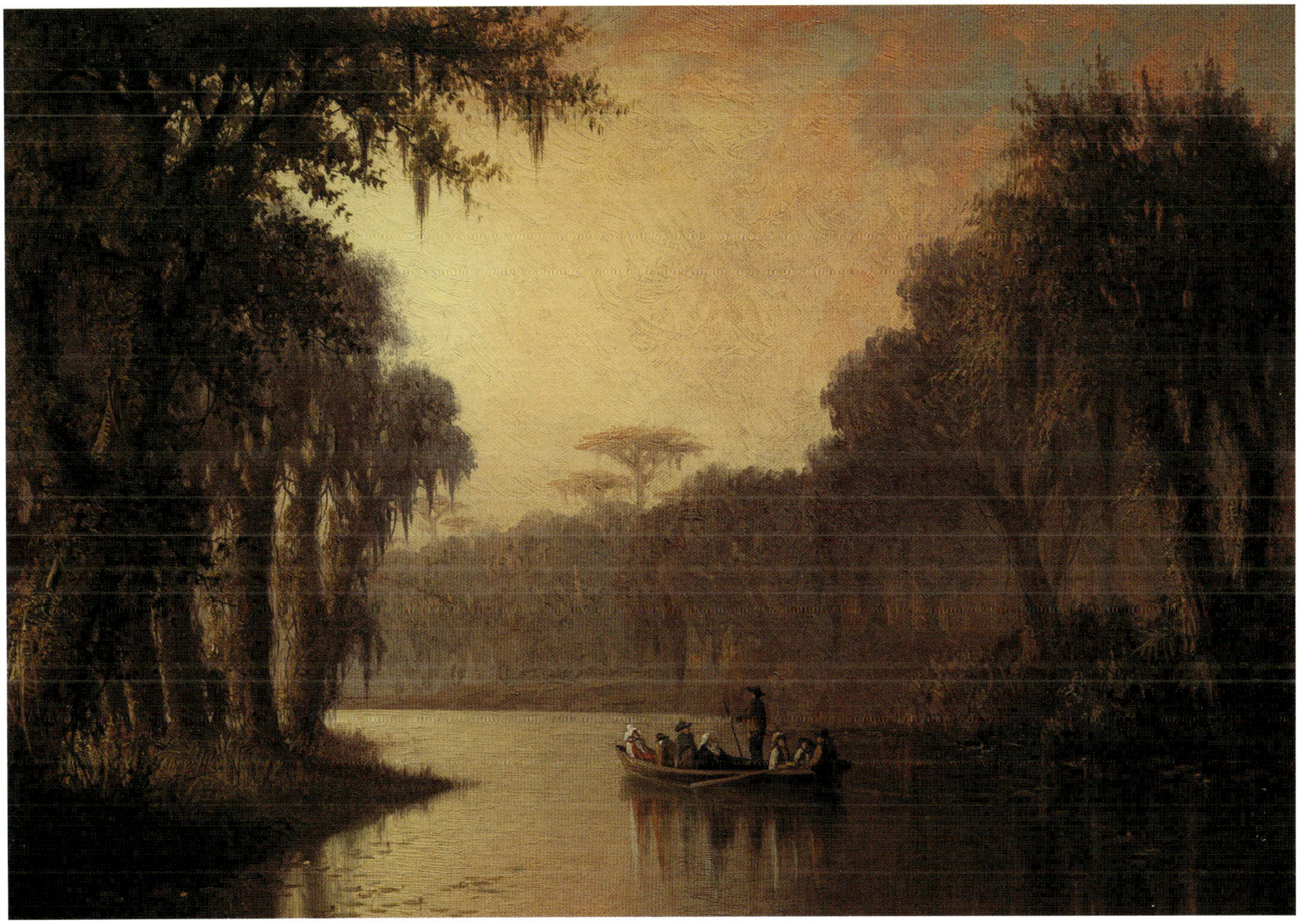

**Plate 46**
Joseph Rusling Meeker,
*Evangeline*, 1884,
Oil on canvas, 25 ½ x 31 ½ inches (framed),
Collection of Bill Gunther,
Photography by Roman Alokhin.

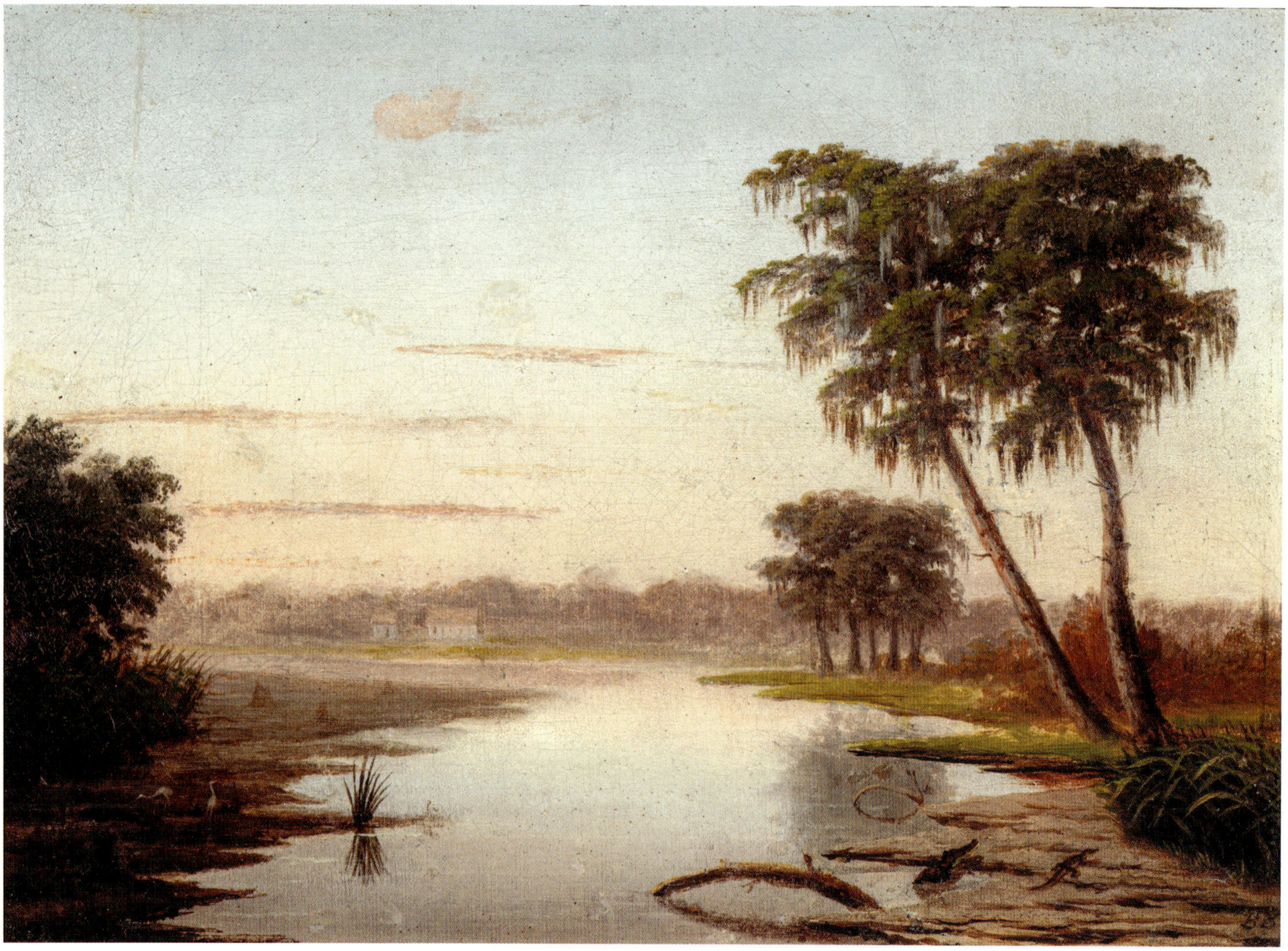

**Plate 47**
Blanche Virginia Blanchard,
*Untitled (Louisiana Landscape)*, circa 1880,
Oil on canvas, 13 x 17 inches (framed),
Collection of Tommy Spinosa,
Photography by Roman Alokhin.

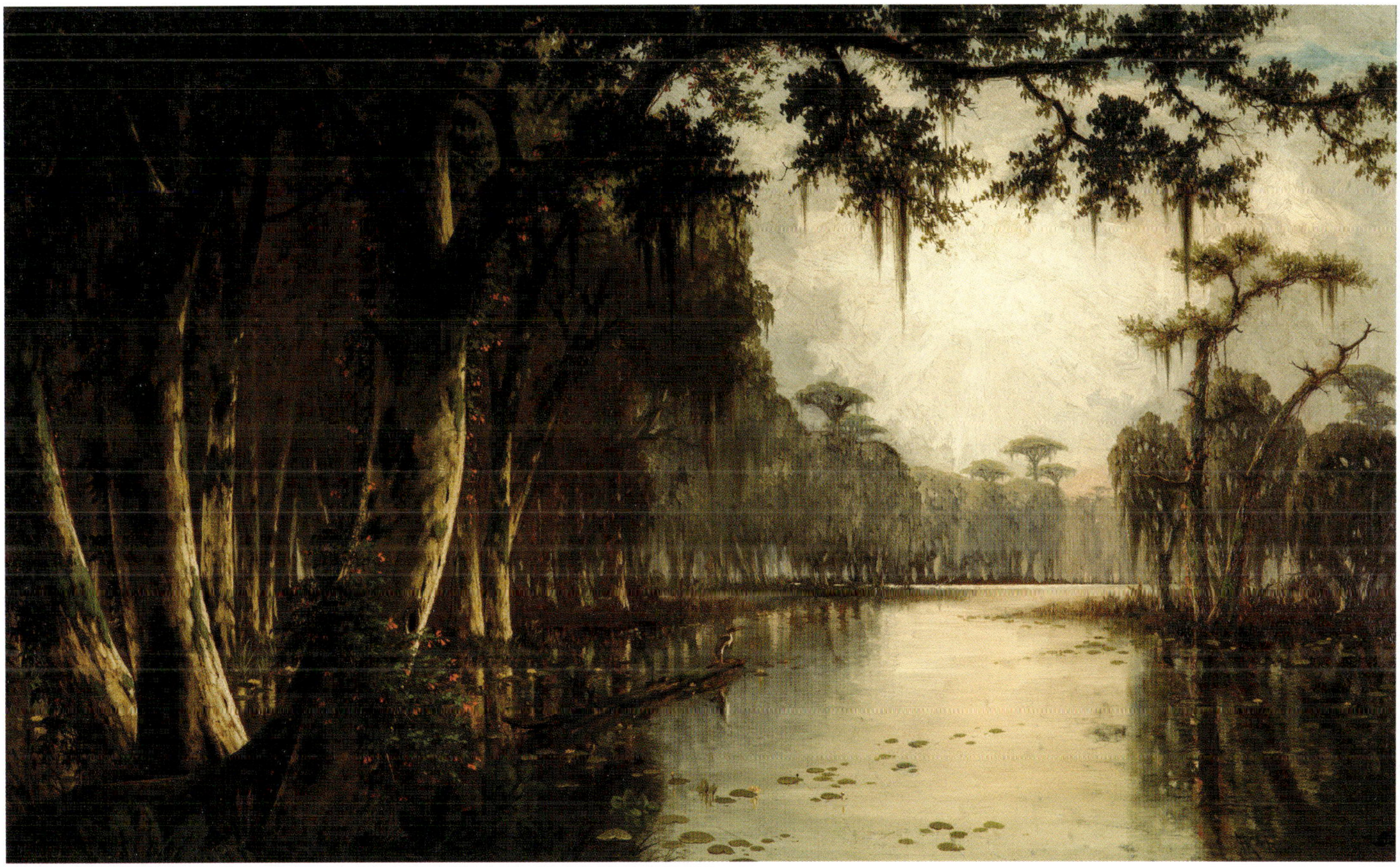

**Plate 48**

Joseph Rusling Meeker,
*Untitled (Louisiana Landscape)*, circa 1880-1900,
Oil on canvas, 45 x 65 inches (framed),
Collection of Bill Gunther,
Photography by Roman Alokhin.

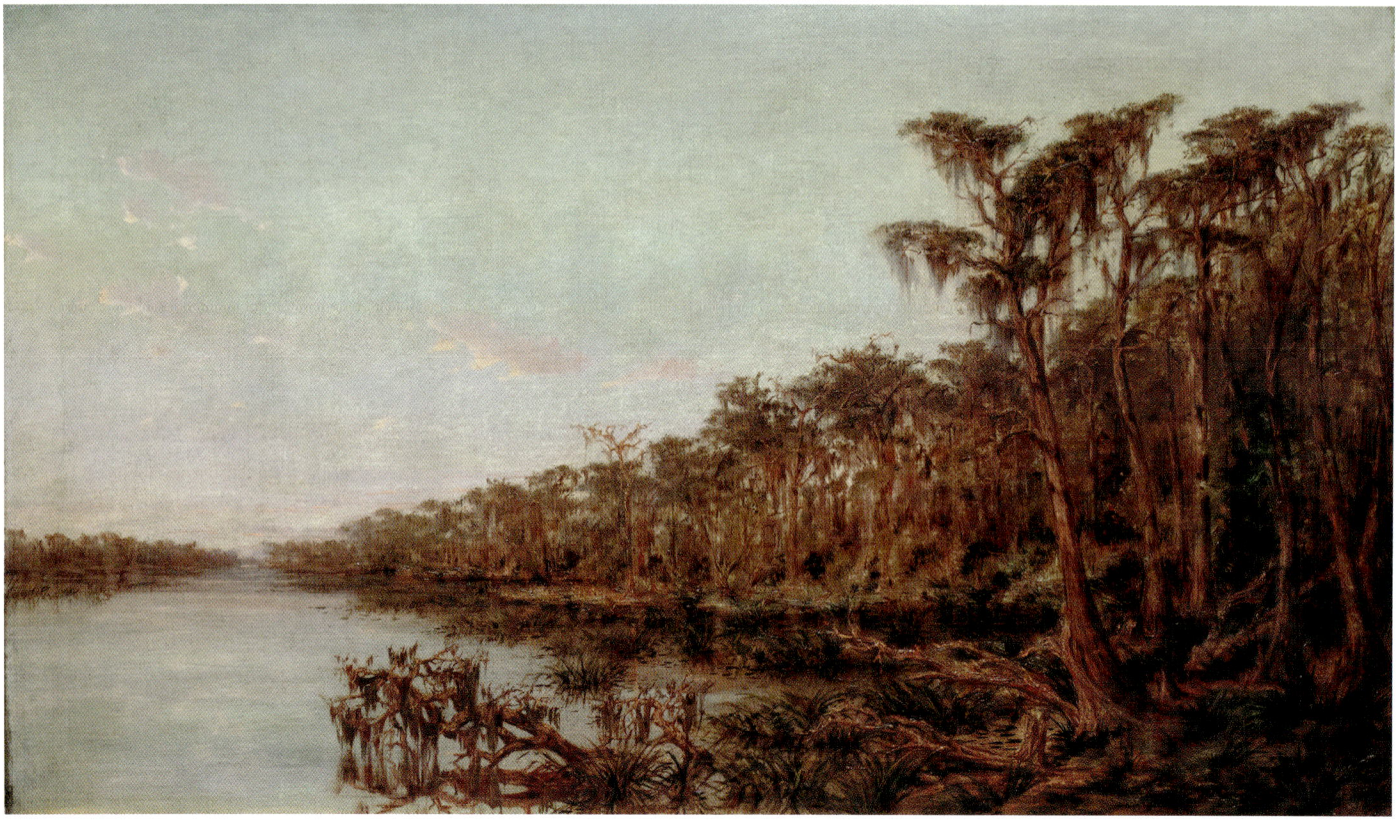

**Plate 49**
Marshall J. Smith, Jr.,
*Cypress Grove, Gulf Coast*, circa 1880,
Oil on canvas, 16 ¾ x 29 inches,
Roger Houston Ogden Collection,
Courtesy of Ogden Museum of Southern Art.
Photography by Patrick Barnes.

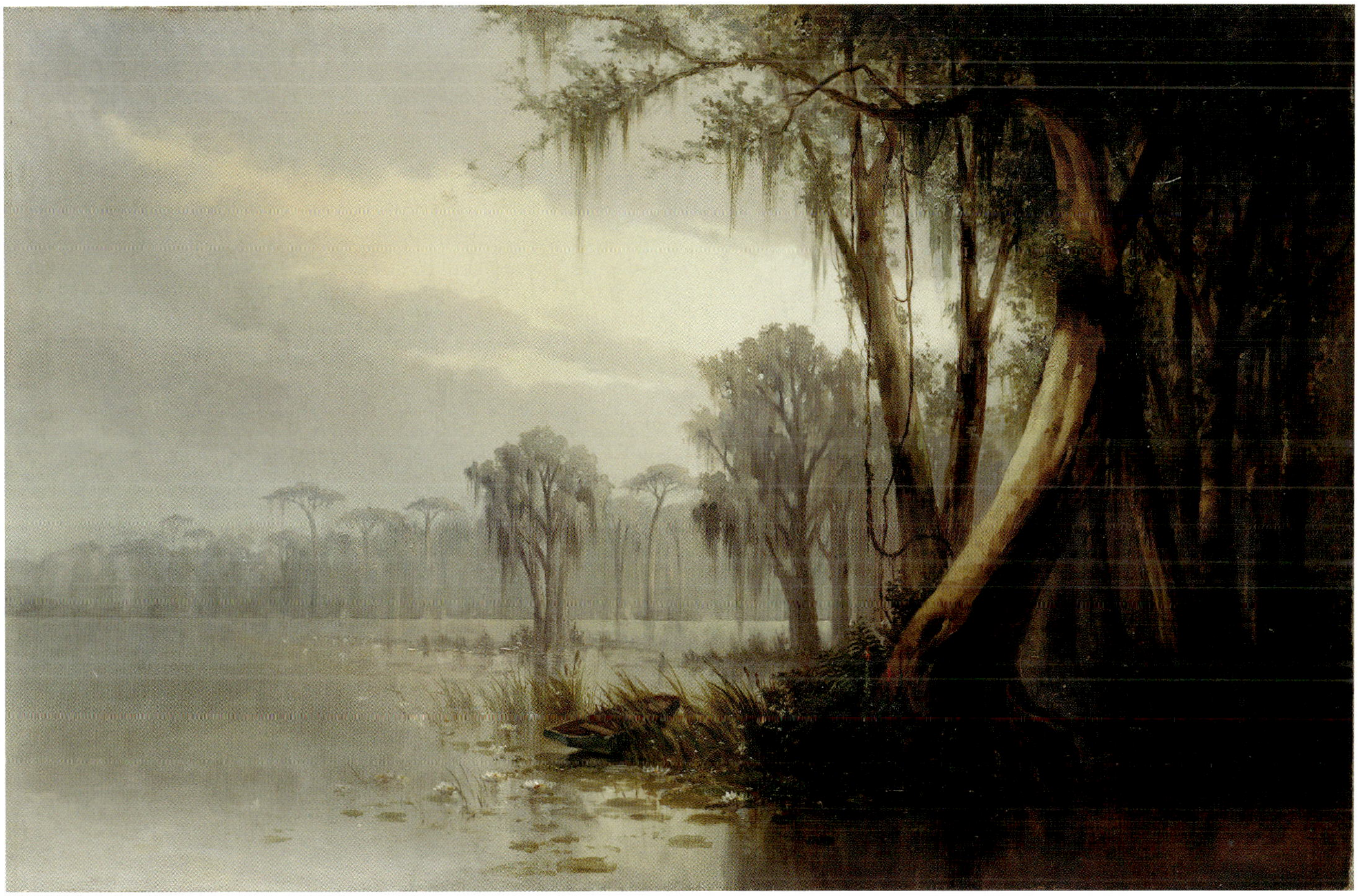

**Plate 50**

Joseph Rusling Meeker,
*After a Storm—Lake Maurepas*, 1888,
Oil on canvas, 32 ¾ x 45 ¼ x 1 ¼ inches (framed),
Louisiana State University Museum of Art, Gift of the
Phi Gamma Chapter of Chi Omega Sorority, 98.14,
Photography by David Humphreys.

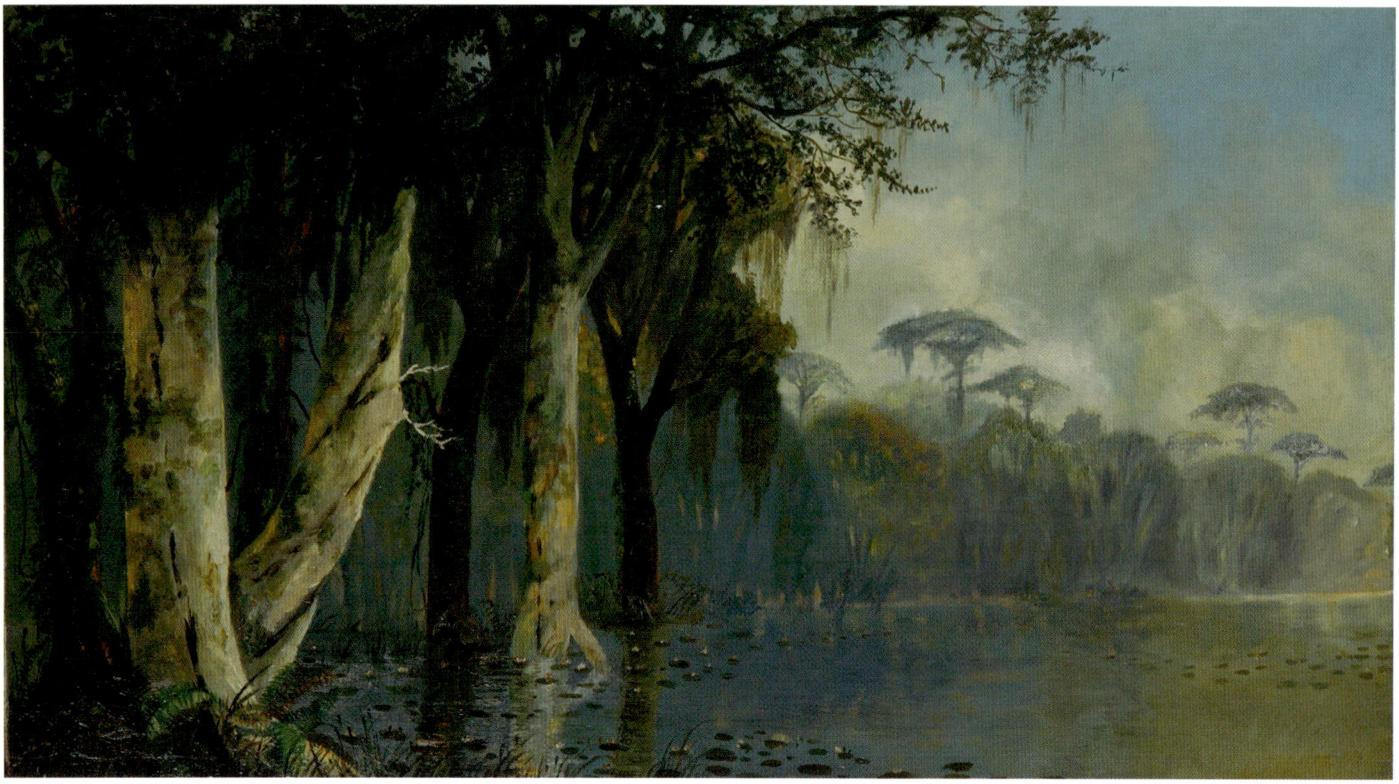

**Plate 51**
Joseph Rusling Meeker,
*Louisiana Bayou*, circa 1885,
Oil on canvas, 19 $^{7}/_{8}$ x 36 inches,
Montgomery Museum of Fine Arts,
Montgomery, Alabama, Association Purchase

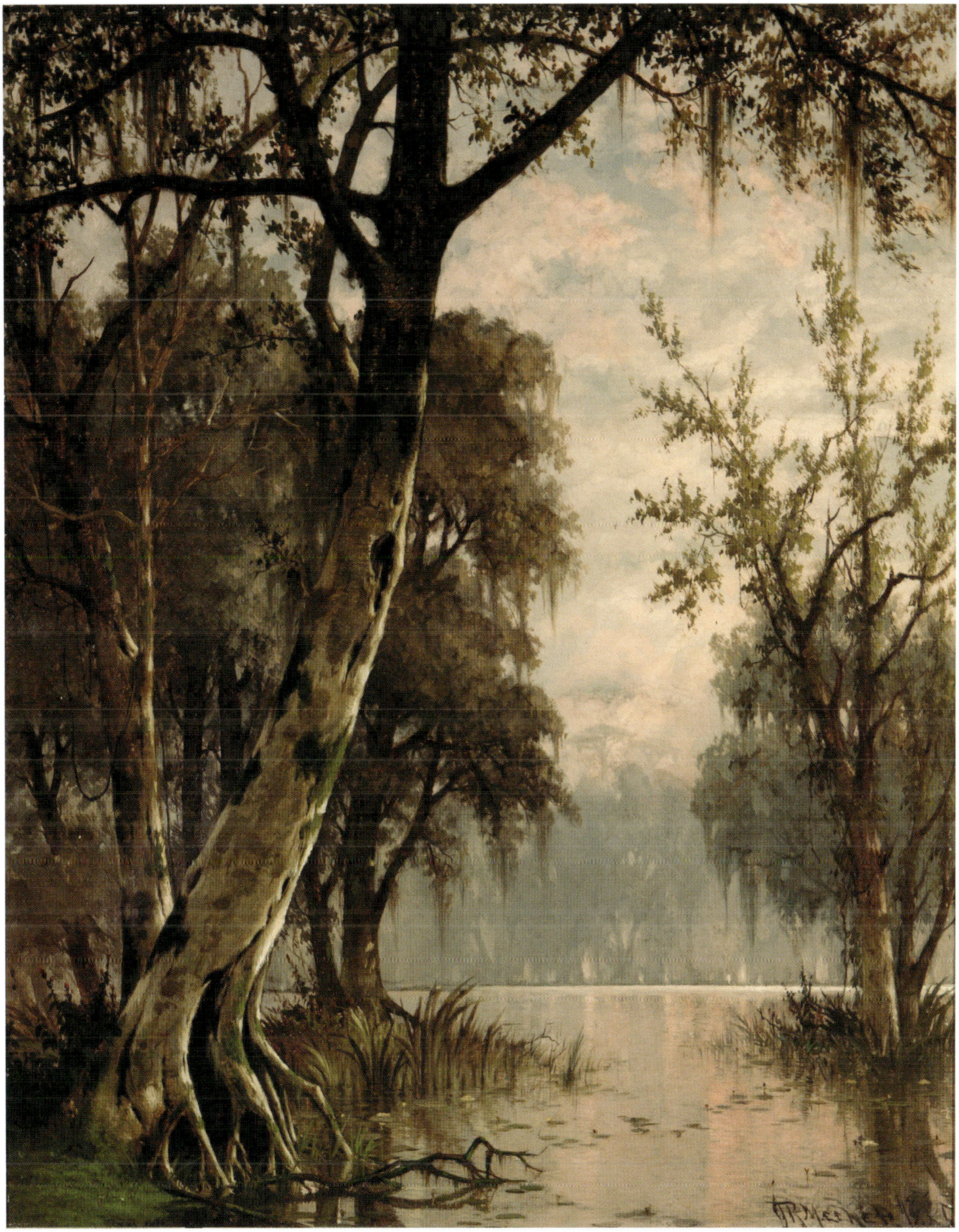

**Plate 52**
Joseph Rusling Meeker,
*Bayou Plaquemines*, 1885,
Oil on canvas, 38 ¼ x 33 inches (framed),
New Orleans Museum of Art,
Museum Purchase, gift of Bernard Bruen,
by exchange, 2003.221

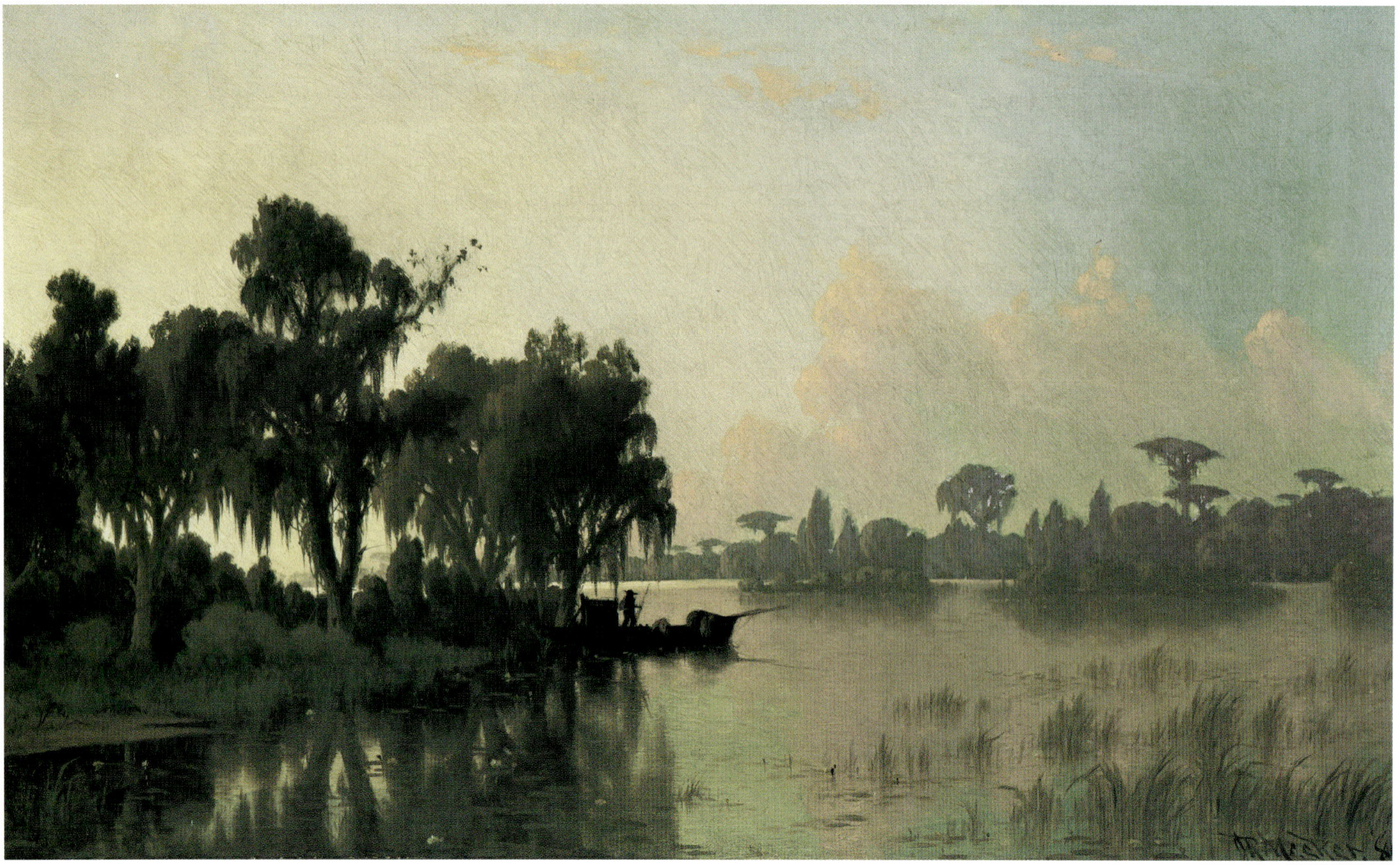

**Plate 53**
Joseph Rusling Meeker,
*Solitary Pirogue by the Bayou*, 1886,
Oil on canvas, 28 ¾ x 41 ½ inches (framed),
Morris Museum of Art,
Augusta, Georgia, 1993.004

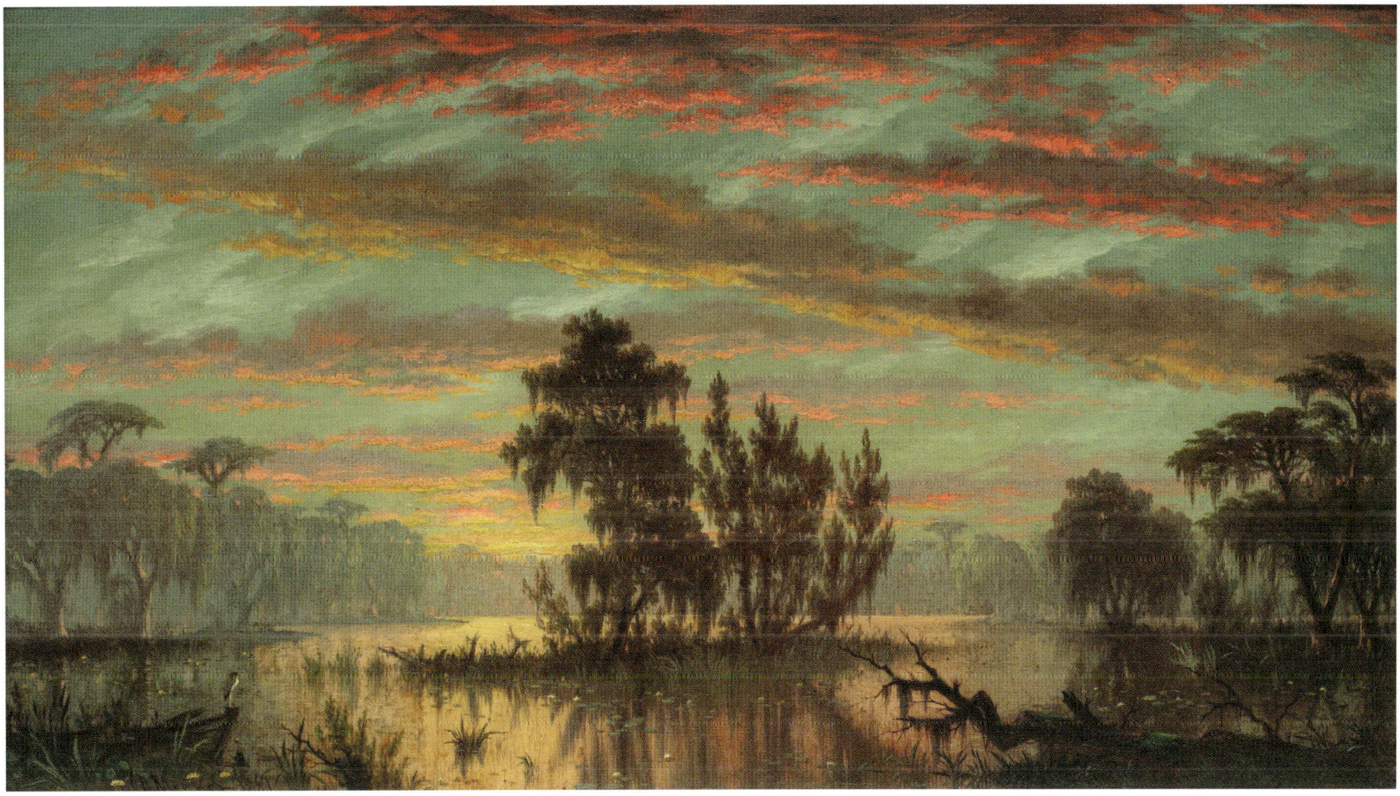

**Plate 54**

Joseph Rusling Meeker,
*Bayou Plaquemines*, 1881,
Oil on canvas, 20 x 30 inches,
Roger Houston Ogden Collection,
Courtesy of Ogden Museum of Southern Art.
Photography by Patrick Barnes.

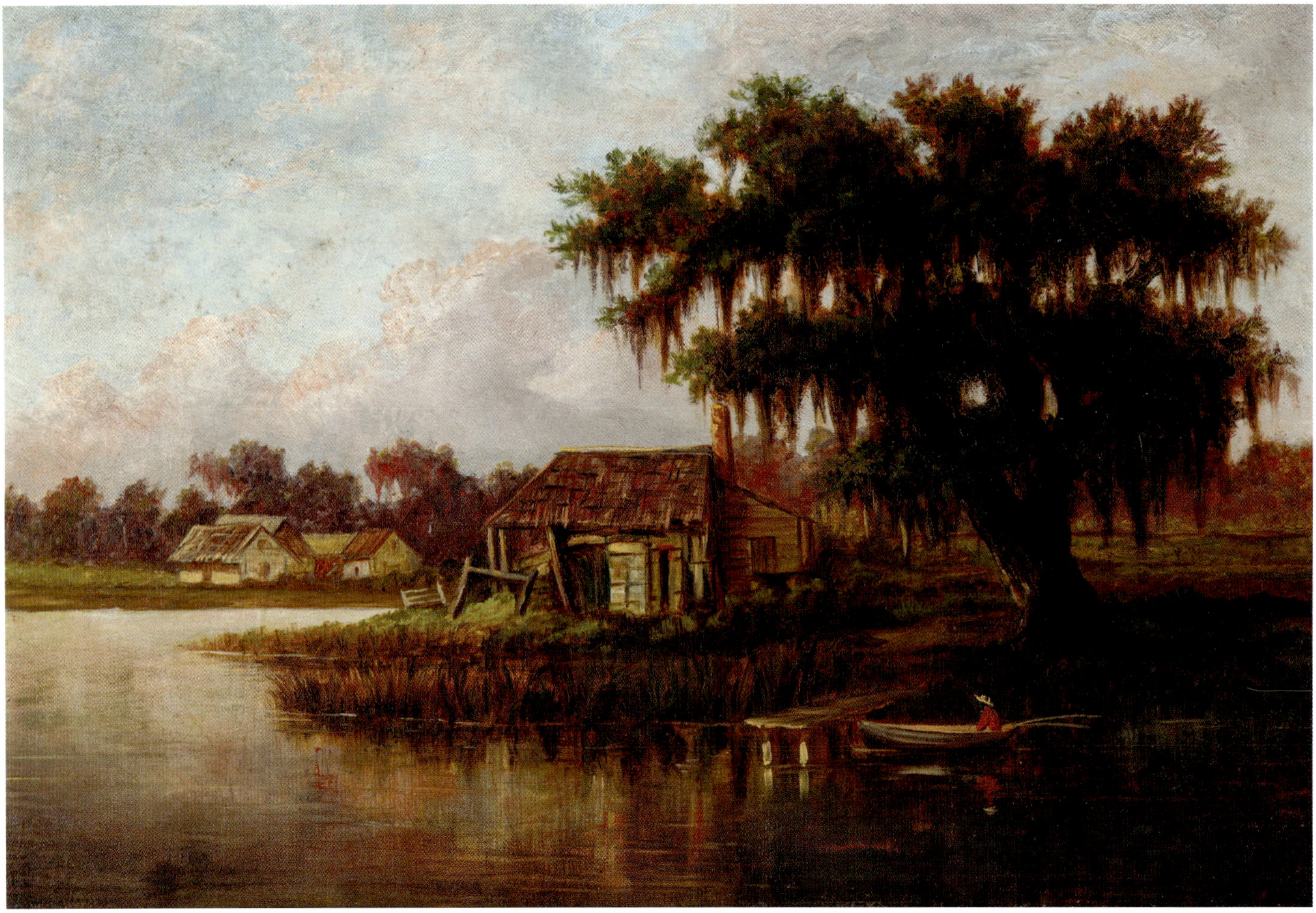

**Plate 55**
Mary Bella Prague Brice,
*Mouth of the Tchefuncta River*, 1897,
Oil on canvas, 17 ½ x 23 ½ inches (framed),
Louisiana State Museum,
Gift of Anne Hastings Moss, 2014.024.12,
Photography by Roman Alokhin.

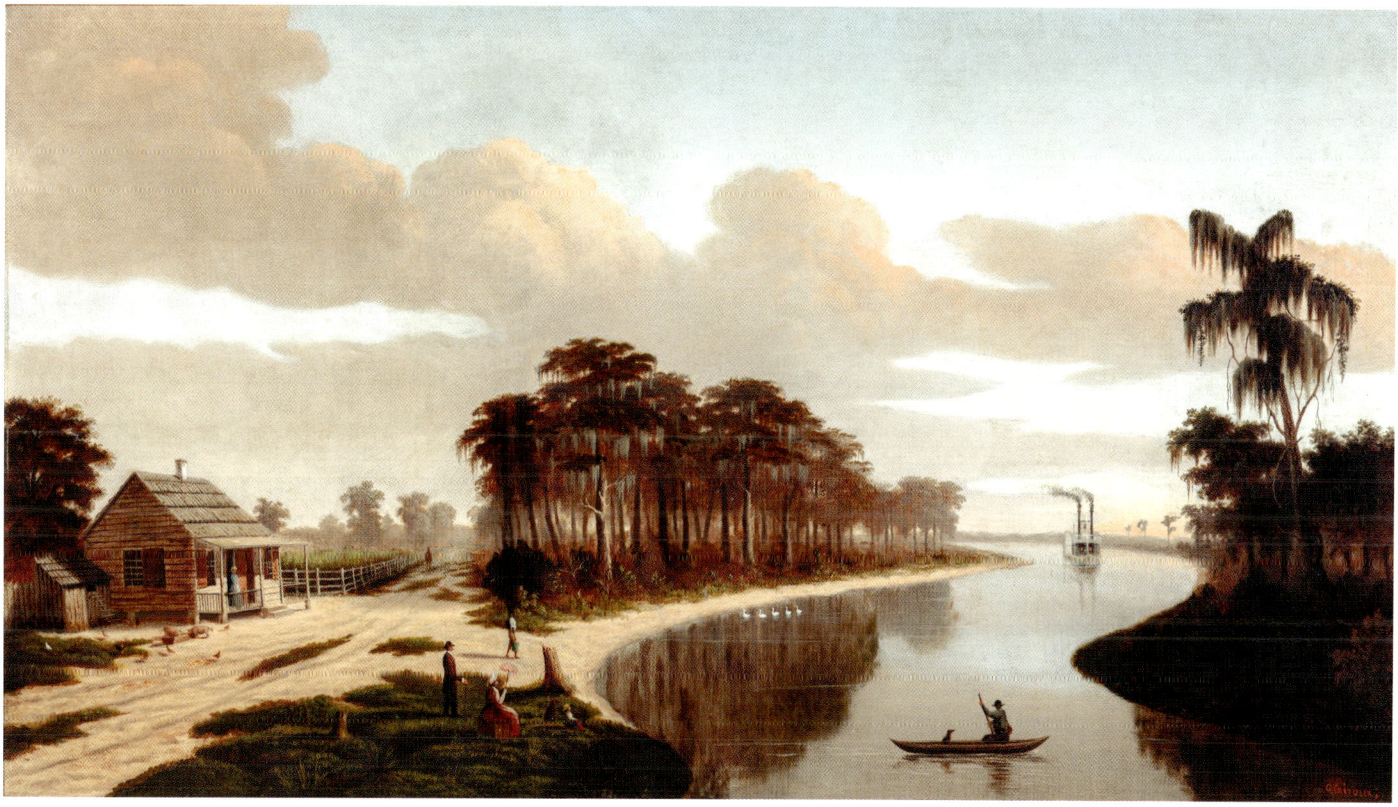

**Plate 56**
Charles Giroux,
*Steamboat Passing a Bayou Farm*, 1880,
Oil on canvas, 27 x 47 inches,
Collection of Donna and Bubba Hines,
Photography by Roman Alokhin.

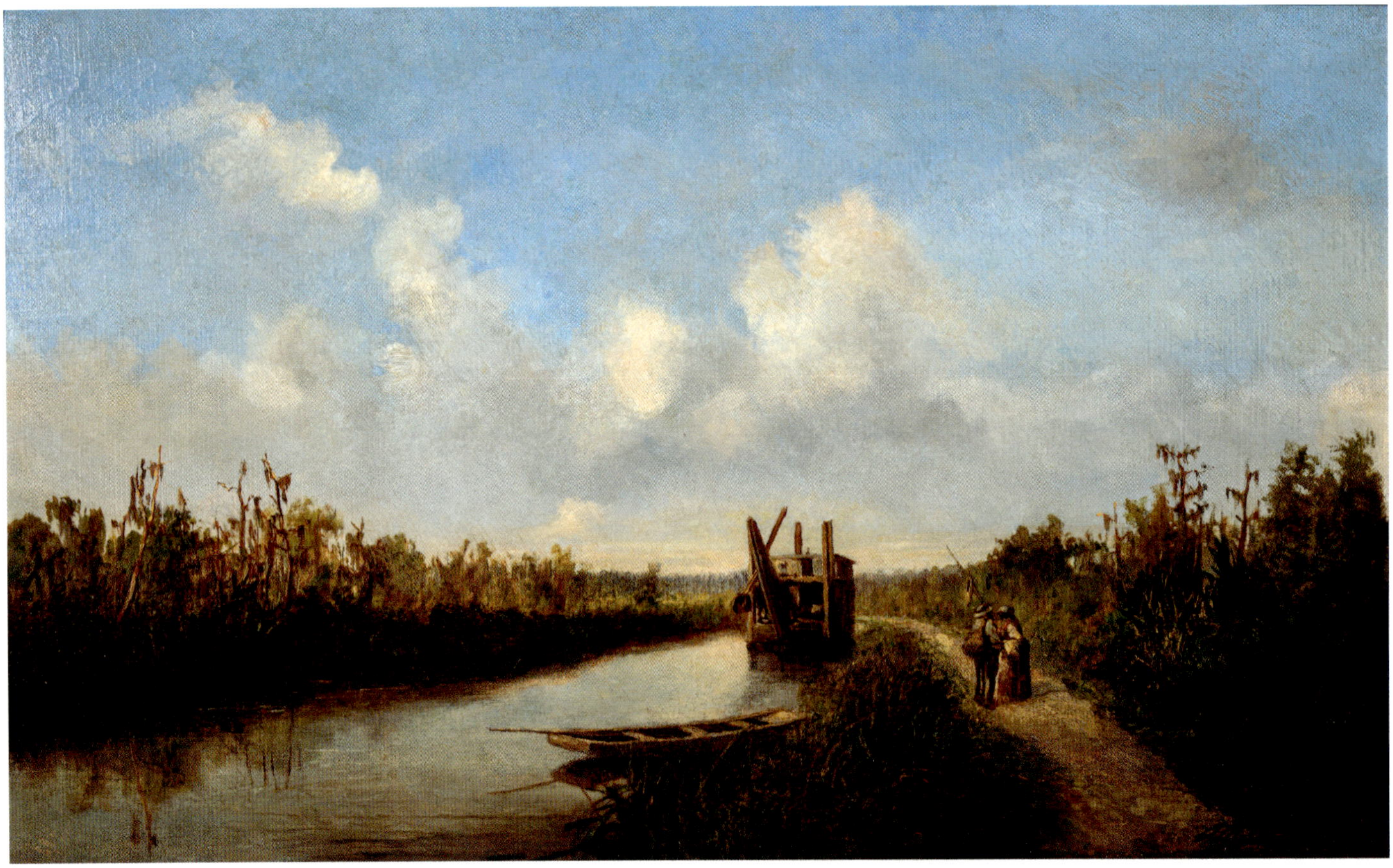

**Plate 57**
Andres Molinary,
*Le Chemin des Chapitoulas*, circa 1875-1900,
Oil on canvas, 29 x 41 ½ inches (framed),
Collection of Bill Gunther,
Photography by Roman Alokhin.

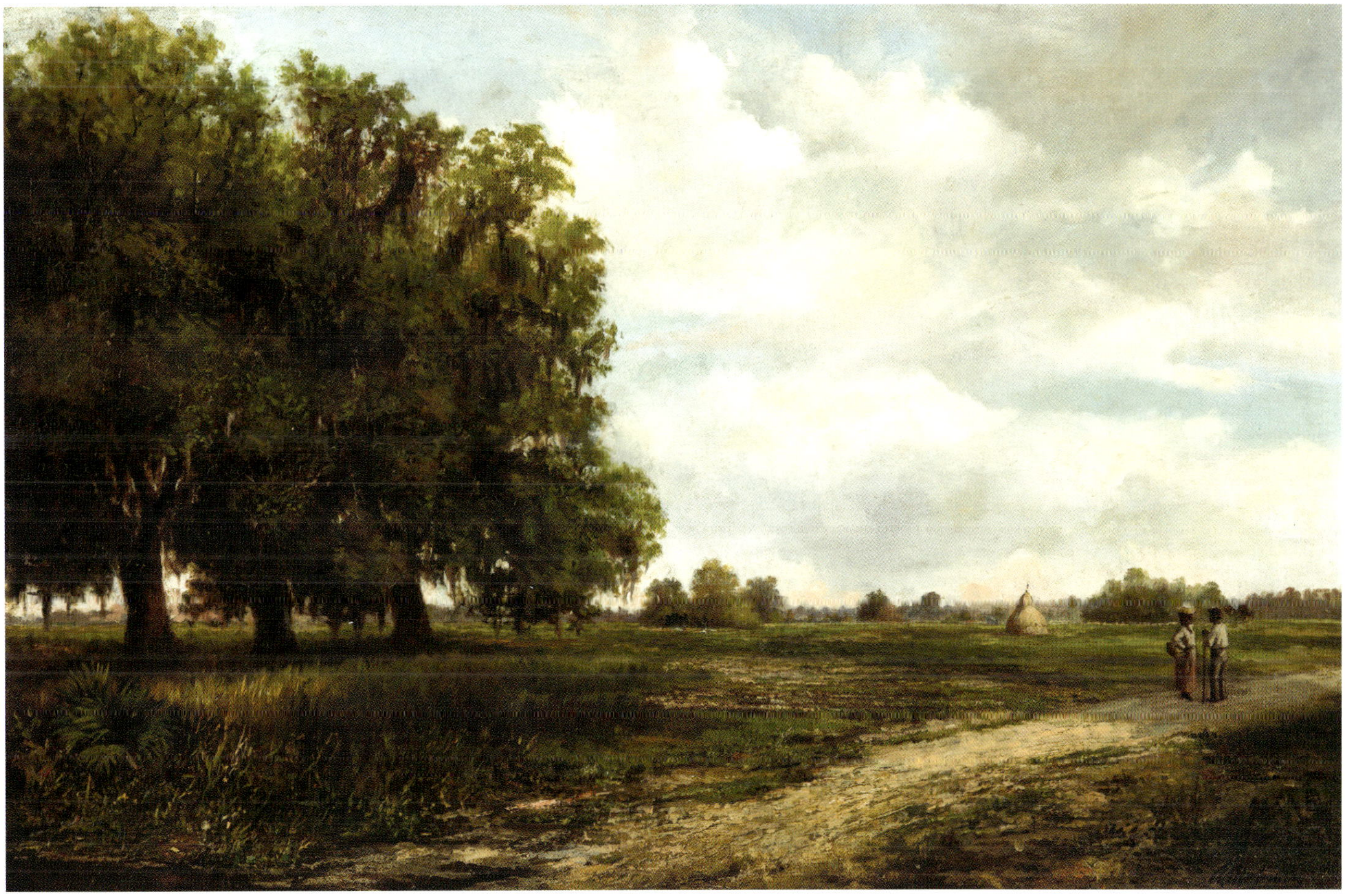

**Plate 58**

Andres Molinary,
*Landscape with Oak Trees*, circa 1890,
Oil on canvas, 33 1/2 x 47 1/2 inches (framed),
Louisiana State Museum,
Gift of Mrs. Paul Godchaux, 12467.44.2,
Photography by Roman Alokhin.

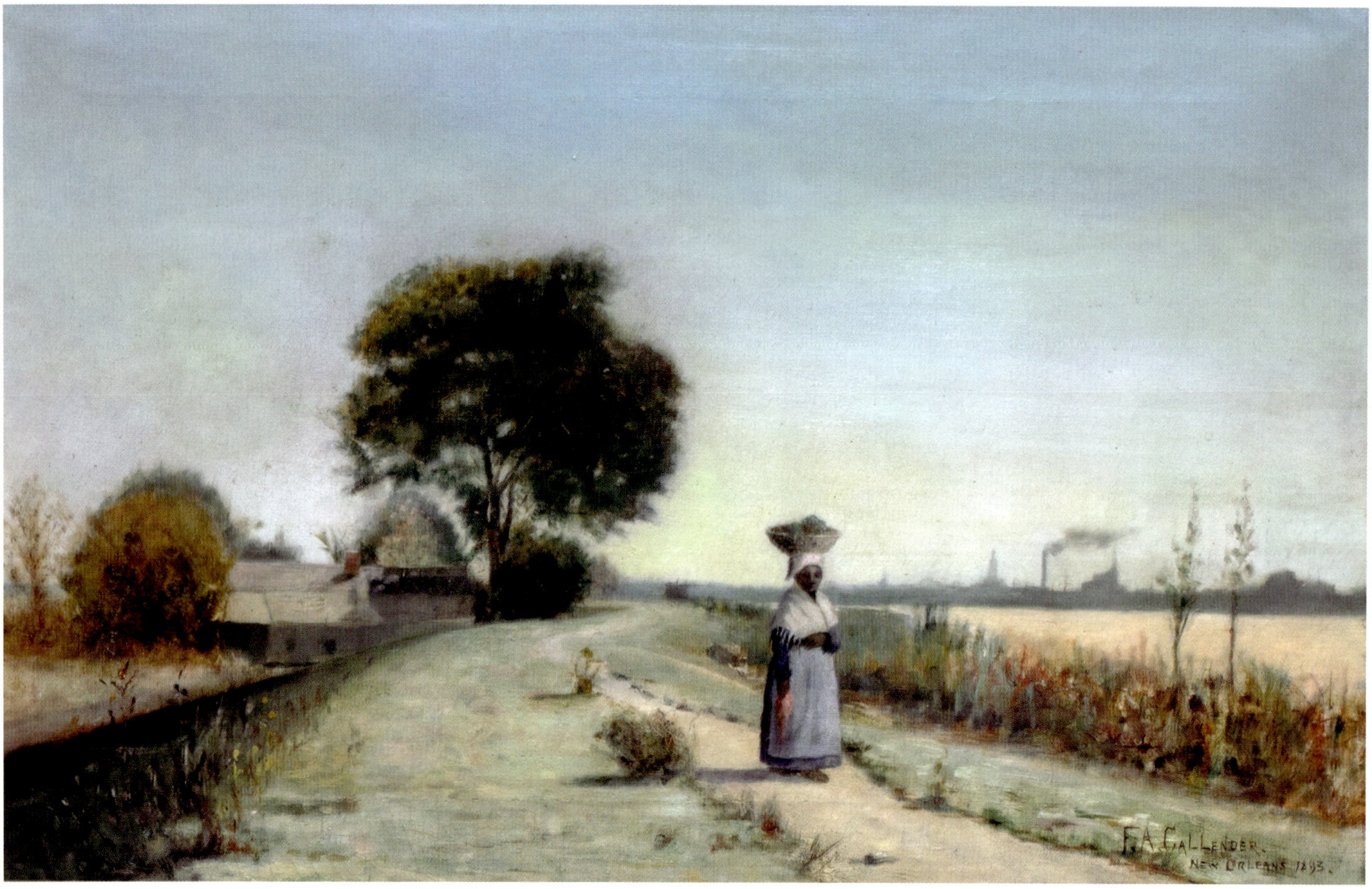


**Plate 59**
F. Arthur Callender,
*New Orleans from Algiers Point*, 1893,
Oil on canvas, 15 x 24 inches,
Roger Houston Ogden Collection,
Courtesy of Ogden Museum of Southern Art.
Photography by Patrick Barnes.

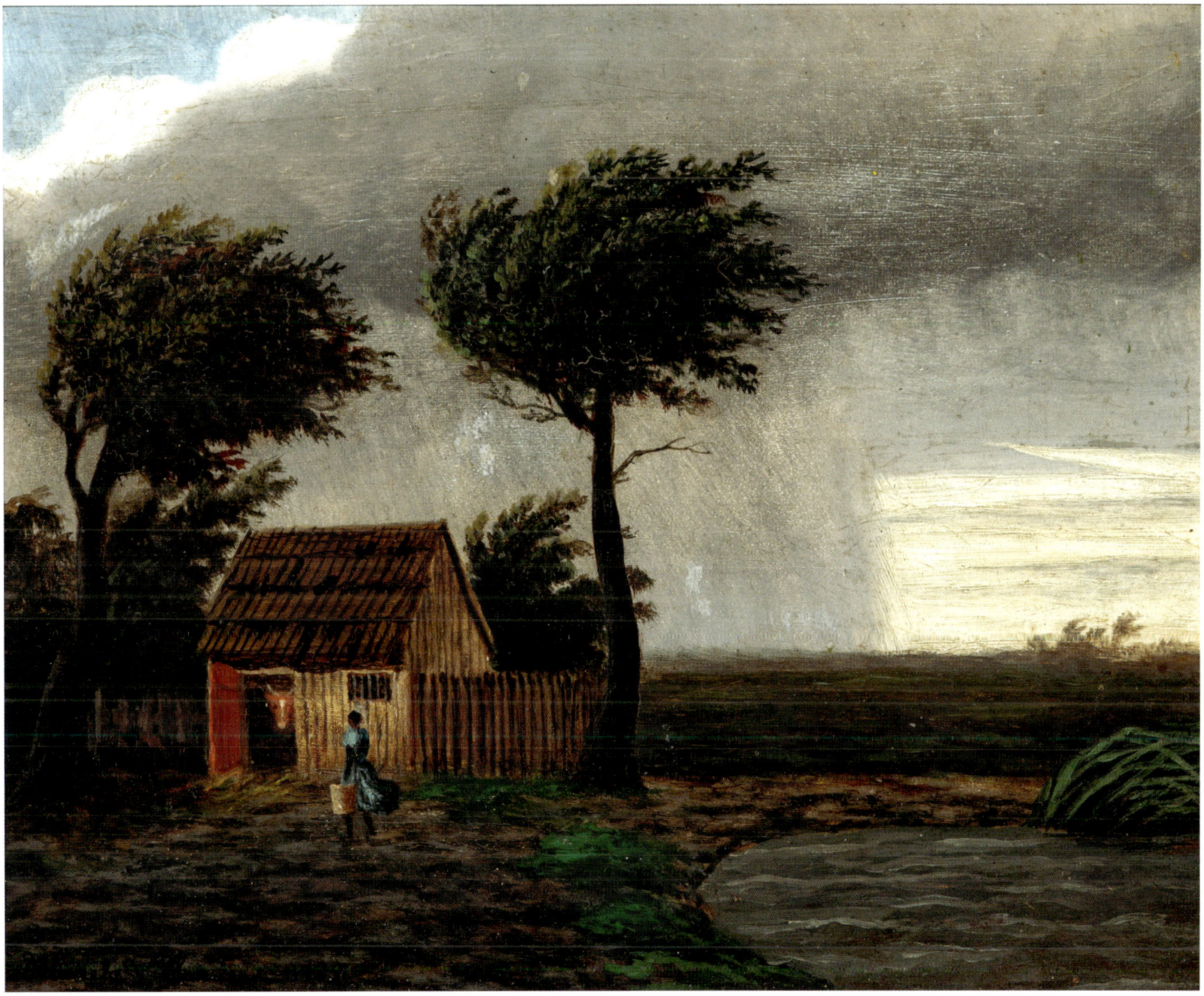

**Plate 60**

Blanche Virginia Blanchard,
*Untitled (Louisiana Landscape)*, circa 1880,
Oil on canvas, 11 ½ x 13 ½ inches (framed),
Collection of Tommy Spinosa,
Photography by Roman Alokhin.

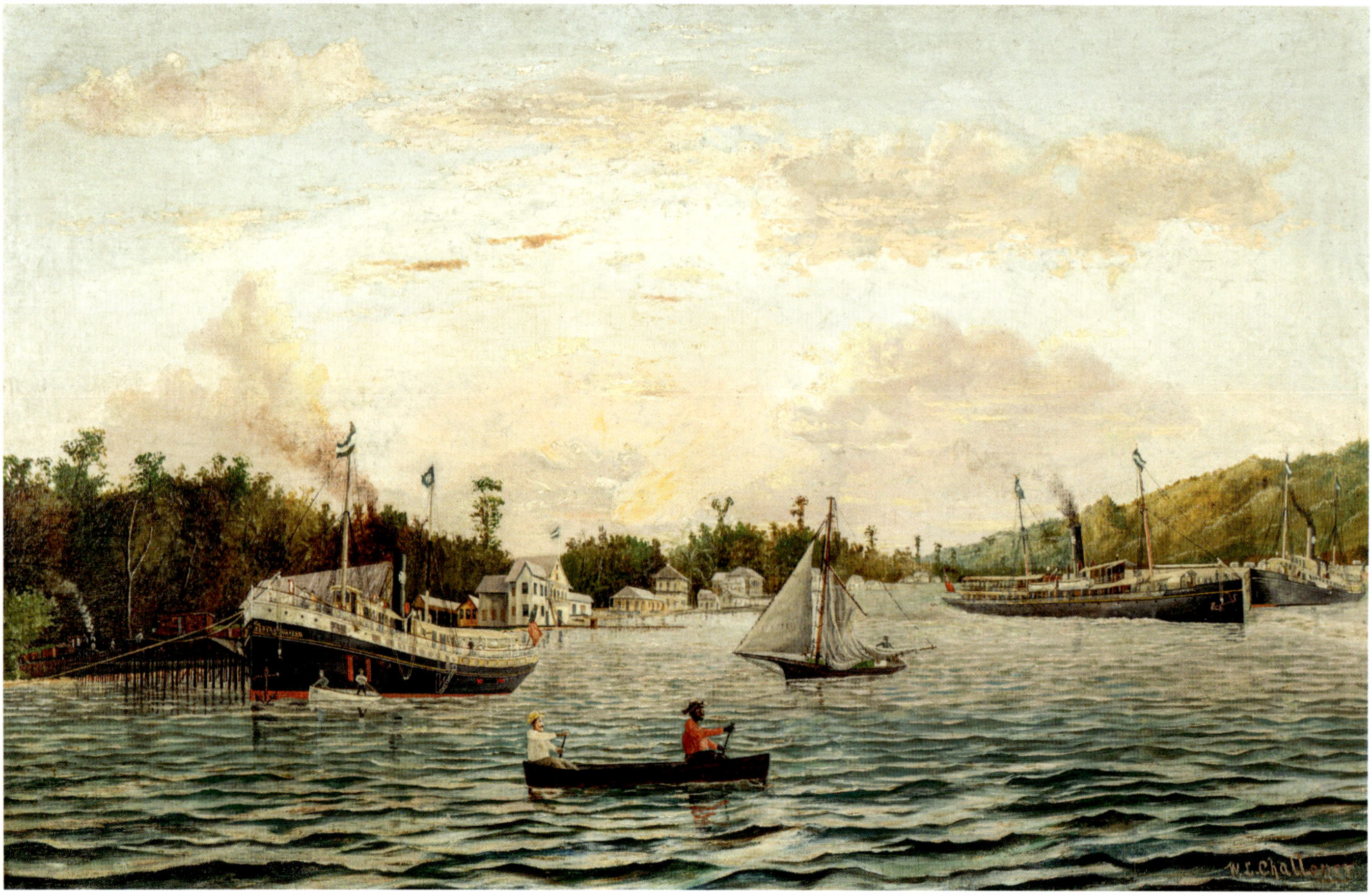

**Plate 61**
Captain William Lindsay Challoner,
*S.S. Breakwater, S.S. Clearwater and S.S. Wanderer in a Harbor [Honduras Port]*, 1897,
Oil on canvas, 30 x 48 inches,
Louisiana State Museum, XX0707,
Photography by Roman Alokhin.

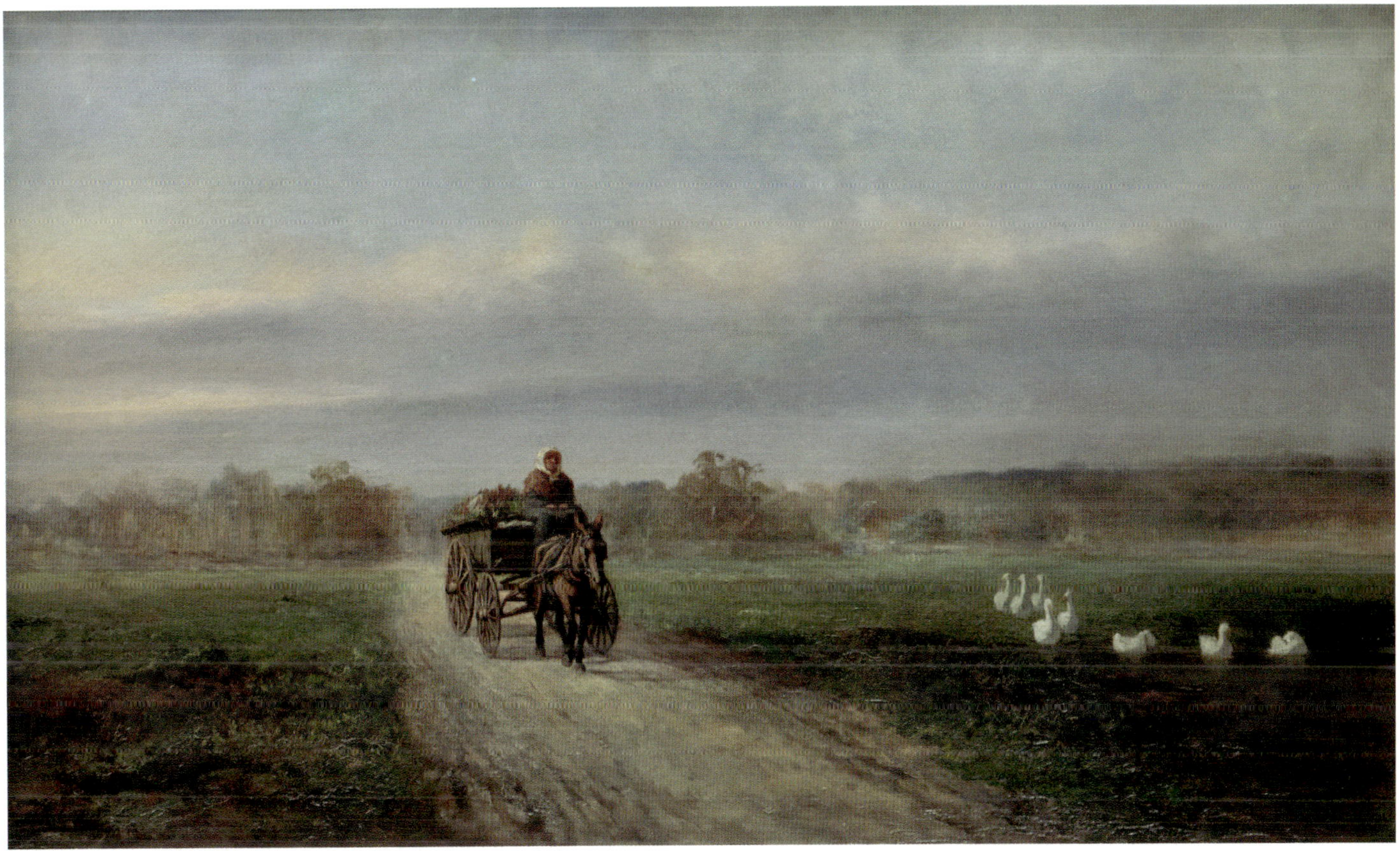

**Plate 62**
Andres Molinary,
*Old Gentilly Road*, 1890,
Oil on canvas, 32 x 48 inches,
Roger Houston Ogden Collection,
Courtesy of Ogden Museum of Southern Art.
Photography by Patrick Barnes.

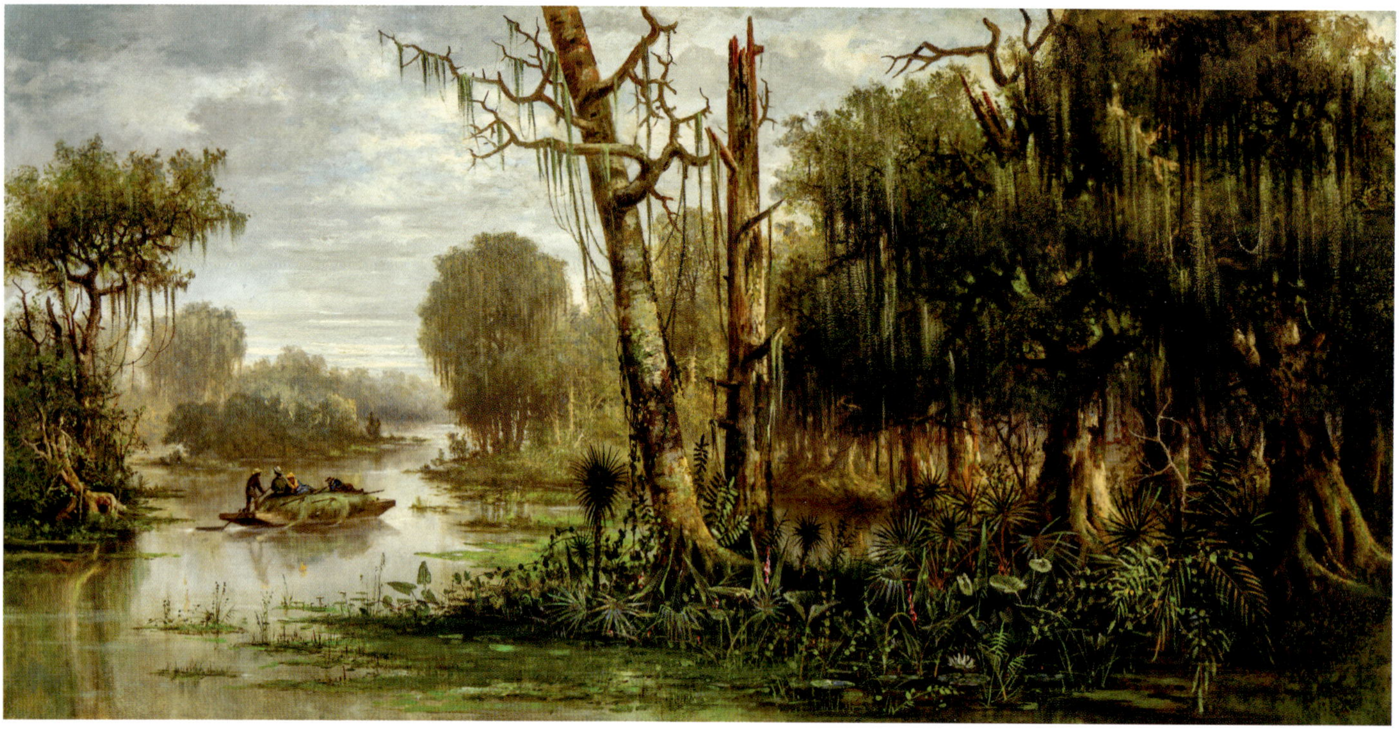

**Plate 63**
Meyer Straus,
*Morning in the Swamp, Bayou Teche*, 1884,
Oil on canvas, 36 x 66 ½ inches (framed),
Louisiana State Museum,
Cabildo Auxiliary Funds Purchase, 1997.001.20.1,
Photography by Roman Alokhin.

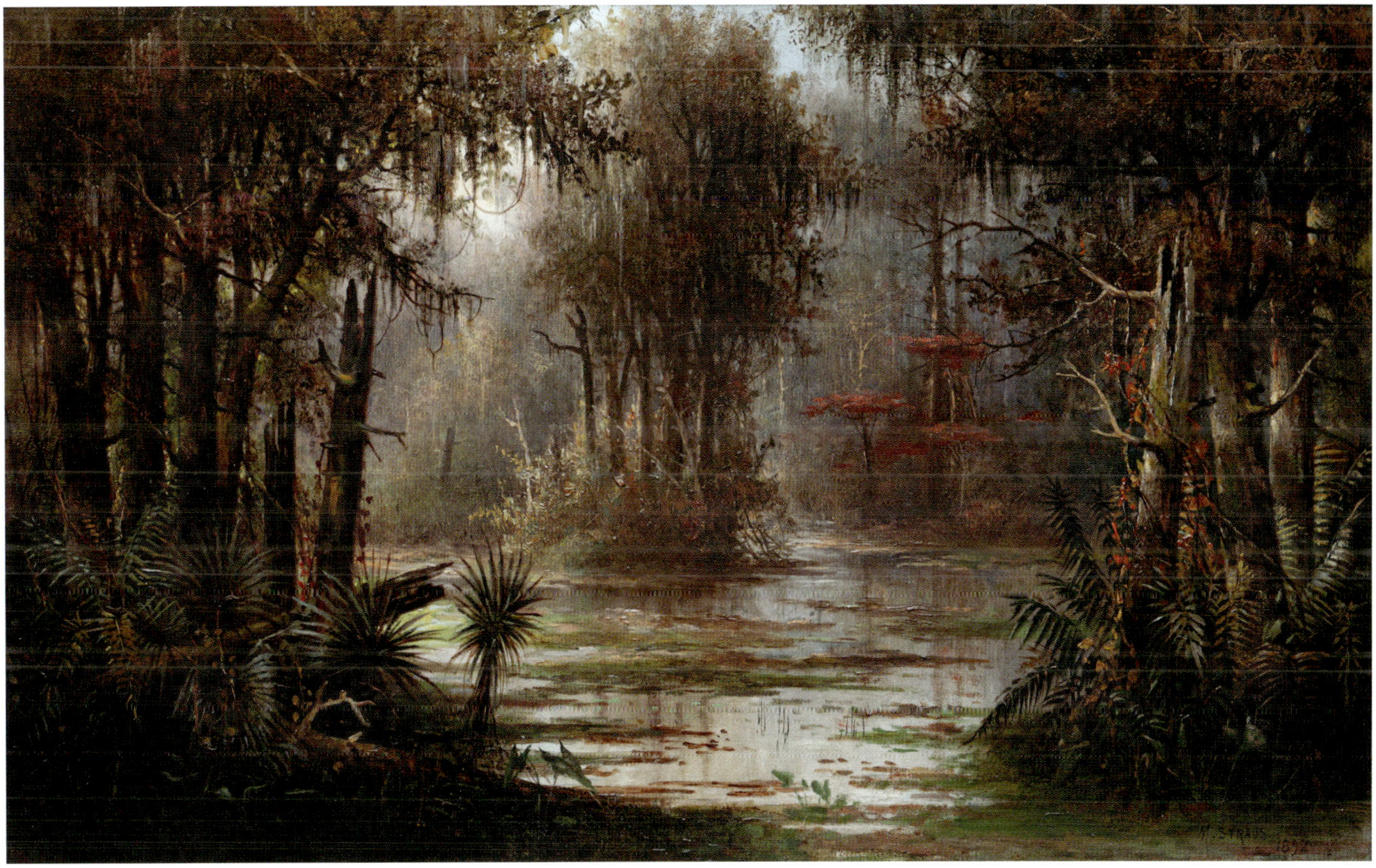

**Plate 64**
Meyer Straus,
*Louisiana Landscape*, 1882,
Oil on canvas, 34 x 48 inches (framed),
Collection of Bill Gunther,
Photography by Roman Alokhin.

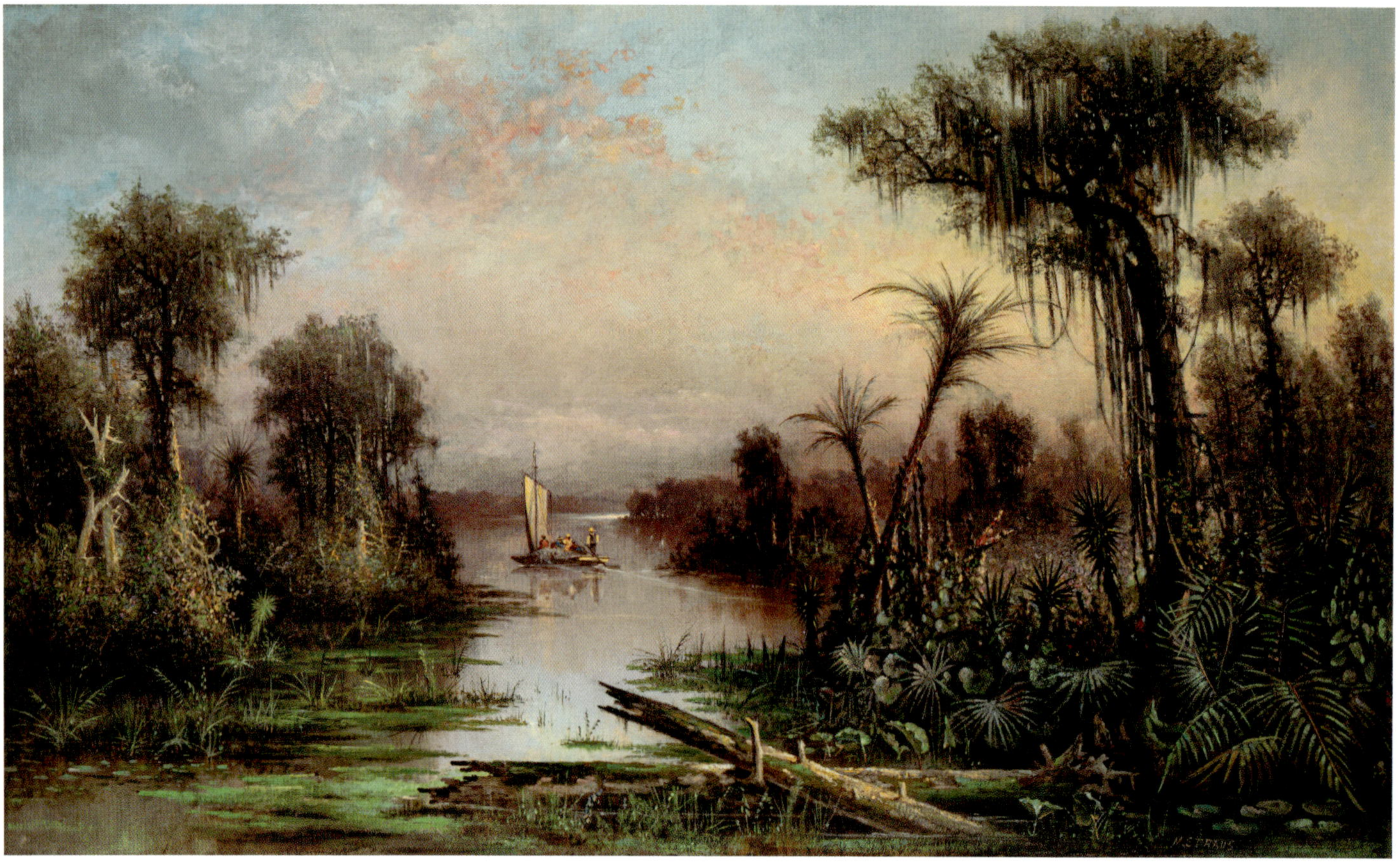

**Plate 65**
Meyer Straus,
*Louisiana Landscape*, circa 1880-1900,
Oil on canvas, 47 x 67 inches (framed),
Collection of Bill Gunther,
Photography by Roman Alokhin.

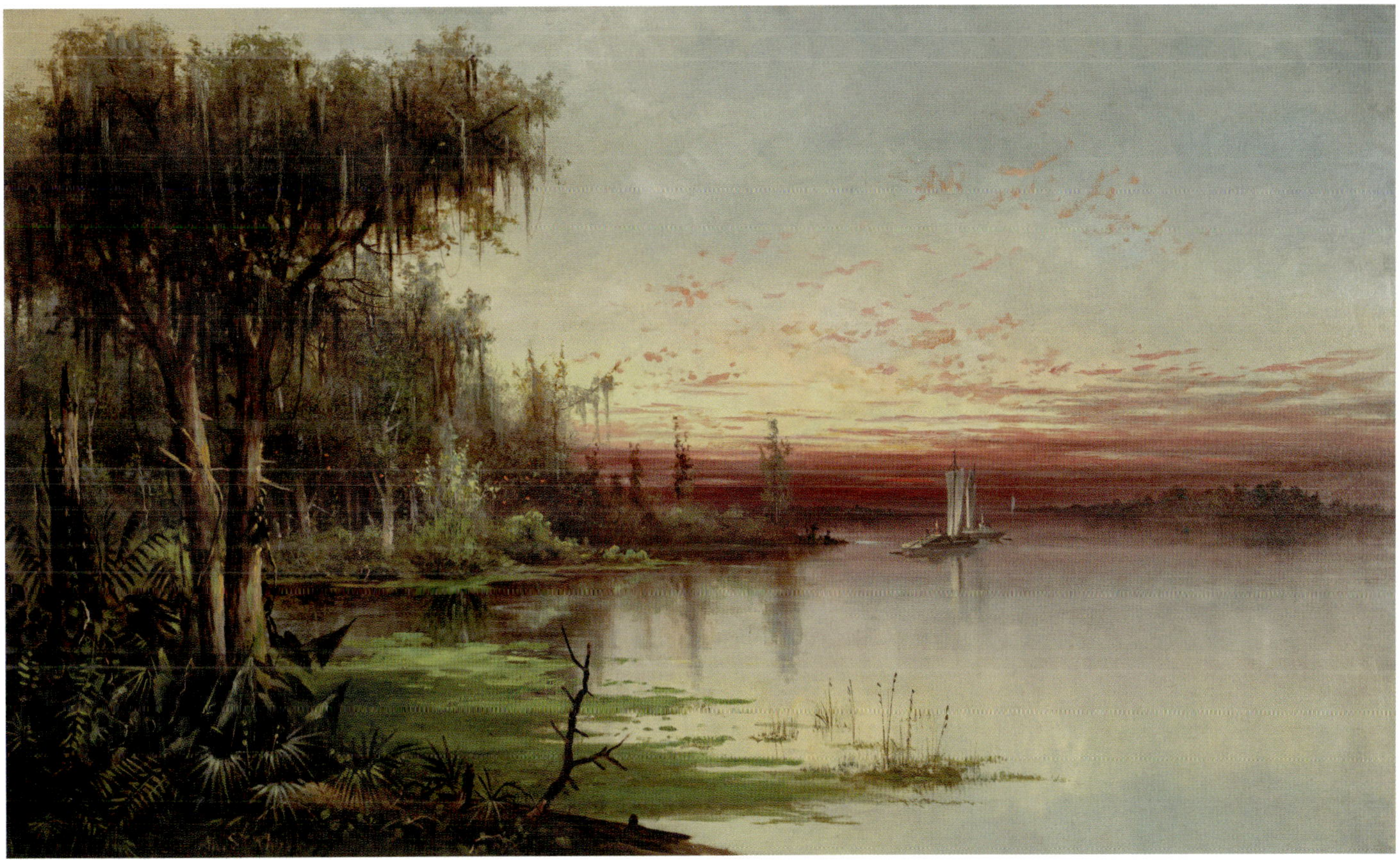

**Plate 66**
Meyer Straus,
*Louisiana Landscape*, circa 1880-1900,
Oil on canvas, 42 ½ x 62 inches (framed),
Collection of Bill Gunther,
Photography by Roman Alokhin.

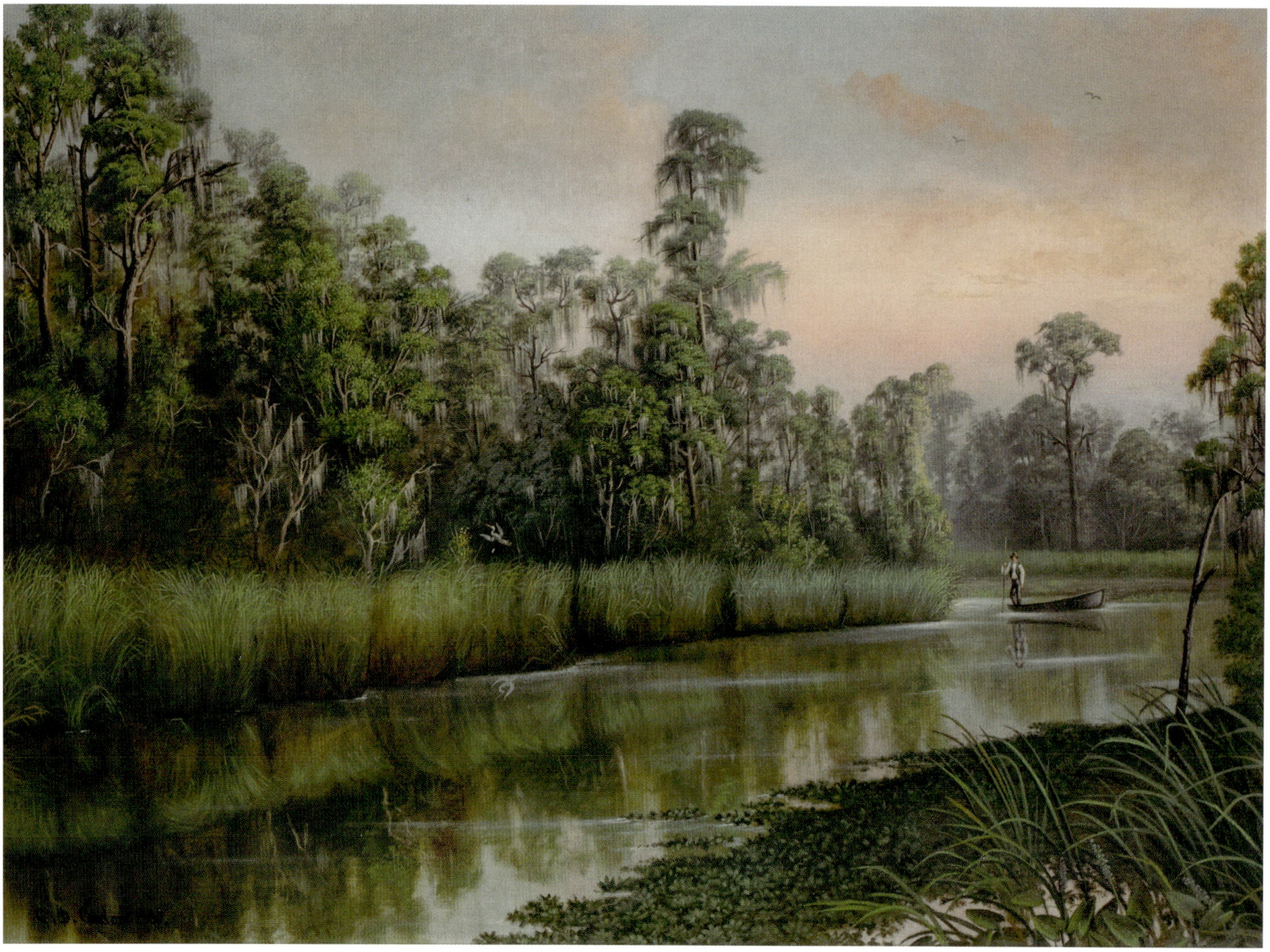

**Plate 67**
George David Coulon,
*Bayou Beauregard, St. Bernard Parish*, 1887,
Oil on canvas, 24 x 33 inches,
Roger Houston Ogden Collection,
Courtesy of Ogden Museum of Southern Art.
Photography by Patrick Barnes.

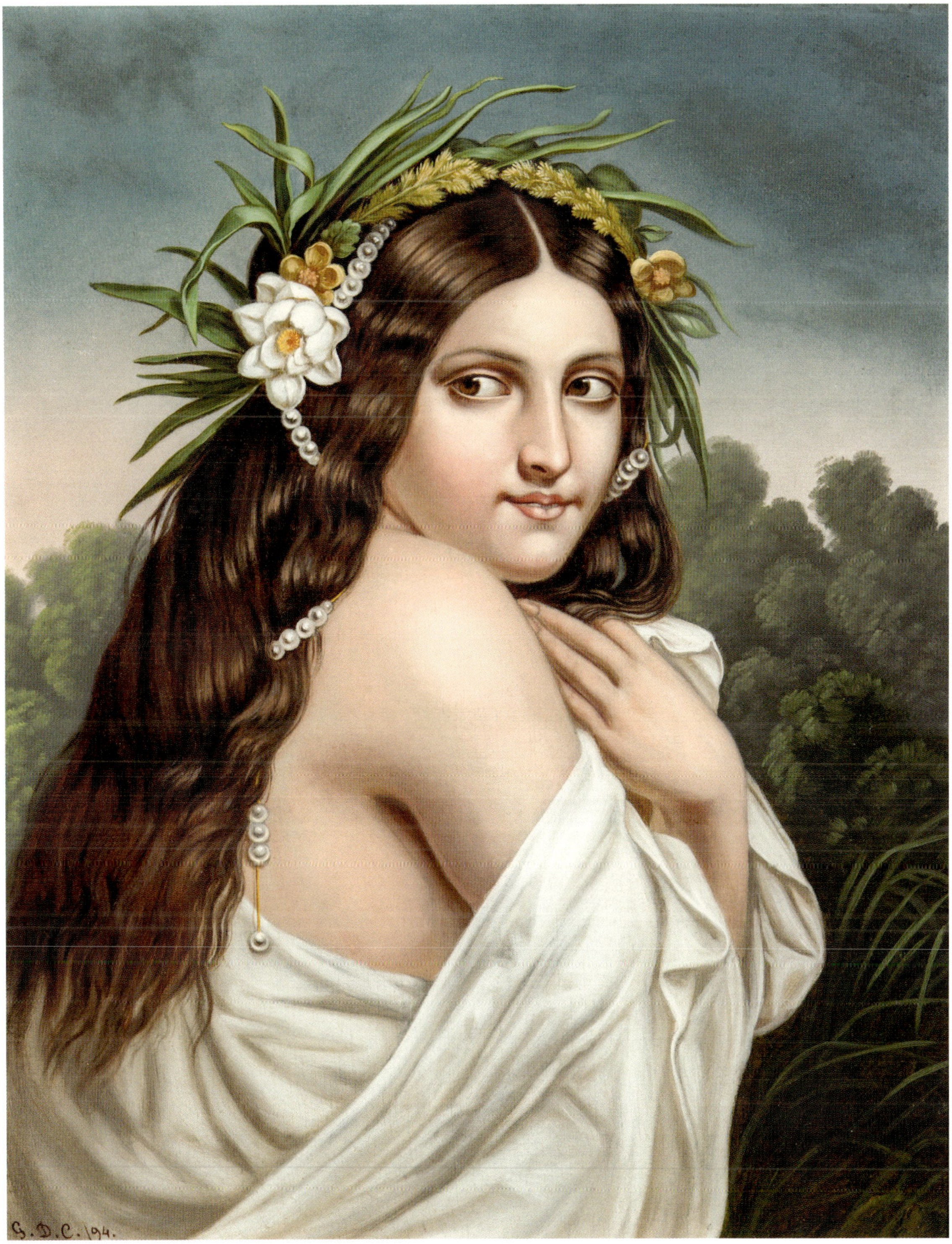


**Plate 68**

George David Coulon,
*Spirit of Louisiana*, 1894,
Oil on canvas, 33 ¼ x 28 ¼ x 3 inches (framed),
New Orleans Museum of Art,
Gift of the Fine Arts Club of New Orleans
on the occasion of their 60th Anniversary, 76.69

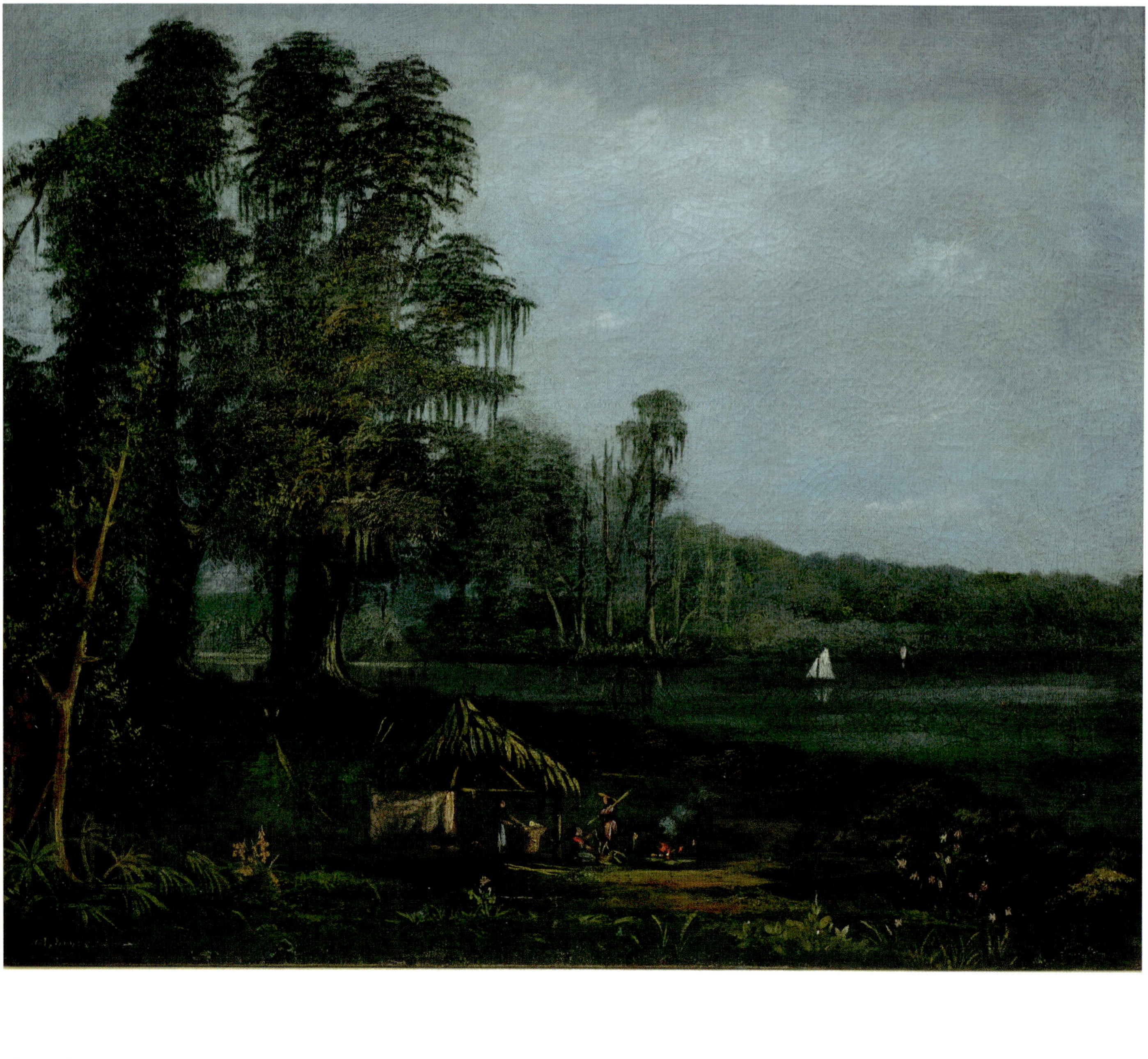

**Plate 69**
Alphonse J. Gamotis,
*Indian Village on the Shores of Lake Ponchartrain*, 1900,
Oil on canvas, 20 x 24 inches,
Roger Houston Ogden Collection,
Courtesy of Ogden Museum of Southern Art.
Photography by Patrick Barnes.

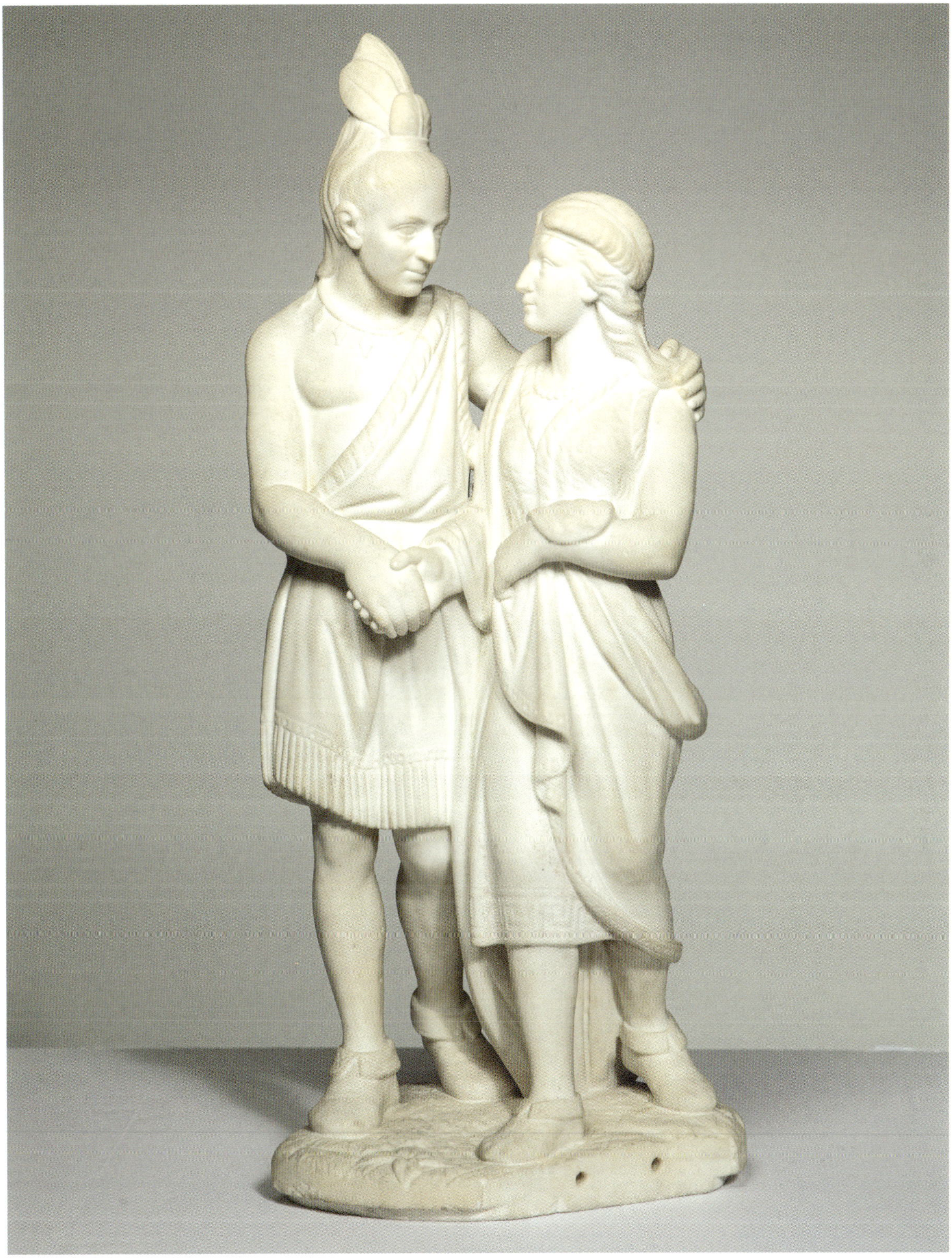

**Plate 70**
Edmonia Lewis,
*The Marriage of Hiawatha*, 1874,
White marble, 31 ½ inches,
Walter O. Evans Collection of
African American Art

# EXHIBITION CHECKLIST

John Antrobus (British, 1831-1907)
*A Plantation Burial*, 1860
Oil on canvas, 52 ¾ x 81 $^{5}/_{16}$ inches
The Historic New Orleans Collection, 1960.46

John Antrobus (British, 1831-1907)
*Untitled (Louisiana Landscape)*, circa 1860
Oil on canvas, 10 x 8 inches
Collection of Jennifer and Fred Heebe

John Antrobus (British, 1831-1907)
*Untitled (Louisiana Landscape)*, circa 1860
Oil on canvas, 10 x 8 inches
Collection of Jennifer and Fred Heebe

Atakapa-Ishak Peoples
*Basket*, circa 1870
Natural fibers, 16 x 8 x 8 inches
Collection of Don Fuson

Toussaint François Bigot (French, 1794-1869)
*Alchapalia, Louisiana*, 1848
Oil on canvas, 29 ½ x 36 inches
Roger Houston Ogden Collection
Courtesy of Ogden Museum of Southern Art

Blanche Virginia Blanchard (American, 1866-1959)
*Untitled (Louisiana Landscape)*, circa 1880
Oil on canvas, 13 x 17 inches (framed)
Collection of Tommy Spinosa

Blanche Virginia Blanchard (American, 1866-1959)
*Untitled (Louisiana Landscape)*, circa 1880
Oil on canvas, 11 ½ x 13 ½ inches (framed)
Collection of Tommy Spinosa

Blanche Virginia Blanchard (American, 1866-1959)
*Untitled (Louisiana Landscape)*, circa 1880
Oil on canvas, 11 ½ x 13 ½ inches (framed)
Collection of Tommy Spinosa

Alfred L. Boisseau (French, 1823-1903)
*Marche d'Indiens de la Louisiane*
*(Louisiana Indians Walking Along a Bayou)*, 1847
Oil on canvas, 28 ¼ x 44 $^{3}/_{8}$ x 2 inches (framed)
New Orleans Museum of Art
Gift of William E. Groves, 56.34

Alfred L. Boisseau (French, 1823-1903)
*Portrait of a Young Lady, possibly Mrs. Alfred LeMore, née Marie Xavier Athenais Chretien*, 1849
Oil on canvas, 39 ½ x 32 inches
Collection of Mr. and Mrs. Dwight Winstead,
Chretien Point Plantation

Robert Brammer (Irish, active New Orleans 1841-53)
*Mississippi Panorama*, 1842-53
Oil on canvas, 29 x 36 inches
Collection of Stacy and Jay Underwood

Robert Brammer (Irish, active New Orleans 1841-53)
*Mississippi Panorama*, circa 1850
Oil on canvas, 32 x 37 inches (framed)
Ogden Museum of Southern Art
Gift of the Roger H. Ogden Collection

Robert Brammer (Irish, active New Orleans 1841-53)
*Wooding Up, Rodney, Mississippi*, circa 1842-53
Oil on canvas, 41 x 48 inches (framed)
Collection of Bill Gunther

Mary Bella Prague Brice (American, 1833-1923)
*Mouth of the Tchefuncta River*, 1897
Oil on canvas, 17 ½ x 23 ½ inches (framed)
Louisiana State Museum,
Gift of Anne Hastings Moss, 2014.024.12

Agostino Brunias (Italian, 1730-1796)
*View on the River Roseau, Dominica*, 1770-80
Oil on canvas, 33 $^{1}/_{8}$ x 62 $^{3}/_{16}$ inches
The Art Institute of Chicago
Gift of Emily Crane Chadborne, 1953.1

William Henry Buck (Norwegian, 1840-1888)
*Bayou Têche*, 1877
Oil on canvas, 16 ¼ x 24 $^{3}/_{8}$ inches
The Historic New Orleans Collection, 1975.1

William Henry Buck (Norwegian, 1840-1888)
*Bayou Têche*, 1877
Oil on canvas, 16 ¼ x 24 $^{3}/_{8}$ inches
The Historic New Orleans Collection, 1975.2

William Henry Buck (Norwegian, 1840-1888)
*Lake Ponchartrain Shore*, circa 1860-1880
Oil on canvas, 17 ½ x 29 ½ inches
Collection of Michael and Virginia White

William Henry Buck (Norwegian, 1840-1888)
*Louisiana Pastoral: Bayou Bridge*, circa 1880
Oil on canvas, 26 x 40 inches
Roger Houston Ogden Collection
Courtesy of Ogden Museum of Southern Art

William Henry Buck (Norwegian, 1840-1888)
*Summer Resort*, circa 1880
Oil on canvas on board, 32 ½ x 28 ½ inches (framed)
New Orleans Museum of Art
Museum Purchase through the
Ella West Freeman Foundation Matching Fund, 71.5

William Henry Buck (Norwegian, 1840-1888)
*Swamp Scene*, 1887
Oil on canvas, 16 x 28 inches
New Orleans Museum of Art
Gift of Miss Mary Bell Swanson Mayer, 80.41

William Henry Buck (Norwegian, 1840-1888)
*Untitled (Louisiana Landscape)*, n.d.
Oil on canvas, 25 ½ x 37 ½ inches (framed)
New Orleans Museum of Art
Bequest of Bernard Bruen, 16.7

William Henry Buck (Norwegian, 1840-1888)
*World's Industrial and Cotton Centennial Exposition (New Orleans, Louisiana World's Fair), 1885*, 1885
Oil on canvas, 23 ¾ x 27 ¾ inches (framed)
New Orleans Museum of Art
Museum purchase through the
Ella West Freeman Foundation Matching Fund, 71.11

William Henry Buck (Norwegian, 1840-1888)
*World's Industrial and Cotton Centennial Exposition (New Orleans, Louisiana World's Fair), 1885*, 1885
Oil on canvas, 23 ¾ x 27 ¾ inches (framed)
New Orleans Museum of Art
Museum purchase through the
Ella West Freeman Foundation Matching Fund, 71.10

F. Arthur Callender (American, d. 1917)
*New Orleans from Algiers Point*, 1893
Oil on canvas, 15 x 24 inches
Roger Houston Ogden Collection
Courtesy of Ogden Museum of Southern Art

Dominico Canova (Italian, 1800-1868)
*Mother Louisiana*, circa 1850
Oil on canvas, 56 x 48 inches
Roger Houston Ogden Collection
Courtesy of Ogden Museum of Southern Art

Albert-Erneste Carrier-Belleuse (French, 1824-1887)
*Woman in Reeds (Undine)*, circa 1865
Bronze with green and gold patination, 30 x 18 x 9 ½ inches
New Orleans Museum of Art
Gift of John G. Agar in memory of his father,
William Agar, 15.51

Captain William Lindsay Challoner (British, 1852-1901)
*S.S. Breakwater, S.S. Clearwater and S.S. Wanderer in a Harbor [Honduras Port]*, 1897
Oil on canvas, 30 x 48 inches
Louisiana State Museum, XX0707

Chitimacha Peoples
*Basket*, circa 1850-1900
Natural fibers, 8 x 14 x 14 inches
Collection of Don Fuson

Choctaw Peoples
*Basket*, n.d.
Natural fibers, 15 x 19 x 19 inches
Collection of Don Fuson

Choctaw Peoples
*Storage Basket*, n.d.
Natural fibers, 26 x 15 x 15 inches
Collection of Don Fuson

Richard Clague (French, 1821-1873)
*Back of Algiers*, circa 1870-73
Oil on canvas, 21 x 27 ¼ x 2 ½ inches (framed)
New Orleans Museum of Art
Gift of Eugenia Uhlhorn Harrod in memory of her
husband, Major Benjamin Morgan Harrod, 13.5

Richard Clague (French, 1821-1873)
*Batture Shanty*, 1870
Oil on canvas, 22 x 26 ⅛ x 3 ¼ inches (framed)
New Orleans Museum of Art
Museum Purchase through the
Ella West Freeman Foundation Matching Fund, 71.3

Richard Clague (French, 1821-1873)
*Fisherman's Camp*, n.d.
Oil on wood panel, 18 ¾ x 22 ¾ inches (framed)
New Orleans Museum of Art
Gift of Mrs. Benjamin M. Harrod, 13.6

Richard Clague (French, 1821-1873)
*Rural Louisiana Farm Scene*, circa 1850
Oil on canvas, 23 ¼ x 31 ¾ inches
Collection of Michael and Virginia White

Richard Clague (French, 1821-1873)
*Trapper's Cabin, Manchac*, 1870
Oil on canvas, 14 x 20 inches
Roger Houston Ogden Collection
Courtesy of Ogden Museum of Southern Art

Richard Clague (French, 1821-1873)
*Untitled*, circa 1857-1868
Pencil and ink on paper, 12 x 15 inches (framed)
New Orleans Museum of Art
Gift of S. A. Trufant, 28.2.14

Richard Clague (French, 1821-1873)
*Untitled*, circa 1857-1871
Pencil and ink on paper, 12 x 15 inches (framed)
New Orleans Museum of Art
Gift of S. A. Trufant, 28.2.23

Richard Clague (French, 1821-1873)
*Untitled*, circa 1857-1868
Pencil and ink on paper, 12 x 15 inches (framed)
New Orleans Museum of Art
Gift of S. A. Trufant, 28.2.47

Richard Clague (French, 1821-1873)
*Untitled*, circa 1857-1868
Pencil and ink on paper, 12 x 15 inches (framed)
New Orleans Museum of Art
Gift of S. A. Trufant, 28.2.48

Richard Clague (French, 1821-1873)
*Untitled*, circa 1857-1868
Pencil and ink on paper, 12 x 15 inches (framed)
New Orleans Museum of Art
Gift of S. A. Trufant, 28.2.56

Richard Clague (French, 1821-1873)
*Untitled*, circa 1857-1868
Pencil and ink on paper, 12 x 15 inches (framed)
New Orleans Museum of Art
Gift of S. A. Trufant, 28.2.57

Richard Clague (French, 1821-1873)
*Untitled*, circa 1857-1868
Pencil and ink on paper, 12 x 15 inches (framed)
New Orleans Museum of Art
Gift of S. A. Trufant, 28.2.79

Richard Clague (French, 1821-1873)
*Untitled*, circa 1857-1868
Pencil and ink on paper, 15 x 12 inches (framed)
New Orleans Museum of Art
Gift of S. A. Trufant, 28.2.97.a

Richard Clague (French, 1821-1873)
*Untitled*, circa 1857-1868
Pencil and ink on paper, 15 x 12 inches (framed)
New Orleans Museum of Art
Gift of S. A. Trufant, 28.2.102

Richard Clague (French, 1821-1873)
*Untitled*, Nov. 28, 1871
Pencil and ink on paper, 12 x 15 inches (framed)
New Orleans Museum of Art
Gift of S. A. Trufant, 28.2.26

Richard Clague (French, 1821-1873)
*Untitled (Korosko, Egypt)*, March 25, 1857
Pencil and ink on paper, 12 x 15 inches (framed)
New Orleans Museum of Art
Gift of S. A. Trufant, 28.2.45

Richard Clague (French, 1821-1873)
*Untitled (Le portage dans la Back Bayou)*, 1860
Pencil and ink on paper, 15 x 19 inches (framed)
New Orleans Museum of Art
Gift of S. A. Trufant, 28.2.13

Richard Clague (French, 1821-1873)
*Untitled (Sakie Royale, Rhoda)*, 1857
Pencil and ink on paper, 12 x 15 inches (framed)
New Orleans Museum of Art
Gift of S. A. Trufant, 28.2.1

Richard Clague (French, 1821-1873)
*Untitled (Spring Hill)*, 1871
Pencil and ink on paper, 15 x 19 inches (framed)
New Orleans Museum of Art
Gift of S. A. Trufant, 28.2.110

Richard Clague (French, 1821-1873)
*Untitled (Spring Hill)*, circa 1871
Pencil and ink on paper, 15 x 12 inches (framed)
New Orleans Museum of Art
Gift of S. A. Trufant, 28.2.36

Richard Clague (French, 1821-1873)
*Untitled (Spring Hill)*, circa 1871
Pencil and ink on paper, 12 x 15 inches (framed)
New Orleans Museum of Art
Gift of S. A. Trufant, 28.2.85

Richard Clague (French, 1821-1873)
*Untitled (Spring Hill)*, Nov. 17, 1871
Pencil and ink on paper, 12 x 15 inches (framed)
New Orleans Museum of Art
Gift of S. A. Trufant, 28.2.43

Richard Clague (French, 1821-1873)
*Untitled (Spring Hill)*, Nov. 1871
Pencil and ink on paper, 15 x 12 inches (framed)
New Orleans Museum of Art
Gift of S. A. Trufant, 28.2.118

Richard Clague (French, 1821-1873)
*Untitled (Spring Hill)*, Nov. 1871
Pencil and ink on paper, 15 x 12 inches (framed)
New Orleans Museum of Art
Gift of S. A. Trufant, 28.2.118

Richard Clague (French, 1821-1873)
*Untitled (Spring Hill)*, Dec. 1871
Pencil and ink on paper, 19 x 15 inches (framed)
New Orleans Museum of Art
Gift of S. A. Trufant, 28.2.31

Richard Clague (French, 1821-1873)
*Untitled (Sycamore, Rhoda)*, 1857
Pencil and ink on paper, 12 x 15 inches (framed)
New Orleans Museum of Art
Gift of S. A. Trufant, 28.2.35

George Henry Clements (American, 1855-1935)
*Louisiana Swamp*, 1879
Oil on canvas, 26 ½ x 22 ½ inches (framed)
Collection of Donna and Bubba Hines

George David Coulon (French, 1822-1904)
*Bayou Beauregard, St. Bernard Parish*, 1887
Oil on canvas, 24 x 33 inches
Roger Houston Ogden Collection
Courtesy of Ogden Museum of Southern Art

George David Coulon (French, 1822-1904)
*Spirit of Louisiana*, 1894
Oil on canvas, 33 ¼ x 28 ¼ x 3 inches (framed)
New Orleans Museum of Art
Gift of the Fine Arts Club of New Orleans on the occasion of their 60th Anniversary, 76.69

Coushatta Peoples
*Basket*, circa 1870
Natural fibers, 8 x 16 x 16 inches
Collection of Don Fuson

Coushatta Peoples
*Basket*, n.d.
Natural fibers, 18 x 29 x 29 inches
Collection of Don Fuson

Robert Seldon Duncanson (American, 1821-1872)
*Uncle Tom and Little Eva*, 1853
Oil on canvas, 27 ¼ x 38 ¼ inches
Detroit Institute of Arts
Gift of Mrs. Jefferson Butler and
Miss Grace R. Conover, 49.498

Asher Brown Durand (American, 1796-1886)
*Forenoon*, 1847
Oil on canvas, 73 ¼ x 61 ¼ x 5 ¾ inches (framed)
New Orleans Museum of Art
Gift of the Fine Arts Club of New Orleans, 16.4

Henry Chapman Ford (American, 1828-1894)
*Water Lilies and Spanish Moss*, 1874
Oil on canvas, 30 x 48 inches
Collection of Jennifer and Fred Heebe

Alphonse J. Gamotis (American, 1842-1919)
*Indian Village on the Shores of Lake Ponchartrain*, 1900
Oil on canvas, 20 x 24 inches
Roger Houston Ogden Collection
Courtesy of Ogden Museum of Southern Art

Charles Giroux (French, 1828-1885)
*Steamboat Passing a Bayou Farm,* 1880
Oil on canvas, 27 x 47 inches
Collection of Donna and Bubba Hines

Harriet Goodhue Hosmer (American, 1830-1908)
*Medusa,* circa 1854
Marble, 27 ¼ x 21 x 9 ½ inches
Minneapolis Institute of Art
The Walter C. and Mary C. Briggs Purchase Fund, 2003.125

Everett B.D. Fabrino Julio (American, 1843-1879)
*Life Along a Louisiana Bayou,* n.d.
Oil on canvas, 15 ¼ x 30 ¼ inches
Roger Houston Ogden Collection
Courtesy of Ogden Museum of Southern Art

Everett B.D. Fabrino Julio
*Swamp Scene,* 1876
Oil on canvas, 21 ½ x 36 ½ inches (framed)
Louisiana State Museum
Gift of Friends of the Cabildo, 1980.100a-b

Judah LeVasseur (French, active New Orleans 1837-42)
*Fishing on Lake Managua, Nicaragua,* circa 1840
Oil on canvas, 31 ½ x 21 ½ inches (framed)
Private Collection

Judah LeVasseur (French, active New Orleans 1837-42)
*Fishing on Lake Managua, Nicaragua,* circa 1840
Oil on canvas, 31 ½ x 21 ½ inches (framed)
Private Collection

Edmonia Lewis (American, 1844-1907)
*The Marriage of Hiawatha,* 1874
White marble, 31 ½ inches
Walter O. Evans Collection of African American Art

Joseph Rusling Meeker (American, 1827-1889)
*After a Storm—Lake Maurepas,* 1888
Oil on canvas, 32 ¾ x 45 ¼ x 1 ¼ inches (framed)
Louisiana State University Museum of Art
Gift of the Phi Gamma Chapter of Chi Omega Sorority, 98.14

Joseph Rusling Meeker (American, 1827-1889)
*Bayou Plaquemines,* 1881
Oil on canvas, 20 x 30 inches
Roger Houston Ogden Collection
Courtesy of Ogden Museum of Southern Art

Joseph Rusling Meeker (American, 1827-1889)
*Bayou Plaquemines,* 1885
Oil on canvas, 38 ¼ x 33 inches (framed)
New Orleans Museum of Art
Museum Purchase, gift of Bernard Bruen, by exchange, 2003.221

Joseph Rusling Meeker (American, 1827-1889)
*Evangeline,* 1884
Oil on canvas, 25 ½ x 31 ½ inches (framed)
Collection of Bill Gunther

Joseph Rusling Meeker (American, 1827-1889)
*Louisiana Bayou,* circa 1885
Oil on canvas, 19 7/8 x 36 inches
Montgomery Museum of Fine Arts, Montgomery, Alabama Association Purchase

Joseph Rusling Meeker (American, 1827-1889)
*Solitary Pirogue by the Bayou,* 1886
Oil on canvas, 28 ¾ x 41 ½ inches (framed)
Morris Museum of Art, Augusta, Georgia, 1993.004

Joseph Rusling Meeker (American, 1827-1889)
*The Acadians in the Atchafalaya, "Evangeline,"* 1871
Oil on canvas, 32 1/8 x 42 3/16 inches
Brooklyn Museum, A. Augustus Healy Fund, 50.118

Joseph Rusling Meeker (American, 1827-1889)
*The Land of Evangeline,* 1874
Oil on canvas, 40 ½ x 52 5/8 inches (framed)
Saint Louis Art Museum
Gift of Mrs. Wright Prescott Edgerton in memory of Dr. and Mrs. W.T. Helmuth by exchange, 163:1946

Joseph Rusling Meeker (American, 1827-1889)
*Untitled (Louisiana Landscape),* circa 1880-1900
Oil on canvas, 45 x 65 inches (framed)
Collection of Bill Gunther

Andres Molinary (American, 1847-1915)
*Landscape with Oak Trees,* circa 1890
Oil on canvas, 33 ½ x 47 ½ inches (framed)
Louisiana State Museum
Gift of Mrs. Paul Godchaux, 12467.44.2

Andres Molinary (American, 1847-1915)
*Le Chemin des Chapitoulas,* circa 1875-1900
Oil on canvas, 29 x 41 ½ inches (framed)
Collection of Bill Gunther

Andres Molinary (American, 1847-1915)
*Old Gentilly Road,* 1890
Oil on canvas, 32 x 48 inches
Roger Houston Ogden Collection
Courtesy of Ogden Museum of Southern Art

Marie Adrien Persac (French, 1824-1873)
*Boat on the Mississippi,* 1840-60
Watercolor on paper, 12 x 17 inches
Collection of Michael and Virginia White

Marie Adrien Persac (French, 1824-1873)
*Bois de Fleche Plantation,* 1861
Gouache and collage on paper, 16 x 22 ½ inches
Louisiana State Museum
Gift of Mrs. Olga Delomme Wagner, 1990.049.1

Marie Adrien Persac (French, 1824-1873)
*Hope Estate Plantation,* circa 1857
Gouache on paper, 24 ½ x 34 ½ x 2 ¼ inches (framed)
Louisiana State University Museum of Art
Gift of the Friends of LSU Museum of Art, 75.9

Marie Adrien Persac (French, 1824-1873)
*Olivier Plantation, Orange Grove,* 1861
Gouache and collage on paper, 18 $^{1}/_{8}$ x 23 ¾ inches
Louisiana State Museum
Loan of Mrs. Rene T. Beauregard, 07155

Théodore Rousseau (French, 1812-1867)
*A Swamp in the Landes,* after 1844
Oil on panel, 30 $^{1}/_{16}$ x 36 $^{1}/_{8}$ inches (framed)
The Walters Art Museum, Baltimore, 37.991

Harold Rudolph (American, 1850-1884)
*Louisiana Bayou,* 1872
Oil on canvas, 16 $^{7}/_{16}$ x 22 $^{5}/_{16}$ inches
New Orleans Museum of Art
Bequest of Eugene Lacoste, 15.92

Marshall J. Smith, Jr. (American, 1854-1923)
*Bayou Plantation,* circa 1879-1900
Oil on canvas, 17 x 36 ¼ inches
New Orleans Museum of Art
Gift of William E. Groves, 66.22

Marshall J. Smith, Jr. (American, 1854-1923)
*Cypress Grove, Gulf Coast,* circa 1880
Oil on canvas, 16 ¾ x 29 inches
Roger Houston Ogden Collection
Courtesy of Ogden Museum of Southern Art

Meyer Straus (German, 1831-1905)
*Louisiana Landscape,* circa 1880-1900
Oil on canvas, 47 x 67 inches (framed)
Collection of Bill Gunther

Meyer Straus (German, 1831-1905)
*Louisiana Landscape,* circa 1880-1900
Oil on canvas, 42 ½ x 62 inches (framed)
Collection of Bill Gunther

Meyer Straus (German, 1831-1905)
*Louisiana Landscape,* 1882
Oil on canvas, 34 x 48 inches (framed)
Collection of Bill Gunther

Meyer Straus (German, 1831-1905)
*Morning in the Swamp, Bayou Teche,* 1884
Oil on canvas, 36 x 66 ½ inches (framed)
Louisiana State Museum
Cabildo Auxiliary Funds Purchase, 1997.001.20.1

Unidentified Artist
*Oak Basket,* circa 1900
Natural fibers, 42 x 20 x 20 inches
Collection of Don Fuson

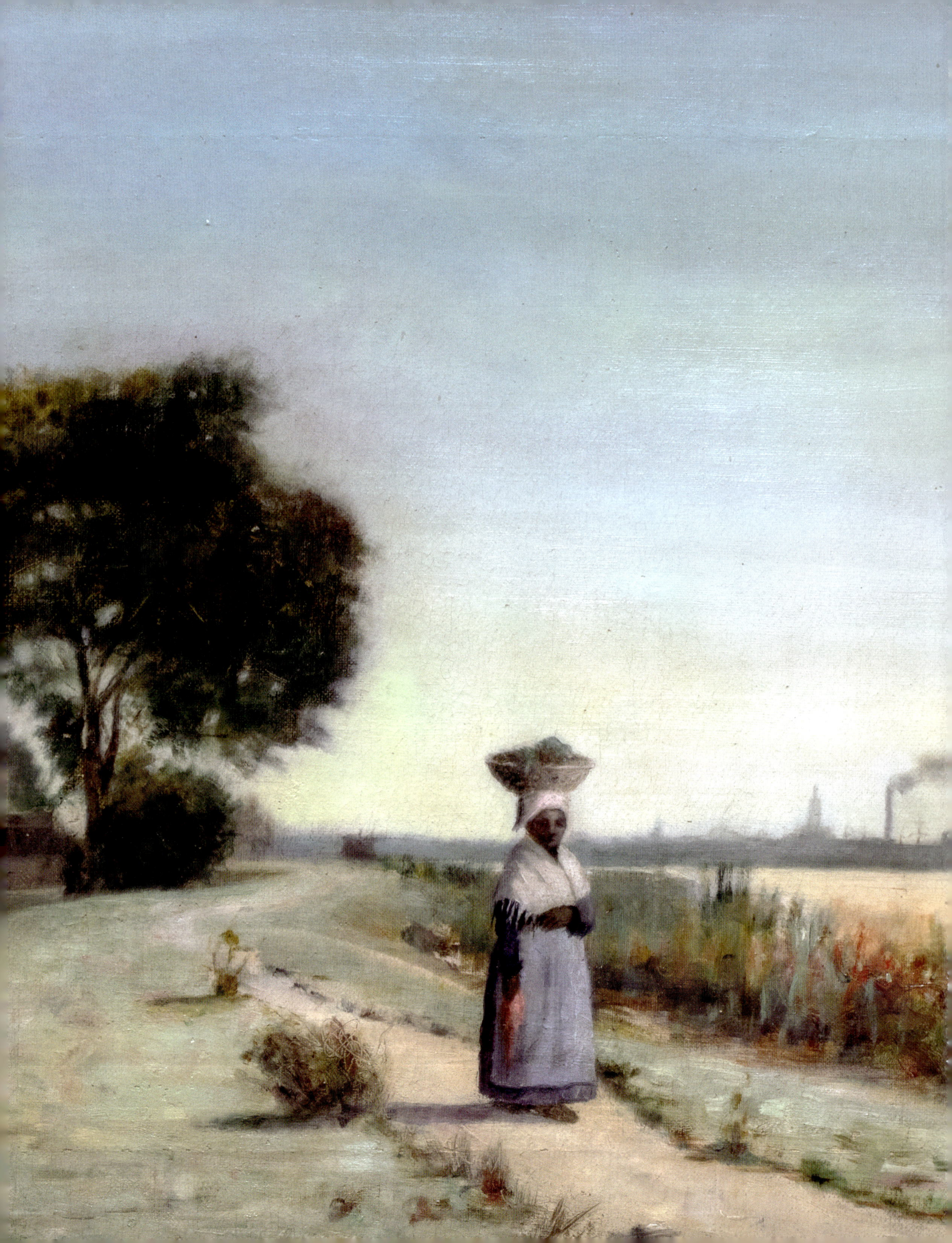

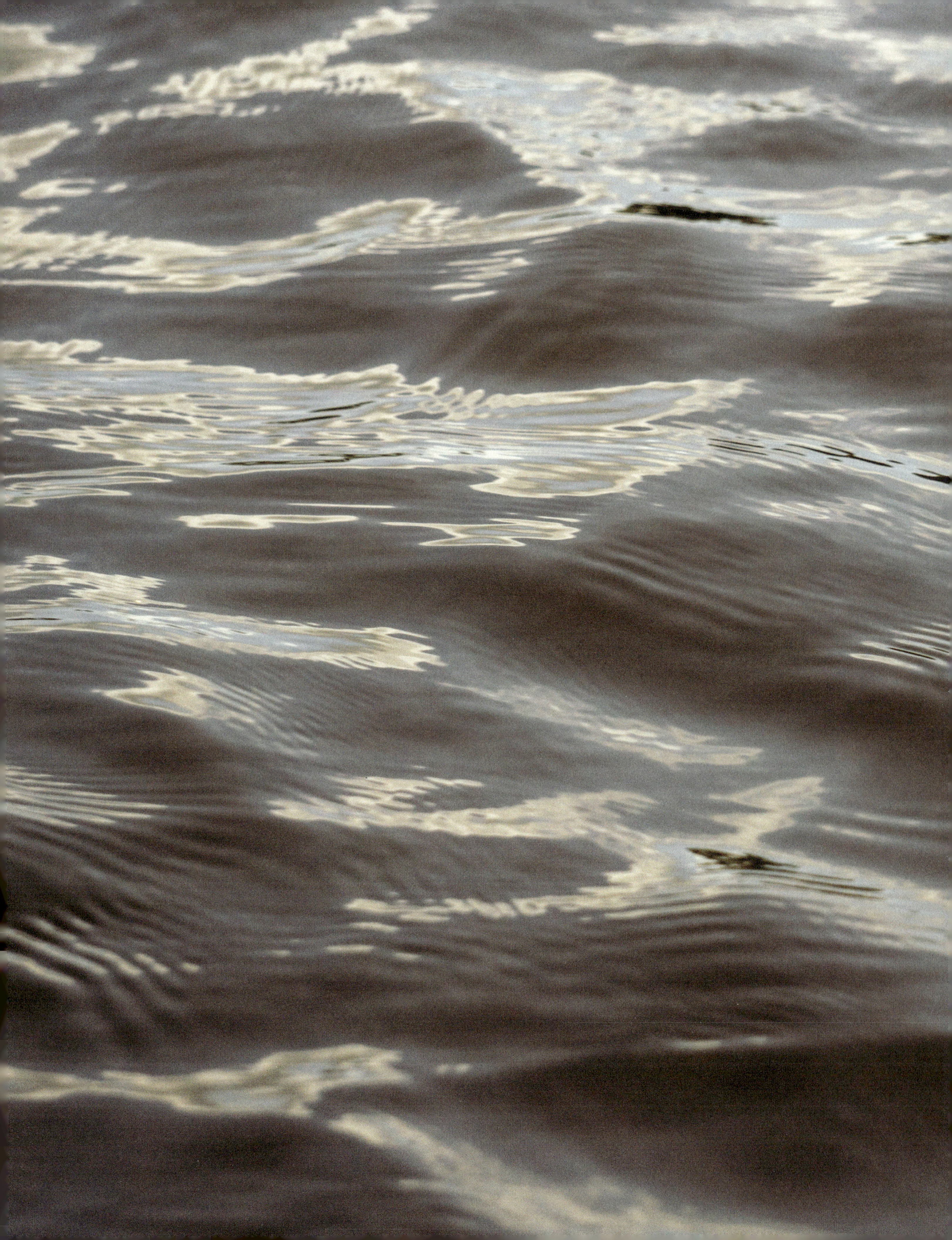